Ambedkar on Law, Constitution and Social Justice

Ambedkar on Law, Constitution and Social Justice

EDITOR

MOHAMMAD SHABBIR

RAWAT PUBLICATIONS

Jaipur • New Delhi • Bangalore • Guwahati • Kolkata

ISBN 978-81-7033-908-3

Reprinted, 2017

Published by
Prem Rawat for **Rawat Publications**
Satyam Apts., Sector 3, Jawahar Nagar, Jaipur - 302 004 (India)
Phone: 0141 265 1748 / 7006 Fax: 0141 265 1748
E-mail : info@rawatbooks.com
Website: rawatbooks.com

New Delhi Office
4858/24, Ansari Road, Daryaganj, New Delhi 110 002
Phone: 011-23263290

Also at *Bangalore, Hyderabad* and *Guwahati*

Printed at Chaman Enterprises, New Delhi

Contents

Foreword

Social justice, being a multi-dimensional concept, has been viewed by scholars of law, philosophy and political science differently. According to the theory of justice, the essence of justice maintains the standard of right and wrong, proper and improper and the ruler should respect basic and political liberties, while the utilitarian philosophers seek justice in the doctrine: 'greatest good of the greatest number' and 'maximum pleasure and minimum pain'. To John Rawls, justice is in 'fairness'. Justice is not merely general welfare of society, but is concerned with welfare of each individual of society.

Framers of the Constitution of India adopted a holistic view of social justice, which is enshrined in the preamble, fundamental rights and directive principles of state policy of the Constitution.

The possibility of ensuring social justice in contemporary era is linked not only with a vibrant and dynamic economy that is capable of meeting ever rising demands for goods and services but to social order too that is informed by a value system as well as endowed with a political will to devise and give effect appropriate distributive justice. It suggests removal of social inequalities that impede the effective exercise of freedom for securing well-being. Also, it implies the fulfilment of the needs of various groups of diverse background. Social justice has significance in the context of Indian society which is divided into castes and communities and they create walls and barriers of exclusiveness on the basis of superiority and inferiority. Such inequalities pose serious threat to Indian democracy. The concept of social justice takes within its sweep the objective of removing inequalities and affording equal opportunities to all citizens in social, economic and political affairs.

India, while passing through the process of development, is in the quest for finding out ways for a better and just socio-economic order. The search for a new model of socio-economic order is the need of the hour. Recent trends in globalization, urbanization, mobilization of the poor in search of better life conditions and social justice movements compel us to think afresh.

Gender inequality is the question not just of economic equality or mere social justice at large. It is not just a issue of women, but an overall human issue. The role of women as a catalytic agent for social change will have to be accepted in the process of attaining social justice.

The present book *Constitution, Law and Social Justice* incorporates research-oriented materials from diverse disciplines on various aspects of law, constitution and social justice. I have every reason to believe that this book will not only be a meaningful addition to the existing literature of social justice, but also inevitable for the judges, law teachers, lawyers, researchers, social scientists, social justice activists, legislators, NGOs and students of law.

I admire Professor Mohammad Shabbir's efforts for bringing out this scholarly work. This book is being published under the auspices of Dr. Ambedkar Chair of Legal Studies &

Research, Department of Law, Aligarh Muslim University, Aligarh, which has already brought out a number of useful publications. Dr. Shabbir, Ambedkar Chair Professor of Law deserves appreciation from all those who champion the cause of social justice sharing the philosophy of Bharat Ratna Baba Saheb Dr. B.R. Ambedkar.

Sanjay Sinh
Former Minister
Government of India
New Delhi

82, Lodhi Estate
New Delhi

Preface

Dr. Mahatir Mohamed, the legendary Prime Minister and architect of modem multi-ethnic harmonious Malaysian nation, in his farewell speech, made a laconic observation that has immense relevance in India too. He said: "what determines success (of a nation) is the culture or the value system which is accepted and practised". In Indian context, we have not yet reached our constitutional destinations of justice, liberty, equality and fraternity. The great obstacle in the odyssey has been the chimerical value system based on rigid caste compartmentalization with its Siamese twin brother of diabolical oppression that crippled Indian society. Here shines the statesmanship of Dr. Ambedkar who opened his firmly-footed crusade against the caste compartmentalization and for liberty, equality and fraternity eight decades ago. The post-independence era of India, full of sound and fury signifying nothing particularly on social front, has clearly proved the political wisdom and farsightedness of Dr. Ambedkar. Neither a statesman, nor a social activist nor an academician can overlook Ambedkar's ideals and vision in any serious deliberation over the betterment of the nation and its tongueless suppressed majority.

This work has been conceived as an endeavour to scan the constitution, law and the concept of social justice through the prism of Ambedkar's vision and ideology. On the symbiotic relationship between the exceptional individual and the momentum of history Hegel rightly observed: "The great man of the age is one who can put into words the will of the age, tells his age what its will is, and accomplish it. What he does is essence of the age; he actualizes it". Ambedkar was a cent per cent Hegelian in this sense. He reflected through his vision and mission the will of the age. He wonderfully crystallized the zeitgeist in the parchments of the Constitution to a great extent. Ambedkar himself said that a great man must be motivated by the dynamics of a social purpose and must be the scourge and the scavenger of the society. Ambedkar was a Herculean scavenger who tried his best to clean the filthy and dirty Aegean stables of the caste-ridden Indian society.

A probe into socio-legal aspects of human rights without due reference to the numerous struggles for human rights and dignity led by nameless individuals and named leaders like Dr. Ambedkar, would be meaningless. Ambedkar clearly expressed the significant role of struggle in the movement for rights by saying: "Lost rights are never regained by begging and by appeals to the conscience of the usurpers, but by relentless struggles." Here, Ambedkar opts a radical realist approach contrary to the Gandhian idealist method.

In Ambedkar one can see the sublime stage of the struggle against Indian apartheid, i.e., the caste system. The struggle against the sub-humanization of the Dalits under the caste stratification has been a long process that started with Buddha and Mahavira in 6th century BC. The struggle continued through Kabir and Guru Nanak. In 18th and 19th centuries, the contact with the western liberal ideology gave a more vigorous and concrete shape to the struggle. Mahatma Jyothibha Phule in Maharashtra, Sri Naryana Guru in Kerala and E.V. Ramaswamy Naiker in Madras represent this stage of the struggle. But all these leaders had a glaring limitation – they could not encounter the caste system in its totality. While Phule exhausted his energy only on social front, Sri Narayana on social and spiritual fronts and Naiker on social and political fronts.

But Ambedkar surprisingly countered the caste system in its totality. His wide learning in law, political science, economics and sociology enabled him to scan the phenomenon in its naked totality. Ambedkar's struggle against the Indian apartheid combined social, economic, political, legal and spiritual facets. His conversion to Buddhism was, in fact, a great breakthrough to the struggle and a fatal flow to the caste-based oppression. Dr. Ambedkar had announced at the Yeola conference in 1935: "Unfortunately, it was not my fault that I am born a Hindu untouchable. But I will not die as a Hindu."

On October 11, 1956 at Deekshabhumi, Nagpur, Ambedkar embraced Buddhism and fulfilled his promise. He thereby gave much-needed spiritual basis to the Dalit struggle for human dignity. Dr. Ambedkar, in early stage, like Sri Narayana Guru, attempted to counter the Brahmin hegemony by the tactics of sanskritization. The solemnization of the first marriage of an untouchable with Vedic rites was held at Bombay in 1927 under the hegemony of Dr. Ambedkar. Ambedkar's trusted lieutenant, Keshav Adrekar, was the bridegroom. This act was an Ambedkarian version of 'Aruvipuram Prathishta' but his further experience proved the futility of the sanskritization and he finally escaped from the caste-ridden Hindu fold.

His conversion has to be perceived in a larger historic perspective. He had conceived it as a prelude to the coming whirlwind of social and political revolution. It is evident from Ambedkar's statement: "History bears out the proposition that political revolutions have preceded by social and religious revolutions. The religious reformation started by Luther was precursor of political emancipation of the European people. In England, Puritanism founded the new world. It was Puritanism which led to the war of American independence. The same is true of the Muslim Empire. Before the Arabs became a political power, they had undergone a thorough religious revolutions started by the Prophet Mohammad (peace and blessing be upon him). Even Indian History supports the same conclusion. The political revolutions led by Chandragupta was preceded by the religion of Buddha. The political revolution led by Shivaji was preceded by the religious and social reforms brought about by the saints of Maharashtra."

The right to self-determination has been embodied in both the International Covenant on Economic, Social and Cultural Rights and the International Covenant on Civil & Political Rights. Dr. Upendra Baxi exposes the futility of the right to self-determination as it has been manipulated by the ruling elite: "It is thus clear that the very notion of self-determination as the insegnia of the right of each and every state to equality by international law, within a community of states, bears an ambivalent relation to human and social sufferings. The notion of self-determination attributes to people a will to statehood, the doctrine of equality among sovereign states assumes that 'state' can indeed represent people. In so far as these notions signify the illegitimacy of colonialism and imperialism human rights friendly. However, we all know situations where predatory sovereignty formations thriving on an ad hoc 'instant' regime of the dominant 'legalities' based on force and fraud tyranny and terror render people rightless." Dr. Ambedkar had prescience of this character of the national freedom. That is why, he gave priority to the social emancipation of the oppressed sections of society over the issue of political freedom of the nation.

His vision is evident from the dedication of his book "who were the *Shudras*", and how they come to be the fourth *varna* in the Indo-Aryan society?" He wrote there: Inscribed to the memory of Jyothibha Phule (1827-1890), the greatest *Shudra* of Modern India who made the lower classes of Hindus' conscience of the slavery to the higher classes and preached the gospel that for India, social democracy was more vital than independence from foreign rule". Ambedkar's stand has been fully vindicated by the history of post-independence India as the human rights discourse in its enunciation of human rights does not relate to language of human pain and suffering. In contrast, people's struggles against regimes practising the policy of cruelty stand rooted in the direct experience of pain and suffering. Ambedkarist struggle for human rights has not been statist or state-orientated. It has been to give voice to human sufferings. In this regard, it has been an integral part of contemporary human rights movement. Dr. Ambedkar declared during the historic Mahad *satyagraha* in 1927: "At the outset, let me tell those who oppose as that we did not perish because we could not drink water from this Chowder Tank. We only want to go to tank to prove that like others, we are human beings." Ambedkar's struggle was to restore human personality to the mammoth majority of Indian population who have been denied it by oppressive supremacists. The humanization of the sub- humanized has been the very core of contemporary human rights movement. The continuing struggle of Afro-American community, led by Martin Luther King and Malcom, has targeted at the same objective. Here also, Ambedkarian struggle confluences with the global movement of the oppressed. During the Mahad *satyagraha*, Ambedkar burnt *Manu Smriti* – the Bible of supremacist oppression for centuries in India. Dhananjay Keer, Ambedkar's celebrated biographer, commented on this brave action in this way: "This act was one of the greatest sacrilegious blows ever since the days of Luther upon the egoistic bigots, custom mongers, and no-changers on earths. December 25, 1927 is therefore a red letter day in the annals of India as it was on this day Ambedkar burnt the old *Smrithi* and demanded a new one in order to reshape the Hindu code governing the life of vast a people." It is the poetic justice of history that the sacred duty of writing the new *Smrithi* of India, i.e., the Constitution was finally assigned to Ambedkar. Dr. Ambedkar deliberately gave due weight to the social justice and social equality in the new *Smrithi*. No one can see such a detailed social manifesto or meticulous provisions like abolition of untouchability in any other Constitution. The drafting of the Constitution was in fact Ambedkar's struggle for social justice. But, deplorably, the operators of the constitutional machinery have failed to deliver the output of justice, equality, liberty and fraternity. After Ambedkar, the Indian Dalit segment could not get a leader of Ambedkar's stature or an intellectual of Ambedkar's vision. Thus, Ambedkarian struggle has been orphaned after Ambedkar, which is perhaps the greatest tragedy of history of the post-independence India.

Ambedkar was neither a day dreamer, nor a donnish armchair statesman, but was a pragmatic philosopher in order to cure the social inequality and injustice. Prescribing state socialism, he insisted that it should be imposed by the law of Constitution, so that it should be beyond the reach of a parliamentary majority to suspend and amend it. He further stated that by this one could achieve the triple objects – establish state socialism, retain parliamentary democracy and avoid dictatorship. The fundamental rights and the directive principles in the Constitution have been incorporated for this purpose. Sir Ivor Jenning perceived the ghosts of the webs stalking in these areas of the Constitution. But anyone can see the spirit of Ambedkar throbbing in these parchments of Constitution. But India's new 'Nawabs' and 'Maharajas' having feudal soul and democratic flesh have been performing exorcism against this glorious spirit by their wicked political and economic black magic.

Dr. Ambedkar sets out four premises which may be called the foundation of political democracy: (i) the individual has an end in himself; (ii) the individual has some inalienable rights which must be guaranteed to him by the Constitution; (iii) the individual shall not be required to relinquish any of his constitutional rights as a pre-condition to receive a privilege; and (iv) the state shall not delegate powers to private persons to govern others. These basics of political democracy have been cunningly sabotaged by the ruling elite of present India by the neo-*laissez faire* economic policy. Individual has been reduced into a mere means of production. Even rights guaranteed by the Constitution and the international Covenants on Economic, Social and Cultural rights, as rights to livelihood, work, trade union, strike, humane conditions of work etc. have been undermined in the name of liberalization, privatization and globalization carnival. The economy has been totally assigned to the mercy of demand-supply mechanism and profit mongers. Thereby, the ruling elite artfully torpedoed Ambedkar's scheme of social justice and political democracy. The poor always springs out of economic might. By delighting economic power to private players indiscriminately, the Indian cabal has undone what Ambedkar and other farsighted founding fathers achieved for the people. "Law is the abode of worldly happiness", said Ambedkar. This laconic and poetic definition of law would be a black swan in the black forest of jurisprudence. Ambedkar is dealing here not with 'is' aspect of law, but with 'ought' aspect. When law turns into an instrument of oppression and perpetuation of inequality, it loses its soul. In the era of POTA species of law, we have to remould it into the Ambedkarite jurisprudential dream. Ambedkar's jurisprudential wisdom enabled him to convince that law alone could not emancipate the Indian oppressed. He never held such quixotic theory. He perceived law and the Constitution as mere enforcement machinery of rights, not as a real source. He held that "rights are protected not by law but by the social and moral conscience of society. If social conscience is such that it is not prepared to recognize the laws which law chooses to enact, rights will be safe and secure. But if the fundamental rights are opposed by community, no law, no parliament, and no judiciary can guarantee them in the real sense".

Ambedkar further said: "There is world of difference between one who is learned and one who is an intellectual. The former is class conscious and is alive to the interests of his class. The latter is emancipated being, who is free to act without swayed by class consideration what India needed, is not a legion of the learned, but at least a handful of intellectuals, in Ambedkarian sense who can fight for justice and thereby can remould the future of India in the right way – an India that Ambedkar dreamt."

This work robbing into the Constitution, law and the concept of social justice in its totality, has been envisaged as a humble step towards that target and not as academic pedantry. This treatise has been shaped with professional devotion making it inevitable to social activists, social reformers, social scientists, researchers, lawyers, law academics, law students, judges, jurist philosophers, law reformers and legislators.

Dr. Ambedkar Foundation, Ministry of Social Justice & Empowerment, Government of India, deserves appreciation for its initiative to accomplish this anthology successfully.

I register my sense of gratitude for excellent publication to Rawat Publications, Jaipur, India.

Mohammad Shabbir
Ambedkar Chair Professor of Law
Dr. Ambedkar Chair of Legal Studies & Research
Department of Law
Aligarh Muslim University
Aligarh, India

Introducing the Dr. Ambedkar Chair

Department of Law, Aligarh Muslim University, Aligarh

The sub-committee on education, constituted for centenary celebrations of Baba Saheb Dr. Bhim Rao Ambedkar, in one of its recommendations in the year 1992, suggested for setting up Dr. Ambedkar Chairs in different disciplines in different institutions/universities. In pursuance of the recommendation and followed by the decision, Dr. Ambedkar Chairs were set up for undertaking study and research programmes on various aspects of the philosophy, thoughts, ideologies, missions and ideals of Dr. B.R. Ambedkar, by Dr. Ambedkar Foundation, Ministry of Social Justice and Empowerment, Government of India.

In the AMU's Department of Law too, Dr. Ambedkar Chair of Legal Studies and Research was set up to pay tribute and constructive homage to the memory of Bharat Ratna Baba Saheb Dr. B.R. Ambedkar, a great leader, law-giver, constitution-maker, social reformer, scholar, thinker, philosopher and jurist. The prime object of setting up of Chair is to provide necessary facilities to undertake studies and research by intellectuals, academicians, scholars, researchers and students to understand, assess, analyze and disseminate ideas, ideologies, thoughts and missions of Dr. Ambedkar, and also to provide opportunity to develop appropriate methodologies and strategies to translate them into practical propositions. The study and research under the Chair should focus on the socio-legal and economic status of the Scheduled Castes and Scheduled Tribes, minorities, weaker sections and other marginalized groups of Indian society, concentrating on the impact and outcome of various measures, strategies and programmes adopted by the various agencies of the government from time to time. The entire research exercise should focus on bringing out meaningful outcome to suggest remedial measures and facilitate the relevant organizations to adopt these measures for the formulation of meaningful policies and programmes.

To achieve these objectives, the functions of the Chair include study and research in the allocated thrust area (Personal Laws and Uniform Civil Code, Human Rights, Law, Constitution, Weaker Sections, Minorities, Scheduled Castes and their Development, Social Justice, Gender Justice, Women & Law, Role of Judiciary and Its Limitations, Jurisprudence and Criminal Justice System). It organizes seminars, workshops, symposia, conferences, lectures and penal discussions. It provides a forum to academicians, intellectuals, researchers, scholars and students for undertaking theoretical and field studies by applying the appropriate research methodologies. It assigns short-term and long-term research projects to post-graduate students and research scholars. Post-graduate dissertations and doctoral theses leading to Ph.D., are allocated to the Chair. Productive activities of the Chair include publication of books, journals, articles, research papers, research outcomes, case studies and monographs in the allocated thrust areas. The Chair undertakes any other studies and research projects assigned by the Foundation from time to time, according to its laid down terms and conditions. Such research studies can be entrusted by the Chair to other relevant institutions with the approval of the Foundation. The Chair provides research guidance to post-graduate, M. Phil and research scholars. The Chair, with the prior approval of the Foundation, may enter into national/international collaborations for undertaking studies and research on subject (s) relevant to the objectives and functions of the Chair and its allocated thrust areas.

To carry out these objectives and to execute the functions of the Chair, the Foundation maintains the provision of human resources to assist the institutions wherein the Chair is created.

Dr. Ambedkar Chair Professor is obligated to promote study and research activities in concerned discipline wherein the Chair is created in general, and in allocated thrust areas in process of carrying out the objectives and functions of the Chair. The Professor handles the case studies, short-term and long-term research projects satisfying the objectives of setting up the Chair in the discipline, undertakes the publication of books, journals, articles, monographs, case studies and research projects of the allocated thrust areas. He is mandated to supervise and provide guidance to post-graduate students' dissertations, M. Phil dissertations and doctoral theses leading to award of Ph.D./LL.D. in allocated thrust areas. The Professor also organizes seminars, symposia, conferences, workshops, lectures and penal discussions out of the topics/themes/issues of the allocated thrust areas in discipline of the Chair. The Chair Professor, besides his normal duties as Professor of Law in the Department of Law, also handles the academic, administrative and financial responsibilities associated with the Chair. The Chair Professor is assisted by the Research Officer and other supporting staff of the Chair in process of carrying out the objectives and functions of setting up the Chair. Research Officer, Research Fellows and Research Assistants are assigned studies and research by the Chair Professor out of the thrust areas in the assigned discipline of the Chair.

Dr. Ambedkar Foundation, Ministry of Social Justice and Empowerment, Government of India, allocated the following thrust areas for study, research, publication and organizing lectures, seminars, symposia, workshops and penal discussions: Dr. Ambedkar's role and contribution in law and constitution-making, constitution and development of the weaker sections of the society, especially the scheduled castes, scheduled tribes, marginalized groups and their development, problems of minorities, women and law, law and social justice, personal laws and uniform civil code, law and social change, effectiveness and limitations of the judicial system, human rights, gender justice and women empowerment, human rights and dalits and jurisprudence criminal justice system.

The creation of Dr. Ambedkar Chair at the Aligarh Muslim University, Aligarh is a matter of honour and distinction for which it rightly deserves in terms of its matchless contributions to the field of legal study and research.

Mohammad Shabbir

Acknowledgements

I express my deep sense of gratefulness to the following persons who deserve special mention: Mr. Naseem Ahmad, Vice-Chancellor, AMU, Aligarh, Mrs. Sonia Gandhi, Chairperson, UPA, New Delhi, Dr. Sanjay Sinh, Former Union Minister, New Delhi, Prof. H.A.S. Jafri, Member, Rajasthan Public Service Commission, Ajmer, Prof. Nazeer H. Khan, Former Ambedkar Chair Professor of Law, AMU, Aligarh, Prof. Balraj Chauhan, Lucknow University, Lucknow, Prof. V.K. Agarwal, Kurukshetra University, Kurukshetra, Prof. B.N. Pandey, Banaras Law School, BHU, Varanasi, Mr. Zafaryab Jilani, Advocate, Lucknow, Prof. F.U. Khan, AMU, Aligarh, Mr. A. Rahman, Advocate, Supreme Court, New Delhi, Mr. Kapil Sibal, Union Minister, New Delhi, Mr. Anil Saraswat, Advocate, Aligarh, Dr. P.S. Varshney, Aligarh, Dr. Khan Noor Ephroz, Advocate, Aligarh, Dr. Iqbal Ali Khan, AMU, Aligarh, Dr.Abdul Matin, AMU, Aligarh, Ms. Rakshanda Mobeen, Dr. Ambedkar Research Fellow, AMU, Aligarh, Mr. Khuram, AMU, Aligarh, Dr. Faizan Mustafa, AMU, Aligarh, Mr. Najeebul Hasan Khan, Research Fellow, AMU, Aligarh, Dr. A.S. Anand, Chairman, National Commission for Human Rights, New Delhi, Mr. Tarlochan

Singh, Chairman, National Commission for Minorities, New Delhi, Dr. Kamal Halili Hassan, UKM, Malaysia, Mr. Sangh Priya Gautam, Former Union Minister, New Delhi, Dr. Hasan Mateenul Islam, AMU, Aligarh, Prof. Akhtar Haseeb, AMU, Aligarh, Mr. Ram Vilas Paswan, Union Minister, New Delhi, Dr. Ashraf Husain, Kirishi Vigyan Kendra, Gorakhpur, Dr. Muhammad Mumtaz Ali, IIU, Malaysia, Madam Noor Aziah, UKM, Malaysia, Mr. Udit Raj, New Delhi, Mr. Nasrullah N. Khan, Malaysia, Mr. M.G. Pandithan, Malaysia, Dr. K.P. Singh, Washington, USA, Dr. Rahul Deepankar, USA, Prof. P.S. Sanghal, New Delhi, Prof. Mohd. Daud Bakar, IIU, Malaysia, Dr. Hooker, Michael Barry, Australia, Prof. M.N. Faruqui, Kharagpur, Dr. Zeenat Kausar, IIU, Malaysia, Dr. Tahir Beg, Barielly, Dr. L. Jawahar Nisan, USA, Ms. Santosh Kumar, USA, Kazi Ashfaque Ahmad, Australia, Prof. Shad Farooqui, University Technology Mara, Malaysia, Prof. Upendra Baxi, Warwic Law School, UK, Dr. Mohamed M. El-Gherani, Libya, Dr. Nik Ahmad Kamal Nik Mahmod, IIU, Malaysia, Mr. C.N. Singh, Pratapgarh, Haji Ramzan, Ali, Advocate, Pratapgarh, Mr. S.H. Khan, Member Secretary, Gharibnawaz Foundation for Education of Muslims, M.P., Mr. N. Manohara Prasad, New Delhi, Dr. Naimullah, ATM Public School, Aligarh and Dr. T.S. Rahi, Lucknow.

Dr. Sanjay Sinh deserves special thanks and gratitude for contributing 'foreword' which enhances the grandeur and grace of the book.

My acknowledgement is also due to Dr. Khan Noor Ephroz, my companion of life and associate in my academic pursuits. My affectionate tribute to my son G.M. Saad and daughter Ayesha Mohammad, whose natural claim in my time could not be devoted to them according to their priorities, as I was involved exclusively in winding up the book.

Though I have made a modest attempt with utmost professional devotion at my command, nonetheless, I am painfully cautious of my limitations. Critics are, therefore, welcomed to point out flaws, and their suggestions for improvement will be gratefully utilized in the next edition of the book.

I am thankful to Mr. Pranit Rawat of Rawat Publications for his professional devotion in bringing out this book fulfilling the word-class academic standard.

Mohammad Shabbir

Contributors

Nik Ahmad Kamal Nik Mahmod, Associate Professor, Dean, Ahmad Ibrahim Kulliyyah of Laws, International Islamic University, Malaysia.

K.P. Singh, University of Washington, Seattle, 231 Gowen Hall, WA 981 95-3521, USA.

Rahul Deepankar, M.D., 555 W. Court Street, Med Centre, Suite 214, Kankakee, Illinois, USA.

M.N. Faruqui, Professor in the Computer and Communication Systems Engineering, UPM, Malaysia and former Vice-Chancellor, AMU, Aligarh.

M. Shabbir, Professor of Law (Ambedkar Chair Professor of Law), Incharge, Dr. Ambedkar Chair of Legal Studies and Research, Department of Law, AMU, Aligarh.

L. Jawahar Nesan, Department of Civil Engineering, Faculty of Engineering, University Putra Malaysia, Selongor Darul Ehsan, UPM, Serdang, Malaysia.

James Massey, Honorary General Secretary and Director of the Dalit Solidarity Peoples, New Delhi and a former member of the National Commission for Minorities, Government of India.

M.L. Gautam, Secretary (Labour), Government of Maharashtra, Mumbai.

C.R. Prasad Rao, UGC Visiting Professor, Department of Sociology, Social Work and Human Resource Management, Nagarjuna University, Nagarjunanagar (A.P.).

Prakash Louis, Executive Director, Indian Social Institute, New Delhi.

D.S. Prakasa Rao, Associate Professor, Dr. B.R. Ambedkar College of Law, Andhra University, Visakhapatnam.

M.A. Kishore, Former Chairman, Department of Political Science, Faculty of Social Sciences, AMU, Aligarh.

Suresh Mane, Senior Lecturer, Department of Law, University of Mumbai, Mumbai.

Abdul Matin, Reader in Sociology, Department of Sociology and Social Work, AMU, Aligarh.

Usha Kapoor, Reader in Public Administration, Guru Nanak Dev University College, Jalandhar City.

Zafar A. Khan, Research Officer, Dr. Ambedkar Chair of Legal Studies and Research, Department of Law, AMU, Aligarh.

Khurram, Lecturer, Political Science, Department of Political Science, AMU, Aligarh.

Md. Zafar Mahfooz Nomani, Lecturer, Faculty of Law, AMU, Aligarh.

S.D. Sharma, Reader in Law, R.K. Kanwal Building Kautali, Khatyari, Almora, Uttaranchal.

Priti, Senior Lecturer, M.J.P. Rohilkhand University, Bareilly.

S.S. Dhaktode, Principal, Siddharth College of Arts, Science and Commerce, Mumbai.

1

Equal Protection of the Law

The Malaysian Experience

NIK AHMAD KAMAL NIK MAHMOD

Article 8(1) of the Federal Constitution of Malaysia provides: "All persons are equal before the law and entitled to the equal protection of the law". Article 14 of the Constitution of India states: "The State shall not deny to any person equality before the law or the equal protection of the laws within the territory of India". There are clear phraseology distinctions between the two provisions and the positive manner the Indian provision is put, connotes perhaps a stronger force in it compared to the Malaysian provision. This paper seeks to review the application of the equality principles in Malaysia in the light of similar approach in India. The focus will be on the judicial approach to the issue of protective discrimination that has been constantly besetting the equality principles. The writer seeks to first compare the Malaysian and Indian provisions on equality and then proceed to discuss the relevant cases decided by Malaysian courts on the issue. In that light the writer will draw from some Indian courts decisions on the matter.

Comparison between Malaysia and India

Like in India, right to equality is incorporated in the chapter pertaining to fundamental liberties in the Federal Constitution of Malaysia. Nonetheless, the Indian Constitution has five Articles on provisions of equality while there is only one main Article in the Malaysian Constitution. Article 8 of the Malaysian Constitution is comparable with Article 14 of the Indian Constitution.[1] One important development in Malaysia is the amendment made in 2001 to include prohibition against sexual discrimination. Such prohibition has been in Articles 15 and 16 of the Indian Constitution since its promulgation.[2]

Among the significant differences between Article 8 and Article 14 is the word 'State', which is absent in the Malaysian context. In India, 'state' covers the central government and all the member states as noted in *Charanjit Lal Chowdhury v Union of India.*[3] In Malaysia, no judicial interpretation has been made on its coverage but it may be presumed that the Malaysian Article 8(1) has application to any governmental unit.[4] Article 8 of the Malaysian provision focuses on 'equal protection before the law' which concentrates on protections against discriminatory legislation. The Indian provision encompasses both legislative and executive acts as can be seen in the Supreme Court decision of *S.S.M. Amirabbas v State of Madhya Bharat*[5] when it was said that: "...denial of equality before the law or the equal protection of the laws can be claimed against executive action or legislative process but not against the decision of a competent tribunal. The remedy of a person aggrieved by the decision of a competent judicial tribunal is to approach for redress a superior tribunal, if there be one".

In its scope the Indian provision is further enlarged by Article 15(1), which provides: "The State shall not discriminate against the citizen on grounds only of religion, race, caste, sex, place of birth or any of them" and Article 15(2), which provides: "No citizen shall, on grounds only of religion, race, caste, sex, place of birth or any of them, be subject to any disability, liability, restriction or condition with regard to (a) access to shops, public restaurants, hotels and places of entertainment, or (b) the use of wells, tanks, bathing ghats, roads and places of public resort maintained wholly or partly out of State funds or dedicated to the use of the general public". Malaysia's Article 8(2) provides that:

> Except as expressly authorized by this Constitution, there shall be no discrimination against citizens on the ground only of religion, race, descent or place of birth in any law or in the appointment to any office or employment under a public authority or in the administration of any law relating to the acquisition, holding or disposition of property or the establishing or carrying on of any trade, business, profession, vocation or employment.

This clause is put in the negative; that is to say, it is put together with a condition that discrimination is allowed only if the Constitution authorized such discrimination. Nonetheless, by way of implication the Malaysian general words of Article 8(1) has intended that any law that seeks to discriminate the people may be held unconstitutional. This in a way has similar implication to that of Article 15(2) of the Indian provision.

Clause 3 of the Article is however, positively asserted. It states that, "There shall be no discrimination in favour of any person on the ground that he is a subject of the Ruler of any State". This reflects the unique positions of federalism in Malaysia. There are nine hereditary Malay Rulers in the 13 states in the Federation and state governors are the heads of the other four. The word 'Ruler' implies that persons who are subject to Malay rulers are protected from discrimination but persons who are subjects of governors are not. In the light of the main clause of Article 8, it could not be the intention of the framers of the Constitution.

Clause 4 provides that, "No public authority shall discriminate against any person on the ground that he is resident or carrying on business in any part of the Federation outside the jurisdiction of the authority". Similar provisions are not available in India but by way of implication and the general terms used by Article 15 and the interpretation of the word 'state' in the case *Charanjit Lal Chowdhury v Union of India,*[6] it appears that the position is well covered.[7]

Despite the negative way Article 8(1) of the Malaysian provision is drafted, the overall reading of the provisions speaks for its affirmative protection to equality before the law.[8] The Indian position has both the positive and negative underpinnings. Positively, all persons in the same position and situation enjoy similar benefits provided by the law. In the negative sense, the Article protects all persons from any legislative acts that impose discriminatory obligations upon the minority group or unfair acts by the members of the executive.

In summation, no matter how both constitutions have been drafted, the way the courts in both countries interpret these provisions have far bigger implications than what the letters of the written constitutions are.

Protective Discrimination

The focus of the writer is on the issue of protective discriminations in the Malaysian Constitution as interpreted by the courts. Protective discriminations as provided by Article 8(5) are as follows:

> This Article does not invalidate or prohibit (a) any provision regulating personal law; (b) any provision or practice restricting office or employment connected with the affairs of any religion, or of an institution managed by a group professing any religion, to persons professing that religion; (c) any provision for the protection, well-being or advancement of the aboriginal peoples of the Malay Peninsula (including the reservation of land) or the reservation to aborigines of a reasonable proportion of suitable positions in the public services; (d) any provision prescribing residence in a State or part of a State as a qualification for election to any authority having jurisdiction only in that State

> or part, or for voting in such as election; (e) any provision of a Constitution of a State, being or corresponding to a provision in force immediately before Merdeka Day[9]; (f) any provision restricting enlistment in the Malay regiment to Malays.[10]

This clause allows other provisions in the Constitution to discriminate based on the criteria laid down in the sub-clauses. The criteria to discriminate are broadly put, namely, personal law, race and creed, residence in a state and election to post in a state, and the Malay regiment, a special unit in the army reserved for Malays only.

The Indian provisions allow similar form of discrimination. Instead of naming specific race or creed, Articles 15(4) and 16(4) used the terms "special provisions for the advancement of any socially and educationally backward classes of citizens or the scheduled castes and the scheduled tribes". The view is that both provisions do not confer a right but gives discretionary power to the State to make special provisions for these special groups.[11]

The Malaysian constitution allows further discrimination in Article 12(2) and Article 153. These articles allow law to be made contrary to the equality principles. Article 12(2) states:

> Every religious group has the right to establish and maintain institutions for the education of children and provide therein instruction in its own religion in any law relating to such institutions or in the administration of any such law; but federal or state law may provide for special financial aid for the establishment or maintenance of Muslim institutions or the instruction in the Muslim religion of persons professing that religion.

Article 153 provides details of protective discrimination for the Malays, namely, special position in the federal public service; education scholarships; education and training; permit or license for trade and business. These privileges are enforceable by law as well as by directions of the King (Yang di-Pertuan Agong).[12] Law that provides for privileges in permit, license and other reservations shall not be authorized to deprive any person whose license, permit or reservation is accrued or enjoyed.[13]

The protective discrimination provisions in Article 153 are entrenched provisions that require not only two-third majority votes of members of both Houses of Parliament but also the consent of the Conference of Rulers, which is composed of Malay hereditary rulers from nine states and the governors of five other states.[14] This is not the case for the amendment of Article 8 and Article 12, which only require the votes of two-third majority in both Houses. It is further entrenched by the facts that Article 10 that provides for freedom of speech prohibits the raising of any question on these privileges and reservations. It is enacted in the Sedition Act 1948 which categorizes it as 'sensitive issues' and may subject the person who raised or criticized these privileges to the charge of sedition.

Malaysia like many other commonwealth countries is a country with 'plural societies'. Read observed that it may be necessary to permit discrimination in the application of personal, customary or religious laws.[15] In Malaysia the Malay-Muslim community constitutes about 63 per cent of the total population followed by 18 per cent Chinese, 7 per cent Indian and the rest are other ethnic groups and indigenous communities of the East Malaysian states and also the aborigines of the states in West Malaysia. The Malays and the natives of the states of Sabah and Sarawak (East Malaysia) are called *bumiputra* or the 'sons of the soil' and these are the groups that are given special rights and privileges by the Constitution.[16] Read observed that it may be necessary to permit discrimination in the application of personal, customary or religious laws.

The rationale behind providing special privileges for the *bumiputra* and other indigenous races is the social structure of the various races in Malaysia. The main premise of these special privileges is the economic imbalances between the *bumiputra* (and other indigenous groups) and the Chinese communities. The Chinese with their entrepreneurship skills and financial strength have controlled the economy of the country leaving the *bumiputra* and other communities far behind.[17] Pursuant to these provisions, the New Economic Policy (NEP) was introduced in the 1970s, providing opportunity for *bumiputra* entrepreneurs to participate in trade and business with government help. Among its strategies, is a requirement that industry and business provide for at least 30 per cent equity to *bumiputra* businessmen. The main goal of the NEP is to ensure that the *bumiputra* controls at least 30 per cent of the economy. This seems achievable but the recent world economic downturn had affected Malaysia and the *bumiputra* entrepreneurs and resulted in the decline of *bumiputra* equity ownership of the economy. Beside the needs to reinvent the strategy of achieving the economic targets, the government has also sought to restate the policy on privileges and reservations to the *bumiputra.* Recently, the policy on admission to institutes of higher learning that practices priority places for the *bumiputra* has been modified to the effect that admission in accordance to the mechanism of meritocracy was introduced. This can be seen as the first step towards gradual modifications of the principle of protective discrimination.

In India, as previously observed, the Constitution provides for protective discrimination in the form of reservation for backward classes and tribes and reservation for scheduled tribes and castes[18], and also for women and children. It is justified on the basis of fairness, to promote integration between the various strata of the societies, equitable distribution of wealth and also on the ground of fair competition consistent with the principle of meritocracy.[19] The Indian Constitution does not provide a definition for the terms 'backward classes', and thus gives the legislature the task to provide a reasonable definition. Whereas Articles 341 and 342 allow the President to define 'scheduled castes' and 'scheduled tribes'.

Problems of Classification

What is the legal premise adopted by the courts in Malaysia when dealing with issues of discrimination? The Constitution has various provisions that allow some forms of discrimination and this seems to be politically accepted by the masses in Malaysia. The courts on the other hand, are the guardian of the Rule of Law and sentinels of democracy.[20] Judges have a significant role to play in ensuring that the fundamental safeguards provided by the constitution is fortified with strict interpretation of the clauses that provide for fundamental liberties. It is therefore necessary for the courts to justify the existence of discrimination and provide guides for the gray areas on the principle of classification. The premise used is the obscure doctrine of classification on the basis that equality can never be absolute. It is said that classification is the constituent element in equality principles to justify exceptions to the general norms. The effect is that equality did not mean that the law and policy could not categorize people and treated them differently. Those who are put in the same category shall not be discriminated whilst people in different categories could be discriminated. In justifying the different treatment applied to different races in a country, the common reason used is the principle of positive discrimination. The first Lord President of Malaysia, Suffian L.P. in *PP v Khong Teng Khen*[21] stated that:

> The principle underlying Article 8 is that a law must operate alike on all persons under like circumstances, not simply that it must operate alike on all persons in any circumstance nor that it must be general in character and universal in application and the State is no longer to have the character and universal in application and the State is no longer to have the power of distinguishing and classifying persons for the purpose of legislation – the law may classify persons into different categories. All that Article 8 guarantees is that a person in one class should be treated the same as another person in the same class". In Malaysia the highlight of the positive discrimination has been

on the special privileges to the *bumiputra*. Nonetheless there are other provisions that provide the same, such as special rights to the aborigines and also privileges to the King and the Malay rulers.[22]

Suffian L.P. again went on to explain the effect of Article 8 vis-à-vis positive discrimination. He said that specific discrimination is permitted within Article 8 and Article 153 that apply to both legislative and executive acts and both in procedural and substantive laws. He further said that the main question to ask is, is the law discriminatory and if the law is not, if for instance, it obviously applies to everybody, it is good law, but if it is discriminatory then because the prohibition of unequal treatment is not absolute but is either expressly allowed by the constitution or is allowed by judicial interpretation, the further question is, is it allowed? If it is, law is good and if it is not, the law is void. The court's positivist underpinning is clearly seen here, namely, what the law allowed, is permissible; what is not, is certainly void or unconstitutional.

In ensuring that positive discrimination is further pegged on sound rational principle the learned Lord President went on to refer to the Indian Supreme Court in *Shri Ram Krishna Dalmia* case[23] that expounds the principle of 'reasonable' or 'permissible' classification, namely, (i) the classification is founded on intelligible differentia which distinguishes persons that are grouped together from others left out of the group; and (ii) the differential has a rational relation to the object sought to be achieved by the law in question. The classification may be founded on different bases such as geographical, or according to the objects or occupations and the like. What is necessary is that there must be a nexus between the basis of classification and the object of the law in question. It was an irony that the evaluation of the principle of positive discrimination was not related to the special privileges of the Malay in *Khong Teng Khen*,[24] rather on the issue of transfer of jurisdiction in a criminal case. In fact, the courts in Malaysia never had an opportunity to consider the issue. The principle of reasonable or permissible classification has however been litigated in relation to other matters.

A similar approach is seen in *PP v Datuk Harun Idris.*[25] It involved a decision by the public prosecutor to transfer the case from one High Court to another. It ruled that equality was not absolute and that it did not mean that all laws had to apply uniformly to all persons to all circumstances. It is the court that has the final say over parliamentary or executive actions that affect equality.

The concern is how the courts digress reasonable classification to allow breach of the equality principles on the ground of protective discrimination, namely, the principle of intelligible differentia. Although the theory of classification is easy to state, its application is beset by many difficulties.[26] One of them is the broad nature of the term 'reasonable classification' that allows plenty of room for judicial value judgment. This can be seen in several decisions in Malaysia. In *Malaysian Bar & Anor v Government of Malaysia*[27] the issue at hand was the validity of the amendment to the Legal Profession Act 1976 that discriminates lawyers who has less than seven years standing as member of the Malaysian Bar to stand as committee member of the Bar. The majority judges were of the view that this discrimination is consistent with the reasonable classification test on the ground that durational classification of this nature is based on professional experience and thus clearly founded on intelligible differentiation. Therefore, there, exists a strong nexus between experience and legislative policy or object of the Act.[28]

The alternative view was manifested in the dissenting judgment of Salleh Abas, L.P. The learned Lord President (as he then was) said that such classification failed the test of reasonable classification on the ground that it is a suspect classification. He drew an authority from a US court decision of *Korematsu v US*[29] that decided that the classification is suspect if it has 'mere' rational connection between the basis and the object of the impugned legislation, and is, therefore, a forbidden classification.[30] This is distinguishable with the traditional test of classification that it is permissible if it is not shown to be arbitrary. The majority judges were however of the view that the traditional test is maintained by the US Supreme Court. The court is stricter in the field of fundamental rights than in other areas in that a compelling governmental or state interest must be shown in the classification or burden imposed on a particular group of individuals.[31] Thus far, this alternative approach has not found any support by the courts in Malaysia.

There are other problems besetting the reasonable classification and the 'nexus test'. Classification can be either under-inclusive or over-inclusive.[32] As observed by Tussman and deBroek:

> The purpose of a law may be either the elimination of a public 'mischief' or the achievement of some positive public good. To simplify the discussion we shall refer to the purpose of a law in terms of the elimination of mischief, since the same arguments hold, in either case. We shall speak of the defining character or characteristics of the legislative classification as the trait. We can thus speak of the relation of the classification to the purpose of the law as the relation of the trait to the mischief.[33]

This formula requires that the discriminatory law must pass the test that the 'trait' matches the 'mischief' This may not be easy to achieve given the facts that in some cases some people do not have the trait and some people who have the trait are not included in the classification. Applying the test to the facts of the *Malaysian Bar* case, the inconsistency is clearly illustrated. The amendment to the law prescribed durational classification as the basis of discrimination. The trait in Tussman and deBroek term means that lawyers who want to run for the Bar Council committee shall have a standing of at least seven years in the profession. Whilst the corresponding mischief is perhaps to ensure that only experienced members of the Bar should be at the helm and experience is weighed on seven years standing as a legal practitioner. Thus, the durational classification accepted by the court in this case assumed that lawyers who are in practice for seven years or more are better qualified than those who have less years to lead the bar. This is perhaps arbitrary by making a generalization between years of service and one's ability to lead the Bar Council.

Kevin Tan and Thio Li-Ann rightly put it, *inter alia:*

> (The) legislature may be able to define its objective so narrowly that the courts will find it difficult to find fault with the classification. If the objectives are themselves discriminatory, e.g., based on race or religion, or descent, then the test of classification is impotent and cannot be used to strike down the discriminatory legislation.[34]

As far as the constitution provided discriminations in Article 8(5), Article 12(2) and Article 153 are concerned the need to justify on the ground of intelligible differentia seems of mere academic importance. The parameter is well put by Abdul Malek Ahmad JCA in *Ahmad Tajudin bin Hj Ishak v Suruhanjaya Pelabuhan Pulau Pinang*[35] when he said that:

> We may, we think, safely begin with the proposition that any discrimination that is sanctioned by the Constitution is beyond challenge. For, the supreme law has, after propounding doctrine of equality in Article 8(1), gone on to carve out exceptions to it. Any discrimination that falls within these exceptions is therefore not actionable.

The problem lies in pegging the justification of intelligible differentia in situations other than those mentioned as illustrated in the case of *Malaysia Bar.* Then again it is too much an expectation that the courts in Malaysia would be willing to go against the established age-old test of reasonable classification.

In *Government of Malaysia v VR Menon*[36] the question at hand was the amendment to the Pension Adjustment Act 1980 that discriminated between pensioners who were residents and pensioners who were non-residents. The amendment excluded non-resident pensioners from receiving additional benefits. In *Ahmad Tajuddin bin Haji Ishak v Suruhanjaya Pelabuhan Pulau Pinang*[37] applied the same test and held that discrimination per se is not actionable. It has to be proven that it was an unfair discrimination not founded on intelligible differentia. In both cases the approach taken by earlier cases of *Khong Teng Khen* and *Datuk Harun Idris* were religiously followed. No attempt has been made to reconsider the current trend in dealing with the intelligible differentia test.

There are, however, decisions that favoured equality and outlawed discrimination. In *Public Prosecutor v Tunku Mahmood Iskandar*[38], the High Court overturned a lower court decision and convicted crown prince. The High Court found that the sentence was highly inadequate and contravened the provision of equality and it did not reflect the gravity of the offence. The High Court in *Datuk Harun* case[39] decided that the provision that allows the Attorney General to virtually choose the court to try the accused person was in breach of the right of equality and therefore unconstitutional. It was, however, overturned by the Federal Court on appeal.

A Change of Approach

The prevalent approach of the Indian court's on equality principle was manifested in *E.P. Royappa v State of Tamil Nadu*, where Bhagwati J. in the Supreme Court said:

> Equality is a dynamic concept with many aspects and dimensions and it cannot be cribbed, cabined and confined within traditional and doctrinaire limits. From a positivistic point of view, equality is antithetic to arbitrariness. In fact equality and arbitrariness are sworn enemies, one belongs to the rule of law in a republic while the other, to the whim and caprice of an absolute monarch. Where an act is arbitrary, it is implicit in it that it is unequal both according to political logic and Constitutional law and is therefore, violative of Article 14.[40]

The Indian Supreme Court decisions have always been of high value to Malaysian courts. Ong CJ in *Karam Singh v Minister of Home Affairs*[41] said; "we find Indian judges, for whom I have the highest respect, impress me as indefatigable idealists seeking valiantly to reconcile the irreconcilable whenever good conscience is pricked by an abuse of powers". The Malaysian court has also observed that opinion among Indian judges is often sharply divided, and sometimes Indian Supreme Court retreats from previously held position and favours views that were in a minority but a few years previously.[42] This sharp division of opinion has been used as an excuse to select only principles that the Malaysian agree irrespective of whether this opinion came from the majority or the minority view.

This does not however prevent the courts to continue to refer to the Indian decisions especially those coming from the Supreme Court as these decisions are considered to be very useful and highly instructive to the interpretation of Malaysian constitutional provisions. This includes the court willingness to depart from previous established principles in favour of recent approach of the Indian Supreme Court. In *Tan Tek Seng v Public Service Commission*[43] the Court of Appeal preferred the *Maneka Gandhi v Union of India.*[44] This decision has made significant departure from the earlier approach taken by Indian courts, which were followed by earlier Malaysian case such as in *Datuk Harun v P.P.*[45] The established concept of reasonable classification was jettisoned and the new stand was taken as summed up in the case of *Shri Sitaram Sugar Co Ltd v Union of India:*[46]

> Any arbitrary action, whether in the nature of a legislative or administrative or quasi-judicial exercise of power, is liable to attract the prohibition of Article 14 of the Constitution... Unguided and unrestricted power is affected by the vice of discrimination. The principle of equality, enshrined in Article

> 14 must guide every State action, whether it be legislative, executive, or quasi-judicial.

The question is whether the approach is a new approach. It is to be borne in mind that arbitrariness vis-à-vis doctrine of equality is not a new concept altogether. It is more of a judicial formula in restating the established principle of reasonable classification. Bhagwati J. observed in *RD Shetty v Airport Authority:*[47]

> The doctrine of classification which is invoked by the court is not a paraphrase of Article 14 nor is it the objective and end of that Article. It is merely a judicial formula for determining whether the legislative or executive action in question is arbitrary and therefore, constituting denial of equality. If the classification is not reasonable and does not satisfy the two conditions referred to above, the impugned legislation or executive action would plainly be arbitrary and guarantee of equality under Article 14 would be breached.

In appears that unreasonable classification is equated with arbitrariness and thus putting arbitrariness within the parameter of unreasonableness. It is submitted that to deal with the issue of discrimination on the basis of arbitrariness only of a particular legislation or policy, is to run into the danger of oversimplifying it. In this light, pegging the concept of protective discrimination on the line of reasonable classification and arbitrariness, one could not help in reaching two different conclusions. For instance, it is reasonable to classify between an economically backward race and an advanced race on the premise that discriminatory laws and policies would alleviate them from poverty. On the other hand, it would also be arbitrary to put the backward race together into one box and generalize all of them as backward given the fact that there are some of them who are not really backward.

It seems that the advantage of using arbitrariness as a scale is to avoid the pitfalls of comprehending whether the law is reasonably classified or otherwise. That is to say, whether the law treads on objective evaluation of its criteria, namely, (1) the classification is based on intelligible differentia, and (2) the differentia has a rational nexus with the object, which the law seeks to achieve. Again, like the approach to discrimination via reasonable classification, it is difficult to run away from judicial value judgment. Yet, the evaluation of discrimination via arbitrariness test is less complicated and easier to apply. The likelihood that any discriminatory legislation to be outlawed is more compared to the previous experience.

Would the acceptance to the approach in *Maneka Gandhi* case and *Shri Sitaram Sugar* case change the trend of judicial decisions dealing with equality issues in Malaysia. It is submitted that it would not. Unfortunately, the equality question was a minor issue in *Tan Teck Seng*. No doubt, the judicial creativity was apparent in that case but it found no support in cases after that. This is evident in the *Ahmad Tajuddin* case.[48] The court chose to revert to the old principle of reasonable classification laid down in *Khor Teng Khen* and *Datuk Harun* case. Nonetheless, the 'first impression' on the issue of whether an unfair discrimination is actionable is worth visiting.

In *Ahmad Tajuddinm* case, the issue was about the promotion of members of the public service to a higher rank based on offers made by the relevant Service Commission. Those who replied to the offer were given promotion but not those who did not answer the offer. It was argued that the promotion should be automatic and the failure to grant them promotion was an act of discrimination. The Court of Appeal decided that based on the doctrine of classification, there was no breach of Article 8 of the Malaysian Constitution. Abdul Malek Ahmad J.C.A. observed that for an unfair discrimination to be actionable, the following elements must be proved to exist: (1) there must be some form of discrimination, (2) the discrimination must be unfair, and (3) there must be resultant harm or injury.

Drawing from various Indian courts' decisions[49] the term 'unfair discrimination' according the learned judge is where the discrimination is accompanied by an element of harshness or unfairness, which the learned judge went on to elaborate as "unjust or unreasonable or unfair bias in favour of one against another".[50] He went on to elaborate the position applying the reasonable classification test and concludes:[51]

> At the end of the day, an objective assessment of the facts of a particular case should leave the court with the impression that a plaintiff has received harsh, unreasonable or unfair treatment in the hands of the defendant.

Taking the analysis by the court on the terms 'unfair discrimination, one could not help but conclude that the direction taken by the Court of Appeal was purely alternative to the objective evaluation of reasonable classification test but it cautiously ensures that the approach does not depart from the established rules in the reasonable classification test. The same seems to be the stand taken by Bhagwati J. on the 'arbitrariness' rule in both the *E.P. Royappa* case and the *Maneka Gandhi* case.

Conclusion

It is an accepted principle that right to equality does not mean that all people should be treated equally. All the law requires is that persons in the like circumstances should be treated alike. Every person in a particular class should be treated alike, so that no person is singled out for discriminatory treatment.

The concept of equality in Malaysia pre-supposes the acceptance of principles of 'reasonable' or 'permissible' classification that is further enhanced by the concept of affirmative action. This is no doubt a clear manifestation of accepted inequality allowed by the Constitution. The special privileges accorded to particular races and particular section of the society in Malaysia is achieved through rigorous methods of political wrangling, concession and manoeuvers. After 45 years of independence, these 'inequalities' have been subject to tremendous scrutiny vide politically and strangely not judicially. Unlike India, Malaysian protected groups are not in the minority. On the contrary, the *bumiputra* constitutes more than 60 per cent of the population and they are also the ruling class in the government. In that light, the constitutional protections will continue to exist despite recent moves by the government in power to revisit these privileges in a more critical manner.

On the other hand, other aspect of 'inequalities' is subject to judicial onslaught as highlighted from the cases above. The reliance on Indian decisions on this matter has been prevailing. Nonetheless, the courts in Malaysia are still grappling with factors such as history, customs, social and economic orientation, or simply prevailing prejudices.[52] Applying the reasonable classification test, judges are faced with unenviable tasks of deciding the question: reasonable from whose point of view? The danger is, as rightly described by Groves:

> The test of reasonableness assigns the relative values to these principles, which may well be in conflict, at the time of the constitutional challenge.... [and] too much deference to the presumption of constitutionality, which is often manifested by a liberal interpretation of "reasonable", destroy the effectiveness of the equality provision.[53]

The way forward is to treat equality within its own social and political surroundings and to accept the fact that each society, which professes its tenets, need not be like every other. On the other hand, it should also be accepted that there are in existence universal values that applies in all like circumstances.

Notes

1. Articles 14, 15, 16, 17 and 18 of Indian Constitution.
2. Since comments by R.H. Hickling, the former Law Revision Commissioner of Malaya in Hickling, "Some Aspects of Funda-

mental Liberties Under the Constitution of the Federation of Malaya" (1963) MLJ AN at xlix.

3. AIR 1951 S.C. 41.
4. Grove, Harry E., "Equal Protection of the Laws in Malaysia and India" (1963), *Am. Jnl. of Comparative Law*, Vol. 12, p. 385.
5. AIR 1960 S.C. 768 at 770.
6. Ibid.
7. See H.M. Seervai (1991), *Constitution of India: A Critical Commentary*, 4th Ed., H.M. Triparthi, Bombay, p. 442 (para. 9.16).
8. See a critical overview of this in S.M. Huang-Thio, "Constitutional Discrimination Under the Malaysian Constitution" (1964), 6 Mal. LR 1.
9. Independence Day (31 August 1957).
10. The Reid Commission, the Constitutional Commission that drafted the Malaysian Constitution proposed a limited duration for the special privileges stated above and to be put under Parliamentary review after that. Objections were expressed on behalf of the Malays and this was later removed.
11. H.M. Seervai, *Constitution of India: A Critical Commentary, (1991)* 4th. Ed., Vol. 1, N.M. Triparthi Private Ltd, Bombay, p. 557 (para 9.170). See *C.A. Rajendran v Union of India* (1968) 1 SCR 721. It has been held that reservation allowed should not exceed 50%. See *Indira Sawhaney v Union of India,* AIR 1993 S.C. 477.
12. Article 153(6) "where by existing federal law a permit or license is required for the operation of any trade or business the Yang di-Pertuan Agong may exercise his functions under the law in such manner, or give such general directions to any authority charged under that law with the grant of such permits or licenses, as may be required to ensure the reservation of such proportion of such permits or licenses for Malays as the Yang di-Pertuan Agong may deem reasonable, and the authority shall duly comply with the directions".
13. Article 153(8) "Notwithstanding anything in this Constitution, whereby any federal law any permit or license is required for the operation of any trade or business, that may provide for the reservation of a proportion of such permits or licenses for Malays, but no such law shall for the purpose of ensuring such a reservation – (a) deprive or authorize the deprivation of any person of any right, privilege, permit or license accrued to or enjoyed or held by him; or (b) authorize a refusal to renew to any person any such permit or license or a refusal to grant to the heirs, successors or assignees of any

person any permit or license when the renewal or grant might in accordance with the other provisions of the law reasonably be expected in the ordinary course of events, or prevent any person from transferring together with his business any transferable license to operate that business; or (c) where no permit or license was previously required for the operation of the trade or business, authorize a refusal to grant a permit or license to any person for the operation or any trade or business which immediately before the coming which immediately before the coming into force of the law he had bona fide carrying on, or authorize a refusal subsequently to renew to any such person any permit or license, or a refusal to grant to the heirs, successors or assignees of any such person any such permit or license when the renewal or grant might in accordance with the other provisions of that law reasonably be expected in the ordinary course of events". There is also another special privilege given to the Malays such as that in Article 89, lands classified as Malay reserved lands and not transferable to non-Malays.

14. Article 159. The five governors are appointed by the Yang di-Pertuan Agong on the advice of the chief minister of each state. The constitutional monarch Yang di-Pertuan Agong holds office for five years and he is elected by the Conference of Rulers. The five governors are excluded when the election process is carried out.
15. James S. Read, "Bills of Rights in the Third World: Some Commonwealth Experiences".
16. The Federal Constitution defines 'Malay' as "a person who professes the religion of Islam, who habitually speaks the Malay language, conforms to Malay custom..."
17. The manifestation of the dissatisfactory state of economic affairs and the special privileges to the Malays were said to be among the reasons of May 13th 1969 racial clash that witnessed killings of innocents and destruction of property in Kuala Lumpur and various other towns in Malaysia.
18. See a speech made by Dr. B.R. Ambedkar in one of the sessions of the Constituent Assembly when he expressed his view on special provisions for scheduled tribes and castes and backward classes. Constituent Assembly Debate, Vol. XII, p. 980.
19. See Vijay Kumar, "Protective Discrimination and Development", Paper presented in the National Seminar on *Constitutional Model of Equality and Fraternity: The Indian Experiences*, March 29-30, 2003, at Aligarh Muslim University, India. See also Y. Satyanarayana, "Affir-

mative Action Program: Recent Trends", Paper presented in the National Seminar on *Constitutional Model of Equality and Fraternity: The Indian Experiences*, March 29-30, 2003 at Aligarh Muslim University, India wherein he mentioned that affirmative action programme has been frequently justified in terms of compensatory justice for the scheduled castes and scheduled tribes and other backward classes.

20. Shad S. Faruqi (1990), "Fundamental Liberties in Malaysia: An Overview", Mimeograph, Kulliyyah of Laws, International Islamic University, Malaysia.
21. (1976) 2 MLJ 166.
22. Ibid, p. 169.
23. AIR 1958 S.C. 538.
24. Above note 13.
25. (1977) 2 MLJ 155.
26. H.R. Seervai, above note 7, at p. 454 (para. 9.33).
27. (1987) 12 MLJ 165.
28. per Mohamed Azmi SO and Wan Hamzah SCJ.
29. (1943) 320 US 81
30. Emphasis added.
31. This ground of governmental interest was applied in *Government of Malaysia v VR Menon* (1990) 1 MLJ 277 where the Supreme Court of Malaysia considered the discrimination provided by the Pensions Adjustment Act 1980 between pensioners who are residents and pensioners who are non-residents.
32. Kevin Tan and Thio Li-Ann, *Constitutional Law in Malaysia and Singapore*, Butterworth Asia, 1997, p. 760.
33. Joseph Tussman and Jacobus deBroek, "The Equal Protection of the Laws" (1949) 37 Calif LR 341.
34. Above note 24, pp. 760-761.
35. (1997) 1 MLJ 241 at 258.
36. (1990) 1 MLJ 277.
37. (1997) 1 MLJ 241.
38. (1973) 1 MLJ 128.
39. Above note 18.
40. AIR 1974 S.C. 555. He later reiterated this stand in *Maneka Gandhi v Union of India* AIR 1978 S.C. 597. See also *RD Shetty v Airport Authority* AIR 1979 S.C. 1628.

41. (1969) 2 MLJ 129.
42. Suffian, L.P. in *Datuk Harun* case. Above note 24.
43. (1996) 1 MLJ 261.
44. AIR 1978 S.C. 597.
45. Above note 18.
46. (1990) 3 SCC 223 at 251.
47. AIR 1979 SC 1628.
48. Above note 36.
49. *All India Sainik Schools Employees Association v The Defence Minister-cum-Chairman, Board of Governors, Sainik Schools Society, New Delhi & Ors.* AIR 1989 SC 88, *Indian Oil Corp Ltd v Premier Road Carriers Ltd.* AIR 1983 Ca 445, *Dost Mohammad v Union of India* 1981 Lab IC 1210, *Ranbir Singh v Chief Commercial Superintendent* AIR 1961 Punj 26.
50. Above note 36, p. 258.
51. Ibid.
52. Groves, at 390.
53. Ibid.

2

Origin of Untouchability

Efforts to Separate Fact from Fiction

K.P. SINGH

Due to the lack of hard evidences, the origin of the untouchability in South Asia is a subject of many debates. The most popular theory traces the origin of four-*varna* system through the Indo-European speakers, roughly in the period 1400 B.C. The main source of this theory is *Rig Veda,* which is being dubbed as 'myth' by Edmund Leach and Sucheta Majumdar and which explains the origin of caste system in cosmic terms.

According the *Rig Veda,* the oldest of the four *Vedas*, the distinction of the four *varnas* dates back to the origins of the human race:

ब्राह्मण: अस्य मुखम् आसीत, बाहू राजन्य: कृत।
ऊरु तत् यत् वैश्य, पत्भ्याम् शूद्रो अजायत॥

(Rig Veda, X 90. 12)

That is to say, at the time of creation, the Brahmin was born from mouth of the *Purusha* (the primeval man), the Kshatriya from his arms, the Vaishya from his thighs, and Shudra from his feet. Nevertheless, in order to analyze justly the origin of untouchability, it becomes imperative to examine the religious texts, travellers' accounts, etc., of the ancient times.

Dharamsutras (600-300 BCE)

The orthodox Brahmins refined the four-*varna* system ideologically over a period of times. The *Dharamsutras*, which were compiled between 600 and 300 BCE, represent the crystallization of these efforts by the orthodox Brahmins whose homeland was the upper Ganga basin. However, from the very beginning, the four-*varna* system was filled with contradictions. Therefore, the Brahmins had to revise the basic principle to conform to the realities of daily life, resulting unavoidably in quite loose interpretations and relaxation of the rules. In the *Dharamsutras*, we can see such difficulties incurred by the Brahmins in defining the status of Shudra.

According to the rules contained in the *Dharamsutras*, because Shudras were born from the feet of the Universal Soul, they were destined to serve three upper *varnas* born from his mouth, arms, and thighs (*Rig Veda Samhita, 4487*). Defining the duties of these four *varnas, Rig Veda* mentions:

ब्रह्मणस्य तपो ज्ञान तपः राजन्य रक्षणम्।
वैश्य तु तपो वार्ता तपः शूद्रस्य सेवम्॥

(Rig-Veda Samhita XI. 235)

They were to support themselves and their families with the small compensations received for the services that they rendered. Despite all these rules and regulations intended to segregate Shudras in ancient Indian society, in their every day life the twice-born *varnas* were unable to adhere to them thoroughly. Having outlined these rules and restrictions, the *Dharamsutras* then discussed how to compromise in practice, by offering some haziness for getting around them. There were in general two kinds of haziness: *Prayachistta* (penance or purification) and exceptions to the rules. In order to address the phenomenon of inter-*varna* sexual intercourse, and also to give privileges to the Brahmins, the *Dharamsutras* recognized the practice of two types of marriages, i.e., *Anuloma* and *Pratiloma* The *Anuloma* was a marriage to a woman of lower *varna (Gautama Dharamsutra IV, 17, 27-28)*, while in contrast, the practice of *Pratiloma* was a marriage to a woman of higher *varna*, which continued to be discouraged and scorned, and *Shudra* male who had had sexual intercourse with a twice-born woman was heavily punished by having his penis severed and his wealth confiscated, and if the woman has a husband or patron of some kind, these above two punishments will be followed by death *(Gautama Dharamsutra XII, 2-3)*.

The Buddhist Millennium (300 BCE-400 CE): Buddhist Scriptures and *Arthashastra*

The Buddhist scriptures and the Kautilya's *Arthashastra*, both of which were created after the death of Buddha, came into existence during the process of the formation of new urban societies in the mid-Ganga basin. The former were compiled by the Buddhist clergy, the representatives of the heterodox sects of those days, while the latter was the work of political thinkers. And they both describe a model of society different from the one contained in the *Dharamsutras* compiled by orthodox *Brahmins* with their roots in the agrarian regions of the upper-Ganga basin.

During this era of Buddhist millennium, a set of folk-stories, the Jataka tales, were also compiled by the Buddhist monks. The story of "A Lost Friend Found by a Song", is a document of social commentary of that time in India. This Jataka tale consists of two Chandala friends who were hated for their identity and origin. Once a villager invited a teacher to offer him food. But due to rainfall in the previous night, he could not attend and instead sent his two pupils. There they pretended being *Brahmins* and had food. Somehow, *Sambhuta* – one of them thought that the food was cool enough and put it into his mouth. As the food was very hot, his mouth got burnt. Immediately, the other friend Citta told him in his own (Chandala) language to spit that out. The villager-host got suspicious and questioned them about their language. The moment the villagers came to know that those two were Chandalas, they beat them up very severely and threw them out of the village. After this incident, they left for the woods and embarked on a series of rebirths, until they were finally born as Brahmins and Khatriyas. However, remembering about their past, the tale ends with their declaration that of the "impermanence of things created", suggesting that life is too important to be spent hating others for their birth based status.[1] The contents of the tale are very significant. Many of the Jataka tales described discrimination parallelling the more-recent untouchability.

The *Arthashashtra,* which is said to have been written by Kautilya, the chief minister of the Mauryan dynasty that rose up in Magadha, takes the *varna* system as the ideal basis of society and lists the obligations of each *varna.* The obligations of the Shudra are described as service to the twice-born, occupations in the craft and stage acting and *Vartta* (engaging in economic enterprises). Many of the provisions of the *Arthashashtra* resemble those contained in the *Dharamsutras* concerning social discrimination against the Shudras. The *Arthashashtra* goes beyond other *Dharamshashtras* in spelling out relatively more punishments for Shudras than for other *varnas*[2] and relatively greater protections for Brahmins than for other *varnas* in the idealized society. The punishment to Shudra for putting on a sacred thread and other signs of the twice-born is extremely severe – death[3]. The *Arthashashtra* also suggests that Chandalas be employed in guarding forests.

In ancient India the references were made to the stigmatized groups by such general terms as *Antya* or *Antyaja* (the far end or lowest people) and *Bahya* (outcasts). As early as the *Dharamsutras,* the Chandalas were defined as "people who would pollute the twice-born by either direct or indirect contact". Any twice-born person who did come in contact with them would have to perform purification rites. The word Chandala does not denote one single homogenous class of people. It is one word for many classes of people, all different from one another in their ostensible origins. Nevertheless, there are two kinds of Chandalas mentioned in the *Dharamsutras*. One is Janam Chandala that is a Chandala by birth and other is Karam Chandala that is a Chandala by conduct. Vashishtha says that "the atheist, the miser, the ungrateful and the one who cherishes anger for long – these are the four Chandalas by conduct and only the fifth is by birth".[4]

The Jain texts also mention about Jungitas or excluded people to whom Diksha or initiation was refused in Jain Sangha. They were Jati-Jungitas (born untouchables), Karma-Jungitas (untouchable by conduct) and Sarira-Jungitas (untouchable in body). Hunters, painters, fisherman, tailors and acrobats are classified as Jungitas by birth. Those who reared birds like peacock and fowls or animals like pigs, those who practiced hunting, acrobatic exercises and barbers' work as avocations are called Jungitas by conduct.[5]

In Buddhist scriptures, people considered to be inferior to the Shudra are often referred as Chandalas, Nesadas, Venas, Rathakaras, and Pukkusas.[6] According to *Gautam Dharamsutra*, a son begotten by a Shudra and a woman of a superior caste is called a *Patita* (outcaste). The son of a Brahmin by Shudra woman is called Nishada[7] by Buddhayana. The offspring of a Nishada male and Shudra female is called *Pulkasa*, and son of begotten by a Shudra on a female of the Nishad caste is known as *Kukkuaka*.[8] An offspring of Kashtriya man and Shudra woman is called as an *Ugra*.[9] The child born of a Vishaya male and Shudra female is called a *Rathakara*.[10]

In the *Shashtras*, five different hypothetical origins for Chandalas are identified:

- The offspring of Shudra father and Brahmin mother,
- The offspring of an unmarried women,

- The offspring of a union with a Sagotra woman,[11]
- The offspring of who after becoming an ascetic, returns to the householder's life,[12]
- The offspring of a man a barber father and a Brahmin mother.[13]

Closer contact, like sexual intercourse with a Chandala woman, required more difficult penance, including fasting. Chandalas, like Shudras, were completely excluded from the religious (Brahministic) practices of the twice-born.

According to the Jatakas, members of *varna* society, especially those belonging to the upper strata beginning with the Brahmin, were to take pains to avoid contact with Chandalas. In Jatakas we discover the stories of daughters of Brahmin and wealthy merchant washing their eyes after looking upon a Chandala, a Brahmin who was so hungry that he ate food left by a Chandala then died from embarrassment *(Jataka-II, 82-84).* The Jatakas describe Chandalas as segregated form the rest of the community, living in-groups on the outskirts of cities and villages. Buddhist scripture also mentions people among them who live by acrobatic performances and those who possessed especial magical powers.

Although the Jatakas are, ultimately, unverified folk stories, the frequency and consistency of the described patterns of discrimination against them suggest that there may have been historic accuracy to the Jatakas' descriptions.

The Hindu Legal Code (500-100 BCE)

The theoretical basis of the four-*varna* system as described in the *Dharamsutras* was systematized in the *Manu Smriti,* which was complied between 500-100 BCE. This legal code, which from antiquity has been the most respected guide to Hindu social life, lays out in an even more substantive manner than the *Dharamasutras* provisions about discrimination against the *Shudra Varna* and the Chandalas and their exclusion from the rest of the Indian society.

The *Manu Smriti* continues the burden of the *Rig Veda* with regard to the *varna*. The Brahmin, however, is the pick of the bunch. It is for him almost that all Creation creates and acts. He not only enjoys the top position in the *varna* hierarchy, even declared "in all justice (*dharmateh*) the lord of the entire creation,"[14] and lord of the *varna* due to the performance of special rite[15] (*samskara*). He may not be learned (*avidvansca vidvansca*); he all the same as veritable is a 'great god' (*daivatam-mahat*).[16] And thus being *param daivta* (great god), the "Brahmins are to be reverenced."[17]

However, contrary to the above position enjoyed by the Brahmins, Manu has been fanatically severe on Shudras. The Shudra finds his due place in the summary dispensing of the sage. "The Shudra among men and horse among animals; therefore those two, the horse and the Shudra, are the conveyances of beings; therefore the Shudra is not fit (ordained) for sacrifice."[18]

According to the Hindu law code, the Chandala, the representative of the untouchable of ancient times, was the progeny of a Shudra father and a Brahmin mother, i.e., the offspring of the most condemned *Pratiloma* marriage. But this theory of origin of the untouchables is far more the product of the *varna* conception of the orthodox Brahmins than anything based on historical facts.

The Brahmins used ideas of ritual purity to legitimize their supreme position in the top-society rank as priests by stressing their own purity and sanctity. This emphasis on purity gave rise to people on the opposite end of the society who were considered to be impure.

However, the provisions set down in the *Manu Smriti* concerning the Chandalas specify that they must reside outside of the village and can interact only with members of their own group. They are to wear the clothing worn by the deceased, eat the food out of broken dishes laid on the ground for them by the twice-born, and wear personal ornaments of black iron, etc.

India's Eyewitness Accounts of Untouchability: Magasthenes' *Indika* (305 BCE)

The *Indika* of Magasthenes is a source material that tells us about Indian society around the time when the *Arthashashtra* was written. According to the descriptions written by this Greek ambassador sent to the court of Chandragupta, the first king of Mauryan dynasty, seven kinds of meros (the Greek word) existed in India at that time. Indians could enter only occupations within their own meros and were forbidden to marry outside meros lines. The seven meros observed were (1) philosophers, (2) cultivators, (3) herders and hunters, (4) artisans and merchants, (5) warriors, (6) overseers or spies, and (7) high-level bureaucrats. Magasthenes' descriptions of meros differs in significant ways from the idealized, like Buddhist scriptures and the *Arthashashtra* are vague as to the distinction, Brahmins endorsed four *varnas*, suggesting important discrepancies between the 'real world' and certain Brahmins' views of how they might like the world to be.

Late 300-400 CE

There have been several other Chinese travellers who have provided descriptive accounts of social situation in the Indian sub-continent during 300 to 400 CE. Nevertheless, during 400 AD, the Chinese traveller Fa-Hsien described a word in which the "*Chandalas...* were fisherman, hunters, and sell flesh meat" (42-43).

630-640 CE

After two centuries, another Buddhist monk from China, Hsuan Tsang, travelled to India. In his travel accounts, he described Chandalas as 'evil men' (Hsuan Tsiang, 21). He also mentions of four types of classifications of the people, i.e., Brahman (*Po-lo-men*), Kshattriya (*T'sa-ti-li*), Vaisyas (*Fei-she-li*), and Shudra (*Shu-t'o-lo*). In these four classes purity and impurity of/rank was assigned to every one of his place (138).

Fictionally, the untouchability itself has been rationalized in Hindu religious thought as the ultimate logical extension of the concepts of *Karma* and rebirth that are supposed to determine all caste identity. One was born into an untouchable caste because of the accumulation of especially heinous sins in previous birth. This burden of sin made the untouchable a hazard to higher caste persons, who would be polluted by contact. The ancient legal text, *Manu Smriti* (the laws of the mythic codifier, Manu) prescribed draconic punishment for untouchables who so defied others. The untouchable was assigned economically and socially critical tasks that were, however, considered 'polluting' themselves – sweeping, tanning leather, and handling a plough that could destroy insect life. According to the prevailing myth, the untouchable was forbidden to hear sacred text (Manu prescribed pouring molten lead in the ears of offenders) even though untouchables played menial roles considered essential to many rituals.

Thus, it should be noted, however, that *Vedic* religion is a fictional entity about which nothing whatever is genuinely known. *Vedic* text may have a bearing on this system of ideas, but they are not primary in either a chronological sense or a theological sense. The Aryan invasion never happened at all. It is only a constructed fiction to serve the vested interests of the people. The term Arya as used in the *Vedic* and later scriptures were never used in the sense of an ethnic or linguistic category. It simply had the meaning of 'noble' or 'superior' as evidenced by such combination as 'aryas of dasa descent' and use of the term in Buddhist and Jain writings to indicate the 'noble truths of Buddhism' (S. Majumdar, 1989). However, to the upper caste Hindus of India, the fiction of Aryan theory of Indian history and the caste system became cherished scientific fact of their superiority over low caste people and consequently they have practiced untouchability. Though we have received several archeological contrary facts during the twentieth century but the fiction of Aryan origins still haunts the minds of upper caste Hindus.

Untouchability in South Asia During Two Thousand Years Preceding 1947

Though Buddhism does not appear to have practiced discrimination against the Shudras, it seems that it did discriminate against the Chandalas. The evidence can be drawn from the following story from Anadanasa, a collection of Buddhist stories similar to those given in the Jatakas around the first century CE. According to the story Prakriti, a Chandala girl, falls in love with Ananda, Buddha's favourite disciple, offers herself for marriage. Buddha suggests that the best course for her was to join the order of monks, like Ananda, which she does. But she is not accepted in the order before being purified. Nilakanta Shastri writes, "that is, the Buddha removed from her all traces of sin that had brought about her low birth, and having thus purified her he made a *Bhikshuni* (nun) of her – sufficiently clear statement that even according to the reformer, the Chandala girl was not fit for the practice of asceticism as she was and that, as preliminary condition, she had to be released from that state of sinfulness and bondage and ignorance."[19]

700-1050 CE

On his travel during the seventh "century to the Indian sub-continent, Xuanzang noted that in India there are four castes: the pure and ascetic (Brahmins), the nobility (Kshatriyas), the merchants (Vaishyas) and cultivators (Sudras). Each of these forms an exclusive social group".[20] However, during the eleventh century, Alberuni – the Afghan traveller, also mentioned in his travel account about the four *varna* system. Explaining about the social position of Chandalas in Indian caste system, he says that "they are occupied with dirty work, like cleansing of the villages and other services... they are illegitimate children; for according to general opinion they descend from a Sudra father and Brahmin mother as the children of fornication".[21] This confirms that during Alberuin's visit to India, the Chandalas were kept at the same social position in the society that they had centuries ago.

Rajara-I, the Chola King ruled from 985 to 1016CE and extended his territory from Kaveri delta to the extreme south of Indian peninsula by defeating the Pandayan Kingdom and later occupied northern parts of Sri Lanka. He built a temple of *Shiva* in Thanjavur and granted villagers worship in his temple. Inscriptions on the temple describe his grant and also mentions about non-taxable land in those 40 villages around the temple. In the inscription, is found the references to 'Tina-Cheri' along with other categories of residential area. Cheri in Tamil means 'street' or 'residential area', and the relative participle Tina means 'untouchable'. Tina-Cheri as a whole, therefore, means the residential areas of untouchables. However, apart from these inscriptions of Rajara-I, there seems to be very few direct references to untouchables or untouchability in Tamil inscriptions.[22] However, during the later period of 10th CE, references are found about the Paraiyas and Pulayas, which are called as untouchable communities by the non-Paraiyas and non-Pulayas.

Nevertheless, during the 12th century and later, class or occupational distinctions were crystallized. Artisans, servants, priests and money lenders were the main groups. Under these circumstances, it was necessary for the orthodox Brahmins to abandon their traditional ideas about Shudra *varnas*. What happened was that the village-based Brahmins began to conduct ceremonies, beginning with life cycle and yearly rituals, for local Shudras and became independent for their livelihood on the compensation received for these services. Therefore, a situation arose in which excluding Shudras from religious ceremonies in accordance with the traditional law codes would result in Brahmins losing their means of livelihood. Brahmins who were being so pressured to make concessions, finally compromised with reality by opening the *Mahabharta*, *Ramayana*, *Puranas*, and other religious texts respected as holy Hindu scriptures, to Shudras. That is to say that, Shudras were allowed to listen to the lessons, taught by Brahmins from these scriptures and attend ceremonies at which they could recite the holy *mantras* taken from them. However, only Brahmins were permitted to preside over these rituals. In the midst of this evolution from Brahmins to Hinduism the new *mantras* were given more importance over the Vedic *mantras*, and the religious discrimination against the Shudra almost lost effect.[23] The Hindu society, which accepted the Shudras as members, continued to develop; but in this the number of untouchables excluded from the four *varnas* increased. Many aspects of the social discrimination reserved for the *Shudra* in ancient Indian society now got transferred into the principles of untouchability.

As Alberuni has mentioned earlier, we can say that such changes were already in progress during the eleventh and twelfth centuries. It would, therefore, be correct to understand and examine these changes as a part of the transition or evolution from ancient untouchability concentrated on the Chandalas to the medieval untouchability. These were characterized by discrimination against many socially stratified castes scattered throughout the local region in segregated communities on the outskirts of agrarian villages. The following four points can accordingly be offered to explain what generally happened in such transition.

To begin with, within the tribes who lost their hunting and collecting territories due to the expansion of agrarian society (with the *Shudra* its major force cultivators), there were those who could not make the transition to agriculture and were thus forced to make their livelihood on the periphery of agrarian society engaged in necessary task (often looked upon as too impure for the four *varnas* to participate in) to supplement agricultural life.

Secondly, from sixth and seventh centuries, characterized by the establishment of a feudal order based on the regional decentralization of political authority and decline of urban commerce in favour of regional economies, village organization went though significant changes into strongly self-subsistent communities supported by many artisans, and service rendering castes. Within this process, some artisan castes broke up, and their members migrated to villages all over the region. The untouchable and other inferior groups living on the periphery of agrarian society were also caught up within this village organization, moving to the outskirts of individual villages and maintaining their tribal organization in the form of castes.

Thirdly, the ideology of purity and pollution, which was developed by the religious leaders of Hindu society, the Brahmins, contributed to the social stratification in villages organized according to many castes. Along with the development of this ideology, strata of inferior castes and artisans who were previously not looked upon with different degrees of pollution, resulted in exclusionary behaviour among them.

Finally, the existence of untouchables functioned to reduce the tense relationship arising from inequality within the village community and brought about a certain amount of stability. This process of order and stability of this village community brought about the order and stability of the regional society and ultimately of the medieval state. Therefore, developments of untouchability were responses to the expectations of ruling classes and landlords. The role played directly or indirectly in the development of untouchability during this time by the ruling classes on both the state and local level was a very important one.

1000-1600 CE

The period between 1000-1600 CE witnessed a new era of protest against the practice of untouchability. The untouchables who were deliberately degraded by the Brahmanic forces had never accepted their position. At first their response to untouchability came to the fore in the form of the *Bhakti Cult*. The *Bhakti Cult,* which originated in later 7th century CE in South India and spread in northern India later during 10th century CE, was an antithesis of the *Vedantic* philosophy propounded by Shankracharyas. They believed in *Dhyan* and *Karma* as the only two ways to achieve salvation. The high castes, especially the Brahmins had the monopoly over both the ways of salvation. The saints belonging to the *Bhakti* Cult stood up against the *Vedantic* philosophy. They believed in spiritual equality and Bhakti or devotion to God as one of the means to achieve salvation. They substituted songs, music, dancing, waving the lights for *Vedic Mantras.* However, there were two main Bhakti traditions prevalent in India. There were the (a) *Niguana Bhakti* tradition comprising Kabir and others and (b) *Saguna Bhakti* tradition prevalent in southern and western India. The Saguna was less confrontational and maintained a commitment to traditional belief and worship, including the adoration of idols.[24]

From time to time, the plight of untouchables touched various social reformers in India who worked for amelioration in different ways. The reformers protested against the exclusiveness of the caste system and notions of superiority and inferiority, which it bred.

Among the early reformers, Basavana or Lingayats (1106-1168CE), Ramanand (1400 CE), Kabir (1440-1518CE), Ravidas or Rai Das (late 15th CE), Nanak (1469-1533CE), Chaitanya (1485-1533CE), Eknath (1533-1599CE). However, the untouchable saints like Ravidas, Chokhamela, and many others were attracted toward the *Bhakti* Cult.[25] However, Chokhamela and Kanaka, the untouchable saints, were not allowed to enter the temple of Vithal at Pandharpur and the temple Krishan at Udippi respectively. Nonetheless, M.G. Ranade said that "the effect of their teaching was to humanize society and to introduce and emphasize the doctrine of mutual toleration."[26]

Nevertheless, the untouchables who were getting disgusted due to their all-sided oppression in Hinduism, naturally must have been inclined to shun it and embrace Islam which was philosophically more fascinating due to its monotheism and egalitarianism, in addition to being a religion of the ruling community. The rise of Sufism and preaching and propagation of Islamic principles by the Sufi saints in a virtually indigenous and attractive way also must have attracted the untouchables toward Islam.

1600-1900

The untouchables resorted to conversions as a means to get rid of Hinduism, which brought all miseries to them in various forms including the practice of untouchability. Moreover, they expected to get a new social status, which was an obvious motivational force for conversion to Islam, Christianity or Sikhism, in addition to certain material benefits.

In order to relinquish the untouchability and caste system, some of the untouchables, especially the sweepers and *Bhangis* belonging to Lalbegi and Malkana castes converted to Islam. They adopted Islamic names and rituals, but at the same time retained their old Hindu rituals and ceremonies. The Muslims were reluctant to have blood relationship with them.

In 1675, some of the untouchables especially the *Chuhuras* (scavengers) in Punjab had converted to Sikhism. It is said that the *Chuhuras* rescued the body of Guru Tegh Bahadur, the ninth Guru, who was executed by Aurangzeb. They carried the corpse of the Guru to Amritsar. Thus, after having observed the courage of the *Chuhuras* sepoys in carrying the corpse of the Guru, the tenth Sikh master, Guru Govind Singh, allowed them into the faith; and as a result, they were called *Mazhabi* or 'faithful'. Most of the *Chuhuras* followed the first converts.[27]

The social and religious reforms continued throughout the nineteenth century. Raja Ram Mohan Roy (1772-1833) founded the Brahmo Samaj, which attacked the caste system. The Brahmo Samaj preached "Ek Dharam (one religion), Ek Jati (one caste), and Ek Bhagwan (one God)".[28] Another social reformer of nineteenth century was Mahatma Jyoti Rao Phule (1827-1890). Being a Shudra himself, he attacked on the caste system and untouchability and sought a complete destruction of social structure. In Gulamgiri (slavery), he examined the motives and objects of the cruel and inhuman laws framed by the Brahmin, "who under the guise of religion has finger in everything, big or small, which the Shudra undertakes".[29] Mahadeo Govind Ranade (1842-1901), another major social reformer, envisioned that downfall of India was due to weaknesses in the Hindu social system. He had a clear understanding of inter-relations between social and political issues. He argued that there were no rights in the Hindu community; there were privileges for few and disabilities for the vast majority. He struggled to create rights and strove to improve the moral tone of Hindu society.[30]

Similarly in Bengal, the life of Ramakrishna Paramhansa left an indelible mark. He was a simple priest, with no formal education, a man in direct tradition of Indian saints. In his gospel, he used expressions such as "the devotees have no caste, one accept food even from a Priah, if the caller is a devotee of God". His famous disciple, Swami Vivekananda, established the Ramakrishna Mission in 1896. The mission translated Ramakrishna's teachings into action by devoted services to the poor regardless of their caste or religion. In his views, "all members of society ought to have equality of opportunity. For inequality is the bane of human nature, the curse upon mankind, the root of all misery – this the source of all bondage, physical, mental and spiritual".[31]

Gopal Krishna Gokhle founded the Servants of India Society which was another group pledged to social reforms. Its members were pledged to a life of service to India. Some of its members worked in the villages and helped the untouchables. Gokhle said in 1903 that "every well-wisher should consider it his duty to rouse self-respect in these classes and place facilities for education and employment within their reach".[32] However, some of Indian princes were also statesmen who undertook measures for eliminating untouchability in their States. Sayji Rao Gaekwad III (1863-1939), Maharaja of Baroda, and

Chhatrapati Shahu, Maharaj (1874-1922) of Kohlapur, were the most prominent among these.

The Portuguese missionary, St. Francis Xavier attempted a large scale conversion of lower classes on the coastal areas of Western India (1542).[33] Later on the Church of England got engaged very actively in proselitization among the lower castes. Nonetheless, the untouchables who were victims of aggravated forms of untouchability especially in Travancore, became a Christian's majority. According to 1891 census there were a total of 2,284,172 Christian converts in India; out of them 1,491,584 were in British provinces and 7,92,714 were in native states.[34] It could presumably be said that the process of conversion to Christianity must have started before the pre-rebellion period.

However, conversion to Islam, and Christianity proved to be good, but only in a limited sense. Muslim community included two classes namely Ashraf and Ajlaf meaning Muslims who traced their ancestry outside of India and Muslims whose pre-Muslim ancestors had lived in India. Even therein existed one more – the Hindi speaking regions namely Arzal, which included persons "engaged in filthy occupations like sweepers, scavengers, Mehtars, Mahars, Mussalis, etc.,"[35] and they were subjected to untouchability. Even among Indian Christians there existed two classes, one converted from higher castes and other from lower castes. It was but a fact that only high caste converts could derive more and more benefits from the missionaries than the lower castes converts.

Conversion to Buddhism

Conversion as a way out of the untouchable status was not new in India. Islam, and more especially Christianity, drew large numbers of their converts from lower caste, and Sikhism in the twentieth century actively encouraged untouchable conversions. Actually, conversion to Buddhism was not yet known, although its numbers in Madras and on the Malabar coast were small. The Madras Buddhists generally declared themselves as

Hindus, but in Cochin in 1931 the Census commissioner reported 96 Buddhists, mostly educated Malayai Iluvans, an untouchable caste, who disgusted with the social disabilities to which their caste was subjected within Hindu fold, became Buddhist converts.[36]

Indian scholarship, from the 1880s onwards, stimulated both European studies in Buddhism and as part of Indian heritage. In 1935, Dr. Ambedkar announced his decision to quit Hinduism. But at that time Buddhism was not seen as a viable alternative for the Mahars. But Ambedkar was aware of the increased intellectual interest in Buddhism. He himself had received as an examination prize in 1907 a biography of the Buddha in Marathi from its author, a Bombay school teacher.[37] Once speaking himself in 1935, he said that "unfortunately, I was born a Hindu. It was beyond my power to prevent that, but I solemnly assure you that I will not die a Hindu".[38] However, after the above announcement, it took about 20 years for Ambedkar to embrace Buddhism on 14 October, 1956 in Nagpur.

Untouchability During the British Rule

When in 19th century the British established their rule over most of India, their policy too was one of non-interference but there was a pressure on them to change the social order in India. But the policy of non-interference was formed in 1857. However, some of their policies had an impact on the social order. For example, they established a nationwide legal system, which resulted in the movement of disputes from caste and village tribunals to the government's courts, which supported the norm of equality before the law. Therefore, the British Law, in principle, did not recognize the caste structure as far as criminal/commercial law was concerned.

However, when the caste Hindus took it upon themselves to enforce their exclusive rights and privileges against the lower castes, the courts were reluctant to provide remedies against such actions, which included social boycott.[39] The higher courts endorsed the high caste dominance in settled ways, while at the lower levels there was often active governmental support for the demands. In civil laws, the British legal principle of 'precedent' meant enforced 'legitimacy' of whatever hierarchical practices were in place when the British acquired control of territory.

Nevertheless, with the spread of schools and growth of a class of educated Indians, many new egalitarian social ideas began to spread. The new class began to question many assumption and beliefs of Indian society. Many of them devoted themselves to renewing social institutions with a view to promote equality and social justice.

By the early twentieth century, the communal quota began to be viewed as a step toward equality. Though the state of Mysore inaugurated the first regime of communal quota in 1918 the reservations were only for non-Brahmin 'backward castes'. Some relief was given by the 1919 reform. Of much greater importance is the fact that the voice of some untouchable leaders began to be heard around this time in political assemblies.[40] While Mahatma Gandhi described untouchability as an ugly outgrowth of Hinduism and appealed to caste Hindus to do penance and purify themselves and Hinduism. Dr. Ambedkar at the same time addressed the untouchables and directed their attention to the potentialities of action to be taken by the government. Hence we see the conflict between those who tried to assimilate the untouchables into Hinduism and their leaders who opposed it, focussing on government.[41]

The communal award of 1932 has to be seen in this context. It granted the demand of the untouchables for a separate electorate in areas where they were concentrated, in addition to the regular votes they would cast as members of the general electorate. Gandhi objected to this award, because that would signify a perpetual split in Hinduism, perpetuating stigma of untouchability and making impossible their assimilation into mainstream Hinduism. He could not accept these demands because the Congress could not afford to lose the Hindu base of its support. Hence the Congress-led governments of 1937 attempted to reform Hinduism.[42] In 1938, for the first time in British India, governments intervened to secure the opening of temples when the Bombay and Madras legislatures passed temple entry Acts. Encouragement to the education of the untouchables increased and measures were taken to secure for them some posts in government service. Before independence, 27 Acts had been enacted by various legislatures to give more legal rights to those who had till then experienced social and religious disabilities.[43]

Untouchability in India since 1947

Many social scientists and serious observers of Indian society believe that a large proportion of those now identified as 'Untouchables' today have descended from people who suffered severe oppression in the past. Many also believe that there are today, as there have been historically, a body of people who are so ill-treated and so distinct from other Indians that they can be separated out and labelled 'Untouchables' or some synonymous term. Many also believe that 'Untouchables' are a social category into which some families have moved and out of which some families have moved over the years. To focus on the practice of untouchability and to separate fact from fiction, I have chosen to divide my answer into three sections, namely, (a) Untouchability and Legal Practice (b) Untouchability and Social Practice (b) Sanskritization, Westernization and Industrialization.

Untouchability and Legal Practice

At the transfer of power in 1947, it was widely accepted that discrimination on the basis of caste would have no place in independent India. Consequently, the Indian Constitution in its very preamble assures every citizen of social, economic and political justice and equality of status and opportunity. Article

17, forbids the practice of untouchability in any form. Among the fundamental rights, Article 14 enunciates the right to equality; Article 15 prohibits discrimination on grounds of religion, race, caste, sex or place of birth.[44] Article 25 (2)(b) assures all classes and sections of Hindus access to Hindu religious institutions of a public character. The Directive Principles of State Policy, which serve as guidelines for the State in making laws, contain specific provisions, viz., Article 3 8, 39, 39A, which enjoin on the State, the duty to ensure the creation of a just social order, and Article 42, which asks the State to promote with special care the educational and economic interests of the weaker sections especially the Scheduled Castes.

However, in spite of having numerous reform movements, constitutional provisions and legislative measures, the levels of discrimination against untouchables are far from encouraging. Caste prejudices and the practice of untouchability continue in rural as well as urban areas of India.

Untouchability and Social Observance

Untouchability has remained a complex social problem for many years. Since the independence of India in 1947 particularly, it has assumed critical significance because of the confluence of several factors. Many scholars have argued that nature of untouchability has changed substantially (Beteille, 1981; Galanter, 1984; Nandu Ram, 1994). This is true, and there are evidences to support this contention. The problem is, why the issue of untouchability should surface so frequently despite the penetration of modern Secular State? An answer to this question requires vigorous inquiries into several dimensions of untouchability. One dimension, in my understanding, is assessment of the ideology or the theoretical approach of the leadership of the untouchables in the past. Obviously, the two great leaders who recently devoted a significant part of their lives toward the question of untouchability are Mahatma Gandhi and Dr. B.R. Ambedkar.

Ambedkar and Gandhi on Untouchability

Both Gandhi and Ambedkar addressed themselves to the problem of the removal of untouchability and the uplift the untouchables. Yet, they differed in their approaches and strategies so much that one criticized the other bitterly. Gandhi believed that untouchability was not an authentic part of Hinduism; the sooner Hindu understood this, the sooner untouchability would disappear. He believed that untouchability could be removed only when the majority Hindus realize that it was a crime against God and man and are a shamed of it.[45] Hence, for him the battle against untouchability included a religious component.[46] He, therefore, called for a charge of heart among the Hindus as an act of explanation and reparation for the centuries of oppression. And by change of heart he meant acceptance of his interpretation of a purified Hinduism on the part of high castes.[47] Ambedkar viewed untouchability as an institutionalized expression of socio-religious oppression and exploitation by the dominant elements. He traced the roots of the problems in the structure of the Hindu society and characterized it as a by-product of the Hindu four-*varna* system. He believed that the untouchable is a by-product of both the *varna* system and the caste system, hence there will be untouchables as long as there are castes. At the end of his life, Ambedkar concluded that nothing can emancipate the outcaste except the destruction of the system.[48] For many years, he tried to improve the lots of untouchables by means of struggles. He argued that "the salvation of the depressed classes will come only when the caste Hindu is made to think and is forced to feel in that he must alter his ways". Further he stated that "I want a revolution in the mentality of the caste Hindus".[49]

During all these years up till June 1947, Ambedkar sensed that the Congress has usurped the politics of Untouchables while he had largely lost. To show the world the hollowness of the Congress claims and actions, he prepared an exhaustive questionnaire on 6 July, 1946 which he gave to B.K. Gaikwad, President, Bombay Provincial Scheduled Caste Federation, to take up with the Congress and Gandhi. In the questionnaire, he stressed the violation of the Poona Pact, and asked about the place of Untouchables in the *Swaraj*, if they were minority, what political safeguards would be provided for them, and why they could not have separate electorate.

Gandhi replied to the questionnaire under the caption "Scheduled Castes" in *Harijan* of 3 November, 1946. As the place of the Scheduled Castes in *Swaraj*, he said, "In the Swaraj of my conception the place of untouchables will be the same in every respect as that of the so-called caste Hindus." In August 1946, the Viceroy, Lord Wavell, invited Nehru to form the Interim Government in which Dr. Ambedkar and Jagjivan Ram were included in the Ministry.

The period from 1947 to 1951 was for Ambedkar period of creative cooperation with Congress Government. He now assumed the role of a practical statesman to grant the untouchables equal status and fundamental rights in the Constitution of India. Nevertheless, there was a change now in Ambedkar's attitude towards Hinduism. When a large number of Scheduled Castes in Pakistan were not allowed to come to India and they were forcibly converted to Islam, Ambedkar issued a press statement to the *Free Press Journal* on November 28, 1947, "I would like to tell the Scheduled Castes who happen today to be impounded inside Pakistan to come over to India by such means as may be available to them. The second thing I want to say that it would be fatal for the Scheduled Castes whether in Pakistan or in Hyderabad to put their faith in Muslims or the Muslim League. It has become a habit with the Scheduled Caste to look upon the Muslims as their friends because they dislike the Hindus. This is mistaken view ... All those who are forcibly converted to Islam would be received back in the fold and treated as brethren... Whatever the tyranny and oppression which Hindus practiced on them, it should not warp their vision and swerve them from their duty."

This statement of Dr. Ambedkar shows that he was very close to the views of Gandhi at this time. Much of nationalist press eulogized this change in attitude of Dr. Ambedkar. It clearly showed that at this time in his life, Dr. Ambedkar believed that the Scheduled Castes could remain within the fold of Hinduism and hope to receive fair treatment.

The era of cooperation with the Congress ended for Dr. Ambedkar in 1951, just before independent India's first general elections. He resigned as Law Minister and participated in the first general election as an opponent of the Congress. However, his party, the Scheduled Castes Federation, did not secure many of the votes. On losing elections, he advised his supporters not to lose heart and told that the "success of the principle and programmes is the victory of the party".

Dr. Ambedkar's forecast has literally come true in at least one way. Today, every political party sets its eye on the powerful vote bank of the Scheduled Castes. Any adverse swing in this vote can violently tilt the swing against any established party. The politic of untouchability has come to stay. Every political party in its manifesto gives a prominent place to the welfare and upgradation of the Scheduled Castes. However, the Indian Constitution adopted several measures to ensure the equal participation of underprivileged castes. The first Prime Minister of India, Jawaharlal Nehru told the Constituent Assembly that "the first task of this Assembly is to free India through a new Constitution, to feed the starving people, and to clothe the naked masses and to give every Indian the fullest opportunity to develop himself according to his capacity".[50] Consequently the Constitution provided for protective discrimination under various Articles (15, 16, 29, 38, 46, 330, 332, 334, and 335) with a view to accelerating the process of building an egalitarian social order. The protective discriminations or reservations have three components: (1) political reservations, (2) educational reservations, and (3) job reservations.

Articles 330 and 332 provide for reservations of seats for Scheduled Castes and Scheduled Tribes in the Lok Sabha and Legislative Assemblies for the States. Initially, the reservations were for ten years, but they have been periodically extended at present, Articles 15(4) and 29 provide the reservations to these underprivileged castes into the educational institution for their admissions. In India there are two types of educational institutions: (1) public institutions and (2) elite institutions. The former are without adequate facilities, and the latter, which have facilities, serve a small section of the society, most of which belong to upper castes.[51] Under Article 16(4), 320(4) and 333, 15 per cent and 7 per cent of the positions are reserved at all levels in the government and public sector for SCs and STs. Somehow, the reservations in jobs has never been fulfilled yet.

Without going into the details, in my opinion Ambedkar was a more pragmatic, cautious and astute leader. Being an untouchable himself, he was closely aware of the humiliation and degrading conditions of the untouchables both in rural and urban areas. Nevertheless, whatever differences existed between Gandhi and Dr. Ambedkar they were minor or marginal ones. Both believed in ending untouchability. Gandhi focused his attention on attitudes of the higher castes. Dr. Ambedkar focussed on mobilizing the so-called untouchables. Of course, in my opinion, Dr. Ambedkar was a step ahead of Gandhi because he saw the fulfilment of the goals of quality, freedom, and dignity by mobilizing the masses, i.e., untouchables. Both Gandhi and Dr. Ambedkar linked untouchability to the religious sphere. Gandhi tried to view the abolition of untouchability more in religious-moral terms, while Dr. Ambedkar first tried to view it in historical terms but later sought a solution in the legal and finally religious realms. In post-independent India, the viewpoints of both Gandhi and Dr. Ambedkar exist and often influence the debate on untouchability.

Both Gandhi and Dr. Ambedkar were great men. While Gandhi was the father of the Indian nation, Dr. Ambedkar was the father of the Indian Constitution. While Gandhi was an apostle of peace and non-violence, Dr. Ambedkar became a Buddhist, which preached universal peace and non-violence. It is unfortunate that Gandhi died on January 30, 1948 and could not see for himself the progress made by the Scheduled Caste. Dr. Ambedkar was fortunate enough to see for himself some initial limited progress made by the Scheduled Castes arising out of the safeguards provided in the constitution, but he finally concluded that for India's Untouchables to achieve equality they should leave Hinduism and adopt Buddhism. And in October 1956, he himself adopted Buddhism.

Sanskritization, Westernization and Industrialization

Sanskritization, westernization and industrialization are processes of social change in modern India, and it is not possible to understand one without reference to the other. M.N. Srinivas, an anthropologist, during his study on Coorgs of South India, labelled the first two processes. In the process of Sanskritization, Srinivas observed that some of the lower and untouchable castes were adopting the way of life of Brahmins. They were leaving their own rituals, customs, and other social practices to which they thought degraded by adopting the rituals and customs to which they thought as pure, clean, and civilized. For instance, some of them quit eating meat, started washing their hands before taking meals, wearing *dhoti* and *Janeu* (sacred thread) etc. Contrary to this process, Srinivas, mentions about the process of Westernization in which the Brahmins were imitating the Westerners by leaving their own culture, rituals and other social practices. For instances, they started dining on the dining table, wearing shirts and pants, etc. According to Srinivas, "Sanskritization is both a part of the process of social mobility as well as the idiom in which mobility expresses itself. When there is Sanskritization, mobility may be said to occur within the framework of caste, whereas Westernization mobility implies out side the caste."[52] M.N. Srinivas' concepts of Sanskritization and Westernization have been criticized by several social scientists for being value laden and over-simplified.

However, no matter if some untouchables have sanskritized themselves and adopted specific elements of Brahminical culture and rituals, most of them continue to be discriminated against in the name of their caste-based origin. Industrialization has played some important part in reducing the untouchability in urban sector. But still, ill practices of untouchability are found in the urban areas and discrimination against Untouchables continues in urban slums. For instance, the Untouchables used to work with leather but now one may find other non-untouchable castes also working with leather. Nevertheless, though they work with the leather as it was the job of untouchables, but still they practice the untouchability. In Bata Shoe Company, there might be some Brahmins working on the leather as part of their job. But as they come out of the factory, they become pure Brahmins. Even at work, they cannot accept an other untouchable worker who is doing the same kind of job. In any case, industrialization has played a significant role in reducing untouchability though it has converted it into different forms. But in rural areas, in economic terms, Untouchables are field labourers or workers in a large number of so-called unskilled occupations. For centuries they have looked like a particularly downtrodden proletariat, some time lumpen proletariat.[53] Not only that, they have also been subjected to various kinds of oppressions in their day-to-day life. According to Oliver and Marika, "another tension between orthodoxy and social practice is represented by the exploitation of Untouchable women by their high-caste masters: evidence from our own time suggests that this practice has been habitual rather than merely occasional. Not the least contradictory aspect of such connection is that the Untouchable woman was never so degraded or ritually polluted as to be sexual unapproachable: Untouchability was always curse, never a protection."[54]

Untouchability in Contemporary India

Ever since India became independent, there have been a number of Amendments to the Constitution of India to improve the socio-economic and political status of India's backward classes in addition to the scheduled castes and scheduled tribes. In August 1989, V.P. Singh, the then Prime Minister of India, announced to implement the recommendations of Mandal Commission which was set up in 1978 and submitted its report in 1980. V.P. Singh's decision led a wide-spread protest, especially by the members of upper castes.[55] However, after the implementation of the Mandal Commission's recommendations, the incidents of violence against low caste people have increased. The caste Hindus' purification of the Sampoornand statue in Varanasi in 1978 after the 'polluted' touch of an untouchable leader Jagjivan Ram and the recent killings of low caste people by the upper caste private army Ranbir Sena, and by the police in Bombay, demonstrate that caste based prejudices and untouchability persist in the minds of many caste Hindus.

Conclusion

The Indian untouchables have been denominated by several terms for the Chandalas to the Dalits. Though they have been victims of their low caste identity, but after independence, they have been seriously engaged in different kinds of activities to get rid of their untouchability. The fact is that the government has made several legal provisions to protect low caste people from the oppression. But unfortunately these laws do not get translated completely into reality. Today, some of the low caste people get butchered and killed. All too often, their higher caste attackers are not held accountable. Again this fact becomes another fiction when culprits move around without accountability.

Notes

1. Jataka Tales: A Lost Friend Found by a Song, pp. 235-39.
2. Vasishtha Samhia, XIX.
3. Ibid. IX, 224.
4. Fuhrer (ed.), Vasishtha, p. 21.
5. Kosambi, D. D., Bhagwan Buddha, pp. 351-53.
6. Anguttara Nikaya, 1. 107, ii. 85.
7. Budhhayana, pp. 1, 9.17.3.
8. Ibid. I. 9.17, 13-14.
9. Ibid. I. 17, 4-5.
10. Ibid. I. 17-6.
11. Ved Vyasa Smiriti, pp. 9-10.
12. Yama Parasura Madhavya quoted by Dr. Ambedkar. The Untouchables, p. 138.
13. Anusasana Parva. 29-17. (Maha Bharata).
14. सर्वस्यैवास्य सर्गस्य धर्मतो ब्राहमण: प्रभु: Manu I. 93.
15. संस्कारस्य विशेषाच्च वर्णानां ब्राह्मण: प्रभु: Ibid. X.
16. Ibid. IX, 317.
17. सर्वथा ब्राह्मणा: पूज्या: परमं दैवतं हि तत् Ibid. 319.
18. Ibid. 1. 6.
19. Nilakant Shastri, A.K. (1974), *Aspects of India, History and Culture*, Oriental Publishers, Delhi, pp. 61-62.
20. Watters, T. (1961), Tr., *On Yuan Chawng's Travels in India*, Delhi, Indian edn. p. 168.
21. Schau, Edward C. (1962), *Alberuni's India*, Lahore, pp. 135-6.
22. Noboru, Karashima, "The Untouchables in Tamil Inscriptions and Other Historical Sources in Tamil Nadu", in H. Kotani (ed.), *Caste System, Untouchability and Depressed*, pp. 21.
23. Kane, P.V., *History of Dharamsastra*, Vol. I, pp. 893-96.
24. Mendelson and Vicziany (1998), *The Untouchables*, p. 23.
25. See Zelliot, Eleanor (1996), *From Untouchable To Dalit.*
26. M.G. Ranade, *Rise of the Maratha Power*, p. 76.
27. Das, Bhagwan (ed.) (1980), *Untouchable Soldiers*, p. 44.
28. Chakravorty, S.C. and Ray, S.N., *Brahmo Samaj: The Depressed Classes and Untouchability*, p. 2.
29. Adhikari, Gopal, *Joti Rao Phule Samagra Grantha* p. 272.
30. *See* Mahadeo Govind Ranade, *Rise of the Maratha Power.*

31. Phadke, Y.D., *Social Reforms in Maharashtra*, p. 62.
32. Ranade, M.G., *Rise of the Maratha Power*, p. 76.
33. Pannikar, K.N., *The Foundations of New India*, p. 36.
34. Smith, George, *The Conversion of India,* p. 201.
35. Das, Bhagwan, *Thus Spoke Ambedkar,* Vol-IV, p. 143.
36. Zelliot, Eleanor (1996), From Untouchable to Dalit, pp. 187-96
37. Ibid. 192
38. Keer, Dhananjay (1987), *Dr. Ambedkar: Life and Mission,* New Delhi. p. 138.
39. Galanter, Marc (1984), *Competing Equalities: Law and Backward Classes in India*, p. 20.
40. Ibid. 27.
41. Ibid. 29.
42. Ibid. 31.
43. Ibid. 36.
44. Elder, Joseph W. (1996), "The Constitution and Social Structures on India" in K.S. Muth and A. Dasgupta (eds.), *The Perennial Tree: Select Papers of the International Symposium on India Studies,* p. 262.
45. Kumarappa, Bharatan (ed.) (1954), *The Removal of Untouchability by Mahatma Gandhi,* p. 57.
46. Lynch, Owen M. (1974), *The Politics of Untouchability,* p. 134.
47. Forrester, Duncan B. (1980), *Caste and Christianity; Attitude and Policies on Caste of Anglo-Saxon Protestant Mission in India,* p. 102.
48. Keer, Dhananjay (1971), *Dr. Ambedkar: His Life and Mission*, p. 189
49. Ibid. 221.
50. Quoted by Granville Austin (1972), *The Indian Constitution: Corner Stone of a Nation,* Oxford.
51. Nelson, John Peter (1972), "The Impact of Education on Social Stratification in India", *Journal of Social Research,* Vol. XV, No. 2 (September).
52. Srinivas, M.N. (1962), *Caste in Modern India and Other Essays,* Asia Publishing House. New Delhi, p. 9.
53. Mendelsohn and Vicziant (1998), *The Untouchables,* Cambridge University Press. London, p. 9.
54. Ibid. 11.
55. Elder, Joseph W. (1996), "The Constitution and Social Structures on India" in K.S. Murty and A. Dasgupta (eds.), *The Perennial Tree: Select Papers* of *the International Symposium on India Studies*, p. 274.

3

Regeneration vs. Reservation

A Dalit Struggle in India

RAHUL DEEPANKAR

India has been a nation of reservations and, by reservation, I mean the system of fixed identities, immovable social positions and reserved privileges and obligations. India's history, culture, economy and polity are not only the monuments of above said system of reservations, they also continue to be determined by it. Social system of Hinduism designed and dominated by Brahminism, created a four prong vertically hierarchical 'Varnashram'. Four varnas of this system namely Brahmin, Kshatriyas, Vaishyas and Shudras had their birth-based fixed social status and duties. Brahmins held the highest position and the functions of education and spiritual leadership. Kshatriyas held the second highest position and warriorship was their duty. Vaishyas were given the third place and duties of production and commerce. Shudras, the people at the bottom, along with avarnas (people outside the varnashram) were given the position of no esteem, considered untouchables and sometime unseeables, were prohibited from introduction to education and were given the duties of serving the top three varnas. For over three thousand years this system became mother of thousands of castes and subcastes, it has been sanctified by religion and implemented with the force of God. This naturally resulted in complete social, spiritual, educational and economic deprivation of untouchables, leaving them unable to recognize or fight for their own humanity. Even the foreign rule over India first by Muslims and later by Britishers, which lasted over a millennium, either ignored or even exploited the existing inequitable system for selfish gains.

These very oppressed classes of people have been called by various names in the past such as Atishudras, Antyaja, Antyevas, Avarnas, Non-Hindus, Protestant Hindus, Down-trodden, Harijans, Scheduled Castes and now Dalits.

From ancient times to British rule in India, there were very few who understood or took revolutionary steps to change the fate of Dalits. Social reformers came and went but the only message Dalits got was "God loves you equally". The implied meaning was that God may love you equally, but your unequal position is created by God and you dare not think of changing it.

It was only during the rise of political movement for freedom, the congress party and leaders like Gandhi saw the advantage in unifying all segments of society behind the cause of freedom. This need forced them to give recognition to the ills of caste system and the signs of collective guilt on the part of non-Dalit, high castes were visible for the first time. Some serious thinkers, like Dr. Ambedkar, have described the Congress party's and Gandhi's gestures and promises merely as symbolic. Furthermore, religious roots of the system are so deep that even Gandhi limited his opposition only against untouchability and not against Varnashram, the very mother of the evil of caste.

Nonetheless, there became an obvious need to do something to help and lift the weakest at the bottom. During later days of freedom struggle before independence Provincial governments had started some relief measures for Dalits. It was only during proceedings of constituent assembly prior to final draft of constitution for free India, that specific provisions were established to protect and promote the interests of Dalits. Dr. B.R. Ambedkar, the chairman of drafting committee of the constitution, is credited for convincing the founders to include specific quotas in form of reservations in educational institutions and governmental services for scheduled castes and scheduled tribes.

It is my attempt, in this paper, to see how the reservation policies have impacted Dalits. Though there have been many aspects of Dalit's lives which have been affected by these policies, the best example of understandable and quantifiable change can only be seen in the employment data which reflects the share of Dalits in government services. The paper also introduces the growing current debate whether the reservation be continued or dropped.

Constitutional Provisions

During extended debates in the constituent assembly, strong moral and intellectual arguments were put forward by likes of Dr. B.R. Ambedkar, which highlighted the conditions and needs of Dalits. As a result, the constitution of free India, which had its preamble based on principles of justice, liberty, equality and fraternity, was made to include definitive and specific provisions to help preferentially those who have been systematically oppressed throughout the history of India. Following mentions throw light on these specific provisions.

Article 15: Provides the prohibition of discrimination on grounds of religion, race, caste, sex or place of birth. The clause (4) of the same article provides the state the freedom to create remedial and promotional policies in favour of weaker sections of the society.

Article 16: Provides equality of opportunity in matters of public employment, however, Clause (4) of the same article of the Constitution provides the state the full freedom to provide preferential treatment in the form of reservations of appointments or posts for backward classes, thought by the state to be under-represented in these services.

Article 17: Provides for the abolition of untouchability and also makes the practice of untouchability an offence punishable in accordance with the law.

Article 29 (2): Provides full protection of interests of minorities and prohibits discrimination in admissions in educational institutions based on religion, race, caste and languages or any of them.

Directive Principles of State Policy

The Constitution not only provides the philosophical concepts to guide the state, but also provides specific directives in order to protect and promote the interests of weaker sections such as scheduled castes, scheduled tribes and also the minorities as exemplified below.

Article 38 (2): Provides the directive to the state to strive for equalization of income, status and facilities, not only amongst individuals but also amongst the groups.

Article 39 A: Provides for equal justice to all and in addition has a provision for free legal aid to those who cannot afford.

Article 46: Provides specific directives to the state to preferentially promote educational and economic interests of scheduled castes, scheduled tribes and other weaker sections.

Provisions for Political Representation

The Constitution not only secures the share of Dalits in education and jobs but also provides for the promotion of their political participation.

Article 330: Provides for the reservation of seats for scheduled castes and scheduled tribes in the house of people.

(1) Seats will be reserved in the house of people for:
   (a) The scheduled castes.
   (b) The scheduled tribes except in autonomous districts of Assam.

(2) Provides for the number of seats reserved for scheduled castes and scheduled tribes according to the proportion of their population in any state or union territories.

Article 332: Provides for the reservation of seats for scheduled castes and scheduled tribes in the legislative assemblies of the states on the same principle as stated in Article 330.

Constitutional Provisions of Special Significance

The following articles in the Indian Constitution have become of special significance in the ongoing debate over reservations.

Article 334: Provides that reservation of seats and special representation for scheduled castes and scheduled tribes would cease after fifty years.

Article 335: This article is of special importance because it provides for the consideration into claims of schedules castes and scheduled tribes to be consistent with maintenance of efficiency of administration.

This article, as will be pointed out later, has given significant discretionary and discriminatory powers to the people in positions of authority, to the detriment of Dalits.

Dalits' Upliftment After Independence

Much has changed for the better after independence and introduction of the modern constitution. Standard of living in general has improved though the disparity between haves and have nots has grown wider. Social rigid grip on Dalit's participation in national polity has increased at a revolutionary level.

In a society that is struggling to breakaway from traditional and unenlightened way of thinking, the election of K.R. Narayanan, a Dalit, as the president of the nation, the election of Mayawati twice as chief minister of most populous state Uttar Pradesh and a plethora of Dalits elected to cabinets of all federal and state governments, is the evidence of more than symbolic change.

This can only inspire greater ambition and hopes in the hearts and minds of future generations of Dalits.

Government Jobs and Dalits

As reported by Ministry of Welfare Research Project 1996, central and state governments have taken several steps for the welfare and upliftment of scheduled castes and scheduled tribes since independence. These include improving educational opportunities, allotment of land, assistance to cultivators, support to small scale industries, assisting craftsmen, and as spelled out in 'directive principles', the reservation of seats in state directed jobs.

Most of these programmes are hard to be analyzed since their implementations have been erratic, opposed by high castes and sabotaged by passive-aggressive attitudes of bureaucrats who mostly belong to high castes. For example, during Mayawatis' chief ministership, the transfer of already allotted land pieces to Dalits required police force. Even that could not give enough confidence to poor and powerless Dalits to keep the land because of fear of repercussions and backlash later.

For the purpose of the discussion within the limited scope of this paper, the available data on share and progress of government jobs held by Dalits provides the most understandable and measurable impact of reservation policies. I am using the available data from welfare ministry research project 1996, which contains factual observations of period between 1956 to 1992. In 1950 the union government fixed a quota of 15 per cent reservation for scheduled castes and 7.5 per cent for the scheduled tribes for central government jobs. This total of 22.5 per cent reservation has been in almost all services and public sector undertakings under the central government. In states, the reservation is proportionate to the populations of scheduled castes and scheduled tribes.

According to the data available from welfare ministry, in 1956, 2,12,754 scheduled castes persons were employed in government services which increased to 6,04,347 in 1992. The total number of scheduled tribe people increased from 22,549 to 2,02,068 in 1992. During the same period non-SC/ST, general category employees grew from 11,84,748 to 27,23608. This translates into increase of percentage from 14.98 per cent in 1956 to 17.12 per cent in 1992 for SCs and from 1.59 per cent in 1956 to 5.72 per cent in 1992 for STs.

On the surface, these numbers may give an appearance that this talk is much ado about nothing. After all, don't these bottom numbers stand close to what was intended in the constitution? The devil is in the details.

Composition and Share of Services

All position of employment under the government have been grouped in four categories. For decades these groups were called as class one, two, three and class four. For political correctness reasons, they are now called Group A, B, C and D. None the less their meaning remains the same. Group A represents the top executive positions like I.A.S., I.P.S., Directors of corporations, general managers of public sector undertakings and the secretaries of various ministries. Group B includes middle management positions of bureaucrat such as section officers sub-district level police and judicial administrators and mid-level technocrats and inspectors of schools, etc. Group C consist clerical staff, teachers, craftsmen, technicians, policemen, etc. The bottom group D is made up of peons, sweepers, labourers, watchmen, grounds keepers, housekeepers, and toilet cleaners, etc.

From 1950 to 1980, half of the scheduled caste employees were concentrated in D group and almost all of the rest in group C. The share in group B and A was negligible. From 1980 to 1992 the share of scheduled castes in group C has gradually grown to 61 per cent of total scheduled caste employees in the country. Group A share of scheduled castes was 71 per cent in 1956 which gradually grew to 9.8 per cent in 1992. This is progress but also the failure of almost half-century in achieving the goal of 15 per cent. The share of scheduled castes in group B has grown from 2.01 per cent in 1956 to 12.17 per cent in 1992, again remaining short of the goal. The change in group C is from 7.03 per cent in 1956 but reached the intended goal of 15 per cent in 1990, however because of significant changes in government policies (discussed later), the share fell to 12.9 per cent in 1992. Group D, however, is a different story. Scheduled castes started, above the intended goal at 22.10 per cent in 1956 but regressed to 17.19 per cent in 1958, again rose up to below the start point at 21.48 per cent in 1990 only to lose the share to 20.73 per cent in 1992. It may not be hard to understand how ex-untouchables started with higher share of jobs at the bottom of job hierarchy. What is significant and deserving of further analysis is that their share regressed during the period of progress in group C, B, and A. Also the phenomenon of drop from 1990 to 1992 is again demonstrated here.

Similar patterns are seen in the data of scheduled castes employment in public sector undertakings with more prominent pattern of drop from 1990 to 1992 in group C and D. Also, scheduled tribes experience follows the same pattern except with greater decline in the share from 1990 to 1992.

Reservation-Induced Progress in Government Employment by Dalits

Howsoever we see these observations, it is clear that there has been a change for the better, reflected in the rise of employment due to reservation, so much so, that the government job has become the most favoured goal of every educated Dalit. Almost negligible share of employment held by Dalits especially in group A to B in mid-1950s reflects two facts. One, that education level of Dalits was extremely poor, and two, that anti-Dalit prejudices and discriminatory practices of decision makers in the government, made it impossible for Dalits to make a breakthrough.

It was only the miracle of constitution and increasing political pressure that made possible for Dalits to crack open this rocky shell of high castes' power grip over the government machinery. The fact that Dalit's employment in group D was already above the proportion of their population and stated goal of 15 per cent demands attention. All the people, whether living in India or study Indology anywhere, know that social status and prestige in India are determined, not by how well you do your job, but by what is the status of your job and whether you have been blessed by high caste birth. Naturally high caste person will not accept menial, dirty (impure) and a low level job even if one is poor and hungry. What is more curious is that Group D includes job description similar to the duties prescribed to Shudras, so then, why hundred per cent of jobs were not occupied by Dalits? The answer is very simple, Brahmins had all the education, and they are not fools. Even the activities of Group D could be and can be divided into touchable jobs and untouchable jobs. Toilet cleaning, sweeping, boot polishing, scavenging and disposal of dead animals, etc., were the jobs that could be easily thrown at the Dalits but to expect high caste Hindus and even ruling Brahminized Muslims to accept Dalits as cooks, food handlers, water distributors, office tea servers or even as domestic house keepers was unthinkable. So the Varnashram made it possible for Dalits to have some jobs, in fact it created the compulsion to do so. On the other hand, Varnashram driven ethos could not allow anything beyond the least desired jobs, even in group D.

Though the progress has been positive, the growth of share of Dalits in State employment remains slow due to multiple factors. Majority of Indian population remains at or around poverty level. In such an environment it is natural to have fierce fight to grab whatever one can. Vast majority of decision makers in high positions belong to upper cast Hindus. Backlash to the policy of reservation, self interest, old prejudices, bribery, despotism, and corruption together or individually work against the fulfilment of quotas reserved for Dalits. Many times the seats are falsely kept unfilled to be filled later by non-Dalits on the pretext that suitable Dalit candidates could not be found.

The data published by two judges, B.D. Purohit and S.D. Purohit, in 1990 indicated that in several instances there is total exclusion of Dalits on the pretext of constitutional Article 335. There is complete absence of Dalits in scientific and technical posts in the departments of space, atomic energy, and electronics. In certain institutions of higher education, such as IITs, IIMs and central universities, while the reservation is made in non-academic positions, the teaching posts have been exempted. The same data also shows that central government has exempted a number of non-scientific and non-technical posts, such as, private secretaries, personal assistants, etc., to the prime minister and other ministers from the reservation labeling them as "the exceptional circumstances and special nature" of jobs.

The most striking example of Dalit's exclusion from a major national service is 'Defence'. This has been done under the banner of Article 335 and well accepted by top sociopolitical and legal thinkers. Palkhivala, a noted lawyer of national fame, says, "The country's armed forces are pride of the nation – the only institution which has not been devalued and degraded. What kind of Army, Navy and Air Force shall we have when field marshals and generals, and admirals and air marshals, have secured admissions and promotions on caste considerations?"

There are definite questions which can justifiably be raised regarding merit and proper qualifications for all sensitive positions. However the real meaning of Palkhivala's statement can only be understood by analyzing it further. There are certain assumptions implied in his statement:

(a) That the Indian army which consists of high castes is based entirely on merit.
(b) If we accept assumption 'a' then we have to assume that fighting talent is limited to the people of high birth only.
(c) That the Dalits if admitted to the army through reservation are unteachable and untrainable to do the job and

hence can only be promoted to higher posts through reservation.

(d) That current promotions in the defence departments of army, navy and airforce are exclusively done on the basis of record of performance and excellence.

If we examine all these assumptions further, we will find that the truth is far from Palkhivala's beliefs. Anyone who understands the ways of Indian government functioning, knows that basic qualifications are not enough to get a job in any department. Ability to bribe, having influential family connections and high birth and political patronage are not only essential at the entry point also in promotions. Thus, the idea of merit is corrupted at the onset.

Secondly, the defence personnel is provided with the best of nutrition and training without consideration of expenses despite wide spread poverty in general population. Given these conditions, a Dalit male who can work on a farm from before sunrise till after dark daily without a break or holiday, in rain and in sun, can easily be nourished to optimal physical condition and can easily be trained to be a fighter equal to any one. Those who cannot understand these logical arguments should take a lesson from US Armed Forces. Affirmative action has been generously used for blacks entry into the armed forces of United States. Can anyone find a better organized and more feared armed forces on the globe? Can anyone say that Col. Powell, who was helped by affirmative action, was an inferior leader or incompetent as Chairman of Joint Chiefs of Staff?

On the other hand, can Palkhivala explain why India has suffered defeat and slavery under foreign invaders for more than a millennium when our defence was the exclusive responsibility of Kshatriyas?

If there is any truth in above said argument then we have to conclude that Indian ethos is still marred with fundamental denial of the basic fact that: "Each and everyone of us is born with equal potential".

Future of Reservation in India

The principal of Siddhartha College, Bombay, Mr. Dhaktode was visiting US in the summer of 1998. At a dinner I asked him, "How do you think the reservation continues when its creator, Dr. Ambedkar, the father of Indian Constitution and fighter for rights of Dalits, wanted it to have limited provision for 10 years in services and fifty years in politics?" The principal Mr. Dhaktode answered, "Probably Dr. Ambedkar knew that once Dalits have tasted the benefits of reservation and also become aware of their political power, the reservation would reincarnate itself over and over".

One can easily see that the conceptual basis and original arguments that created these provisions in Indian Constitution have already been reinterpreted. The new breed of reasons based on current sociopolitical and economic conditions keep emboldening the supporters to fight for the reservations and the opponents promise the battle to end them with their own reasons. First, let us review the reasons that proponents use for continued reservation.

Intractable Social Traditional Ills

As a result of continuous talks of social reforms and resistance against oppression by Dalits, there has been some change in social attitudes especially in the urban area; however, great majority of Indians, almost 70 per cent of them live in villages. The village life is still dominated by traditional concepts of high and low, pure and impure, active obstruction in the way of Dalits achieving education, continued psychological and material oppression of Dalits at the hands of rich and powerful people of high caste in the rural area. Hence, Dalit leaders believe that all those conditions which necessitated the reservations in the first place still stay intact for 80-90 per cent Dalits who live in villages. The most popular Dalit Cabinet minister in free India, Jagjivan Ram said, "My son will not need reservation when he becomes touchable."

Sub-optimal Compliance

Proponents of continued reservation rightfully point out that despite almost half a century of reservations, the share of Dalits in government services has not risen to the stated directive in the Constitution. They claim that equality, which was defined by Dr. Ambedkar, as raising the level of disadvantaged groups to the level of previously advantaged ones, has not been achieved and hence the continuation of these policies is essential.

Rising Caste Solidarity

Dalits have not been monolithic in their social, religious or political orientations but when it comes to the question of ending the reservation, almost universally Dalits oppose it. In it, Dalits find the pretext to huddle together and they also feel the impact of their political power more distinctly than any other issue. On the other hand, high caste people see the loss of opportunities due to reservation, as well as feel the irritation of tolerating Dalits in positions of prestige and power. This makes them almost unified in their response against the reservation. As expected this polarity of attitudes has resulted into variety of conflicts which are frequently violent, resulting in the loss of lives almost in each corner of the nation. Dalits interpret these violent reactions on the part of their oppressors is the proof that they must be succeeding. Objectively, one can see this phenomenon as start of long-term intractable social divisions and ongoing conflicts in future. In my personal view this is not an absolute inevitability. There is another possible outcome. I have always believed that the phenomena of caste has exclusively benefitted the minority at the top. Brahmins, Khatriyas and commercial communities of Hindu social system have never felt any reason to abolish 'caste' and its resultant ills. It is my intuitive belief that once this group of social leadership understands that 'caste' is against their self interest, we will see their own initiative to end it and start living under a new equitable social code, which will end the need for constitutional directives in favour of Dalits.

Need for More Protection and Justice

The preceding section should make it quite obvious that the rising conflicts will require a bigger administrative infrastructure to see efficient adjudicative resolution. Dalits strongly believe that because of caste hatred, corruption, despotism and their inability to afford bribes, they do not get their deserved police protection and court justice. Fear of inequality of protection and justice under the law provided to Dalits is easily understood. 'India Today' deserves quoting: "Legal system instead of being part of the solution, has ironically become a part of the problem." One can easily see that Dalits feel the reservation will allow a greater share for them into police force, judiciary, and other administrative positions to give them hope of more protection and justice.

Prevalence of Poverty and Growing Gap between Haves and Have-Nots

India at the time of its birth as a free nation had declared itself to be a "socialist republic" meaning thereby that equalization of status and re-equalization of wealth by new kind of distribution was the implied goal for the future of India. Even if there was no provision of reservations, the majority of Indian population who are and have been living in poverty would have fought through democratic means to create some system of redistribution of wealth simply to survive. With the passage of time the disparity between poor and not so poor has grown to the state of poor who are too many and the rich who are not that many.

Dalits feel that they have no easy means to secure their share of nation's wealth in the continued traditional economic methods. All economic means have been captured and are maintained in the hands of few who already owned them traditionally. Dalits feel that without state's intervention through reservations they have no chance to break down these old economic barriers.

Growing Disparity of Means of Acquiring Abilities to Compete

The people who have experienced or studied Indian educational system know that there are three levels at which education is being provided. The top level belongs to the elites of society in urban areas where private, English medium dominated education is provided at the likes of Delhi Public Schools, convent schools, Doon schools, airforce academy and international schools, etc. Graduates from these schools have no difficulty in competing with students from France or America. The second level of schools which are available to middle class of urban population provide reasonable education to a minority on the national level. With the help of educated parents and with freedom from deprivation, the graduates of these schools can muster enough competitive power to retain their middle class status or even to move to upper class status.

And then there are masses who make up the majority and live either in slums of the city or in the villages. The schools for these masses are either not available or are totally dysfunctional and devoid of any facilities that can prepare a student for a fierce competition. Even in this category the Dalit masses are served by the worst kind of facilities. Growing in lowest socio-economic conditions and receiving very inferior education, Dalit youngsters grow to be subpar in capacity and totally devoid of self-confidence.

Now to imagine a student from the third category to compete with the candidate of the first category in an open competition and hope to succeed is nothing but travesty and betrayal of common sense. Ninety percent of Dalit students belong to the third category. It is quite obvious that these students and their parents will have no reluctance or moral guilt in demanding the continuation of reservations in their favour.

Compensation for the Past Sufferings

Indian social system in general, and Hindu civil code based on 'Varanashram' in particular, can be described briefly as the minority with reserved privileges and power exploiting and stealing by design the labour of the majority. This fact becomes very clear to anyone who finds out the economic and political agenda behind Brahmanism. Dalits are catching up fast to this forbidden knowledge of history through general awareness, political consciousness and secular education. Therefore, Dalits feel a natural righteousness in demanding a compensation for three millinea of loss of possession of humanity and material. In comparison to reservations in favour of higher castes for three thousand years, fifty years of preferential treatment given to Dalits is negligible. The reservation policy becomes the only visible validation of their historical sufferings. They have become convinced that reservation is their right.

New Economic Trends

Forbes magazine once wrote about billionaires of the world which included the only billionaire from India – 'Birla family'. The remarkable note in the article was that during early post independence India, Birla family due to its connections with top political leaders, had licenses for the industries for which the technology had not even developed yet. License Raj, which was practiced in India for forty some years was nothing but continuation of old commercial tradition meaning, only those who could muster enough political, financial and despotic clout were allowed to venture in new commercial activities. Naturally, as a result, Dalits could not touch any of that.

After heavy pressure from inside and international institutions, there has been growing liberalization and privatization in commerce. But without capital and know-how resulting from traditional barriers, Dalits feel unable to participate in an open market economy. It is only through preferential treatment in granting loans and admission to vocational training institutions that Dalits feel they can become real partners in the affairs of nation's economy.

Reservations and Nation's Polity

Ninety per cent of post-independence period has been the rule of the Congress Party at the centre. It is a common knowledge that Congress Party's support mainly came from Dalits, minorities and a minority of Brahmins. It is but natural that Congress leaders saw obvious expediency in the symbolism of continued reservation for Dalits as opposed to bringing about fundamental changes in social attitudes and traditions of economic activities. Some have also argued that continuing reservation has maintained the old Brahminic hegemony by keeping Dalits attached to the crumbs of reservations based on caste instead of becoming casteless citizens by rejecting Hinduism for equal human dignity.

Because reservations have become the most important means for survival and progress for Dalits, particularly the educated ones, not only Congress but all other parties never get tired of promising more reservations and for longer periods. All political parties find this issue to be the most convenient substitute for better efforts to provide real means of progress and hope for better life as equal and dignified partnership for Dalits.

Politics of Dalits

Every Indian politician of Dalit background is the ideal archetype of Dalit. Everyone of them has grown with the philosophy of victimization and follows the same stereo-typical rhetoric. Typically, all Dalit politicians and political parties including B.S.P. promise bigger and stronger support for continued reservation. It is based on two very basic realities. One, that no Dalit can contest elections successfully without reserved constituencies which are exclusively set aside for the scheduled castes or scheduled tribes and, two, that without supporting reservations no Dalit politician can draw majority support from ignorant and impoverished Dalit masses. Any talk of opposition to reservations by any politician whether valid or not is nothing but a political suicide. Also constitutional Article 334 provides for ending the political reservation after fifty years; this makes it obvious that for Dalit politicians, continuation of reservations is not only the political expediency but also the question of self-survival.

Now, let us look at the arguments that oppose reservations and are often used by conservative ideologues and socio-political elements who follow 'Hindutva' as their ultimate cultural ideal.

Social Change

Opponents of reservations feel that there has been significant change in traditions of social interaction for the better, reducing disabilities from caste. They mainly use examples of urban societies where anonymity has grown and untouchability is out of practice. Here and there we also see an intercaste marriage. Moreover attributes that attract power and prestige in urban areas has more to do with money and job position rather than 'caste'. Hence, they believe, the original conditions that created reservations are no more operational.

It is easy to see that this argument comes from urban elites who have least contact with or understanding of rural life where 80-90 per cent Dalits live. Arguably, there has been some attempts by Dalits to Sanskritize themselves in order to appear like high castes but most sociologists will agree that anonymity and secular commercial activities visible in cities is unthinkable in villages. Village life is still dependent on concept of pure and impure and endogamy.

New Generation's Perspective of 'Equality'

The right to equality under the law is a fundamental right of every citizen. Special provisions created under Article 15 (4) and 16 (4) seem to violate the letter of the law. However, the founders of free India understood the historical inequities of society that disabled Dalits to utilize this new equality of opportunity. Therefore, the understanding of equality in their minds included equalization of achievement as well as equalization of opportunity.

This understanding is lost on the new generation. They claim "equality means equality" regardless of any historical inequalities or current imbalance. They also see intolerable unfairness and inequity when a better qualified candidate is rejected to make place for reserved seat to accommodate a Dalit with lesser marks or credits.

The politically driven race to increase reservations as high as seventy per cent or more in states like Tamil Nadu, Karnataka, Madhya Pradesh, and Andhra Pradesh gives actual strength to this argument that the concept of equality under the law is violated beyond tolerable limits.

The Creamy Layer

This argument remains at the top in all debates at cocktail parties, academic conferences and political discussions, so much so that even the laws have been proposed to end the reservation privileges for Dalits, who have advanced educationally and economically. It is also argued that some Dalits who have become well off and others who enjoy higher positions like IAS, IPS, IFS, doctors and engineers, etc., do not suffer the disabilities of discrimination and lack of means and facilities. The argument goes further that this creamy layer also eats up the advantages of reservation that could help the really poor and weak segments of Dalits.

Despite the counter arguments that even with the use of reservation taken by creamy layer, the intended goals under the constitutional directives have not been met, the supporters of reservation find themselves on the defensive side of moral and fairness aspect of this argument.

Unintended Negative Consequences of Reservations on Dalits

This argument is shared by both the high caste opponents, intellectuals and also by enlightened liberal Dalit supporters of the reservations. They consider the following effects as negative to the progress of Dalits and hence the reasons for discontinuing the reservations, at least as they exist now.

A. Reservations create an accommodation of and reward the submaximal efforts by Dalits who enter various competitions.

B. The people who get positions due to reservation are stereotyped as inferior by their colleagues and thereby always are assigned superficial duties which further thwarts their personal growth and possible future promotions.

C. The future generations of Dalits, or at least those who are relatively free from oppression do not see any examples of in order to emulate. This prevents development of self-confidence and deepens the inferiority complex.

D. The reservations create a mindset in Dalits which prefers studies in non-scientific subjects to prepare them for clerical and non-technical jobs which disables them from competing in commerce, growing market of technology and advance crafts. This can only exaggerate their inabilities to participate in the globalized and privatized economy.

E. The reservation, by its potential to promote inefficiency, retards national growth in general. In turn the inefficient and poor economy can only increase real impoverishment which Dalits shoulder the most. As my friend, Kuldip Nayar a noted liberal journalist and member of parliament says, "Without increasing the total wealth of nation, socialistic system of redistribution despite its apparent fairness, can only distribute poverty and nothing more".

Lack of Dignity Despite Religious Conversion

Both opponents and supporters of reservations point out that main reason of religious conversion is the search for self-respect and human dignity. The reservations are now available to those who have discarded Hinduism and have become neo-Buddhists, or Sikhs, as long as they declare themselves as scheduled castes on applications. The attraction of reservations keeps this segment of Dalits enslaved to the old identities and also gives extra life to the heinous system of Varna and caste. In the end, ironically, the reservation becomes the hindrance in achieving personal freedom and dignity through religious conversion.

Diminishing Role of State in Creation of Employment

That with new economic policy, changes of privatization, liberalization and also divestment away from non-profitable ventures, the government's ability to provide employment has declined significantly. No one disagrees that this phenomenon will only grow with far greater speed. As a result, Dalit's ability to depend on state to provide jobs will suffer a great setback leading to more frustration and discontent along with increased unemployment. Thus, the opponents of reservations believe, that staking future on reservation, Dalits will waste precious time without self-development on dangerous and deceptive false hopes.

Globalization

The economic dynamics of economic globalization has changed the rules of competition and success from intranational to international arena. Historical collective guilt of high caste people is not shared by the multinationals. Their basic requirements in an applicant for the job has more to do with his or her educational and technical abilities and nothing to do with the caste. Even more importantly the government which can apply the rules of preferential treatment based on caste will have no authority to compel globally competing companies to adopt any policy that can appear as threat to their competitive edge, whether real or perceived. Therefore, the opponents contend that indefinite dependence on reservation by Dalits will create a slippery slide backwards.

Culture of Thwarting Meritocracy and Excellence in Dalits

Unless one believes that Dalits are born with inferior capacity and potential, it is quite evident that reservations requiring suboptimal achievement in academics sends the message to young Dalit generation that they really do not have to aim as high as their non-Dalit counterparts. This breeds a culture of submaximal goals and compromised efforts. This not only impacts the current generation but also the future ones by limiting their ambitions and inspiration. The opponents rightfully point out that if the culture of merit and excellence is not allowed to grow amongst Dalits, many future generations will be lost to inferior performance and mediocre achievements.

Social Conflict, Disharmony and National Disintegration

The experience in last twenty years has born out the fact that there is severe backlash to the preferential treatment given to Dalits. There has been perilous polarization of communities in almost all states of the nation. Pandemic of violence has erupted all over. All major states of Uttar Pradesh, Bihar, Gujarat, Maharashtra, Madhya Pradesh, Tamil Nadu and Karnataka, etc., have seen heinous violence directed against Dalits. Also, nations judicial system has failed to provide justice to those who have been injured the most, Dalits. The opponents of reservations, explain this as the result of anger, frustration and envy against perceived unfair favouritism given to Dalits through reservations. Some serious Dalit thinkers, however, see it as a validation as well as price for their success in getting part of their share they deserve. The opponents also believe that if the system of reservations extends further and every caste and community (Muslims and Christians, etc.) claims the share according to their proportion of population, the national integration process will suffer greatly. India, they say, will remain a conglomeration of nations based on caste and ethnic identities.

Conclusion

The makers of Indian Constitution, who also happened to be the founding fathers of free India, gave, for the first time in history, the official recognition to the inequities of the history and multifaceted exploitation of Dalits. Collective guild and persuasion by moral and political arguments of the time produced specific remedial steps in the form of constitutional directives, resulting in policy of reservations.

The success of reservations, though suboptimal, reflects state's power to bring about change, rising political power of Dalits and increased interest in education. The failures, on the other hand, indicate less than desirable culture of meritocracy and excellence amongst Dalits and recalcitrant, hostile attitudes of high caste people in power who run the government institutions responsible for implementing these changes.

Now, in changed times of demand for equality without qualifications and increasing global competition, the collective guilt has been substituted by backlash. Regardless of differing views and growing rigid attitudes on both sides of the reservation issue, the debate is bound to become more and more heated. This debate has also become progressively more important for the dream of social harmony and national integration.

Burden of moving away from reservations falls on the shoulders of actors on both sides. High castes and socio-religious leaders have the moral obligation to remove all that is responsible for creating Dalits, as they are, and Dalits have no future without self-development. The most suitable words to end this exercise comes from Shelby Steele regarding affirmative action in USA: "Racial representation is not the same thing as self-development, yet affirmative action fosters a confusion of these two needs."

4

Caste System

A Major Impediment to the Development of Dalits in India

M.N. FARUQUI

Caste Dilemma

Indian civilization, one of the oldest in the world, had some remarkable features of survival and development of abstract ideas. Unfortunately, despite its glorious history of enlightened development some of the basic human rights, as we know them today, have been denied to a fairly large group of people. Over the last 3,000 years or so they have been enslaved as perpetual bonded labour and ostracized from the society as 'untouchables'. They have lived in inhuman conditions of extreme poverty and have been subjected to torture, rape and other physical abuse. Recently, they have been called 'Scheduled Castes', 'Harijans' and 'Dalits' and independent India has tried to ameliorate their conditions through some 'positive affirmation' and 'positive discrimination'. However, the struggle of Dalits to improve their lot through education has only provoked the fury of the upper castes who have resorted to violence when they have perceived a self-reliant attitude developing amongst the Dalits.

Caste has an inglorious track record and has done quite a bit of damage to the society. Looking at it from an enlightened view the low-caste stigma has instilled in them a feeling of inferiority complex psychologically and diminished the self-respect in their own eyes. This has naturally hampered and stunted their mental growth and they have lost any motivation for doing well and excelling in their activities. Socially and economically it has produced millions of human beings who are segregated from the Hindu society on the principle of pollution and who only survive as a menial class living in abject poverty.

Mahatma Gandhi felt the crippling effect of this enormous split in the Hindu society, when he realised that the untouchables are Hindus in name only. They technically do not form a part of it since they are not allowed to pray in the Hindu temples, could not even utter the words of the scriptures and had different set of gods and goddess in their own pantheon. One of the major contributions of Gandhi was that he tried to bring these untouchables into the Hindu fold by calling them 'Harijans'. There were serious flaws in his concept of the remedial action necessary and we will analyze and show later the essential problems faced with his approach. A rather rough description would be to say that these efforts were cosmetic in nature without addressing the real dilemma of the caste system that condemns some 250 million Dalits to a life of abject poverty and social inequality, and legitimizes the daily violence visited upon them. Towards the close of the nineteenth century, Dr. Ambedkar was born into this community of untouchable, Mahars. He lived and worked almost at the same time as Mahatma Gandhi but differed from him strongly in the perceptions and solutions for the difficulties faced by the Dalits. Surprisingly for his community he managed to get a first rate education under a very trying and biased atmosphere of the then schools and colleges. Despite Dr. Ambedkar's relatively privileged upbringing, his father was educated and was serving in the British army, he was not entirely sheltered from his untouchable ancestry. In school he was made to sit in a comer of the classroom, stressing the fact that an untouchable student should not be allowed to learn with students of the upper-castes. Moreover, his teachers refused to touch him fearing pollution. But even in those colonial days when even the rich and upper caste people were not getting the opportunity for education abroad he did go to some prestigious colleges like Columbia University, USA and Greys Inn in UK for studies.

Untouchables

After his return from England he became a leader of the oppressed untouchables whom he tried to liberate from the unfair persecution and cruelty of the upper castes and the misery of the caste system. He devoted his life to the betterment of the lot of the untouchables and fought the enormous gaps in political expression, law, social activity, economic ability, labour opportunities, and education. He tried to make changes into the system from the inside hoping to bring round the caste Hindus to accept a better deal for the Dalits.

It can be said that he devoted his entire life to the betterment of the Dalit community and his major contribution in the drafting of the Indian Constitution bears his stamp of concern for the downtrodden community. The upliftment of a community of 250 million people dispersed over the whole subcontinent and suffering from the injustices of a system that had survived over the previous three thousand years is not a small task.

For quite sometime Dr. Ambedkar had loosely supported efforts aiming to reintegrate untouchables into the Hindu fold without the stigma of pollution. This included temple entry movements, movements to participate in village Hindu festivals, as well as efforts to gain access to village wells and tanks traditionally reserved for upper-caste inhabitants. However, in 1927 Dr. Ambedkar severed himself even from these efforts entirely. He symbolically burned the *Manu Smriti*, the law book that most strictly codifies the caste and the caste rules. Under his leadership, the ideas of reintegration into the Hindu fold, and indeed, the idea that Dalits were Hindu's altogether, were rejected. A new vision of Dalit culture and the introduction of Dalit politics replaced these earlier notions of Dalit liberation.

Dr. Ambedkar began to believe that nothing could emancipate the Dalit community unless there was a complete annihilation of the Hindu caste system. Failing that he felt that not only the rejection of the caste but a complete denial of the Hindu religion was the only method of escape for the millions of untouchables who suffered under the Hindu caste system. Despite holding such strong views he continued to hope that something better may be worked out for the Dalits. Thus in 1935, though Dr. Ambedkar publicly announced that "he was born a Hindu" but would "not die as a Hindu" he remained and thought himself to be a Hindu practically throughout his life. He converted to Buddhism two years before his death in 1955.

Ideological Differences with Gandhi

In the early days of the Indian Independence, Dr. Ambedkar fought with Gandhi over the priorities of the new Indian government because Gandhi had a different set of priorities and did not see the untouchable problems to be that urgent. Mahatma Gandhi did contribute his mite towards helping the Dalits. He gave them the name Harijan though by now the Dalits have rejected this designation. He cleaned the toilets of Dalits thereby shocking the upper castes and fought with his supporters and benefactors to ensure that Dalits could stay in his *ashram* in Ahmedabad. However, Gandhi did not see the problems from the angle of an untouchable Dalit. Also, he could not fight the prejudice against the Dalits in India while condoning casteism within the Hindus? Unfortunately, many Indians did not share the principle or logic of eradicating the caste system for the sake of helping the Dalits. They were keen to overthrow the 100-year-old British *raj* and also sought to preserve their 3,000-year-old caste prejudices.

Gandhi's main aim was political, which culminated in the Independence of India. One can see today that while he defeated the British and gained freedom for the Indians, his work regarding the Dalits remained incomplete and he could not free them from the yoke of untouchability. The sheer pressure of time and the political tasks were such that Gandhi could never devote sufficient time and energy for the cause of the Dalits. But more important was the fact that he would have risked offending his main supporters, the caste Hindus. Hence, Gandhi made contradictory statements like saying that he believed in the *varnashram* (caste system), but opposed untouchability at the same time.

Many apologists of Gandhi have tried to explain his attitudes by saying that may be he could do little else since he was a leader and only a representative of his people so that he could never be too different from their aspirations, or too radical in their view. He may have taken them in the direction of eradicating untouchability but Indians then were extremely caste conscious and Gandhi was a leader of India's masses. Unfortunately even now the situation is not much different and a higher caste Hindu, is to a large extent, conscious of his superior status. The people did follow Gandhi in the fight for independence from the British rule but they were not with him in the fight against the caste prejudices. People were unwilling to reform Hindu society beyond certain symbolic gestures and even Gandhi could not force them.

Dr. Ambedkar too, had a clear but slightly different agenda. He wanted to give the untouchable community an identity untainted by the stigma of pollution and untouchability. He wanted the maximum benefits for his people, and realized that caste Hindus would be less amenable than the British. In his way of thinking his opponents were not the British but the caste Hindus who were unwilling to change or compromise.

An important component of Dr. Ambedkar's ideology was his strong belief in the power of education. This education was meant to be both social and academic. In the social sphere he stressed the importance of cleanliness, equality between men and women, as well as abstinence from alcohol and carrion. All of these elements were meant to aid Dalits in gaining self-respect and a sense of pride in their identity. Caste, he felt, hampered economic growth and the social development of rural India would not be possible while the village is divided along caste lines. Therefore, he suggested that feudal estates based on casteism must be broken up and the land be distributed to the people who till it.

Gandhi's approach to the question of untouchables was more akin to that of Christian missionaries seeking conversion rather than of empowerment. He wanted Harijans to be accepted as part of Hindu society. With this in view, he advised the Harijans to be clean and to give up alcohol and meat eating. Gandhi would not countenance the weakening let alone abolition of the caste system.

Dr. Ambedkar's goal was very clear. If the Hindu society was not willing to accept the Dalits as equal human beings he would have nothing to do with Hinduism itself. As mentioned above he wanted to annihilate the caste system and that not being possible he advised his followers to change to Buddhism. He wanted to help his people, the Dalits, and he had to help them because no one else was willing to do so, least of all the Brahmins and Banias who thronged the Rashtriya Swayamsevak Sangh (RSS) and the right-wing parties, or the Congress. His famous scathing remark about the Gandhi's way of thinking was that Gandhism is the philosophy of the leisure class.

Dr. Ambedkar also felt that no social reform movement could be successful unless annihilation of caste is made as its principal objective though he did not believe in violent overthrow of the upper-caste government in power. But Mahatma Gandhi held the view that mere abolition of untouchability would bring about the desired result.

Away from Savarkar

Before we leave this topic it will be worthwhile to examine the opinions of some revolutionaries like Savarkar who were opposed to the ideas of Mahatma Gandhi in the political arena. Savarkar attempted to keep the Mahars into the Hindu fold by defining 'Hindutva' as a separate idea from Hinduism. Savarkar argued that Hinduism means the Hindu religion or the *Vedic* or *Sanatan Dharma.* Hindutva on the other hand means the quality or property of being a Hindu, i.e., one who belongs to any of several theological or philosophical sects born in India. Thus, Hindutva in his definition embraces Buddhist, Jains, Sikhs and members of all other indigenous school of thought. In a desperate bid to keep the Mahars within the fold of Hindu religion Savarkar advised the Mahars that the real progress of Mahars could be achieved only by retaining the Mahar caste. Moreover the need to protect his so-called 'Hindutva' from Islam or Christianity renders Savarkar's distinction between Hinduism and Hindutva invalid because he is found using Hindu religion and Hindutva quite interchangeably.

It has been argued that Savarkar's Hindutva does not refer just to religious identity but is supposed to refer to the socio-cultural identity of Hindus. But socio-cultural identity does not make sense unless it is a part of the self-consciousness of the concerned community or it is a voluntarily accepted identity by the community in question. Otherwise, it will not be a real identity but a fake and an imposed identity. Hindutva as understood by Savarkar is not the part of the self-consciousness of Buddhists, Jains and Sikhs and so on and hence Hindutva is an imposed and artificial identity for them.

Savarkar's strategy of dissolving more than 3,000 castes into one pan-Hindu identity involves pan-Hindu temples, pan-Hindu dinners, inter-caste marriages, anti-untouchability programmes and the removal of injunctions on caste-ridden vocations and sea-voyage. But Dr. Ambedkar is also aware that inter-caste dining or even inter-caste marriages are not enough to eliminate casteism. He was of the opinion that for realizing the desired goal of casteless society through inter-caste marriages it is necessary to destroy the belief in the sanctity of Hindu *shastras*. And for destroying this belief, he suggests that people should not only discard the *shastras*, but they should deny their authority as well, like Lord Buddha and Guru Nanak did.

Dr. Ambedkar and Independence Movement

A highly educated and liberated intellectual like Dr. Ambedkar was so disillusioned and disgusted with the caste system and the prejudices of the upper caste Hindus that he did not participate in the freedom struggle. Much has been made of this point and Arun Shourie in his book *Worshipping False Gods* has virtually denounced him. Quite aside from the point, Shourie has a habit of censuring and condemning every other religion except Hinduism. He always takes a perverse pleasure in noting down small deviations, errors and angularities in others and makes very sarcastic and critical comments on it. Why he did not subject Hinduism to the same critical, and one may say derisive study, does not peak well for his so-called unbiased views. Thus, in this case also what Shourie says about Dr. Ambedkar maybe is true, but that really is not the debate. Dr. Ambedkar did not take part in the Independence Movement because he was primarily concerned with the plight of his people who were then treated as 'untouchables', 'unapproachables' and 'unseeables'. It can be said that India got her freedom from the British but for millions of Dalits and Adivasis the situation has not changed much even after 50 years of independence. For them, the British Raj has been replaced by a Brahminraj. Hindus cannot accept Dr. Ambedkar because Dalit emancipation for them means weakening of the Brahmins' and upper castes' power and privileges.

Dr. Ambedkar's problem was in deciding, as far as the Dalits were concerned, freedom from whom? The withdrawal of the British, he felt would not deliver the Dalits from their upper caste oppressors. To that extent he lent his support to the British government during the Second World War when Gandhi had launched his 'andolan' for complete freedom. He even sided with Muslim League and Mohammed Ali Jinnah against the Congress and Gandhi.

To assume that whosoever did not take part in the freedom struggle was not a patriot is not a correct reading of the situation in India. For example, most of the educated Indians, other than the lawyers and doctors in private practice, were invariably in the employment of the British government and their active participation in any political movement was unthinkable.

Constitution of India

Dr. Ambedkar is often respectfully referred to as the father of the Indian constitution by his followers. Despite his opposition to the freedom movement he was appointed as the Law Minister in the Jawahar Lal Nehru's cabinet of independent India. Though Dr. Ambedkar was certainly not responsible for the entire document, he was appointed as head of the constitutional committee after India's independence, and secured for the Dalits important clauses within the Indian constitution such as the prohibition of untouchability enumerated in Article 17.

In a zeal for praising the contribution of Dr. Ambedkar to the drafting of the Constitution of India it is forgotten that whatever draft of the Constitution was made by him and whatever clause he put there the Constitution was approved by the Constituent Assembly as a whole. The Dalits were given some special privileges and that untouchability was abolished. But then the Constituent Assembly had an overwhelming majority of Hindus – caste Hindus. If they were not sympathetic to the cause of Dalits – for whatever reason either political or an inner remorse at the conditions of Dalits in India – the 'wonderful' constitution of Dr. Ambedkar would not have come into existence. So despite all the praise on one side, vilification on the other, the fact remains that it was the 'caste' Hindus who gave themselves a constitution that had guarantees written into it for many including Dalits. Dr. Ambedkar was the one who piloted it and wrote some of the important Articles in it. How far the Constitution has been put into practice and has been made a reality for the large community of the downtrodden Dalits is a matter of debate and conjecture? Some of the well-to-do amongst them have benefitted quite a lot but the poor untouchable has a long way to go before the sins of the previous centuries can be washed away.

Conclusion

Dr. Ambedkar pointed out that in Hinduism there was this difficulty of knowing why one is Hindu. The essence of his argument was that a man who does not belong to a recognised Hindu caste could not be a Hindu. Such an argument immediately excluded the Dalits from the Hindu fold. This is also borne out by the fact that both, Gandhi and Savarkar tried to legitimize and 'bring' the Dalits into the Hindu society and religion while Dr. Ambedkar wanted the caste system itself to be destroyed. He considered the Gita a political book aimed at upholding the teaching of the *Vedas* and raising Brahmanism to a supreme position.

It has been argued, though I feel that it has been offered more as an apology, that Dr. Ambedkar's conversion to Buddhism was not a religious conversion but was a strategy for creating negative consciousness among the *'Dalits'* against the hegemony of the dominant castes. In fact Dr. Ambedkar had categorically made it clear that Buddhism is one of the essential elements in the process of bringing about political revolution leading to the overthrow of such domination. From hindsight we can say that conversion away from Hinduism has not proved to be the beneficial panacea to the Dalits. Economic solutions in the modem times are not dependent upon ones religion though historically people who have adopted the 'victor's' religion have generally benefitted. Economically, a

Dalit does not gain anything by calling himself a Muslim, a Christian or a Buddhist. But as it has been said that a man does not live by bread alone, the social condition of the Dalit does improve once he is no more an untouchable in his new faith. At least his image in the eyes of the society gets better and he may be able to improve his economic situation also with time.

The Constitution of India gave assurances for the upliftment of the Dalits (called by the British epithet of Scheduled Caste) and abolished 'untouchability'. However, no effort has ever been made to abolish the caste system itself through legal means. Untouchability therefore remains and is being observed in one form or the other and caste consciousness with its evil effects continues to have sway over every activity in the Hindu society and lamentably Muslim society in India as well. The acceptance of the recommendations of the Mandal Commission has unleashed such forces that have further fragmented the society and has strengthened the very roots of the caste system. In the fight for the supremacy of the different castes within the Hindu society and securing maximum benefits for ones own caste, the poor Dalits have been relegated to the background. No doubt a lip service is paid to their cause and come elections or World Bank reminders the collective conscience of the caste Hindus wakes up to the plight of these unfortunate people. It is also no doubt true that a section of the Dalits have benefitted from the schemes and reservations made by the Constitution but much more requires to be done. Baba Sahib's dreams remain unfulfilled.

Finally, I would like to say that the slogan of the "socialistic pattern of society" has also failed to deliver. Nehru's dream of a secular India has breathed its last over the demolition of the Babri mosque. Secularism has become an empty slogan and even the right wing parties involved in that demolition call themselves 'secular'. The anti-caste movement of Dr. Ambedkar remains relevant and is possibly the only way that a liberal and egalitarian society can be built in India.

5

Uniform Civil Code and Judicial Activism

Muslim Personal Law Perspective

M. SHABBIR

The 'Uniform Civil Code' is one of the Directive Principles contained in the Constitution of India. It directs the state "to endeavour to secure for the citizens a uniform civil code throughout the territory of India".[1] It created controversy since its very inception. The multiplicity of diverse nature of Indian society caused alarming reactions; happy, unhappy and mixed on the issue of the Uniform Civil Code'. Ever since the process of the constitution making, rather till date, voices for and against have surfaced from various quarters, but the latter have been successful in pushing the issue of the Uniform Civil Code into oblivion and limbo. Nevertheless, the apex judiciary from time to time, has reacted sharply, favouring its enforcement even at the cost of its 'judicial discipline'. The latest pronouncements of the Supreme Court on the 'Uniform Code' in *John Vallamattom and Anr. vs. Union of India*[2] (herein-after *John Vollamattom Case)* and *Smt. Sarla Mudgal, President, Kalyani* and *others vs. Union of India & others*[3] (herein-after *Smt. Sarla Mudgal Case)* which set burning example of unwarranted, indefensible and uncalled for 'judicial activism'. The Constitution of India ensures equality[4] to all citizens irrespective of their caste, sex, creed, religion and place of birth. Freedom of religion, its practice and propagation, freedom of culture, freedom to manage religious affairs and educational rights are guaranteed as fundamental rights to all citizens especially to minorities by the Constitution. Despite such effective constitutional safeguards, communal harmony and the peaceful co-existence of different communities and amity of citizens are affected on negative tenor.

The Constituent Assembly Debates in the Constitution making process reveal that the constitution makers debated the concept, relevance and utility of the Uniform Civil Code at length. The Muslim members of the Constituent Assembly opposed the move of the Uniform Civil Code with all possible intensity at their command. In this background, the for and against arguments are to be discussed for the objective evaluation of the Uniform Civil Code and its relevance in India.

The Constituent Assembly debated the Uniform Civil Code under Article 35. Mohammad Ismail Saheb moved the following proviso for addition to Article 35 under which it was placed then:

> Provided that any groups, section or community of people shall not be obliged to give up its own personal law in case it has such a law.

He advocated that the right to adhere to own personal laws was one of the fundamental rights. He asserted that personal laws were part and parcel of religion and culture. Any interference with the personal laws, would tantamount to interference with the very way of life of those who had been observing such laws for generation to generation. To strengthen his argument, he cited precedents of Yugoslavia, the Kingdom of the Serb, Croats and Slovenes which were obliged under treaty to guarantee to Muslims being in minority in the matter of family laws and personal status:

> The Serb, Croats and Slovene state agree to grant to Mussalmans in the matter of family law and personal status, provisions

> suitable for regulating these matters in accordance with the Mussalman usage.

To enrich his argument, he named similar protective clauses of other European Constitutions which dealt with the minorities. However, he pointed out that such clauses were narrow in scope as they dealt with the minorities only. He emphasized that his proposed amendment was a comprehensive one as it dealt with "any group, section or community of the people" and not confined to minorities only.

His proposed amendment sought to secure the rights of people in respect of their existing personal laws. He contended that in favour of the Union Civil Code, the only plank of argument was: "to secure harmony through uniformity". But he strongly refuted the very idea of regimentation of civil laws including personal laws of all people, irrespective of their caste, creed, religion and culture. In his view, the move of regimentation of personal laws of all the citizens for the purpose of the Uniform Civil Code was counter productive. By following their own personal laws, people of different castes and communities would not be in conflict with each other.[5]

Despite meaningful advocacy of Mohammad Ismail Saheb in favour of his proposed amendment, it was objected by S.C. Majumdar, member of the Constituent Assembly. With the contention that his proposed amendment was in direct negation to the letter and spirit of Article 35 under the concept and nature of the Uniform Civil Code was debated in the Constituent Assembly. The Vice-President of the Constituent Assembly sustained the objection of Majumdar. Resultantly, Ismail Saheb could not succeed. Under the circumstance, he reflected his feeling with the following observations[6]:

> ...for creating and augmenting harmony, it is not at all imperative to compel people to give up their personal laws.

Naziruddin Ahmad, another member of the Constituent Assembly moved a proviso to Article 35 which reads:

> Provided that the personal law of community which has been guaranteed by the state shall not be changed except with the previous approval of the community ascertained in such a manner as the Union Legislature may determine by law.

Elaborating his proposed proviso, he remarked that the Uniform Civil Code would not create inconvenience to Muslims only, but to all religious communities who have religious oriented laws and other laws which were inseparably inter-woven with their beliefs and practices. He argued that the very concept of the Uniform Civil Code clashed with the religious and cultural freedom guaranteed to every citizen as fundamental rights.

Surveying the legal developments in the Indian subcontinent, he pinpointed certain provisions of the Civil Procedure Code, 1908 which had already interfered with the Muslim Personal Laws. However, the British administration as he pointed out, during its 175 years rule, did not interfere with the institution of marriage, dower, divorce, maintenance, guardianship, paternity and acknowledgement, administration of estate, wills, gift, *waqf* and inheritance. However, laws that were enacted in the area of Muslim Personal Laws during the British administration of justice, were mostly on the initiative of the Muslim community.[7]

He appealed that advocacy for protection of personal laws and keeping them out of purview of the Uniform Civil Code must not be taken as a proposition of idealism, but as a matter of stern reality. The move of the Uniform Civil Code, he warned, would lead to confusion, misunderstanding and resentment in various sections of the society. In this perspective, his note of caution is pertinent to be quoted:[8]

> What British in 175 years failed to do or was afraid to do, what the Muslim rulers in course of 500 years refrained from doing, we should not give power to the state to do.

Mahboob Ali Baig Sahib Bahadur, member of the Constituent Assembly proposed the following proviso for addition to Article 35:

> Provided that nothing in this article shall affect the personal law of the citizen.

Concentrating on the institution of Muslim marriage, M.A. Ayyanger, member of the Constituent Assembly intervened and remarked on it as a "matter of contract". The remark of Ayyangar tempted Mahboob Baig to argue forcefully. He asserted that the matrimonial contract was enjoined by the Holy *Qur'an* and the traditions of the Prophet (Peace and blessing be upon him). He also revealed by his educative remark that if the Muslim marriage was not solemnized according to the dictates of the two primary sources of the Islamic matrimonial jurisprudence, it would be void *(Batil).*

He stated that the Islamic matrimonial laws were in operation on Muslims since the introduction of Islam to India and Muslims practiced accordingly with the approval of relevant authorities in all its states. Besides Muslims, he argued about other communities too, whose religions were mixed with their personal laws. He stated that Indian concept of secularism, which the Constitution of India recognized as one of its basic postulates, tolerated the existence of all religions with equal honour and dignity. He emphasized that in secular state like India, different communities must have the freedom to practice their own religion and culture, and they should be allowed to observe their own personal laws.[9] B. Pocker Sahib Bahadur, member of the Constituent Assembly, supporting the motion of Mohammad Ismail Sahib, proposed the addition of the following proviso to Article 35:

> Provided that any group, section or community of the people shall not be obliged to give up its own personal law in case it has such a law.

He evaluated his proposed 'proviso' as 'moderate and reasonable'. He clarified that his proposed proviso was not reasonable to the Muslim Community only, but to other communities too, with reference to matrimonial issues, divorce, succession and endowments. In his opinion, the reason for success of the British administration of justice who ruled India for about 175 years was the maintenance of their policy of non-interference with the personal laws of all communities. He perceived the Uniform Civil Code a 'tyrannous provision' and alarmed the people not to tolerate it. He asserted that his observation was not only voicing forth the sentiments of the Muslim community, but also echoing of those sections who had belief that the Uniform Civil Code interfered with their theological oriented laws and religious practices. He questioned the authority of the Constituent Assembly for discussing the religious and cultural issues to conceive the Uniform Civil Code. In his opinion, the Constituent Assembly had not been mandated by the people of India through the medium of election process to mutilate the substance and form of their personal laws for the sake of the Union Civil Code. He alleged if such a body like the Constituent Assembly interfered with the religious faith and practices of the people, it would be a 'tyrannous venture'. He observed that since the different communities had different laws, and in such situation which community's law would constitute the model or standard to evolve the Uniform Civil Code? He highlighted that every community had different personal laws.

He estimated that intra- and inter-differential position of different communities in the area of law dealing with marriage, matrimonial remedies, dissolution, etc., constituted potent obstacles in the way of actuating the Uniform Civil Code.

Commenting on the clause meant for the Uniform Civil Code, he opined:[10]

> By this one clause you are revolutionizing the whole country and the whole setup. There is no need for it.

In his view the proposal for the Uniform Civil Code was antagonistic and incompatible to religious and cultural freedom guaranteed to citizens as fundamental rights. His emphatic observation to the effect is noteworthy.[11]

> There are ever so many multitudes of communities following various customs for centuries or thousands of years. By one stroke of the pen you want to annul all that and make them uniform. What is the purpose served by this uniformity except to murder the conscience of the people and make them *feel* that they are being trampled upon as regards their religious rights and practices. Such a tyrannous measures ought not to find a place in our Constitution.

Hussain Imam, member of the Constituent Assembly, focussing on the diversity of India opposed the move of the Uniform Civil Code and pointed out:[12]

> India is too big a country with a large population so diversified that it is almost impossible to stamp them with one kind of anything. In the north, we have got extreme heat. In Assam we have got more rain than anywhere else in the world... In Rajputana desert, we have no rain. In a country so diverse, is it possible to have uniformity of civil laws?... Concurrent jurisdiction to the provinces as well as to the centre in matters of succession, marriage, divorce and other things. How is it possible to have uniformity when there are eleven or twelve legislative bodies... to legislate on subject according to requirements of their own people?

His last part of the debate was a full of appeal:[13]

> The apprehension felt by the members of the minority community is very real. Secular state does not mean that it is anti-religious state. It means that it is not irreligious but non-religious and as such there is a world of difference between irreligious and non-religious. I... suggest... the Drafting Committee to come forward with such safeguards... as will meet the apprehensions genuinely felt... and I have every hope that the ingenuity of Dr Ambedkar will be able to find a solution to this.

Thus, members of the minority community strongly argued for the exclusion of personal laws from the ambit of the Uniform Civil Code. Nevertheless, despite their convincing arguments and deep resentment, they could not get success and ultimately the assurance of Dr. B.R. Ambedkar, the Chairman of the Drafting Committee of the Constitution making body, the Constituent Assembly, proved a solacing factor.

K.M. Munshi, member the Constituent Assembly, observed that the Uniform Civil Code is opposed on two grounds:

1. That the Uniform Civil Code is violative of religious and cultural freedoms, and
2. That it was tyrannous to minorities, especially Muslims.

He relied on clause (2) of Article 25 of the Constitution which reads:

"Nothing in this article shall affect the operation of any existing law or prevent the state from making any law:

(a) regulating or restricting any economic, financial, political or other secular activity which may be associated with religious practice.

(b) Providing for social welfare and reform..."

He clarified that it had already been decided that in the case of religious freedom under clause (1) of Article 25 of the Constitution attracted 'social welfare and reform', the parliament would be competent to enact laws. Thus, he on strength of clause (2) of Article 25 observed:[14]

> The whole object of this article is that when the parliament thinks proper an attempt may be made to unify the personal laws of the country.

To refute the Uniform Civil Code as 'tyranny to minorities', he argued that in Muslim countries, minorities' personal laws were not recognized as 'sacrosanct' to prevent the legislative body from enacting laws. He gave example of Turkey and Egypt wherein minorities were not permitted to have their distinct personal laws. Also, he gave the example of European countries wherein civil codes were applicable to all those who went there, irrespective of their belonging to majority or minority communities. Conclusively, he beseeched to divorce religion from personal laws.[15]

> We want to divorce religion from personal laws, from what may be called social relations or from the rights of the parties as regards inheritance or succession What have these things got to do with religion, we really fail to understand.

He failed in the realization of the place and significance of religions in the Indian society. He failed to recognize the due place of religion in the society and exhorted to unify and consolidate the nation by all means.[16]

> But after all we are an advancing society. We are in a stage where we must unify and consolidate the nation by every means..., however, the religious practices in the past have been so construed as to cover the whole field of life, we have reached when we must put our foot down and say that those matters are not religion, they are purely a matter of secular legislation.

Soliciting to Muslim brethren, he opined:[17]

> ... I want my Muslim friends to realize this that the sooner we forget this isolationist outlook on life, it will be better for the country. Religion must be restricted to spheres which legitimately appertain to religion, and the rest of life must be

regulated, unified and modified in such a manner that we may evolve, as early as possible into a strong and consolidated nation.

A.K. Ayyar, member of the Constituent Assembly, explained the scope of the Uniform CivilCode:[18]

> A civil code... runs into every department of civil relations, to the law of contracts, to the law of property, to the law of succession, to the law of marriage and similar matters.

Ayyar urged the Assembly to pass the article dealing with the Uniform, Civil Code. The Assembly passed accordingly, brushing aside the proposal of the Muslim members for the exclusion of personal laws from the ambit of the Uniform Civil Code.

Dr. B.R. Ambedkar, Chairman of the Drafting Committee, tried his best to solace the Muslim members on the issue of the Uniform Civil Code:[19]

> I shall also like to point out that the state is claiming in this matter power to legislate. There is no obligation upon the state to do away with the personal laws. It is only giving the power. Therefore, no one need to be apprehensive to execute or enforce that power in a manner that may be found to be objectionable by the Muslims or Christians or by other communities in India... because sovereignty in the exercise of that power must reconcile itself to the sentiments of different communities. No Government can exercise its power in such a manner as to provoke the Muslim community to rise in rebellion. I think it would be mad government if it did so.

Besides the above observation, Dr. Ambedkar persuaded the Muslim members 'not to read too much into Article 44." He affirmed even if the Uniform Civil Code was implemented, it would be applicable to those who would consent to be governed by it.

Muslim Personal Law from Mughal regime down to the British administration of justice, was duly protected and implemented. It is derived from Islam and the Islamic way of life. It manifests the religious faith and cultural ethos of the Muslim community. It is part and parcel of Islamic religion and culture. The Constitution of India guarantees the religious and cultural freedom.[20] Religion is the matter of faith and conscience. The culture and civilization incorporate the religious ethos. Muslim Personal Law being the very core of Islamic religious faith amalgamates in itself 'belief', 'practice' and 'propagation'. The ambit of religious and cultural freedom[21] enshrined in Part III of the Constitution as the fundamental rights covers the Muslim Personal Law.

Muslims as a community, being the followers of different scholastic thoughts are divided into diverse sects and sub-sects which constitute religious denomination. Each sect of the Muslim has the fundamental right to manage its own affairs in matters of religion under Article 26(b) of the Constitution.[22] Thus, Muslim Personal Law being the integral part of the Islamic religion and Islamic affairs, deserves protection of Article 25 (1) and 26(b) of the Constitution.[23]

Islamic family status, family relations, matrimonial issues and other related matters and their governance, are the core and crux of the Muslim Personal Law. Of course, these institutions reflect the culture of the Muslim community. Under Article 29(1) of the Constitution[24], Muslims are empowered to preserve their distinct culture. Muslim culture is intertwined and intermixed with the Islamic way of life. Muslim Personal Law cannot be segregated from Islam and the Islamic culture. Religious and cultural rights enshrined in the Constitution[25] protect and preserve the Muslim Personal Law. During the British regime, Muslims were allowed to follow their personal laws. Permission to follow their personal laws assumed statutory recognition in 1753 by the Charter of George II, whereby, Muslims could get exemption from the application of the Mayor's Court. By the permission under the relevant provision of the Charter, Muslims could adjudicate their cases on the basis of their personal laws.

Non-interference with the personal laws was not the innovation of the British administration of justice. Rather, the British India inherited it from its predecessor, the Mughal administrating of justice. Muslim rulers were convinced that neither it was just nor equitable to force other communities to give up their personal laws. Consequently, they allowed all religious communities to profess and practice their personal laws. The feasibility and legitimacy of the policy of the Muslim rulers to the effect influenced the British administration in India to promulgate the Muf'assil Regulation, 1772 during the time of Warren Hastings, and later passed the Regulation of 1780 which provides:

> That in all suits regarding the inheritance, marriage and caste, and other religious usages and institutions, the law of Koran with respect to Mohammadans... shall invariably be adhered to.

Again in 1937, the British Imperial Legislature assured the application of Muslim Personal Law to Muslims by enacting The Muslim Personal Law (Shariat) Application Act, 1937. The relevant provisions are noted below:[26]

> Notwithstanding any custom or usage to the contrary in all question.... Regarding intestate succession, special property of females, including personal property, Inherited or obtained under contract or gift or any of the provisions of personal law, marriage, dissolution of marriage including Talaq, illa, Zihar, Lian, Khula, Mubarat, maintenance, dower, guardianship, gift, trusts, trust properties and Waqfs... the rule of decision in cases where parties are Muslims shall be the Muslim Personal Law (Shariat).

Under Article 372, the Constitution of India ensures the application of "all the law in force in the territory of India immediately before its commencement". The Muslim Personal Law (Shariat) Application Act, 1937 is 'law in force' as Article 372 of the Constitution explains to the effect:

> ... all the laws in force in the territory of India immediately before the commencement of this Constitution shall continue in force therein until altered or repealed or amended by a competent legislature or other competent authority.

Further, explanation I of Article 372 of the Constitution states:

> The expression "law in force" in this Article shall include a law passed or made by a legislature or other competent authority in the territory of India before the commencement of this Constitution and not previously repealed...

The very letter and spirit of Article 372 of the Constitution reveal that the Muslim Personal Law is the 'law in force' as it is enacted by the competent legislature. Since its application, the Act has never been 'altered or repealed or amended by the competent legislature or other competent authority' till date, so that it is the 'law in force' or 'living law' according to Article 372 of the Constitution. Entry 5 of list III (Seventh Schedule) of the Constitution does recognize the existençe of numerous personal laws. Muslim Personal Law is one of the existing personal laws in India.

As discussed in preceding para, Muslim Personal Law being the part and parcel of the religion and culture of the Muslim community, is duly protected by part III of the Constitution. In such constitutional scenario, if the state enacts any law which takes away or abridges the personal law of the Muslim community, it shall attract Article 13(2) of the Constitution which reads:

> The state shall not make any law which takes away or abridges the rights conferred by this Part (III) and any law made in contravention of this clause shall to extent of the contravention, be void.

The doctrine of 'reasonable classification' is recognized under Article 14 of the Constitution which deals with the 'equality before the law' and the 'equal protection of the laws.' Muslims in India have their own distinct language, religion and culture, thus, they constitute a 'separate class' as a distinct community. The philosophy of 'reasonable classification' is applicable to them. According to 'reasonable classification', they constitute a 'separate class'. Being a 'separate class', they are constitutionally entitled to have their separate set of personal laws.

It is paradoxical as on the one hand, all citizens are entitled to freedom of conscience and the right to profess, practice and propagate religion,[27] while on the other hand, the Constitution directs the state to endeavour to secure for the citizens a 'Uniform Civil Code' throughout the territory of India.[28] Any section of the citizens having a distinct language, script or culture of its own shall have the right to conserve the same.[29] Every religion's denomination or any section thereof shall have the right to manage its own affairs in matters of religion.[30]

Not only religious belief, but acts done in pursuance of religious performance or practice: rites, ceremonies, observances and modes of worship are protected under Articles 25(1) and 26(b) of the Constitution. The constitutional provisions embody the principle of religious tolerance and serve to the secular nature of Indian democracy which the architects of the Constitution considered the very basis of it.[31] Freedom of conscience connotes individual's doctrines and dogmas pertaining to all matter which are considered by him or her to be essential and conducive to spiritual well-being[32] to carry out religious practices in pursuance of religious beliefs which are considered by that particular religious belief to be its essential and integral part. Such religious practices are constitutionally guaranteed as a fundamental right.[33] Its practice is religious, if it is considered as the essential and integral part of the religion, and depends on the conscience of the follower of the religion and its basic tenets.[34]

The practice of the Muslim Personal Law by the Muslims is the practice of Islam. The practice of Muslim Personal Law manifests the culture of the Muslim community. Muslims of India are guaranteed by the Constitution to preserve and conserve their culture.[35]

Religion is not only a matter of faith, but also prescribes ritual observation, ceremonies and modes of religious performance. The Muslim Personal Law is the integral part of Islam. Marriage, dower, divorce, maintenance, guardianship, paternity, acknowledgement, *waqf*, wills, gifts, pre-emption, administration of estate and inheritance constitute the core of the Muslim Personal Law. All these institutions are derived and developed by the primary and secondary sources of the Shariat. It is an established postulate of the Islamic jurisprudence that in the very concept of Islamic Law, the essence of religion and values of ethics and morals are incorporated. In the Islamic legal system, law, religion and ethics are intermixed and interwoven. Truth in the belief of totality is ordained by the *Qur'an:*

1. But no, by the Lord
   They can have
   No (real faith)
   Until they make thee Judge
   In all disputes between them,
   And find in their souls
   No resistance against
   Thy decisions, but accept
   Them with the fullest
   conviction.[36]
2. Then is it only a part of the Book
   That ye believe in,
   And do ye reject the rest?
   But what is the reward for those
   Among you who behave like this
   But disgrace in this life?
   And on the day of Judgment
   They shall be consigned
   To the most gregarious penalty.
   For Allah is not unmindful of what ye do.[37]

3. Say: Truly, my prayer
And my service of sacrifice,
My life and my death,
Are (all for Allah)
The Cherisher of the Worlds.[38]

4. O ye who believe:
Obey God, and Obey the Apostle,
And those charged
With authority among you
If ye differ in anything
Among yourselves, prefer it
To God and His Apostle,
If ye do believe in God
And the last day;
That is best and most suitable
For final determination.[39]

Besides the Holy *Qur'an*, the other sources strengthen the proposition that in the Islamic system, law and religion are intertwined:

1 Religion, Ethics and Law are, therefore, so intermixed in Islam...[40]
2. The Source of law and religion being the same.[41]
3. The Islamic thought is most typical manifestation of the Islamic way of life, the core and Kernel of Islam itself.[42]
4. Muslim Jurisprudence furnishes us with an example of complete union of law and religion.[43]
5. in Islam law is religion and religion is law because both have the same source and equal authority, being both contained in 'the Divine' Reservation.[44]
6. The personal law of... Muslim finds its source and authority respectively ...Muslim religion.[45]
7. The Muslim generally have deep emotional feelings for their law which they regard as one of the their distinctive possession.[46]
8. Justice Mahmood in *Govind Dayal vs. Inayatullah*[47] observed:

> It is to be remembered that... Muhammadan laws are so intimately connected with religion that cannot readily be disserved from it.

Muslim Personal Law, being the integral part of religion, culture, ethics and morality, has legislative basis[48] and constitutional recognition[49] in India.

Islamic religious faith becomes meaningless if it is not practiced according to the dictates of the Shariat. For example, in Islam, to have faith in five times daily prayers and Haj (pilgrimage) are not sufficient till the moment these are not performed according to Sunnah (action of the Prophet) by the Muslims. According to constitutional scheme, the state is under the obligation to protect the religious and cultural freedom of which the Muslim Personal Law is an inseparable part. Under the Islamic scheme, the ambit of Muslim Personal Law covers marriage, dower, divorce, maintenance, guardianship, paternity, acknowledgement, *waqf*, wills, gifts, pre-emption, administration of estate and institution of inheritance. These are the important components of religious faith and practice as revealed by Allah, the Almighty in His Holy Book, expounded by the Prophet (peace and blessing be upon him), collected, codified and interpreted by the great caliphs and learned Imams. The perfection of Islam is proclaimed by Allah, the Almighty Himself.[50]

> "...
> But fear me,
> This day I have perfected your religion
> For you, completed
> My favour upon you,
> And have chosen for you
> Islam as your religion."

In view of the religious and cultural background of the Muslim Personal law, any attempt by judiciary or any other wing of the Government of India to change or codify or repeal it, would amount to rebellion against Allah, the Almighty, the Prophet (peace and blessing be upon him), great caliphs, learned Imams and its followers.[51] Also, any such attempt would violate the religious and cultural freedom of Muslims which are guaranteed by the Constitution of India.[52]

The Muslim Personal Law and the Uniform Civil Code: The Judicial Approach

The Indian judiciary on the issue of the Uniform Civil Code and the Personal Law has not been consistent. It has adopted diverse approaches on different occasions.

The Division Bench of the Calcutta High Court in *Naresh Chandra Bose vs. Schindra Nath Deb*[53] held that the expression "Law in force" under Article 372 (2) of the Constitution was not limited to statutory laws, but it is extended to cover customary laws and personal laws like that of the Muslim Community. Further, it observed that the Article 44 of the Constitution itself recognized the existence of different sets of personal laws for different communities.

The Supreme Court in *Krishna Singh vs. Mathura*[54] opined that in process of applying the personal laws of the parties, the judges of the High Court 'could not introduce their own concepts of modernity'. In view of the Supreme Court, the Constitution maintained the position of personal laws *status quo*.

The Delhi High Court in *Harvindra Kaur vs. Harmander Singh*[55] appreciated the sanctity of personal laws. The relevant observations of the Delhi High Court are extracted below:

1. The introduction of the Constitutional law in the home (personal law) is most inappropriate.
2. It (Constitution) is like introducing (in area of personal laws) a bull in a China Shop.
3. It (Constitution) will prove to be a ruthless destroyer of the marriage (which is the part of personal law) institution and all that it stands for.

4. In privacy of home and the married life, neither Article 21 (protection of life and personal liberty), nor Article 14 (equality before law) have any place.
5. In sensitive sphere (personal law) which is most intimate and delicate, the introduction of the cold principles of constitutional law will have the effect of weakening the marriage bond.

Academicians have the similar view:[56]

> Inside the privacy of homes, to the cases of parental, marital, filial and fraternal relationships that requirement of our constitutional law, we must appreciate, have only a limited application.

Chief Justice Gajendragadar (as he then was) opined that the non-implementation of Article 44 amounted to a grave failure of Indian democracy. He expressed his conviction for its early implementation. In his view, a Common Civil Code was imperative for evolving a new secular social order.[57]

Justice Hedge, the Judge of the Supreme Court (as he then was) observed:[58]

> Religious-oriented laws were a concept of medieval time, alien to modem societies which are secular as well as cosmopolitan. So long our laws are religious-oriented laws, we can hardly built up a homogenous nation.

The Constitution bench of five judges in *Mohd Ahmad vs. Shah Bano Begum*[59] opined on the Uniform Civil Code, while it was not the issue before the Supreme Court for judicial treatment. The relevant observation held unanimously by the five judges are noted below:[60]

> It is also a matter of regret that Article 44 of our Constitution has remained a dead letter. It provides that the state shall endeavour to secure for the citizens a Uniform Civil Code throughout the territory of India. There is no evidence of any

> official activity for framing a common civil code for the country. A belief seems to have gained ground that it is for the Muslim community to take a lead in the matter of reforms of their personal law A common civil code will help a cause of national integration by removing desperate loyalties to laws which have conflicting ideologies. No community is likely to bell a cat by making gratuitous concession on this issue of the state which is charged with the duty of securing a Uniform Civil Code for the citizens of the country and, unquestionably, it has the legislative competence to do so. We understand the difficulties involved in bringing persons of different faiths and persuasions on a common platform. But, a beginning has to be made if the Constitution has any meaning. Inevitably, the role of reformer has to be assumed by the court because, it is beyond the endurance of sensitive minds to allow injustice to be suffered when it is so palpable. But piecemeal attempts of courts to bridge that gap between personal laws cannot take the place of a common civil code. Justice to all is a far more satisfactory way of dispensing justice than justice from case to case.

Again, a two Judges bench of the Supreme Court in *Ms. Jorden Diegdeh vs. S.S. Chopra*[61] reiterated:

> ...the time has come for the intervention... in these matters to provide for a Uniform Civil Code of marriage and divorce.

Further, Justice O. Chinappa Reddy speaking for the court, referred to the observations of the Chief Justice Chandrachud (as he was then) in *Shah Bano Begum case* and observed:

> It was just the other day that a Constitution bench of this court had to emphasize the urgency of infusing life into Article 44 of the Constitution which provides for a Uniform Civil Code. The present case is yet another which focuses our immediate and compulsive need for a Uniform Civil Code. The totally unsatisfactory state of affairs consequent on the lack of a Uniform Civil Code...

Now, the latest but very controversial verdict of the Supreme Court in *Smt. Sarala Mudgal case*[62] wherein the Supreme Court, preferred to deal with the Uniform Civil Code, while therein the issue of the Uniform Civil Code was not raised for judicial treatment. Factually speaking, Meena Mathur, one of the petitioners was married to Jitender Mathur. Her husband embraced Islam and married Fatima, the name after her conversion to Islam. The marriage was solemnized when both embraced Islam and adopted the Muslim way of life accordingly. Petitioner contended that the conversion of her husband to Islam was just to remarry by circumventing the provision of section 494 of the Indian Penal Code. He asserted that being a Muslim, he could marry to the extent of four, provided he was able to do justice with all the wives according to the dictates of the Holy *Qur'an*[63] and *Sunnah* of the Prophet (peace and blessing be upon him). Another petitioner, Geeta's husband, converted to Islam and married after conversion to a Muslim girl. His first Hindu wife contended that her husband's conversion to Islam was just to facilitate his second marriage as in the Islamic matrimonial system, a male could marry to the extent of four at a time. Geeta, a Hindu wife whose husband converted to Islam married to Deepa, a Hindu girl after her conversion to Islam, contended that the conversions of both to Islam was to facilitate the second marriage. One other, Sunita Ghosh who was married to G.C. Ghosh in 1984 according to Hindu rites. G.C. Ghosh proposed to divorce his wife by mutual consent[64] under the provision of the Hindu Marriage Act, 1955. He disclosed to his wife that he had already embraced Islam and showed the certificate issued by the Qazi testifying his conversion to restrain her husband from remarrying.

Factual narration in the preceding paragraphs reveals that the issue of the Uniform Civil Code was not raised before the Supreme Court for its verdict. Nevertheless, Justice Kuldip Singh preferred to opine on the need and relevance of the Uniform Civil Code in India. For reason best known to

Justice Kuldip Singh and his companion Judge Justice R.M. Sahai who *suo-moto* picked up the issue of Uniform Civil Code and expressed their opinion on it at length. Both expressed their favour for the implementation of it relying on *Shah Bano Case*[65] with their approval. Justice Kuldip Singh ignored the relevance of 'unity in diversity' as one of the peculiarities of India. He did not pay heed to the doctrine of 'Secularism' in the Indian context. He brushed aside the religious and cultural freedom of Indian Muslims guaranteed to them as fundamental rights by the Constitution of India and preferred to observe:[66]

> ...those who preferred to (remain) in India after the partition fully knew that the Indian leaders did not believe in two-nation or three nation theory and that in Indian Republic there was only one nation – Indian nation... and no community could claim to remain a separate entity on the basis of religion.

To secure the Uniform Civil Code, Justice Kuldeep Singh manifested unwarranted zeal and finally made an earnest appeal to the Government of India:[67]

> We, therefore, request the Government of India through the Prime Minister of the country to have fresh look at Article 44 of the Constitution of India and endeavour to secure for the citizens a Uniform Civil Code throughout the territory of India.

On issue of the delay in implementation of the 'Uniform Civil Code', Justice Kuldip Singh expressed his wonder:[68]

> One wonders how long will it take for the Government of the day to implement the mandate of the framers of the Constitution under Article 44 of the Constitution of India.

The irrationality of Justice Kuldip Singh's approach can be gleaned by his observation noted below:[69]

> Article 44 is based on the concept that there is necessary connection between religion and personal law in civilized society. Article 25 guarantees religious freedom whereas Article

> 44 seeks to divest religion from social relations and personal laws. Marriage, succession and like matters of a secular character cannot be brought within the guarantee enshrined under Article 25, 26 and 29.

Further, he observed ignoring the grassroot realities and sanctity of the personal laws:[70]

> The legislation – not religion – being the authority under which personal law was permitted to operate and is continuing to operate, the same can be superseded/supplemented by introducing a Uniform Civil Code. In this view of the matter no community can oppose the introduction of human civil code for all the citizens in the territory of India.

He reminded the Government of its failure:[71]

> The successive Governments till date have been wholly remiss in their duty of implementing the Constitutional mandate of Article 44.

In *John Vallamatton and another vs. Union of India*[71(a)] the constitutionality of the provisions of section 118 of the Indian succession Act, 1925 was challenged before the apex court petitioners were Christians. They were aggrieved by the discriminatory treatment meted out to them regarding property for religious and charitable purposes. Section 118 of the said Act imposes restriction only on the Indian Christians, that is why the impugned provision is violative of Article 14 of the Constitution which ensures equality to all. Section 118 of the Act being unreasonable is arbitrary and discriminatory and therefore, violative of Article 14 of the Constitution. In this case 'Uniform Civil Code' was not the issue raised before the Supreme Court to adjudicate in any manner, but Hon'ble Chief Justice V.N. Khare *suo-moto* brought the matter of Uniform Civil Code and opined that "it is a matter of regret that Article 44 of the Constitution has not been given effect to and the Parliament is still to step in for framing a Common Civil Code in the country. It will help the cause of national integration by removing the contradictions based on ideologies". Such remarks of the Supreme Court was not tenable legally as it was mandated to adjudicate on issues which have been raised before it for adjudication by applying the relevant rule of law. It is not competent to assume the role of legislature and executive disturbing the scheme of separation of power. It is duty-bound to respect the scheme of separation of power. It is not competent to behave as social, economic, political and legal reformer. Issue of Uniform Civil Code and 'national integration' are raised in the case under comment without legal authorization. Such unwarranted zeal is bound to create chaos and confusion. Apex judiciary in the past too has done like that causing agitation at national level. *Shah Bano* and *Smt. Satls Mudgal* case can be illustrated on representative basis to this effect. Such behaviour of the Supreme Court does not satisfy the requirement of legality, reality and legitimacy. By such a disorderly stand of the apex judiciary the cause of national integration is bound to suffer adversely.

Besides other key concepts, secularism, religious and cultural freedom constitute the 'basic structure' of the Indian Constitution. Religious freedom under Article 25 is not confined to freedom of conscience but its ambit covers the right to profess, practice and propagate the religion by the citizens. Indeed, religion is a wide and pervasive concept. It is not confined to 'faith' only because 'practice' and 'propagation' are the part and parcel of the religion. 'Faith' represents the inner aspect of religion, while 'practice' and 'propagation' manifest the 'external aspect'.

Marriage, dower, divorce, maintenance, guardianship, parentage, acknowledgement, waqf, will, gift, administration of estate, inheritance and conversion are the integral part of the Muslim Personal Law. These are religious in nature and content. Giving consent by a Muslim before Qazi for the purpose of marriage is as much a matter of faith and conscience as worship itself. It is the manifestation of faith or conscience when a Hindu converts by reciting Kalama or a Muslim becomes a Hindu by reciting certain *mantras. All* these come within the purview of religious freedom guaranteed under Article 25 of the Constitution of India. Quite possible, some of the religious practices observed by the followers of one religion may appear to the followers of other religions to be excessive or violative of human values or moral ethics or ethics or human rights. However, after all, these are the matters of faith. For the smooth coexistence of multi-religious and multi-cultural societies, adherence to the doctrine of tolerance is imperative. It is pertinent to point out that in the domain[72] of faith or belief, there is little scope or role for logic or reason. It is noteworthy that the freedom of religion is not merely a constitutional guarantee, but also, it is the core and crux of our culture.

According to the observation of Justice Kuldip Singh, a marriage of a Hindu solemnized according to the Hindu prescribed norms or rites, cannot be dissolved by the conversion of the Hindu husband to Islam and his subsequent second marriage with a Muslim female according to Islamic norms. Grounds of divorce for a Hindu husband and wife are enumerated under Section 13 of the Hindu Marriage Act, 1955. Except for the grounds and procedure laid down in the Act, the Hindu spouses cannot opt for any other ground or procedure for the dissolution of marriage. Thus, the conversion of a Hindu husband to Islam and his subsequent second marriage with Muslim female does not affect his first marriage and his marriage after conversion to Islam is void according to the observation of Justice Kuldip Singh. This observation contravenes the guarantees under Article 25, 26 and 29 of the Constitution of India. The very objective of the conversion to Islam frustrates if the converted person is not able to enjoy all the attributes of system in the fullest manner as a Muslim. Such observation obstacles the smooth translation of 'religious practice' and 'religious propagation'. It may be pointed out that Justice Kuldip Singh fails to harmonize in proper perspective the issue of bigamy under Section 494 of Indian Penal Code,

1860. Hindu husband's conversion to Islam, and his second marriage according to the prescribed norms of Islamic matrimonial jurisprudence, 'religious faith' and 'religious practice' are assured to every citizen by the Constitution. Justice Kuldip Singh's unrealistic observation is extracted for evaluation:[73]

> Article 44 (dealing with Uniform Civil Code) is based on the concept that there is no necessary connection between religion and personal laws in a civilized society. Article 25 guarantees religious freedom whereas Article 44 seeks to diverts religion from social relations and personal laws. Marriage, succession and like matters of a secular character cannot be brought within the guarantee enshrined under Articles 25, 26 and 29.

Justice Kuldip Singh singles out Muslims and Christians who are very sentimental to their religious matters and personal laws. He appreciates the sacramental nature of Hindu personal laws, but Hindus, for the cause of 'national unity', have forsaken their sentiments and welcomed its codification by the Parliament.[74] His observation to the effect is noted below for scrutiny:[75]

> The personal law of the Hindus, such as relating to marriage, succession and the like all of a sacramental origin, the same manner as in the case of, the Muslims or the Christians. The Hindus along with Sikhs, Buddhists and Janis have forsaken their sentiments in the cause of national Unity and integration, some other communities wouldn't, though the Constitution enjoins the establishment of a "Common Civil Code" for the whole of India.

Practical experience establishes that minority community is sensitive, especially to their religious, cultural and educational matters. Muslims in India are in minority. Their sensitivities are endorsed by the founding fathers of the Constitution of India. That is why the Constitution of India sanctions religious, cultural and educational rights in favour of minorities including Muslims on the footing of the fundamental rights. If Justice Kuldip Singh believes that adherence to personal laws by the Muslim community in India weakens 'national unity and integration', he is a victim of fallacious assumption. His following observation negates reality and legality of the existence of different religions and cultures of different communities in India:[76]

> Those who preferred to remain in India after the partition fully knew that the Indian leaders did not believe in two-nation or three-nation theory and that in the Indian Republic there was to be only one nation – Indian nation and no community could claim to remain a separate entity on the basis of religion. It would be necessary to emphasize that the respective personal laws were permitted by the British to govern the matters relating to inheritance, marriage etc. only under the Regulation of 1871 framed by Warren Hastings. The legislation – not religion – being the authority under which personal law was permitted to operate, the same can be superseded/supplemented by introducing an Uniform Civil Code. In this view of the matter, no community can oppose the introduction of human civil code for all the citizens in the territory of India.

Companion Judge, Justice R.M Sahai appears to be alive to the sensitivities, realities and magnitude of the problem. His observation reflects to the effect:[77]

> The pattern of debate, even today, is the same as was voiced forcefully by the members of the minority community in the Constituent Assembly. If the non-implementation of the provisions contained in Article 44 amounts to grave failure of Indian democracy, it represents one side of the picture, then the other side claims that logical probability appears to be that code would cause dissatisfaction and disintegration than serve as a common umbrella to promote homogeneity and national solidarity.

Justice R.M. Sahai evaluates religious freedom and secularism:[78]

> ...religious freedom, basic foundation of secularism, was guaranteed by Articles 25 to 28 of the constitution. Article 25 is very widely worded. It guarantees all persons, not only freedom of consciences but right to profess, practice and propagate religion.

However, Justice R.M. Sahai concludes his observation with a contradictory note. His following observation is testimony to the effect:[79]

> ... freedom of religion is the core of our culture. Even slightest deviation shakes the social fiber But religious practices, violative of human rights and dignity and sacerdotal suffocation of essentially civil and material freedom, are not autonomy but oppression. Therefore, a unified code is imperative both for protection of the oppressed and for promotion of national unity and solidarity.

The above observation reveals that Justice R.M. Sahai favours the implementation of the Uniform Civil Code for "protection of the oppressed and for promotion of national unity and solidarity".

Judicial activism means the introduction and elaborating of new ideas, notions and conceptions in the process of deciding the case at hand.[80] The Constitution of India stands for the separation of power. In view of this, the judiciary is least competent to function as a legislature. Why, because courts by the very nature of its function, lack facilities and essential data to make probing enquiries to know the home reality. Reliance on advocates who appear before courts is quite likely to provide partisan or inadequate information. Contrary to it, if courts have to rely on their own knowledge and research, they are bound to be either selective or subjective.[81] Also, courts have no necessary means for supervision and implementing the aftermath of their orders and mandates.

It is hard reality that the courts wish to do justice to the commoner and to shake a wooden bureaucracy, whittling down its prestige by issuing administrative orders which authorities sometimes find difficult to implement. The judiciary has no institutional means to supervise and enforce it. Substantially and infrastructurally, our judiciary is not equipped to be a legislative or an administrative agency.

On the issue of 'judicial activism', the following point of caution is noteworthy:[82]

> ...there are too many dangers to the Judiciary itself from an omnipresent rescuing factors. In its own interest also the Indian judiciary may sooner or later has to propound a policy of non-intervention.

Such policy would not be a sign of weakness or abdication by the judiciary, rather a recognition of the fact that the Constitution has not made the judiciary a substitute for the failure of the other branches of the government and its judicial power has its own constraints imposed by the Constitution of India.

It is an established fact that the Constitution of India is founded on the premise that there will be a responsible government. The executive wing is accountable to the legislature and the later to electorates. Entrusting the legislature with wide and far-reaching powers over the lives, liberties and property of the citizens, the makers of the Constitution of India have made the legislature trustee of powers reposed in it. The judiciary is structured as guardian of right of the people with auxiliary check on the legislature and executive.

The most creative judge, Lord Denning, remarks focusing on the role of a Judge:[83]

"Judges cannot do anything to help the poor or unemployed. They cannot provide housing for the homeless. All social reforms must be left to others..." In *Indira Gandhi vs. Raj Narain,*[84] the Supreme Court of India observes:

> ... courts are institutionally setup as courts of law and lack the power of the legislature or the executive. The Indian Constitution prescribes.... Separation of powers between the three

branches of Government and the Judiciary was never quipped or intended to do the work of other branches.

Justice Sawant (as he then was) commenting on the role of the judiciary remarks:[85]

> The absolute and unlimited power of the judiciary particularly at the highest level without public accountability may endanger democracy itself.

The most articulate Judge, Justice P.N. Bhagwati (as he then was), observes:[86]

> ... the Constitution is the paramount law of the land. Every organ of government, be it the executive or the legislature or the Judiciary, derives its authority from Constitution and it has to act within the limits of its authority...

In process of the Constitution making, stressing the need for an independent judiciary to correct the government and at the same time rather in the same breath, Pandit Jawahar Lal Nehru emphasized on the limits of the Judicial power:[87]

> ... No Judge or Supreme Court can make a third chamber. No Judiciary can stand in judgment over sovereign will of Parliament representing the will of entire community...

Secularism in the context of the Indian Constitution is not a mere passive or negative doctrine, but it is a comprehensive, forward-looking, dynamic and productive doctrine where life, law and religion exhibit mixed manifestation.[88] The Constitution of India sanctions equal citizenship, unity in diversity, no discrimination, freedom of religion and culture, secularism, equality, justice social, economic and political, and fraternity among all communities.

According to the scheme of the Constitution, the state functions through three organs: legislative, executive and judicial. It discourages the concentration of power in any particular organ or the state.[89]

One of the most important functions of the judiciary is to interpret law and statute. In the process of interpreting law and statute, the primary duty of judge is to ascertain the intention of the legislature. It has to discover and act upon the true intention of the legislature. Also, it has to discover and act upon the true intention of the legislature: the *mens* or *sentential legis.* The essence of law lies in its spirit and not in letter. However, the letter is the mode of the external manifestation of intention, hence, the judiciary is under the obligation to admit the *litera legis* as the exclusive and conclusive evidence of *sentential legis.*[90]

The court's function is not to make or alter the law, but to interpret it only. If judges are not entitled to legislate, if their judicial activities are subjected to check and balance and if strict separation of power exists, judges must remain alive to their judicial restraints or judicial constraints. They are urged not to interfere with others by their innovative approach based on their own logic and philosophy. It is neither desirable, nor reasonable to bend the personal laws beyond their elastic limits in order to accommodate certain so-called popular ideas of the day, because over-zealous judges may always find some 'humanitarian' or 'modernist' ground to unsettle the well-established rules of the Muslim Personal Law in order to accommodate their preferences.[91]

It would be appropriate to say: "the duty of the Judge is to administer justice according to law, and not according to his own personal notions of fairplay or fair dealing".[92]

In this context, the Chief Justice, Sir Shah Sulaiman's observations in *Anis Begum vs. Mohd. Istefa Husain* is urged to be considered seriously:[93]

> If one finds a question well thrashed out and in later centuries a particular interpretation is adopted by the leading doctors and text book writers, it would not be proper for us in twentieth century to go beyond such a consensus of opinion and decide a point contrary to such opinion – such a course of action would unsettle the Muhammadan Law.

It is noteworthy that the court has often assumed a reformist stand even though the Constitution does not give it the power to introduce such notions into the problem before it. It is unfortunate that judges regard themselves as leaders in matters of social reform.[94] Seervai, a noted constitutionist of India, opines that judges must enforce the laws whatever they may be, and consideration beyond for infusing own liking and disliking based on their own preferences, is constitutionally not valid.[95]

In India, judges are hardly in the position to assume the role of *Mujtahid*, social reformer and legislator. In this background, if they are not following the judicial discipline 'according to the dictates' of the Constitution of India, people belonging to other communities in general and Muslims in particular, shall be bound to lose confidence in judiciary.

Under the banner of All India Muslim Personal Law Board, Indian Muslims have expressed their resentment after the decision of Supreme Court in *Shah Bano*[96] to the effect. As a matter of caution, it is pertinent to note that if undesirable judicial activism continues, Indian Muslims will be duty-bound to demand for the statutory establishment of the Shariat Courts to be presided over by Muslim Judges, being experts in the understanding and application of Islamic jurisprudence and Islamic law in the area of Muslim Personal Laws. This reality must not be ignored by the Government of India and the same is urged to restore the shattered confidence of Indian Muslims.

Vast sections of the people do adhere to the numerous personal laws. The diversities of family laws of different communities, the tribal's own laws and customs, the belief of the people that the source of law and religion is the same and that faith, law and religion are intermixed and interwoven, prompt people to oppose the Uniform Civil Code from its very inception. The Uniform Civil Code under Article 44 is one of the directive principles of state policy, while Articles 25, 26 and 29 deal with religious and cultural freedoms are the fundamental rights and both conflict with each other. In such conflicting situation, fundamental rights are mandated to prevail.

History preserves as the living testimony that when great emperor, Akbar introduced *'Deen-I-llahi'* and another renowned Hindu emperor, Ashoka introduced *Dhamma,* at the cost of the substitution of the existing personal laws of the people, making endeavour in this direction, both had to vanish and give up with these, due to the counterblast of the people.[97]

Mughals and British rulers of India preserved the personal laws of the Hindu and Muslim communities, because of the dominant view that personal laws were too much identified with the religion and culture of the people. The British regime appointed various law commissions which recommended that the personal laws could not be codified as such exercise would amount to interference with religious and cultural matters of the people.

On issue of the Uniform Civil Code, a noted scholar A.A.A. Fyzee acknowledging the sentiments of the Indian Muslims commented:[98]

> Although, there is recommendation in the Constitution of India, the community is solidly opposed to this course. It would hurt the feelings of vast majority of Muslims in the country and will be considered an Unnecessary interference with their religion.

Attempt to introduce the Uniform Civil Code in India shall be suicidal *per se* and is bound to cause disorder, chaos and disintegration. By such exercise, India's 'unity in diversity' is bound to be jeopardized and imperiled.

The Constitution of India is a man-made law and it has already been amended more than eighty-nine times till date after its commencement within its about fifty-three years' time span. The legality, reality and legitimacy of the Uniform Civil Code apart, it has already been the cause of chaos, confusion and communal disharmony. The very concept of the Uniform

Civil Code has become a potent threat to India's integration. Also, it negates 'unity in diversity' and to the peculiarity of the Indian concept of secularism. In such a circumstance, the ideal solution is the deletion of Article 44 from the Constitution. However, if it is not feasible, alternatively, by its amendment, the Muslim Personal Law is urged to be made out of the purview of Article 44.

It is a matter of great concern that the role of judiciary in the area of Muslim Personal Law particularly in post-independent era, has not been a happy and satisfactory experience. From time to time, its innovative approach coupled with unwarranted judicial activism have caused immense harm to the cause of the Muslim Personal Law. In such a unhappy situation, it is urged to follow the policy of 'judicial restraint' and the scheme of 'check and balance' of the Constitution of India instead of giving preponderance to its own preferences based on prejudices and motivated likings and dislikings in the name of doing lip-service with these concepts like: 'gender justice', 'humanism', 'human rights,' 'equality', 'fair play' 'discrimination' 'unity' and 'national integration'.

It must not be assumed hat there is no flaw in the Muslim Personal Law as applicable in today's India, which needs Islamization. It needs reforms and improvement. What should be the methodology for achieving the desired objective? Lack of unanimity in many ways, e.g., enlightened Muslims of modern approach are opposed to the replacement of the Muslim Personal Law by the Uniform Civil Code as they suggest certain reforms to do away with the deviations from original sources of the *Shariat.* From a methodology point of view, they do suggest the pattern of earlier reforms introduced in Muslim Personal Law. There is another stream consisting of a large section of Muslim lawyers, social activists and Muslim masses in general who oppose the change or reform of any kind in the Muslim Personal Law. They are not convinced to take reform or change due to social, political and legal reasons. Legally, they are of the view that the reform in the Muslim Personal Law can be effected by the Indian legislature which is dominated by the non-Muslims and such legislature due to its prejudices and biases may go beyond the expectations of Muslim minority in the name of democracy.[99] Besides, they are the victims of deep-rooted apprehension and crisis of confidence. If once the Muslims concede that their personal laws are not immutable and give freehand to the Government of India to introduce reform in line to majority community, they being the minority would lose their religious and cultural identity. They believe that these identities are guaranteed to them by the Constitution of India as fundamental rights. In such a case, they do apprehend that the government, instead of introducing desired reform or change with the due consultation of Muslim community, might replace their personal laws by imposing the Uniform Civil Code *suo moto*. It is noteworthy that this crisis of confidence is prevailing persistently since the partition of the country, i.e., 1947 till date. Despite the truth in such apprehensions as pointed out above, the existing Muslim Personal Law in India is in need of reform.[100] It is heartening to note that the All India Muslim Personal Law[101], after the judicial verdict of the Supreme Court in *Shah Bano Case* has realized it and is working for its reform and improvement. No doubt, the process should be accelerated.

It is necessary to examine the validity of the Muslim Personal Law in our current circumstances by taking into account the very core and spirit of *Shariat*. Contemporary realities, misuse of the Muslim Personal Law and the divergent stand of different schools of Islamic jurisprudence on one and the same issue, while application of the provisions of one school appear to be conducive and other schools' provision and its application on the same issue are creating hardship. Also, modernity *per se*, coupled with the challenges of multifarious nature, advancement by the contributions of science and technology, and the *inter* and *intra* conflicts of different existing schools of Islamic jurisprudence, involvement of

Biddat (deviations) in the Muslim Personal Law call for the healthy reform and improvement of the Muslim Personal Law.

The capacity and competence of *Shariat* can satisfy squarely the current complex issues of social, education, economic, religious, cultural, legal, political an scientific nature of our modern civilization. Enlightened Muslim scholars are under the obligation to nullify and do away with the alleged static nature of the Islamic system in dealing with the complex issues of Muslim Personal Law. Indeed, it must not be forgotten that Islam and the Islam system are full of dynamism and capable to meet out all exigencies, problems and adverse situations that may emerge till Doomsday, provided there is an honest application of the original sources with due appreciation of their spirit in proper perspective. Also, the spirit, doctrines, principles and technique enshrined in the *Qur'an, litihad'*[102], *Ijma, Qiyas, Aql, Shura, Takhayyr, Talfeeq, IFTa, Istidlal, Istishab, Istihsan* and *Al-Masalih al-Mursalah* are urged to be relied upon to meet the end of justice in the area of the Muslim Personal Law.

This onerous task can be accomplished successfully by the Federation of Muslim Scholars who must be thoroughly conversant with all possible branches of human knowledge, learning of Islam and also be aware of religio-cultural, socio-legal, politico-economic complexities and intricacies of modern life and scientific developments in national and international milieu. All India Muslim Personal Law board is earnestly beseeched to constitute the Federation of Muslim Scholars hailing from renowned institutions. If the proposed federation adopts the suggested scheme and efforts are sincerely made, the capacity and competence of *Shariat* can reform and improve the existing Muslim Personal Law.

Notes

1. Article 44 of the Constitution of India states: "The State shall endeavour to secure for the citizens a Uniform Civil Code throughout the territory of India".
2. See writ petition (Civil) No. 242 of 1997 and its disposal.
3. Judgment To-day, vol. 4, No. 7, 30th May, 1995, p. 331.
4. See Articles 14 and 15 of the Constitution of India.
5. Constituent Assembly Debates (hereinafter C.A.D.) Vol. VII (1948) p. 549, See also Vasudha Dhagamvar, *Towards the Union Civil Code* (ed. 1st, 1989) pp.117-132, H.A. Gibbs, *Reform of Muslim Personal Law* (ed. 1st, 1988).
6. C.A.D., vol. VII (1948) p. 549-550.
7. A few for example: Dargah Khawaja Saheb Act, 1936, Dissolution of Muslim Marriage Act, 1939, Kazi Act, 1880, Muslim Personal Law (Shariat) Application Act, 1937, Moslem Marriage and Divorce Registration Act, 1935, Muslim Dower Act, 1920, Oudh Laws Act, 1876 and Musalman Waqf Validating Act, 1913.
8. *Supra*, note 6.
9. *Supra*, note 6.
10. *Supra*, note 6.
11. *Supra*, note 6.
12. *Supra*, note 6.
13. *Supra*, note 6.
14. *Supra*, note 6.
15. *Supra*, note 6
16. *Supra*, note 6.
17. *Supra*, note 6.
18. *Supra*, note 6.
19. *Supra*, note 6
20. Article 25(1) states: "...all persons are equally entitled to freedom of conscience and the right freely to profess, practice and propagate religion."

    Article 26 states: "... every religious denomination or any section shall have the right:

    (a) to establish and maintain institutions for religious and charitable purposes;

    (b) to manage its own affairs in matters of religion...

Article 29 (1) states: "Any section of the citizens... having a distinct language, script or culture of its own shall have the right to conserve the same."

21. *Supra*, note 6.
22. *Supra*, note 6.
23. *Supra*, note 6.
24. *Supra*, note 22.
25. *Supra*, note 22.
26. See section 2 of the Muslim Personal Law (Shariat) Application Act, 1937.
27. See Article 25 (1) of the Constitution of India.
28. See Article 44 of the Constitution of India.
29. See Article 29 (1) of the Constitution of India.
30. See Article 26 (b) of the Constitution of India
31. *Sardar Syedna Tahir Saifuddin Sahab vs. State of Bombay,* AIR 1962, SC, p. 853.
32. *P.R. Gandhi vs. State of Bombay,* AIR 1954 EC, p., 388.
33. *Ibid.*
34. *Ibid.* See for detail Abdul Hamid A. Abu Sulayman, Crisis in the Muslim Mind (Islamic Methodology, No. 1) (ed. 1st, 1993, USA) pp. 22, 28, 145, 149, 153, 158.
35. *Supra,* note 31.,
36. *Qur'an IV:* 65 (*Surah Al-Nisa*) trans. Abdullah Yusuf Ali.
37. *Qur'an 11* 85 *(Surah Al Baqarah)* trans. Abdullah Yusuf Ali.
38. *Qur'an VI* 162 *(Surah Al Anam)* trans. Abdullah Yusuf Ali.
39. Qur'an IV 59 *(Surah AI-Nisa)* trans. Abdullah Yusuf Ali.
40. Fyzee, A.A.A., A Modern Approach to Islam (ed. 1981) p.36.
41. *Ibid.*
42. Schacht, J., An Introduction to Islamic Law (ed. 1964) p.1.
43. Fyzee, AAA..., Outlines of Mohammedan Law (ed. 3rd., 1969) pp. 1-2.
44. James Bryce, Studies in History & Jurisprudence (ed. 1901) p. 237.
45. D.K. Srivastava, Religious Freedom in India: A Historical and Constitutional Study (ed. 2nd, 1982) p. 4.
46. TM., The Muslim Law of India (ed. 2nd., 1982) p. 4.
47. (1885) 7 All 775 at p. 781.

48. See The Charter of George 11, 1755, Mufa'ssil Regulation, 1772, The Muslim Personal Law *(Shariat)* Application Act, 1937.
49. See Articles 13,14, 25, 26,29, 44 and 372 of the Constitution. See for detail, Mohammad Shabbir, Muslim Personal Law and Judiciary (1988).
50. *Qur'an V:* 3 (*Surah Al Maidah*) trans. Abdullah Yusuf Ali.
51. See Z.A. Siddiqi, 'Muslim Personal Law' (ed. 1st., 1973).
52. *Supra*, note 22.
53. AIR 1956 Cal. 224.
54. AIR 1980 SC 707.
55. AIR 1984 Del. 66 at 75.
56. See Bhattacharya, A.M., Muslim Law and the Constitution (ed. 2nd., 1994), Mohammad Shabbir, Muslim Personal Law and Judiciary (ed. 1st, 1988) and Tahir Mahmood, Personal Laws in Crisis (ed. 1st, 1986) pp. 17, 47-48, 133.
57. Gajendragakar, Secularism and the Constitution (ed. 1st 1977) p. 126.
58. Sec. S. Hedge, Islamic Law in Modern India (ed. 1st 1977) p. 3.
59. AIR 1985 SC 945.
60. Ibid.
61. AIR 1985 SC 935.
62. *Supra*, note 2.
63. See Qur'an IV: 3 (*Surah Al Nisa*) trans. Abdullah Yusuf Ali.
64. Mutual consent is one of the grounds of divorce available to Hindu husband and wife under Section 13 of the Hindu Marriage Act, 1955.
65. *Supra*, note 61.
66. *Supra*, note 3.
67. *Supra*, note 3.
68. *Supra*, note 3.
69. *Supra*, note 3.
70. *Supra*, note 3.
71. *Supra*, note 3.

71a. *Supra*, note 2.

72. See observation of Mr. Justice Sahai, *Supra*, note 1 at pp. 346-348.
73. *Supra*, note 1 at p. 345.
74. See Hindu Marriage Act, 1955, Hindu Adoption and Maintenance Act, 1956 Hindu Minority and Guardianship Act, 1956 and Hindu Succession Act, 1956.

75. *Supra*, note 2 at p. 345.
76. *Supra*, note 74.
77. *Supra*, note 74.
78. *Supra*, note 74.
79. *Supra*, note 74.
80. See for detail Upendra Baxi, Equality and Freedom (ed. 1978).
81. See Alexander Bicked & Harry, 'Legislative Purpose and Judicial Process: The Lincoln Mills case', Harvard Law Review, vol. 71 (Nov. 1957) pp. 1-39.
82. T.R. Andhyarujina, Judicial Activism and Constitutional Democracy in India (1992) p, 54; see also for separation of power: W. AzIan Ahmad, An Introduction to Administrative Law (ed. 1st, 1995) p. 5.
83. Lord Denning, 'Judges and Judicial Power' (collection of essays in honour of Justice V.R. Krishna Iyer) p. 4.
84. AIR 1975 SC 2299, see also Arif Ahmad vs. State of J&K., AIR 1989 SC 1899-1905.
85. See Judicial Independence: Theory and Reality (Lecture delivered by Mr. Justice Sawant in 1988).
86. *State of Rajasthan vs. Union of India* (1977) 3 SCC 592-661; See Mr. Justice Bhagwati's dicta in *Minerva Mills case* (1980) 3 SCC 625-677; *S.P Sampath Kumar vs. Union of India* (1987) 1 SCC 115-128.
87. C.A.D., vol. VI 1, pp. 1195-196 for lucid exposition on judicial self-restrain, see Stone, J, Social Dimension of Law and Justice (1966) pp. 667-670.
88. *Supra,* note 59 at p. 127.
89. Raina, S.M.N., Law, Judge and Justice (ed. 1st, 1979) p. 72.
90. Salmond, Principles of Jurisprudence (ed. 12th) p. 132; see also Mohammad Shabbir, *Muslim Law and Judiciary* (ed. 1st., 1988) pp.284-286.
91. S.K. Rashid and A. Masood, 'Judicial Reform of Muslim Personal Law: The Thin Edge of the Wedge,' *Aligarh Law Journal*, 11, vol. VI (1978) p. 13.
92. *Supra,* note 42 at pp. 44-45.
93. (1933) 55 AII.E.R., 743.
94. Rajeev Dhavan, The Supreme Court of India: A Socio-Legal Critique of its Justice Techniques (ed. 1st., 1979) pp. 457-458.
95. Seervai, Indian Constitution (ed. 3rd, 1969) p. 86.

96. *Supra,* note 61.
97. See Aftab Ahmad, Uniform Civil Code and Constitution of India, (unpublished paper presented in conference convened by All India Muslim Personal Law Board on 11-13th Sept. 1995 at Bangalore, Karnataka, India).
98. Fyzee, A.A.A., 'The Reform of Muslim Personal Law in India, *Humanist Review,* vol. VIII (1970).
99. Mohammad Shabbir, 'Uniform Civil Code and Muslim Personal Law', *Civil & Criminal Law Journal,* vol. 16, No. 4 (1981), New Delhi, Mohammad Shabbir, 'Uniform Civil Code and Muslim Personal Law: Study in Constitutional Perspective', The Aligarh Magazine: The Problems of Muslims in India (1984, Aligarh), S.J. Hussain, 'Legal Modernism in Islam', *Journal of Indian Law Institute,* VII (1985, New Delhi) pp. 384-387.
100. See for concept of Islamization and its logical and lucid elaboration: Abdul Hamid A. Abu Sulayman, Islamization: Reforming Contemporary Knowledge (1994, IIIT, USA), Imad al Din Khalil, Islamization of Knowledge: A Methodology (1995, IIIT, Beirut).
101. See for detail analysis Maulana Minatullah Rahmani, 'Muslim Personal Law in India, Muslim Personal Law: (edited by F.R. Faridi & M.N. Siddiqi, 1973) pp. 74-79, Maulana Syed Hamid Ali, 'Change in Muslim Personal Law; Scope & Procedure' Muslim Personal Law (edited by F.R. Faridi & M.N. Siddiqi, 1973) pp. 90-92, M. Imam, Minorities and the Law (edited in 1972, The Indian Law Institute, New Delhi), Mohammad Shabbir, Muslim Personal Law and Judiciary (ed. 1st 1988) pp. 323-326, see proceedings of the All India Muslim Personal Law Board's conference held in Delhi, Calcutta, Madras, Kanpur, Delhi, Bombay, Hyderabad and Gurarat.
102. Taha Alwani, *Ijtihad* (1993, IIIT, USA) pp. 4-31.

6

Annihilation of Caste

One More Look

L. JAWAHAR NESAN

I am neither a sociologist nor an anthropologist but a student of the human society and for being that I leave the choice to the readers that they can assign me under any terminological category as they wish. However, I must clarify what prompted me and compelled me to touch the issue of 'caste' although all my academic education pertained to 'engineering and technology'. Much abler and more profound pens have analyzed the issue of caste in the past without leaving any doubt over its genesis and mechanism. Of them, one cannot point out anybody who had surpassed and bypassed the thesis of Dr. Ambedkar on caste. So do I too in this article as to whether his thesis on *Annihilation of Caste* bears any relevance and brings significant success if it is applied in today's environment. If it does, what shall be the way forward ahead of his thesis in annihilating the caste and if it seeks modifications in line with the current situation what are such modifications required of it or if it does not, what could serve as a realistic solution, all have been intended to be explored in this article.

But have I possessed the eligibility or acquired the knowledge to put Dr. Ambedkar's thesis under my scrutiny, I asked myself before I thought of taking this subject through my pen. Much of self-contemplation enabled me to ascertain that I have the eligibility and knowledge to review the work of one of the great professors of the concerned subject on earth. I found myself eligible because I have been from a mass, which is the immediate victim of the caste system. This is not to say that those who are not victims are not eligible to analyze this subject matter but it is because of being a victim one could come up with a most right conception on and solution to the caste system. For instance, if the 'chaturvarnya' system which became an impetus for the evolution of the present day caste system could be upheld by a person no less than Mahatma Gandhi, then it could be rightly said that the victims of the caste system are the most appropriate people eligible to analyze the caste.

I found myself knowledgeable enough to explore this subject not because I hold the terminal academic education but simply for being a student of the society. The use of the word 'student' is so prudent as one could notice, but it is right when a so-called sociologist claims the validity of my knowledge to assess this issue. Being an element of the human society I observe the societies of all cults and religions from the outset without being part of them and thus claim that I have become the student of the society. I am convinced that a person who is already a part of the society hardly studies it as it is, without any bias unless he/she possesses the ability to perceive the things to which he/she is attached with as they are. Especially, the student who is associated with a religious society cannot perceive that society as it is and make its best student while he/she endorses that society with all sacredness and loyalty. Having endorsed none of the religious societies I was able to freely learn them as they were and thus made a good studentship of them.

Evolution of the Caste System and Its Current Status

The planet earth is a formation of several matters and particles and thus forms a system in itself. The whole solar family forms a system composed of planets and sun that are bound to operate within the overall system. Within such a system that facilitates interaction of energies amongst its elements, if one element fails to function properly then the failure of the whole system cannot be prevented. For instance, if the sun fails to emit light nobody can imagine how the earth would survive. This same principle applies to the human system, which is normally composed of individuals, a small group of people, and a group of nations and so on. If a component of a human system deviates from its duties it is supposed to discharge or works against the interests of the other components then it will endanger the very existence of the human system. To illustrate this, a terrorist component (group) being equipped with wrong motives against the human system will undertake all activities to fulfil its motives resulting in the damage of the system. The sociological term for the human system is 'society'. The human society is supposed to be comprised of several components or classes characterized by certain common creed, ethics, communication, love and affection and that with the embodiment of such characters the components are bound to be organic in nature rather 'mechanistic'. The organic nature suggests that the components or classes are open to the society, as the society (environment) changes the components shall also change so that the components will transit to the changed environment as intact, because of the existence of fraternity and communication amongst them. This means if any of the components is not organic or not allowed to be organic within the society, then its isolation by deprivation of or disintegration from the society is irresistible. The mechanistic nature, in other words the endogamic character, of the society assumes a closed setting, where the classes dissociate themselves from the other classes within the same environment, therefore, the elements of the society which attempt to be organic with the others (or within the environment) will be excommunicated in order to maintain the mechanistic character.

In a religious society all components are bound to behave as organic such that when changes are envisaged due to environmental influence, they can sail through the change without affecting the overall system. During the change process, new components (classes) may evolve without affecting the society provided the society facilitates the organic character. A religious society shall therefore encapsulate the organic character, otherwise its disintegration will be irresistible. The religious society is bound to ingrain with the indispensable characters such as fraternity, liberty, equality, love and communication apart from its religious practices. In contrast, most of the religious practices uphold the spiritual or divine characters and entertain the social characters such as love and fraternity as secondary. But social needs are more essential and important than religious needs for the survival of the human society. This can be well conceived by pondering over the genesis and behaviour of the religious society.

The primitive human societal system and the evolution of its civilized form as it is seen today helps clarify how the 'social needs' form the essential basic characters of a society. It is well known that the primitive social system was simply groups of people tied together based on the physiological needs like food, shelter and so on and geographical proximity, but it lacked the need for 'social' – like the need for being loved by or living for the common cause of the people. Gradually, the social needs were nurtured and thus they became the foundation for the evolution of the civilized society. For instance, making affiliation with friends, relatives and others based on love, affection, compassion, morality, faith, ethnic origin and creed and sensing comfort by being with them or being a part of them through some formal groups lead to identify societies. What does it reveal except the necessity of the social need such that when people are surrounded by the people who love them and care for them and have same creeds they sense a feeling of confidence in that group and consequently feel satisfied with the thirst for social. As the population grew and new thoughts were continually inculcated the social demand also became complex and thus led to the formation of societies characterized by variety of non-social interests brought about by ethnicity, race, colour and religions. But when religions caught hold of the people being addicted to them the religious aspect predominated the social aspect and thus today, almost the majority of the people on earth are segregated into several religions and that people are identified and evaluated through religious values rather than social values.

The depletion of the social value and over reliance on the religious value alienated the humanity and caused the prevalence of persecution, injustice and degradation amongst the human system. This is a very common attitude that exists in inter-religions nowadays; for instance, between religions, the religious value predominates because it is the only value that distinguishes their identities. But at intra-religion level both social and religious values are entertained, if not equally, except in Hinduism. One could conclude that most often the religious values brought the people to be bound by respective social ethics but the Hindu religion differs from the others by not even having such religious values that socially bind the people as a society. This is the main reason Dr. Ambedkar dismissed the Hindu religion as a society. If the Hindu religion is not a society then what is it as a whole? It is a set of endogamous societies where each one of them deserves to become a religion, as there is a lack of socialness in it. As explained above any religion, which fails to provide social needs to its components (classes) is fatal, and cannot be said to be a religious society. The lack of such socialness triggers the components to act as separate entities and in the long run these entities dissociate themselves or are excommunicated from the respective religion and make their own, leaving the parent religion meaningless. Thus, it is clear that a religion without socialness proves as a fatal flaw. One could repudiate this standard on the ground that the Hindu religion has survived for millenniums notwithstanding. But on a much deeper investigation one could easily unveil not only the non-existence of the socialness but also the existence of the anti-socialness in the Hindu religion. The symptoms of the anti-socialness are the execution of the act of persecution and the untouchability through an established graded social hierarchy. Perseverance of these anti-social elements has made the suppressed to acquire a syndrome of "Socially Induced Helplessness" (SIH). The SIH is a feeling of lowness and inefficiency that the suppressed experiences such that given an opportunity to socially improve or agitate against prejudices the suppressed will not claim to do so. Having put under the trap of the anti-socialness of the Hinduism for millenniums, the suppressed or depressed experienced a feeling of helplessness which prevent them from agitating against the evils of Hinduism or from dissociating from the Hindu fold physically. But this does not mean that they are mentally associated with Hinduism. In other words if one does not accept a religion consciously how can he/she be said to belong to that religion. Since Hinduism is superimposed on them without their conscience or consciousness and that they too are experiencing the SIH no one can claim them as to have belonged to Hinduism. Thus, having emancipated from the experience of the SIH and eliminated the symptoms of the anti-socialness the suppressed or depressed component might break the Hindu fold and degenerate it to a confined group of minority orthodoxies.

The same standard can be used to measure or trace out the socialness in other religions as well. While exploring the socialness one should note the fact that the religious values have brought the components (classes) to be bounded by respective socialness. The question of whether the so-called socialness exists in other religions can be answered affirmatively although it cannot be said as to have existed perfectly. This assertion could be claimed from the fact that these religions facilitate the organic character amongst its components. The components of these religions are not so preached from those of the others in their own religion and they neither follow any degraded hierarchical system amongst themselves. If at all had there been any clashes or divisions amongst them like the one between *sunni* and *shia* muslims and between the catholics and protestants they were not due to the endogamousness or graded social hierarchy but due to their organic intention of conquering or absorbing one by another. This means one cannot observe the lack of 'socialness' in these religions but their socialness can be seen to emerge when there is an external threat imposed on them. Whereas in the Hinduism the strict observance of different customs by different castes prevents the castes to be social even if there is an external threat to the religion as a whole. Dr. Ambedkar puts this clearly as: "the caste system prevents common activity and by preventing common activity it has prevented the Hindus from becoming a society with a unified life and a consciousness of its own being".

However, other religions cannot be sun as perfectly holding the socialness on its entirety but bearing only a range of it from low to high. For example, the range of socialness existing can be found as high in Buddhism when compared to Islam and Christianity but nil in Hinduism. The nil existence of the socialness in Hinduism is mainly because of the practice of the graded hierarchical system of castes as prescribed by the chaturvarnya. But if the system of chaturvarnya is subjected to the earlier conception arrived in this article that "a religious society shall encapsulate the organic character otherwise its disintegration is irresistible", one can easily conclude that the chaturvarnya does not exist now as it was intended to be, but only its impacts. The main reason for this assertion is that it has disintegrated into more than 4,000 castes. No category of the chaturvarnya is intact in itself but an explosion of different castes with different customs and practices. This proves well within the thesis of Dr. Ambedkar that "any innovation that seriously antagonises the ethical, religious and social code of the caste is not likely to be tolerated by the caste and the recalcitrant members of a caste are in danger of being thrown out of the caste. A novel way of thinking will create a new caste for the old ones will not tolerate it". If this is true, thousands of innovations had created thousands of castes due to the endogamous character is the fact that no one can repudiate. If these thousands of innovations could prevail through the thousands of castes and that if majorities of these innovations are antagonistic with the chaturvarnya then where is the trace of the notion of chaturvarnya as it has been claimed to be in existence still now? Such is the truth, the practice of chaturvarnya is not worth to consider as it has been over ruled by its repellants (innovations). However, one should not forget that the impact of the system of chaturvarnya does still exist in the form of graded employment opportunities and graded social inequalities. But it can be noticed that although majority of the castes do not accept the notion of chaturvarnya they still claim to be Hindus, which is a marked difference in the attitude of the present day castes of lower rank with their past. This proves well that they are still trapped under a state of mental slavery that prevents them from identifying the affinity of the divinity with the chaturvarnya system. The basic injunction of the chaturvarnya is based on its relativity with the divinity is the fact which no one can reject. In the past, people were so ignorant that they could not have differentiated the divinity with the chaturvarnya but nowadays it is a generally accepted notion amongst the *shudras* and untouchables that chaturvarnya is a fallacy. But they still get along with the divinity of the Hinduism – what a contradiction. It can be read from this attitude that people see divinity and chaturvarnay as two different matters but both contribute to each other is the fact.

Another remarkable attitude is that the people who reject chaturvarnya still do not intend to fuse with other castes, why? There can be only two answers; one, the society is habituated not to allow fusion within its components, two, the practice of 'inequality in equality' adopted by the components for their own benefit. The first case suggests that the perpetual endogamic character of the society with which the castes have prevailed over years prevent them to break the barrier and fuse with others. The practice of endogamousness solely will not harm others but if it is practiced in accompaniment with full hatred towards and suppression over others then it cannot be simply referred to the habit but something inherent with an intended purpose. Deeper analysis of answer two should resolve this doubt. It is the attitude of expecting equality from those at the higher level while showing inequality to those at the lower level. This attitude is more serious than the strict observance of chaturvarnya since it recognizes only the castes, which are at higher levels for equality but continue to perpetrate the persecution of the lower ones. Whereas in chaturvarnya except the 'brahmana' all the other three are sandwiched in between their superiors and inferiors. Therefore, this changed attitude might create more confidence and strength in every castes and drive them to not merely imitate the brahmana but to act like them. Since this attitude assumes the existence of no superior castes, as the brahmana assumes, every caste which experiences this attitude will tend to be more tyrannic than ever before, thus ending with the likes of the brahmanas. If this attitude were perpetrated in all castes then the dire consequences would be far from imagination. The intended purpose of this attitude can be dwelt in two aspirations, one is to get the social status improved at par with the brahmana and two, to grapple with the power of political economy. To achieve these two for the non-priestly castes, the easiest way is to continue with the persecution of those at the lower levels but at the same time in order to be not persecuted by the castes at the higher levels they dismiss the chaturvarnya system and thus preach equality. No caste in India forbids this attitude including the so called *shudras* and untouchables. The untouchables for instance imitating the uppercaste prefer inequality amongst its several classes in favour of superiority of one to the other if not persecution of one by the other. If a section of untouchables shows its superiority over its own fellow then where has it the moral right to claim against the graded inequality for its own freedom?

Annihilation of Caste: The Old Thesis

Annihilation of castes has been a perpetual issue over years and that several antidotes had been prophesied as remedies and some of them were indeed practised but they seemed to have not eradicated the caste system or at least eliminated the symptoms of the caste system. Some advocated the practice of the softcore remedies such as inter-dining and inter-marriage and others dictated the hardcore solutions such as the destruction of the shastras and the Hindu religion as a whole. Those who believed in the sanctity of the Hindu shastras could afford to go up to the act of inter-dining to abolish the caste system, which was cowardly. These people having known that this would not help eradicate the caste system adopted it to mislead or divert the people who are concerned on caste system. Those who did not believe in the sanctity of the shastras disregard them as fallacy and found them as the real cause for the casteism and advanced destruction of the Hindu religion. Having prophesied the destruction of the sanctity of the shastras, Dr. Ambedkar disregarded the inter-marriage system as it is repugnant to the beliefs and dogmas, which the Hindus regard as sacred. He further went to state that "if you wish to bring about a break in the system then you must destroy the religion of the shruti and smiritis, nothing else will avail". However, in his "Annihilation of caste", he did not make it very clear as to whom he pleaded to renounce such sacredness and destroy the religion. Had he appealed to the caste Hindus or Brahman, it would have been a meaningless effort as he himself had stated that "some of them stand to lose more of their prestige and power than others do". Neither would it have been a fruitful effort had he appealed to the untouchables or Shudras (who were the worst victims of the caste system) who were at that time so ignorant not even aware of the shastra or chaturvarnya that had been inflicted upon them over an era. Even now this appeal stands irrelevant to the shudras and untouchables, as these classes are so aware nowadays in as much as to the extent of their mass protest against the chaturvarnya. But still they feel comfortable to remain in the Hindu fold, which requires further investigation. However, having disregarded the chaturvarnya by the lower classes why does the caste system still prevail amongst them? The answer to this is what has been discussed in the previous section that is the attitude of 'inequality in equality' created the modified system of social inequality with which people feel comfortable. To add more to it, if the sacredness was put on the caste system just for the sake of the fulfilment of its divinity then its eradication should also erode the caste system. But the sacredness although has a nexus with the divinity, indeed it has a special purpose that is to grapple with the power, wealth and social status. If the caste system still existed after the destruction of sacredness then it means that the submerged purpose of the sacredness is the one, which controls the caste classification, not the sacredness alone as it was thought in the past.

Having the chaturvarnya disregarded by the Shudras and untouchables as social injustice who else will be its followers except the uppercastes or brahmana? If the minority uppercastes are the only strict observers of the shastra then how can the faith on the chaturvarnya be erased, which is in fact non-existent in its original form in other castes? Therefore, the chaturvarnya could be seen as to have treaded backwards and reduced to brahmana and uppercastes because of the disregard of the Shudras and untouchables. If the sacredness on the shastra is confined only to the jurisdiction of the uppercastes then their sacredness will not mean anything as the lower castes have already relinquished their sacredness but still remain in the Hindu fold. However, if the caste system is to be eliminated it must be always remembered that it relies on the Shudras and untouchables.

Even if Hinduism is destroyed the post-destruction period will not be completely able to see the erased trace of the caste system. It may not necessarily exist as a caste system but as a class system accompanied by inequalities if it is not in consonance with principles of liberty, equality and fraternity. In the aftermath of the destruction, castes will be bound to stick with their own classes in the form of attitudinal, cultural, functional and ethical identities on which they have put their faith for years. This in turn will lead them to be loyal to and enthusiastic with their own classes and thus prevent the fusion with others. The best example can be found from the history of Northern Ireland, which has been a problem over centuries between the Catholics and Protestants. Both are the two different classes following the same bible but with different ideologies. Predominated fanaticism drove them to avoid fusion between them. In the Hindu fold the destruction of the sacredness on the shastras on the part of the Shudras and anti-Shudras while may not necessarily shackle the caste system, will lead to a class system where still the disparities can be seen to exist. This must be based on what I propose to state that the "law of conservation of plurality of the society", which can be defined as plurality of the society is inevitable and that due to the stimulus of the change process, plurality in the form of classes may evolve but after the evolution they can neither be destroyed nor be avoided but they can be transformed from one form to another. If this is true, caste system cannot be destroyed but transformed to a class system based on the principles of co-existence. The fact is that there is no guarantee of achieving homogeneousness in any society, especially in a society which has been completely divided in terms of castes and creeds over years.

One may be ready to cease putting faith on the notion of the caste system but it does not necessarily suffice the other prerequisites for him/her to treat others equally and fuse with them. The prerequisites may include social ethics, culture, spirituality, eating system, attitudes and behaviour which in the long run may become the next priority of sacredness for the transformed castes (who gave up the caste system) to identify and segregate themselves as distinct classes. This shows that the caste can only be transformed from one form to another and that due to the change process of social evolution 'plurality' will come on into the society in its own way. If such a transformation of the caste system is set to occur whether the homogenous society is established or not, certainly the evils of the caste system can be got ridden if the transformed classes incorporate the sacredness of liberty, fraternity and equality.

Another solution for the caste problem that was aboard for some time was conversion to other religions. Embracing a religion cannot make a salvation for the caste-ridden society if the real intention of the embracement is to escape from the caste prejudices. Analyzing the conversion from two perspectives can vindicate this; one is the strict observance of the religious principles and rites by the people of the recipient religion and the other is from the perspective of mass conversion. Conversion to a religion must be triggered by the desire to embrace that religion based on the satisfaction of its ideologies, principles and faith – any other motives that drives the recalcitrant members to embrace other religions will not last long in those religions. On the other hand, if the conversion is triggered by the caste prejudice and inequality inherent in the present religion, then the recipient religion should at least be tested not only for its ideological notion and consciousness for providing equality and freedom but also for its people's attitudinal and social behaviours towards the converts. On the ideological ground most of the non-Hindu religions can be called as providing equality amongst its entire people but in reality it is in contrast. For instance, the Christian converts from the lower castes of the Hindu fold have to still go through the same sufferings, as they cannot mix with the converts of the upper castes. Inter-marriages between the lower caste converts and uppercaste converts are punishable to the extent of ex-communication by those belonging to the upper caste converts. Even Indian Islam converts of the lower castes cannot be seen mixing with others, although all are treated equal in their religious rites. Such peculiar characteristics of these religions in India are largely in contrast with their foreign counterparts. The prevalence of this attitude in these religions is because of the import of the upper-caste converts who although could afford to erase the sacredness on the shastras and embrace a new religion could not afford to relinquish caste consciousness. This indicates that if the recipient religion of the lower caste also constitutes the upper caste converts, then some form of caste prejudice is expected to occur, thus making the sufferings of the lower caste converts never ending. No religion in India can escape from this infection, no matter howsoever pure their ideologies and social notions are. The gist of this perspective of the analysis of conversion, therefore, is that there will be no guarantee that the low caste converts will get their due rights and equal treatment in the respective recipient religion in India. On the other hand, for the low castes to embrace other religions there are a lot more other than the issue of equality must be weighed including the notion of the divinity and sacredness, liberty, fraternity, cultural compatibility, and the readiness to adopt the linguistic sacredness associated with the recipient religion.

The second perspective of the analysis, i.e., mass conversion is not so complex to ponder over. The under privileged castes can opt for a 'mass conversion' to a suitable religion to weaken the hegemony of the upper castes Hindus, and that such conversion on a large scale might be thought of reducing the Hindu fold to one of a minority. Unless and until a revolution occurs a mass conversion seems to be quixotic. Even if it happens the radical transition to an another religion would apparently mean that the recipient religion is nothing but a composition of lower castes. Then, gaining equality from both the people of the recipient religion and those of the other religions much depends on their readiness to accept the converts as to have achieved the status to be treated equally. This reaction of the people of the recipient religion towards the low caste converts, much depends on how far they are alien to the Hindu fold in terms of the notion of caste. However, the fact that the changed status of the converts from the eyes of the other religions including the donor religion is questionable. For instance, a low caste Christian convert is still a low caste in the eyes of the other religions and that he/she still ought to go through the same sufferings of social injustice with other religions if not from the recipient religion.

Conversion can still become one of the effective ways to escape from the sufferings of the graded inequality provided all the aforesaid negative impacts are eliminated. In fact the Shudras and untouchables together becoming the prime target of the religions invading India is not a new issue, rather millions of them have been embracing these foreign religions since long time ago. Now the upper-caste Hindus are on a mission of reconverting the converted untouchables back to the Hindu fold. Whether or not they concern about this impudent act but is it the rationalistic path of restoring Hinduism, that they must ask themselves. The religious history of the world has borne evidence that some of the global religions like Christianity and Islam had trespassed on other societies to extend their kingdom. Trespassing sometimes was executed along with charitable assistance but many a times it was by outrageous aggression, but the end result of such trespassing is worthy to consider here. In their mission, they managed to get people of the Hindu faith embracing their religion such that later the converts became no less than any true orthodox Muslims or Christians. If the conversion is to be successful, it must be reinforced by the elements of 'fusion' and 'equality' on the part of the recipient religion as was done by Christianity and Islam, but one should remember that these religions could not afford to offer these elements at full scale. Therefore, one could conclude that trespassing is not new to any religion but how the hunted people are integrated in a religion in the aftermath of the trespassing is the key for their success. The present day Hindu orthodoxies in India have no mechanism in their mission but they will never have an efficient one as long as they continually put faith on the chaturvarnya system. However, the mission of the rejuvenation of the Hinduism by the orthodoxies shows their acknowledgement of the defeat of the Hinduism. There was a time when the upper-castes Hindus never claimed to even accept the untouchables as Hindus and always isolated them from purely adopting the Hindu rites. In contrast now they are on the battlefield to hunt the untouchables for the Hindu fold. Does this not reveal their defeat? Some might perceive them being strong for having undergone such aggressive reconversion of untouchables but the fact is that they are very weaker than ever before and scared of their survival and thus take a defensive action to protect the Hindu religion from deterioration. But with a lack of proper fusion element incorporated in the hunt they will never succeed in their mission. Had they adopted Dr. Ambedkar's suggestion on the reformation of the Hindu religion in their past endeavours, Hinduism now would have been everyone's choice in India.

Annihilation of Caste: The New Theory

To annihilate the caste Dr. Ambedkar prophesied that "caste is a notion, it means a notional change is needed. To change the notion, the real remedy is to destroy the belief in the sanctity of the *shastras*". Having proposed this solution he foresaw the complete destruction of the religion of the *'smiriti'*. But as discussed in detail earlier in this article, although the depressed community has now discarded the sanctity of the chaturvarnya, they still claim to be a part of the Hindu fold and their spiritual interest in Hinduism has increased than ever before. On the other hand one cannot expect the upper castes to give up their belief in the sanctity of the shastras as this will detrimentally affect their superior social status, but the depressed community must do so if they want to stake their claim for equality. However, to reap its full consequence the relinquishment of the sanctity must come on in its entirety without any exclusiveness. The depressed community discarding the chaturvarnya system solely will not destroy the religion, unless the shastra and smiriti as a whole is discarded with full conscious. Disregarding shastra not only means destroying the chaturvarnya but also divinity, which most people will not afford to do. To them, chaturvarnya is a matter of a system imposed by the uppercastes for their own benefit which they can afford to lose, but divinity is a matter related to god whereby dismissing the god on which they put all their faith to get salvation is something which they cannot even wish to retrospect in. Therefore, if one wishes to change the people's notion on the divinity and their spiritual faith in a large scale, it would prove a mere waste of time. The reasons are many but to mention a few; people see divinity and the chaturvarnya exclusively as two different matters and that they are not prepared to accept that chaturvarnya is one of the characteristics of the divinity in Hinduism even though the shastras explicitly reveals this character, people are still entrapped in a state of mental slavery, and people still prefer imitating the upper castes which in combination with their disregard of chaturvarnya lead them to adopt the practice of 'inequality in equality'. These are the main reasons that the shudras and untouchables are still believed to have belonged to the Hindu fold despite the fact that they oppose the concept of the chaturvarnya. Then what is the real remedy to annihilate the caste system? Having found the conventional remedies such as conversion and elimination of sacredness of the chaturvarnya obsolete, the feasible solution must be the physical disintegration of the Hindu fold although it principally exists as a composition of disintegrated islands because of its endogamous character. The physical disintegration means destruction of the system of the chaturvarnya and leaving the castes as separate entities. Destruction of the system in turn means extrication of the 'forced dependency' amongst different castes. Having characterized by strict behaviour of endogamousness, the only factor that links all castes to form as a system is the dependency of the inferiors on the superiors for social, economic and political status. Extrication of the dependency from the caste system will empower every caste to attain the desired social status and that since the only factor that binds them to form as a system is eradicated it will be disintegrated into several entities of their own. This means it does not destroy the castes but only the system; in fact the castes cannot be undone. However, extrication of the dependency alone will not be able to undo the system unless it is accompanied by the relinquishment of the sanctity of the chaturvarnaya.

How to extricate the dependency from the caste system? It can be only through the elimination of the behaviour of Socially Induced Helplessness (SIH). The concept of the SIH has been explained in detail earlier in this article, which is a feeling of lowness, inferiority or inefficiency by the people who have been continuously put under persecution for a long time. Having experienced with this attitude, people will not even attempt to overcome their problems even under the provision of the right environment. Within the context of the caste system, this attitude of inefficiency prevents them from overcoming the problem of dependency. Elimination of the SIH seeks to inculcate the feeling of self-efficacy in the suppressed communities, which in turn seeks them to be educated socially. Social education not only will build confidence in and impart social skills to them but also will make them not to imitate the uppercastes and relinquish the sanctity of shastras. But one should not forget that relinquishment of the sanctity of *shastras* should not necessarily enable them to renounce Hinduism because of the sacred faith they put on the Hindu deities. Of course, the objective of the elimination of the SIH is not to destruct their faith on Hindu deities but to prepare them to be responsible for their own social status. Therefore, upon the elimination of the SIH, both the sanctity of shastras and imitation of the uppercastes can be eradicated by the suppressed communities within themselves. A person can imitate one only when he/she is attracted with the special features of the one being imitated just like the follower imitates the leader. By imitating the leader the followers consciously accept the ideologies and supremacy of that leader, but within the context of the caste system the followers (lower castes) have no option except imitating the leaders (upper castes) because of the SIH persistently experienced by the lower castes. Therefore, the extrication of the SIH should be able to prevent the lowers from imitating the uppers and make them feel self-efficient which in turn will extricate the dependency of the lowers. Thus the removal of the forced dependency will create a physical disintegration of the caste system whereby the disintegrated entities (castes) will in no environment feel inferior to or be depressed by the one who wishes to dominate since the post-removal of the SIH should enable the depressed to grapple with enough social strength to oppose any feudality inflicted upon them. However, the caste consciousness will never end because as discussed earlier if caste is not meant to suppress others it becomes a matter of identity with which people who belong to them feel comfortable. Therefore, the caste consciousness will not take the same form as it was before the disintegration of the caste system but it will conceive the notion of the class system that precludes the dependency factor. Endogamous character might have created castes or classes of different nature but if they carry along with them the factor of forced dependency in terms of graded inequality then they are against the humanity. This means that caste-consciousness or class-consciousness of a society without the notion of the graded inequality is more practical to achieve. But to annihilate the caste system if one aims to eliminate their endogamous character by getting fusion amongst them to form a homogenous society then failure in their mission is unavoidable. Therefore, a social revolution in consonance with the elimination of the SIH amongst the depressed or lower castes and consequent extrication of the forced dependency that exists in the form of graded inequality amongst the castes must become a realistic solution to the caste problem. In the aftermath of such a revolution, inculcation of social fraternity amongst different castes based on the principle of 'integration' will not be quixotic.

Who Should Lead the Revolution?

Revolutions often had the stimulus from those of the affected one because the full commitment and the courage to go through the sufferings during the revolt can be shown only by them. In the past revolutions such as the communist movement in Russia and the French movement, all proved beyond doubt that the losers ought to lead the revolution. The aim of the revolution must be a radical reconstruction of the society based on the new theory of annihilation of caste as propounded in this article. Dr. Ambedkar discarded social revolution to annihilate the caste system in the past as the weaker sections then had not had freedom in having a political weapon and a moral weapon (education) which are indispensable to trigger a change in notions, sentiments and mental attitudes of the people. Therefore at least in his lifetime as a short-term measure he put all his efforts and strengths in the political and economic reconstruction to secure constitutional safeguards for all depressed castes including untouchables. Some might argue that he was inconsistent with his own ideologies that social reconstruction must precede economic and political reconstruction. These revelations are based on shallow analysis but having much deeper insight into it one could see the fact that it was the time that impulsed him to deal with the economic and political reconstruction that had come in his way of social reconstruction. In fact, he emphasised social reconstruction before achieving independence for India as he was of the view that prior to such reconstruction independence would not mean anything to those who are at the lower level of the graded social hierarchy. However, being forced with the compulsion for the political and economic reconstruction in the independent India he had to get the most out of it. This resulted in procuring a package for the benefit of the menials that brought them their proportional representation - a political weapon, in the power structure. Amongst the menials who had the opportunity to enjoy the power structure there was consequential socio-economic improvement in par with the oppressors which in turn led them to imitate the upper castes oppressors. The formation of such an oppressive attitude within the menials is the main enemy to social reconstruction, which must be destroyed immediately. It is a fallacy on the part of the privileged section of the lower castes for having assumed that the political package as secured by Dr. Ambedkar was the end in itself for their never ending social problems. What Dr. Ambedkar had secured was a temporary salvation for their persistent problem and that he never supposed that it was the end but the weapon for achieving a permanent social reformation, which the depressed classes have conveniently ignored for a long time and these were because of the precedence of having acquired the political advantage over the social reconstruction. Had the social reconstruction preceded the political reconstruction the privileged section of the weaker communities would not have taken the wrong direction, leaving the majority of their community under a constant ambience of the social inequalities. Therefore, the ultimate measure to be undertaken is the social revolution in consonance with the new doctrine of annihilating the caste and that if it ought to be successful it is the losers who have to agitate and lead the revolution in an integrated manner. Now the situation is so conducive that the weaker communities could not be prevented to use their political and moral weapons in their struggle against the social prejudice unless they themselves restrain from doing so. The nucleus of the revolution must be the emancipation from both the mental slavery and from the clutches of the shastra, which is possible only when the moral weapon is properly used.

Post-Revolution Integration

The lower castes will have obtained socio-economic strength in the post-disintegration of the caste system so that any confrontation will be resisted equally by the lower castes, which may thus lead to a severe conflict between the upper and lower castes. Therefore, the post-social reconstruction environment should inherently facilitate 'integration' amongst all classes. The notion integration came into being because of the being of the differentiation. A society is always multipolar with diverse interests, ideologies and practices and that peaceful co-existence of all its constituents seeks them to be effectively integrated. Therefore, integration is not simply the avoidance or destruction of differentiation but a problem of approaching, analyzing and managing differentiation without attempting to eliminate them. If any attempt was made to eliminate the plurality of the society in the name of integration then the destruction of the society will be inevitable. This means that the law of integration seeks to undisturb the characteristics of different castes that bear their identities. But the characteristics should not be wrongly interpreted as to have also included the feudal attitude of the uppercastes as the traditional brahmanical attitude is to dominate and suppress others. This lofty attitude will impede people of different castes to execute mutual recognition and respect and thus will create conflict amongst them. Therefore, the new approach of integration must acknowledge and respect different castes while taking into account the fact that different castes are expected to continually evolve, triggered by the change process.

The enthusiastic pro-vedic brahmanical mass when thousands of years back set to make a transition to change the incorporation of the chataurvarnya system it failed to provide equality, mutual recognition, mutual respect and mutual assistance to the then existing Dravidian system. Therefore, the Hindu society is still floundering with continued agitations and resistance from the affected groups. If the chaturvarnya system precluded the graded hierarchy and incorporated the aforesaid mutualities the brahmanical society would have succeeded in their mission with greater respect and dignity. Due to their earlier feudal attitude they earned a name far worst than any racial or communal apartheid in the world. To annihilate the caste system, castes should be integrated by accepting and properly handling differences amongst them in the post-revolution and that if the process of effective integration requires preservation of their differences then it must be done so. To effectively integrate different castes following principles are noteworthy to consider:

- A community that is perpetually put under the caste system should not ignore castes and that the evolution of new castes should be seen as the delivery of the change process.
- Castes, which do not destructively impact upon the society, should have mutual understanding, respect and assistance for mutual co-existence. But it must be noted that regardless of the castes whether being good or bad must be acknowledged as a separate entity, otherwise the ignored caste will cause all ill effects to show its existence.

- All commonalities that exist amongst the castes should be fostered and encouraged so that a sense of unity can be achieved across the variety of castes.
- Castes, which fall away from the 'path of purity', should be weakened by increasing and strengthening the unity amongst the castes which follow that path. The path of purity means the path that dictates one to adopt high ethical standards including humanity, honesty and sincerity and high social standards including liberty, fraternity and equality.
- Castes, which are destructive to the human kind, should be made to fade away by excommunicating them from the society and preventing them from grappling with the wealth and power.

Changes are persistent and inevitable; nothing on earth is eternal such that everything is subjected to change. But within the caste-ridden society it is evident that endogamousness or excommunication is the characteristic that often cause the change, which consequently stimulate the emergence of different castes. These formations may dramatically seek different ways in which the issues relevant to the changes or needs or excommunication are usually dealt with. Consequently this may cause stir, confusion and agitation amongst different castes which are affected by those new developments. Therefore, the new formation should not be undermined or ignored but should be subjected to continuous scrutiny for the validity of their contribution to the humankind. First, analyze them as to what they really mean to the humankind. Second, analyze whether the situation really calls for their emergence. Third, if so, analyze whether they serve their purpose. Fourth, analyze their impact upon the humankind. Fifth, if they bring negative impact, find out the ways to diffuse them without trying to blatantly oppose them at the first instance. Because filled with indignation they might oppose with equal force and thus injure the process of integration but they must be treated properly so that they gradually wane by themselves. Excommunication of such castes by fostering more integrity and solidarity amongst other castes and prevention of those destructive castes from grappling with power will leave them with only two options: either to change their attitude and follow the path of purity in social life or suffer from the fate of excommunication. In all respect, to improve the integrity amongst and achieve peaceful co-existence of all castes, the commonalties along with the principles of fraternity, liberty and equality must be reinforced during the post-annihilation of the caste system.

7

Dr. Ambedkar's Vision of a Just Society

JAMES MASSEY

One of the key themes in most of the writings of Baba Saheb Dr. B.R. Ambedkar was the establishment of an 'ideal society'[1] or a 'casteless society'[2] or a society based upon the 'principle of justice'.[3] Therefore, by taking a clue from his basis of an 'ideal society', we have entitled this essay as: Dr. Ambedkar's Vision of a Just Society. Because in his own words, the "ideal would be a society based on liberty, equality and fraternity"[4] and again while giving the meaning of 'justice', he said: "Justice is simply another name for liberty, equality and fraternity". Therefore, to understand Dr. Ambedkar's vision of a 'just society', we in real sense have to understand the meaning of these three expressions, i.e., liberty, equality and fraternity. But, before making an attempt to understand these three expressions, we need to know the context out of which, a need for a 'just society' arose for him. This mean we have to explore the possibility of understanding, the existing nature of Indian society or social order. Dr. Ambedkar had very comprehensive discussion on the existing 'social order' based upon the Hindu classical religion in some of his works, which included *Philosophy of Hinduism* and *The Hindu Social Order*. These two works now are part of Volume 3 of his Writings and Speeches.[5] One other point becomes very clear from Dr. Ambedkar's writings is that he was not only a very creative and constructive critic, but was also at the same time a thinker, who will come up with the alternative proposals also. This he did exactly in the case of Indian existing social order or society, because he not only pointed out the evils of the existing social order and ask for a complete change, but also offered an alternative model of an 'ideal society' or a 'just society'. This he did in his most well known work namely "Annihilation of Caste". A summary of his alternate or the description of his 'ideal society', we find in his above work in the following words:

> An ideal society should be mobile, should be full of channels for conveying a change taking place in one part to other parts. In an ideal society there should be many interests consciously communicated and shared. There should be varied and free points of contact with other modes of association. In other words there must be social endosmosis.[6]

This much about the general introduction of our subject. But now we will have some detailed discussion on the same. For convenience sake, we have divided our discussion, in the following three parts:

(1) Existing Social Order
(2) An Alternative Society Based Upon Justice
(3) Way to Establish a Just Society

Existing Social Order

About the 'existing social order', first thing we need to remember is that for Dr. Ambedkar, the existing social order means the Hindu Social Order, because the present Indian social order is deeply rooted in the Hindu *varna* (caste) system. Because of the caste reality, according to him the existing social order does not give any important place to an individual person. Therefore, in this society an individual also does not have any real chance of growth or to develop his or her personality as a person. Because of the same reason the rights of a human being (or human rights) do not find any place in the existing social order. It is because this social order "is based primarily on class or *varna* and not on individuals".[7]

The above point, Dr. Ambedkar discussed in detail in his essay "The Hindu Social Order: Its Essential Principles".[8] According to him the original Hindu Social Order recognized only four classes or castes, which included (1) *Brahmins* (priests), (2) *Kshatriyas* (warriors), (3) *Vaishyas* (traders) and *Shudras* (servants). But today, these have become five, because *Panchams* (fifth Untouchables) has been added to the above four. But Dr. Ambedkar, about an individual person's place in this Order says:

> The unit of Hindu Society (existing Indian Society) is not the individual Brahmin or the individual Kshatriya or the individual Vaishya or the individual Shudra or the individual Panchama. Even the family is not regarded by the Hindu social order as the unit of society except for the purposes of marriage and inheritance. The unit of Hindu society is the class or *varna* to use the Hindu technical name for class.[9]

Because of the above position of the *varna* based social order, in it, "there is no room for individual merit and no consideration of individual justice. If the individual has a privilege it is not because it is due to him personally. The privilege goes with the class, and if he is found to enjoy it, it is because he belongs to that class. Contrawise, if an individual is suffering from a wrong, it is not because by his conduct deserves it. The disability is the disability imposed upon the class and if he is found to be labouring under it, it is because he belongs to that class".[10]

Dr. Ambedkar to prove his above point quoted very extensively from the Hindu ancient texts. He added that because the basis of above division of classes was divine according to which these "were created from different parts of the Divine body has generated the belief that it must be Divine will that they should remain separate and distinct".[11]

Ambedkar about the divisions in the existing social order points out that these do not limit up to five divisions only. These get further divided into sub-classes or castes into hundred and thousands. For example, at the time, when he wrote his essay on "The Hindu Social Order", the total population of all the Brahmins was about a crore and a half but they were divided into 1,886 sub-castes. The same way the other castes were also divided.[12] The recent study conducted by the Anthropological Survey of India (1993) of the Scheduled Castes also proves Dr. Ambedkar's above point, because according to it presently there are about 751 identifiable sub-communities (divisions) of the Dalits alone.[13]

He has listed three basic principles on which the existing social order stands. The first principle is 'the principle of graded inequality', which is a 'fundamental principle' of this Order. As mentioned above this order not only divided the society horizontally into thousand of castes or sub-castes or communities but also it more badly divides vertically. According to its given scheme "the Brahmin is placed at the first in rank, below him is the Kshatriya and below the Kshatriya is the Vaishya. Below the Vaishya is the Shudra and below the Shudra is the Ati-Shudra or the Untouchables. This order of precedence among the classes is not merely conventional. It is spiritual, moral and legal. There is no sphere of life which is not regulated by this principle of graded inequality".[14] The last part of this observation is important, because the principle of graded inequality has been carried into the total human life including social, economic and political.[15]

The second principle, which Dr. Ambedkar dealt was that of 'fixity of occupations'. According to this principle, the Brahmins were assigned to study and teach, the Kshatriyas were to protect and fight, and the Vaishya was to look after trade and Shudras were assigned to serve. Here the point needs to be remembered is that every member of each class has to follow the work assigned to his or her class. There was no scope of individual choice. In fact, there were punishments to be given if any member of any class goes against this principle.[16]

The third principle on which the Hindu social order is founded is the fixation of people within their respective classes.[17] This means that every person's caste status or class status was decided by birth – not on one's ability.

Before moving to the next section of this essay, one final point about the existing social order of India needing our attention is about the question, if what Dr. Ambedkar has said above, are the things of the past or are they applicable today also. The answer is in affirmative, because a number of official reports of various commissions appointed by the Government of India have endorsed Dr. Ambedkar's above position. Two of such reports are referred here. For example, L.M. Shrikant's Report of the Commissions for Scheduled Castes and Scheduled Tribes for the period ending 31st December, 1951, opened with these words: "The Caste in Hindu society is still the most powerful factor in determining a man's dignity, calling or profession. Such a rigid caste-system is not found anywhere else outside India".[18] These words of Shrikant tells us that what Dr. Ambedkar said before our country's independence about our existing social order remained true even after the independence. Another Commission's report (known as Mandal Commission, which got ready in 1980, but was made public in 1990), has devoted two full chapters[19] on the same issue with which Dr. Ambedkar is concerned. This report says about the Indian social order:

> Castes are the building bricks of Hindu social structure... Here we are mainly concerned with the manner in which caste has fragmented the social consciousness of Hindu society by dividing it into numerous groups arranged in hierarchical order...It may be further remarked that in this process of divisions, groups called castes have been permanently assigned high or low ranks simply on the basis of birth... The social ranks and their respective duties, ordained by God for humanity, were

> intended to remain fixed and unmovable. Like the limbs of the body, they cannot properly exchange either their place or function.[20]

About the effects of caste system in the Indian society and what change has taken place in it, the report of the Mandal Commission says:

> Even if the caste model described by us represents an ideal State, yet it does not negate the fact that caste system has been the most enduring basis of social organisation in India or, that, it has divided the Indian Society into a large number of hierarchically arranged high and low castes or, that, the lower castes have suffered crippling social handicaps for centuries as a result of the low caste status. Similarly, despite all the modifications that caste has undergone over the ages and, specially after Independence, changes in the caste system are representative more of shifts in emphasis than any material alteration its basic structure.[21]

Now as we have seen from the writings of Dr. Ambedkar as well as the official reports of various commissions, the Indian social order is deeply rooted in the *varna* (caste) system and because of the rigidity of the caste system till now practically no "material alternation in its basic structure" was possible. One of the problem in various efforts has been that very rare attempt has been made to come up with an alternative model of a social order or society. But this has not been the case of Dr. Ambedkar, because he not only suggested the total annihilation of caste or caste based society, but his starting point was an offering of a model of an 'ideal society' or what we call a 'just society'. Already references to his vision of such a society has been made in our introduction of this essay. Therefore, now we will briefly deal with the Dr. Ambedkar's vision of an 'alternative society' based upon justice.

An Alternative Society Based Upon Justice

Dr. Ambedkar has stated at number of places in his writings about the nature of a society, with which he wanted to replace the existing one. For his ideal society, he recognized the two essential principles: "The first is that the individual is an end in himself and that the aim and object of society is the growth of the individual and the development of his personality. Society is not above the individual and if the individual has to subordinate himself to society, it is because such subordination is for his betterment and only to the extent necessary. The second essential is that the terms of associated life between members of society must be regarded by consideration founded on liberty, equality and fraternity".[22] In this observation of Dr. Ambedkar, a main point needs to be noted is that in the caste-based society, an individual person has no place, where in Ambedkar's proposed society individual is the final end. Also, in the caste-based society a person's relationship with the member of his or her class or with the members of other classes were already fixed, but in Dr. Ambedkar's visioned society these relations have to be based on liberty, equality and fraternity. Here, the demand on the society is to protect the individual's human rights. What Dr. Ambedkar has said above, about the two essential principles of his alternative society, in his other works, he has concluded that any good social order or society has also to go through the two tests namely 'the test of justice' and 'the test of utility'. In fact, his judgmental analysis of the caste based or Hindu Social Order was based on these two tests. Again his above stated two essential principles of his society covers the same premises of these two tests.

Beside the two essentials principles or tests, one of the most important components is 'justice' or the 'principle of justice', because according to Dr. Ambedkar "the norm or the criterion for judging right and wrong in the modern society is justice"[23] and again justice, according to Dr. Ambedkar "is simply another name for liberty, equality and fratemity".[24]

Here, one point from these statements of Dr. Ambedkar becomes clear, that is to understand the real nature of Dr. Ambedkar's visioned society, we have to know the meaning of these expressions namely: (a) liberty, (b) equality, and (c) fraternity.

Liberty

He has discussed the meaning of 'liberty' in his number of works. In his essay on the "Hindu Social Order: Its Essential Principles", he has divided liberty into two categories namely 'civil liberty' and 'political liberty'. The first category, 'civil liberty' according to Dr. Ambedkar refers to the following three basic liberties: (1) liberty of movement which is opposite to arrest without due process of law, (2) liberty of speech (which of course includes liberty of thought, liberty of reading, writing and discussion) and (3) liberty of action. The second category, the 'political liberty', according to Dr. Ambedkar "consists in the right of the individual to share in the framing of laws and in the making and unmaking of governments".[25] Dr. Ambedkar while discussing about the meaning of liberty has also added that it must be accompanied by three social conditions, which include social equality, economic equality and there must be knowledge (education) made available to all. All these three social conditions were restricted to a particular class in the old social order based upon the caste system, but these conditions as part of the human liberty form an important part in the new social order.[26]

Equality

The general meaning of the expression equality is 'exactly the same or equivalent in measure amount, number, degree, value, or equality'. But the question has been raised if in the literal sense, all the human beings are same or not. While answering this question, Dr. Ambedkar has agreed that all the persons may not be equal with regard to "physical strength, in artistic skill, in material wealth, or mental capacity", but still "human beings possess, in degree and kind, fundamental characteristics that is common to humanity". The nature and manifestation of the fundamental characteristics, which appear in all human beings, are summed up in the phrase, 'moral equality'. Emphasis must be placed on the term 'moral', because "no rational exponent of moral equality has been disputed. Therefore, in essence of the phrase 'moral equality' asserts in ethical value, a belief to be sustained, and recognition of rights to be respected, because a society without any response for human personalities is a band of robbers".[27]

Fraternity

Given below are three statements of Dr Ambedkar which help us in understanding the meaning of 'fraternity', which along with liberty and equality is the cornerstone of an 'ideal' or 'just society'.

1. In his essay on "Philosophy of Hinduism", while talking about a 'just society' about the meaning of fraternity:

    There are two forces prevalent in Society. Individualism and Fraternity. Individualism is ever present. Every individual is ever asking "I and my neighbours, are we all brothers, are we even fifteenth cousins, am I their keeper, why should I do right to them" and under the pressure of his own particular interests acting as though he was an end to himself, thereby developing a non-social and even an anti-social self. Fraternity is a force of opposite character. Fraternity is another name for fellow feeling. It consists in a sentiment which leads an individual to identify himself with the goods of others whereby the good of others becomes to him a thing naturally and necessarily to be attended to like any of the physical conditions of our existence.[28]

2. In his other essay on "The Hindu Social Order: Its Essential Principles", while discussing 'fraternity' as one of

the key essentials of a 'just society' or what he calls a 'free social order' as compared to the existing Indian caste based social order, says:

> Fraternity is the name for the disposition of an individual to treat men as the object of reverence and love and the desire to be in unity with the fellow beings. This statement is well expressed by Paul, when he said 'of one blood are all nations of men. There is neither Jew nor Greek, neither bond nor free, neither male nor female; for yet are all one in Christ Jesus'. Equally well was it expressed when the Pilgrim Fathers on their landing at Plymouth said: "We are knit together as a body in the most sacred covenant of the Lord... by virtue of which we hold ourselves tied to all care of each others' good and of the whole." These sentiments are of essence of fraternity. Fraternity strengthens socialites and gives to each individual a stronger personal interest in practically consulting the welfare of others.[29]

3. The best summary of his view on fraternity as well as of his 'ideal society' or what we call 'just society', we find in his these words:

> An ideal society should be mobile, should be full of channels for conveying a taking place change in one part to other parts. In an ideal society there should be many interests consciously communicated and shared. There should be varied and free points of contact with other modes of association. In other words there must be social endosmosis. This is fraternity, which is only another name for democracy. Democracy is not merely a form of Government. It is primarily a mode of associated living, of conjoint communicated experience. It is essentially an attitude of respect and reverence towards fellowmen.[30]

This statement of Dr. Ambedkar which is self-explanatory on the meaning of fraternity and his 'ideal society' or his 'alternative society', but then how will this be established? This is the question, which we will be dealing with in the next section of this essay.

Way to Establish a Just Society

After reading Dr. Ambedkar's main writings, one thing becomes very clear, that is he was not just a critic or a person having some new ideas – he was also at the same time a person who also had concrete suggestions for the implementation of the same. For example, in his analysis of the existing social order based on caste, he was very clear what evils it carries, he was also very clear (as seen in the earlier section of this essay) about 'justice' (based on liberty, equality and fraternity) as the basis of his alternate society. Again at the end how to establish an 'ideal' or 'just society', he was very clear. *Varna* (caste) system was the basis of the existing Indian social order and it was this system which was responsible for all the evils of the existing order. It is because of this analysis he talked about the annihilation of caste. But he was also very clear that "it is not possible to break caste without annihilating the religious notions on what it, the caste system, is founded".[31] According to him, this was only possible through a Kranti (revolution), not through a simple reformation. His work on "Annihilation of Caste" suggested the following method/way to lay the foundation for an alternate society or the society rooted in justice. He said:

> Whether you do that or you do not, you must give a new doctrinal basis to your Religion – a basis that will be in consonance with Liberty, Equality and Fraternity, in short, with Democracy. I am not authority on the subject. But I am told that for such religious principles as well be in consonance with Liberty, Equality and Fraternity it may not be necessary for you to borrow from foreign sources and that you could draw for such principles on the *Upanishads.* Whether you could do so without a complete remoulding, a considerable scraping and chipping off the ore they contain, is more than I can say. This

> means a complete change in the fundamental notions of life. It means a complete change in our look and in attitude towards men and things. It means conversion; but if you do not like the word, I will say, it means new life. But a new life cannot enter a body that is dead. New life can enter only in a new body. The old body must die before a new body can come into existence and a new life can enter into it. To put it simply, the old most cease to be operative before the new can begin to enliven and to pulsate. This is what I meant when I said you must discard the authority of the Shastras and destroy the religion of the Shastras.[32]

The above statement of Dr. Ambedkar is the best summary of his suggested methodology of establishing a 'just society' in place of the present caste based Indian society. It does not need any comment but still for the sake of our further understanding of the same, we can list the following three main steps which he suggested to be followed:

(1) *New Doctrinal Basis is the First Step*: Dr. Ambedkar suggested the first step to formulate the new doctrinal basis of the Hindu religion, which according to him, has to "be in consonance with Liberty, Equality and Fraternity." Here it means to reinterpret part of the text of Hindu religion such as *Upanishads*, which carries the philosophical basis of Hindu religion. Dr. Ambedkar's stress here is on the radical reinterpretation, which involves "a considerable scraping and chipping off the ore they contain", which presently go against the principle of fraternity or fellow-feeling and does not allow the practice of "the associated mode of life", which is one of the important basis for the establishment of a just society. Dr. Ambedkar in this regard gave the examples of Sikh and Muslim religions.[33] Because the present doctrinal basis of Hindu religion does not fully allow to be practiced, the principles of liberty and equality, which automatically cancel the people's right of military service, political

power to protect them and the right to educate, Dr. Ambedkar names three rights as: 'physical weapon', 'political weapon' and 'moral weapon', which according to him in the present social order based upon the caste system are "denied to the masses in India".[34] Now how to make available these three weapons to the masses is the first step toward the formation a of New Social Order based upon justice.

(2) *A Complete Change in the Fundamental Notions of Life:* The above stated first step, automatically leads to the second by entering into "the associated mode of life" actually means asking for "a complete change in the fundamental notions of life". It means adopting a new set of 'values of life', which in the strict sense is 'conversion' leading to a 'new life'. Again for the establishment of New Social Order or bringing "a complete change in the fundamental notions of life", he looked into the following three practical possibilities:

   (a) the first action he suggested to abolish the Caste, the various sub-castes should be abolished, because these came into existence only through imitation and excommunication. But he was not fully convinced with his own, this suggested step, because he thought the process may stop with the abolition of sub-castes, therefore:

   (b) he suggested another action, according to which inter-caste dining may be the solution. But again he himself argued against this suggestion. Because there were many castes which allow inter-dining, but it has not succeeded in killing the spirit of caste and the consciousness of caste, therefore:

   (c) he suggested another action, which involved inter-marriage. About inter-marriage, he said: "Fusion of blood can alone create the feeling of being kith and kin and unless this feeling of kinship, of being kindred, becomes paramount, the separatist feeling –

the feeling of being aliens – created by Caste will not vanish. Among the Hindu, inter-marriage must necessarily be a factor of greater force in social life than it need be in the life of the non-Hindu. Where society is already well-knit by other ties, marriage is an ordinary incident of life. But where society cut asunder marriage as a binding force becomes a matter of urgent necessity. The real remedy for breaking caste is inter-marriage. Nothing else will serve as the solvent of caste".[35]

(3) *The Old Body Must Die to Receive New Body:* The second step leading to conversion through a 'u-turn' leading to a new life actually means going through a death experience; which means rejecting completely the old life before entering into new. This according to Dr. Ambedkar was possible if one will be willing to "discard the authority of the Shashtras and destroy the religion of the Shashtras". He strongly suggested: "You must take the stand that Buddha took. You must take the stand which Guru Nanak took. You must not only discard the shashtras, you must deny their authority, as did Buddha and Nanak".[36] Here a point needs to be remembered is that though Lord Buddha and Guru Nanak Devji belonged to a Khastriya caste and the shashtras (scriptures) only allow their caste to study only, but not to teach; yet they both became founder teachers of the two great religions, which mean they took the role if Brahmins and through their this action they rejected the authority of the shashtras.

Concluding Remarks

In three parts of this essay we have discussed the vision of Dr. B.R. Ambedkar's 'Just Society' based upon the three universal principles namely Liberty, Equality and Fraternity. The united name for these principles he used is justice. If one goes through very carefully the various discussions of Dr. Ambedkar, which he undertook in his *Writings and Speeches* (out of which some are referred in this essay), one definitely will not only understand the meaning of the Preamble of the Constitution of India, but will also come to know possibly, who was behind the formulation of the Preamble. Dr. B.R. Ambedkar indeed was the architect of the Indian Constitution and as a Chairperson of the Drafting Committee, he did not introduce in it the right articles and clauses, but gave it the right basic structure. The basic structure of the Indian Constitution, we find in its Preamble. This Preamble has the following four components:

> **Justice**, social, economic and political;
>
> **Liberty**, of thought, expression, belief, faith and worship;
>
> **Equality** of status and of opportunity, and to promote among them all
>
> **Fraternity**, assuring the dignity of the individual and the unity and integrity of the Nation.[37]

Now if one keeps the above four components of the Preamble of the Constitution of India in mind, and our discussion of section two of this essay on "An Alternative Society Based Upon Justice", which means the 'ideal' or 'just society', one will understand the form of government envisaged in the Constitution of India and the vision of a 'just society' of Dr. Ambedkar was the same. Of course while giving the meaning of 'fraternity', Dr. Ambedkar also said (as seen in section two) that "it is only another name of democracy" and about the democracy in his other speech on "Ranade, Gandhi and Jinnah", he said: "democracy was not a form of government: it was essentially a form of society. It may not be necessary for a democratic society to be marked by unity, by community of purpose, by loyalty to public ends and by mutuality of sympathy. But it does unmistakably involve two things. The first is an attitude of mind, an attitude of respect and equality towards their fellows. The second is a social organization free from rigid social barriers".[38] Dr. Ambedkar's this statement on 'democracy' makes the above point very clear – that for him there was no difference between a democratic form of government (particularly, which the Constitution of India upholds) and the alternative society based upon the principle of justice as seen by him. But Dr. Ambedkar's visioned society, it seems, is still a thing of the future. Because, most of the documents, we referred in this essay were written by him about 70 or 75 years ago, but with the gap of 20-25 years. Later at the time of the adoption of the Constitution of India on January 26, 1950, he made the following statement:

> We must make our political democracy a social democracy as well. Political democracy cannot last unless there lies at the base of it, social democracy. What does social democracy mean? It means a way of life, which recognise liberty, equality and fraternity as the principles of life. These Principles of liberty, equality and fraternity are not to be treated as separate items in a trinity. They form a union of trinity in the sense that to divorce one from the other is to defeat the very purpose of democracy. Liberty cannot be divorced from equality, equality cannot be divorced from liberty. Nor can liberty and equality be divorced from fraternity: Without equality, liberty would produce the supremacy of the few over the many. Equality without liberty would kill individual initiating. Without fraternity, liberty and equality could not become a natural course of things. It would require a constable to enforce them. We must begin by acknowledging the fact that there is complete absence of two things in Indian society. One of these equality on the social plane, we have in India a society based on the principle of graded inequality which means elevation for some and degradation for others. On the economic plane, we have a society in which there are some who have immense wealth as against many who live in abject poverty. On the 26th January, 1950, we are going to enter into a life of contradictions. In politics we will have equality and in social and economic life we will have inequality. In politics we will be recognising the principle of one man one vote and

> one vote one value. In our social and economic life, we shall, by reason of our social and economic structure, continue to deny the principle of one man one value. How long shall we continue to live this life of contradictions? How long shall we continue to deny equality in our social and economic life? If we continue to deny it for long, we will do so only by putting our political democracy in peril. We must remove this contradiction at the earliest possible moment or else those who suffer from inequality will blow up the structure of political democracy, which this Assembly has so laboriously built up.[39]

I do not think Dr. Ambedkar's above statement made by him more than 50 years back need further comment from us, because what he said 70 or 75 years back in his work on "Annihilation of Caste" or in "Philosophy of Hinduism" and then what he said above 50 years ago as part of his closing statement to the Constituent Assembly on 25th January, 1950 (one day before the adoption of the Constitution), still is applicable even today as we began a new century of 21st as well as the third millennium. But the call given by Dr. Ambedkar to the nation on 25th January, 1950 still continues to challenge us to work for the removal of the contradictions of life, faced by masses if Indian people in their social and economic life, because as long as these contradictions will continue, the 'just society' or 'ideal society' envisaged by him will be a thing of the future.

Notes

1. Ambedkar, B.R.: Annihilation of Caste with a Reply to Mahatma Gandhi, in *Dr. Babasaheb Ambedkar, Writings and Speeches,* Vol. 1, complied by Vasant Moon, Bombay, 1989, p. 57.
2. Ibid, p. 80.
3. Ambedkar, B.R.: Philosophy of Hinduism, in *Dr. Babasaheb Ambedkar, Writings and Speeches*, Vol. 3, complied by Vasant Moon, Bombay 1987, p. 25.

4. Ambedkar, B.R.: Annihilation of Caste, op., cit p. 57.
5. *Dr. Babasaheb Ambedkar, Writings and Speeches*, Vol. 3, op. cit., pp. 3-150.
6. Ambedkar, B.R.: Annihilation of Caste, op. cit., p. 57.
7. Ambedkar, B.R.: The Hindu Social Order: Its Essential Principles, in *Dr. Babasaheb Ambedkar, Writings and Speeches*, Vol. 3, complied by Vasant Moon, Bombay 1987, p. 99.
8. Ibid., pp. 99-106.
9. Ibid., p. 99.
10. Ibid., pp. 99-100.
11. Ibid., p. 100.
12. Ibid., p. 102.
13. Singh, K.S.: *The Scheduled Castes, People of India*, National Series Vol. 11, Anthropology Survey of India, Delhi, 1993, p. 1.
14. Ambedkar, B.R.: The Hindu Social Order: Its Essential Principles, op. cit., p. 107.
15. Ibid., p. 111.

    Also see: Reservation for Backward Classes, Mandal Commission Report of the Backward Classes Commission, 1980, (Alongwith Introduction, Akalank Publications, Delhi, 1990, p. 25 (In future references used as Mandal Commission Report 1980).
16. Ambedkar, B.R.: The Hindu Social Order: Its Essential Principles, op. cit., pp. 111-13.
17. Ibid., pp. 113-15.
18. Shrikant, L.M.: Report of the Commission for Scheduled Castes and Scheduled Tribes for the period ending 31st December, 1951, Delhi, p. 1.
19. Mandal Commission Report, op. cit., pp. 19-25.
20. Ibid., p. 19.
21. Ibid., p. 23.
22. Ambedkar, B.R.: The Hindu Social Order: Its Essential Principles, op. cit., p. 95.
23. Ambedkar, B.R.: Philosophy of Hinduism, op. cit., p. 22.
24. Ibid., p. 25.
25. Ambedkar, B.R.: The Hindu Social Order: Its Essential Principles, op. cit., p. 98.
26. Ambedkar, B.R.: Philosophy of Hinduism, op. cit., pp. 38-39.

27. Ambedkar, B.R.: The Hindu Social Order: Its Essential Principles, op. cit., pp. 96, 97.
28. Ambedkar, B.R.: Philosophy of Hinduism, op. cit., p. 44.
29. Ambedkar, B.R.: The Hindu Social Order: Its Essential Principles, op. cit., pp. 97, 98.
30. Ambedkar, B.R.: Annihilation of Caste, op. cit., p. 57.
31. Ibid., p. 27.
32. Ibid., pp. 77-78.
33. Ibid., p. 55.
34. Ibid., p, 63.
35. Ibid., p. 67.
36. Ibid., p. 69.
37. Bakshi, P.M., *The Constitution of India with Selective Comments*, Delhi, 1999 (Reprint), p. 1.
38. Ambedkar, B.R.: Ranade, Gandhi and Jinnah in *Dr. Babasaheb Ambedkar, Writings and Speeches*, Vol. 1, compiled by Vasant Moon, Bombay, 1989, p. 222.
39. Constituent Assembly Debates, Official Report, Book No. 5, Vol. XL, 1411-1949 to 26-11-1949, New Delhi, 1999 (Third Reprint), p. 979.

8

Constitution, Law and Social Justice

Dr. Ambedkar's Perspective

M.L. GAUTAM

Social justice is different from mere justice. Justice as a concept in political thought has been the subject matter right from Socrates. According to Tharasy Mechus justice means "that everywhere there is one principle of justice, which is the interest of the stronger". It simply means that 'might alone makes rights'. Government, accordingly in brief exists for the good of the governors, not the governed. However, Plato differed from this definition and held that a function of the doctor is to heal his patients and the sufferers and to protect these people, so the doctor unselfishly concerns himself with the welfare of his people. He also disagreed with Thrasy Mechus that injustice is better than justice. Plato replies that the just person will be a happy and better man in the long run than an unjust man because of the inherent contradictions in the course of the latter.

Justice as a part of welfare state was not used either by Plato or Aristotle. Plato felt that for a stable polity it would be better to assign functions to the people, according to their natural attributes. He says that all men are not born equal. It means that men by nature essentially are unequal. They vary in their capacities in depressions, courage, wisdom and justice.

Plato regards these four things as cardinal virtues. Some persons are born better suited by their courage, some are with the wisdom, some are with the justice and some are with depressions. In a simple language we can say that Plato divides the people into three natural attributes, i.e., courage, wisdom and appetite attributing to the ruling class, the military class and the common class, respectively. To obtain stability in the state he feels that there is an essential equilibrium, and this equilibrium can be maintained if the people discharge their duties as assigned to them by the nature.

Historical Perspective

Social justice, thus, is totally different from the concept of justice as developed in the Greek city states. It is now more a part of a welfare state. Welfare state means that it exists for the people and not people for the state. To explain the concept of law and social justice as propounded by Dr. Ambedkar, it may be worthwhile to refer to the history of social justice in India, especially, during the national movement. It was the National Congress resolved on the issue in 1917. The resolution read:

"This Congress urges upon the people of India the necessity of justice and righteousness of removing all disabilities imposed by custom upon the depressed class, the disabilities being of a most vexatious oppressive character subjecting those classes to considerable hardship and inconvenience."

This resolution of the Congress, thus, was epoch making in sociopolitical history of India. In the same session of Congress, Bhulabhai Desai further explained that "the disabilities under which some of our brethren suffer, are great blow to the equality and brotherhood of man that we preach. From the great height of the resolution that you have passed this morning, with what face will we approach the British Democracy or any other power, if we are unable to uplift our own brethren? They will say 'What lies in your own power, the obliteration of the social degradation of a section of your own people, you have been unable to do!' We can do it by self-help alone and in this matter we need not approach any other power but ourselves. That proves the necessity of the great forward step that this Congress has taken in allowing this resolution to be moved before you. The existence of this great bane is an insult to the name of Hinduism. Therefore, both on the ground of necessity and justice, as well as on the ground of righteousness, for the truth that you cherish, how can you deny them what this resolution demands, when the justice lies in your own hands? And if you fail to do that, with what justice, with what face, will you demand Self-Government?"[1]

Social justice in Indian sense is the result of our social system that we have right from Vedic period. It is said that Vedic period (from 1500 to 1000 BC) was free from caste system. Rigveda simply speaks about three classes, i.e., the Brahamans, the Kshatriyas and the Vaishyas and the fourth *varna*, i.e., Shudras was interpolated at the later stage. During this period, the social stratification was not rigid, as observed by a number of historians including R.S. Sharma. Dr. Ambedkar too, agreed to this fact. However, the social classification became much more distinct, rigid and obvious in post Vedic period, i.e., from 1000 to 600 B.C. Jainism and Buddhism originated at the ills of Brahamanas (post-Vedic literature). They opposed not only *varna* system but also Brahaminical authority. The post Vedic literature, i.e., Dharam. Sutras and Brahamanas including Puranas and Epics ordained the social classification and gave religious sanctions. *Manu Smriti* specifically went to the extent of depriving last varna from property and education – basic source of social status. They were subjected to innumerable humiliations and made servile to the upper *varnas*. Wisdom became the monopoly of the first *varna*. Empirical studies carried out by Dr. Ambedkar, was presented in the Columbia University in 1915, as his thesis, namely, 'Caste: Its Origin, Genesis and Mechanism'. In this thesis, he concluded that it was the superposition of endogamy on exogamy that resulted in origin of castes. In the beginning it was the priestly class which became the enclosed class by observing endogamy. This enclosed class, in the process became the caste. He further analyzed the consequences of the caste system in his celebrated book *The Annihilation of Castes*. To have a glimpse of his thoughts may not be out of tune here. He holds that the Brahamanism not only divided the people socially, i.e., not only the division of labour but labourers too. The labour of a washerman was held higher than the labour of a sweeper or cobbler. Such an unnatural division is not found elsewhere in the world. As discussed above, Plato's classification which was simply meant for utopian ideal state did not go for division of labours.

Men do not become a society by living in physical proximity any more than a man ceases to be a member of his society by living so many miles away from other men. Secondly, similarity in habits, customs, beliefs and thoughts is not enough to constitute men into society. Things may be passed physically from one to another like bricks. In the same way, habits and customs, beliefs and thoughts, of one group may be taken over by another group and there may, thus, appear a similarity between the two. "Similarity in certain things is not enough to constitute a society."[2]

The proposition still holds good in our society. The sweepers or Balimikies, the Nats and Kanzars, are not only far off both physically and socially, even though they follow the same faith, carry the same traditions even much more earnestly than caste Hindus. Take any festival, whether it is Holi or Diwali, Ganpati or any other festival. They are those people who dance in the streets and make a good show of Hindu festivals and Hindu identity. Do they have any social connection or even communication with the rest of castes in the society in the real sense? A society in the real sense, according to Dr. Ambedkar, must have the following three essentials to be a society:

1. An associated life.
2. Common activity or objective.
3. Communication (free social interaction).

He found that all three essentials are not present in the Hindu society. He was of the view that it is not the man who constitute the society but they are the classes which constitute the society. In his words, "men constitute a society because they have things which they possess in common. To have similar things is totally different from possessing things in common. And the only way by which men can come to possess things in common with one another is by being in communication with one another. This is merely another way of saying that society continues to exist by communication, indeed in communication."

This communication between man and man is prevented by the operation of the caste system. It also prevented common activity and by preventing common activity it has prevented Hindus from becoming the society with unified life and conscious of its own being.

The operation of the social order demands the segregation of man to man and not association. Society can neither exist nor progress in the absence of an associated life. Common mental notions for a national objective are very much necessary for cohesive society and cohesive society is a condition precedent for a strong polity.

Describing the consequences of the operation of castes system in India, he says:

> The effect of castes ethics of the Hindus is simply deplorable. Caste has killed public spirit. Caste has destroyed the sense of public charity. Caste has made public opinion impossible. A Hindu's public is his caste. His responsibility is only to his caste. His loyalty is restricted only to his caste. Virtue has become caste-ridden and morality has become caste bound. There is no sympathy to the deserving. There is no appreciation for the meritorious. There is no charity to the needy. Suffering as such, calls for no response. There is charity, but it begins with the caste and ends with the caste. There is sympathy, but not for men of other caste.[3]

We will hold for the time being the critical evaluation of this statement in view of number of legislations passed both social and economic, in pursuance of the objective as enshrined in the Indian Constitution. We proceed further giving some historical background of the social justice. We know that in old Hindu Law or before codification the Brahamins were not subject to punishment. The *Manu Smriti* is the strong evidence to that effect, as how the things were manufactured with a view to have supremacy of a particular class in the society. The more dangerous thing that they did was giving religious sanctions to the Chaturvarnya system, which is still troubling Indian society. Comparing inequalities as prevalent in the western countries and in India, he observed that:

> in Europe it is true that the strong has not shrunk from exploitation, nay the spoilation of the weak, but there, the strong have never contrived to make the weak helpless against exploitation so shamelessly as was the case in India among the Hindus. Depriving property and education from the larger sections of the society they have been completely made disabled for direct action against their pitiable conditions. There have been social revolutions in other countries of the world. Why has not there been a social revolution in India? A simple answer is that the caste system is in the interest of the upper strata of the society. It is human nature that once he is well settled he would not allow to get disturbed.

Talking about ill effects of the caste system he remarked that: "there cannot be a more degrading system of social, organisation than the Chaturvarnya system. It is the system which deadens, paralyses and cripples the people from helpful activity." This is no exaggeration. History bears ample evidence. Social system got so degraded that in southern India some communities became unapproachable and unseeable. Bhattacharya, while commenting on the whole system observed:

> The toddy-tappers of Malbar and East coast, Ishvas and Shanars, were not allowed to carry umbrellas, to wear shoes or golden ornaments, to milk cows or even to use ordinary language of the country."[4]

According to Wilson:

> In Malbar, Brahmins alone were permitted to sit on boards formed in the shape of a Tortoise, and if a member of any other caste were to use such a seat he was liable to capital punishment. Members of all castes except Brahmins, were expressly forbidden to cover the Upper Part of their body above the Waist.[5]

The Census of 1891 speaks the diabolical nature of caste system as follows:

> In the case of women also, until 1865 they were obliged by law to go with the upper part of their bodies quite bare, if they belonged to or other lower caste (Madras Census 1891, p. 224).

Similar conditions prevailed even in 19th and early 20th century. G.W. Forrest has noted that in Bombay State:

> Under the Peshwas, a greater distinction was made in the punishment on account of the Caste of the Criminal than of the nature of the crime itself. Hard labour and death were punishment mostly visited on Criminals of the lower caste.[6]

Thus social injustice is the product of caste system in the society. The question arises as to the approach of Dr. Ambedkar to ensure social justice and at the same time the approach of Gandhi since he too intended to abolish the caste system. Dr. Ambedkar regards Chaturvarva system as main harbouring factor of caste system. Mahatma Gandhi, on the other hand felt that:

> I believe that inter dining or inter marriages are not necessary for promoting national unity. That dining together creates friendship is contrary to experience. In India, children of

> brothers do not inter-marry. Do they cease to love because they do not inter marry? To destroy caste system and adopt western European social system means that, Hindus must give up the principle of hereditary occupation which is the soul of the caste system. Hereditary principle is an eternal principle. To change it is to create disorder. I have no use for a Brahmin, if I cannot call him a Brahmin for my life. It will be chaos, if every day a Brahmin is to be changed into a Shudra and Shudra is to be changed to a Brahmin. The caste system is a natural order of society. In India, it has been given a religious coating. Other countries not having understood the utility of caste system, it existed only in a loose condition and consequently those countries have not derived from caste system in some degree of advantage, which India has derived. These being my views, I am opposed to all those who are to out to destroy the caste system.[7]

Social Justice and the Constitution

Social justice, as provided in the Constitution is so distinctive and expressive that no one is required to search for it. We find the concept of social justice in the Preamble itself. It speaks of justice – social, economic and political. The sequence shows that without social and economic justice, political justice will be illusory. In the background of caste-bound social status in Indian society, one cannot have adequate means of livelihood, since the sources of wealth are concentrated in few upper stratas in the society. Thus, birth decides the source or means of wealth too. In the absence of both, social and economic justice, the political justice remains a mirage. A man in the slum, unless he is a goonda, cannot hope to get into politics of election. He is not even in a position to exercise his franchise. "One man, one vote, and one vote, one value", a doctrine propounded by John Stuart Mill and praised by Dr. Ambedkar in his discussions in the Constituent Assembly, is still a distant ray to large members of the lower strata. To achieve the social and economic justice, we have the concept of protective discrimination, as provided under Article 15, 16 and 335. The apex court was in favour of a favourable interpretation to the concepts embedded in these Articles, but the *Indra Sohoni's Case*, which is famous as *Mandal's Case*, turned the table. Most dangerous and unfortunate decision has come of a Constitution Bench of five judges, headed by Justice Anand, Chief Justice of India. The judgment, for the first time in Indian Constitutional history, has held the Scheduled Castes and Tribes not fit to hold high technical and medical positions. Well, such kind of view of our apex court has shaken the very spirit of the concept of social justice. The French revolted against the feudal kings and established the human concepts of liberty, equality and fraternity. Dr. Ambedkar started searching for these concepts through liberation of suppressed and oppressed from the age old social bondage. Our forefathers succeeded in embedding these principles in the Constitution and supported Dr. Ambedkar by heart and action. Even the hard core Hindus realized the need of place of such concepts in the law of the land.

The opponents have opposed the protective discrimination on the ground that relaxation of standards in the name of social justice would prove dangerous to the health of nation. While, theoretically the argument may have its logical merits, in practice it has been proved illogical. The experience shows that people from this disadvantaged group are not only hard working but also are relatively honest. All big scandals in our beloved nation have been the result of ingenuity of persons who belonged to upper strata in the social ladder in the society.

The evils of social system still operate in the administrative structure, wherein persons of weaker sections are ranked as third class citizens. They are hardly given their due as per merit.

In the area of economic justice, we have Article 39 (B) and (C), which obliges the State to see that source of wealth should not be allowed to concentrate in a few hands only. The economic system should be so operated that it does not result in the concentration of wealth and means of production to the common detriment.

The apex court has upheld the amendment in the Constitution, i.e., Article 31 (C) which protects the economic legislations enacted to fulfil the objectives of Article 39 (B) and (C), even if such legislation is violative of Article 14 and 19 of the Constitution. These provisions in the Constitution still stand in the age of privatization and globalization. Profit making assets are being privatized. The Constitutional provisions are simply adoring the economic beauty of the Constitution. While the Constitution was in the making, Dr. Ambedkar was asked as to why he has not prescribed a specific economic structure in the Constitution. "Let us leave to the future generations to decide as to what kind of economic structure would suit them", he replied.

Article 39, as a matter of fact, looks like a *Panch Sheel*, fully capable of giving socio-economic justice to men, women and children. We have added one more *Sheel*, i.e., (f) by 42nd Constitutional Amendment Act, 1976. In spite of all these *sheels*, we have concentration of wealth and its resources in few hands, we have unequal pay to man and woman, we have flagrant abuse of child labour and his youth. The children of street dwellers in a megalopolis like Mumbai, specially the girls, are abused by the street goons – the moment the child comes to 10 or 12 years of age or even before that, they are abused. The State in India is a silent and a helpless spectator, since our social system is built on superfluous religious concepts. We face the present sufferings because of past *karmas*, teach our *shastras*. We still ordain them.

The concept of law and social justice as conceived by Dr. Ambedkar is still incomprehensive to our tradition-bound society.

N.A. Palkhivala has rightly observed that Dr. Ambedkar while carrying a crusade against the caste system, he did not bear any grudge against Hindus, in general. He observes as follows:

> Dr. Ambedkar was too big a man to harbour thought of vengeance and vendetta, ill-wills or revenge towards those who

had been exploiting casteism from times immemorial. He gave Indian Constitution, which guarantees equality to all as its basic feature, and ensures truly egalitarian society, where no class would be unprivileged, underprivileged on the ground of religion, race, caste, sex, descent place of birth or residence.[8]

The Law and Social Justice

The utility of law was "If the law does not conform to the facts it is so much worse for the law itself", observed Dr. Ambedkar. Following this principle, he codified scattered Hindu Laws into Hindu Code Bill. His Bill was defeated on the floor of the Parliament, in spite of being an official Bill (Dr. Ambedkar was the Union Law Minister). The provisions of the same code were later on incorporated in Hindu Succession Act, Hindu Marriage Act and Guardianship Act. The Utilitarian thinkers justify the existence of the State on the principle of its utility to man. From his youth, Bentham showed a fascinating devotion for social welfare. He was much impressed by the Priestley's Essay on Government and the statement that the 'happiness' of the majority of its members, is the standard by which a State will be judged. Bentham believed that happiness consisted in the presence of pleasure and absence of pain. Institution, therefore, should be so contrived that social conduct was conducive to greatest happiness. He worked out this psychology in his application to morals and law, holding that mankind is placed under two sovereign masters – pain and pleasure. He held that all human instincts are equally natural and that they are good or bad, depend on their results. Bentham believed that men have no duties to abstractions. Dr. Ambedkar too, advocated that the purpose of the State is to promote the general welfare. The State, he regarded, was a necessary Institution, which safeguards the individual and general security of man in the society. Individual liberty cannot be secured or enjoyed in the anarchical society and hence, he gives due importance to the stability of the State.

He pleaded in his writings that the man should follow the constitutional path to redress his grievances. It is because of this reason, he wanted to restructure the social order of the society as a condition precedent to a democratic free state. The purpose of the State to Dr. Ambedkar appears to be the same as to John Stuart Mill, who "laid stress upon the idea that every individual should aim to promote the general happiness. Social well-being was the end of Government, the fostering of virtue and intelligence was the test of its success."

Notes

1. Writing and Speeches of Baba Saheb Dr. B.R. Ambedkar, Vol. 9, Government of Maharashtra, Department of Education, p. 1, 2.
2. Dr. B.R. Ambedkar, *Annihilation of Caste.*
3. Dr. Ambedkar, *Writing and Speeches*, Department of Education, Government of Maharashtra, Vol. 1, 1979, p. 57.
4. Bhattacharya, J., *Hindu Castes*, 1877, pp. 77-79.
5. Wilson, John, *Indian Castes*, 1877, pp. 77-79.
6. G.W. Forrest, Official Writings of Mount Stuart Elphinstone, 1884, pp. 310-311.
7. Writings and Speeches of Dr. B.R. Ambedkar, Vol. 9, p. 276.
8. *We the Nation*, p. 273.

9

Macro Impacts of Reservation Policy

Some Observations

C.R. PRASAD RAO

The Reservation Policy, a practical policy instrument of social justice has had a long contentious history in India. The Constitution of India has only imparted to it enlarged scope, statutory force, and vigilant implement safeguards.[1] Also called a measure of Compensatory, or Protective, or Reverse Discrimination, reservation complexly interfaces with the built-in iniquitous institutions of the Indian society, which it fails to overcome in full force because structured inequalities are present within the reserved categories. The three chief motivations for reservation are: (1) Legitimating the rationale and role of the State; (2) Provision of level playing field for Dalits in the struggle for mobility, and a stake and share in the political, executional and development processes; and (3) A genuine desire to cleanse the collective, historical conscience of the society by compensating for deprivations and disabilities endured, and to integrate the highly pluralistic, divisive, and hierarchical Nation-State. Whereas, the history of reservation is well-documented what is not so obvious and documented is how reservation is impacting the target population in mainstreaming them and how non-target segments of the society are reacting and responding. In other words, how socially just and integrated the society is getting by implementing and extending reservation over the decades? Are the distortions, paradoxes, and uneven impact outcomes? Are latent, unintended, unrecognized, unanticipated functions of reservation merely rendering the remedy with worse functions of reservation surfacing, rendering the remedy worse than the disease? Is reservation merely a handy, soft option of the state policy in fulfilling its constitutional obligations? What is the State-Civil Society interface vis-à-vis Dalits and Reservation? Substantive and methodological answers to these and other impact-linked questions about reservation feedback to policy and legislation provide a significant historical hindsight. Researchers and evaluators do distinguish the success of implementation (in terms of administratively achieved quota fulfilments) from the success of reservation (in substantive and structural terms of impact). Implementation data are very frequently encountered in official reports which speak very little of the impact of the implementation.[2] Occasionally, uncritical use and reporting of reservation statistics takes place. For instance, look at the following data reproduced from an edited book of Seminar papers relating to Jawaharlal Nehru University (Table 9.1).

Correctly and critically interpreted, the above data do not provide any confirmatory evidence of either admission lapses or selection biases for which they were reported. It only reveals that the statutory quota for SC/ST students was not filled and there was a shortfall or backlog. How this backlog/shortfall came about cannot be said on the basis of these figures. The actual commission of discrimination can only be demonstrated when two more additional sets of data were made available in the table, that is, (1) the number of total applicants from SC/ST category, and (2) the number eligible for admission as per whatever admission criteria were in vogue from among the total number of SC/ST applicants. Non-availability or non-eligibility of applicants cannot be interpreted as bias, or lapse, or discrimination. Consider again another data set from the Report of the Scheduled Castes and Scheduled Tribes Commissioner, No.28, 1986-87, p. 502 (Table 9.2).

Table 9.1

Statistics Related to the Fulfilment of SC/ST Quota in M. Phil/Ph. D. Admissions in J.N.U. as on 13 August, 1984

S. No.	School	Total number of students selected for admission	SC/ST students		
			Actual Quota 22.5%	Selected	Shortfall
1.	School of Social Sciences	189	43	23	14
2.	School of Languages	76	17	3	14
3.	School of International Studies	164	37	23	14
4.	School of Computer & System Sciences	15	3	NIL	3
5.	School of Life Sciences	50	7	2	5
6.	School of Environmental Science	24	5	4	1
	Total	498	112	61	51

Source: N. Ashirwad: Dalits in India, in Y.C. Simbadri (Ed.): Global Youth, Peace and Development, Vol. II, 1992, Table-IV, p. 8, Ajantha Publications.

Table 9.2

Statement Showing S.C. and S.T. Representation in Universities (1986-87)

Categories	Total	S.C.	%	S.T.	%
Teaching posts:					
Professors	2,133	13	0.61	1	0.5
Readers/Assoc. Professors	3,261	34	1.04	5	0.15
Lecturers/Asst. Professors	5,341	169	3.16	32	0.60
Research Associates etc.	674	71	10.53	2	0.30
Ministerial Posts:					
Group A	3,525	118	3.35	11	0.31
Group B	4,833	221	4.57	48	0.99
Group C	19,811	1,686	8.51	219	1.11
Group D	17,607	2,628	14.93	616	3.50

Source: G.G. Wankhede: Education, Development and Social Change: The case of Scheduled Castes, Proceedings of the National Seminar on "Indian Society At Turn of the Century: Perspectives From Below", J.N.U., New Delhi, March 25-27, 1999.

On the basis of this data also, it is hard to draw firm, unambiguous conclusion about the prevalence of discrimination. The non-availability/non-eligibility factors are behind the data reported. This is confirmed by the observation that the percentage of representation is higher in the lower cadres which speaks of non-availability/non-eligibility factors.

To quote the paper writer:

> So far the educational progress made by the Scheduled Castes is satisfactory compared to their traditional and historical situation. However, comparing them with non-Scheduled Castes, they lag behind considerably even after 50 years of independence. Various studies have shown that the progress made by them is marginal mainly confined to urban population, and mainly in the general stream of education. Drop out and stagnation are the major problems faced by them. They enroll late, take longer time to complete, and enroll into low standard educational institutions. .... Thus, the educational problems of the Scheduled Castes are two-fold: One at home level; and second at school level (Wankhede, 1999:7).

This is a problem of educational achievement at the secondary stage of education. In higher education, the problem is more acute. These trends of low educational attainments of SCs and STs get directly reflected in employment hierarchies.

It needs emphasizing here that bias can work both ways: positively or favourably, and negatively or unfavourably. I recall two anecdotal experiences involving me as an expert member of University Faculty Selection Committee Meetings. In one case, the vice-chancellor of the concerned university has requested us to select – even out of the way – a particular SC candidate because he was using him as a buffer against militant/inimical forces of the campus. In the second anecdote, involving another university, the vice-chancellor was against our selecting a particular candidate because he was very troublesome. Moderates, extremists and conformists and poor and low achievers exist among the Dalits as they do in many other ethnic communities. Likewise, there are among university teachers and students belonging to SC/ST communities all manner of behaviour syndromes - time servers, trouble makers, trouble shooters, careerists, system saboteurs, and coercers, etc. Such spectra of human elements are present in every organized life including families, social groups, cliques and peers, and so on. In terms of impact studies, the interface of reservation and cultural and behaviour patterns is a crucial dimension. Politics may precede self-analysis, self-reform and self-uplift. To put the idea simply and plainly, does reservation result in bringing to the educational campuses, panchayats, legislatures, parliament, and employer organizations, on a large-scale, certain specific behaviour syndromes of undesired outcomes? Reservations may bring about the levelling of material conditions leaving out aspects of cultures, attitudes, work habits, and creative roles and contributive potentials. The Reservation Policy cannot be expected to balance and reconcile pluralistic demands and interests of different stakeholders of organizations. I very much suspect if NGOs working for the Dalits do implement the reservation principle in their recruitment drives. Political parties formed by Dalits have disintegrated because of internal dynamics. Therefore, a crucial policy question arising out of this discourse is what is a more efficient agency or strategy of social justice and equality? Are there alternative uplift models - Ambedkarite, Gandhian, Leftist, religious, participative, local self-governmental, self-help, corporate adoption, co-operative and NGO? Some sections prefer religious conversion to reservation. And some others depend upon both. Are there indigenous traditions which are more just and egalitarian in their operation and outcome than our modern devices? (e.g., grass roots democratic institutions of traditional society). The discourse takes a more radical and fundamental turn here.

Impact research/evaluation is a "Before-After" scientific measurement, and researchers/evaluators do not come across adequate data for establishing socio-economic status benchmarks against which impacts are measured at the national or state level.[3] Reservation impact carries over vertically snowballing through several successive generations, and spreads horizontally across the family spaces of single generations multiplying eligible and beneficiaries within the confines of single families.[4] This problem arises especially because reservation has been in vogue for at least five decades. The impact varies (i.e., multiplies and intensifies) between the earliest beneficiary families and the fresh beneficiary families while there are many others who have not been impacted at all! A further difficulty lies in respect of the arena of impact: economic, social, educational, political, cultural, psychological and behavioural at the individual and group levels. Cumulative impacts at the individual level, and aggregative impacts at the macro level of groups, group relations, organizations, institutions, political parties, and employer establishments, etc., are very crucial dimensions bearing on policy and legislation issues centering around social justice through reservation.

II

Considered in the aggregate, the Reservation Policy has generated a lot of politics, polemics, legal disputes, social divisions, violent protests and agitations and creamy layers and gloomy spectacles. Strong and articulate vested interests and advocacy groups have emerged both for and against reservations. More and more areas of claim and claimant categories are emerging on the scene. While de-reservation[5] (i.e., exclusion/inclusion issue) is not yet seriously mooted, debited, or implemented yet, the reservation space is increasingly crowded by certain segments and families and inaccessible to other eligible segments of the same reserved caste. While there are forces at work for cornering, consolidating, expanding and multiplying benefits, there are non-reservation aspirants striving and claiming to access the reservation vehicle of mobility. "The reservation culture in India is fast spreading and newer sections of the population are seen demanding separate exclusive enclosures". Caste has been transmuted into a resource of political bargain and, a material lever of uplift. Caste identities and rivalries are being reinforced openly, grossly, and subtly.[6] Whereas economic status is a fluid resource achievable by sponsorship or self-effort or both, caste status which is frozen by birth, is being turned into a political asset. Where achievement and ascriptive identities are consistent, the caste-based risk of conflict and polarizations are sharpened. Reservation, egalitarian ideologies of the militantly assertive kind (e.g., Dalit Panthers), demographics of universal adult franchise, and the democratic politics of the nation sharpen caste identities, caste-based coalitions, and caste rivalries. Similarly heightened and accentuated is the risk of caste prejudice becoming unconsciously subliminal, escaping the net of rational control. The emotional underpinnings of caste hatred get a fresh lease of life. The political process of the nation exploits caste-based demographics (vote banks) and caste-based reservations (policy-mediated politics). Social and psychic marginalization takes place among the beneficiaries of reservation who remain alienated from those outside of the reservation space as well as those who are left behind in the mobility race unable to get onto the bandwagon of reservation. In other words, reservation is fraught with high risks of social fragmentation rather than social integration. The three chief components of mainstreaming are (a) development; (b) politics; and (c) identity including self-respect, identity and equality. Politics or identity sans development is a dangerous uplift strategy.

III

Uplifting of people from backwardness and social disability is a complex social policy and social action programme further complicated by the demographic enormity of the target population. The present Reservation Policy merely helps to co-opt a small minority of the SCs, STs and BCs into the mainstream. Uplifting of the remaining huge mass of the SCs,

STs, and BCs is a stupendous revolutional exercise which can not conceivably be accomplished even by extending reservation interminably and by scrupulously overseeing its implementation. Mobility, equalization, and uplift processes breed dialectical backlashes over time (e.g., rise of racism against blacks and Asian migrants in the USA). Reservation, while it is laudable in its conception, implementation, and achievement, is only a drop in the ocean of backwardness. Alone it is insufficient to meet the challenge of structured inequalities and inequities of the society. Some of the dangers and distortions of the operation of the Reservation Policy have been highlighted here. A social justice measure like reservation is considered an easy, symbolic, or soft option of the State lacking in the political will to bring in and enforce more radical and structural reform/development measures. Further such drives cannot emanate from the State. Civil society participation is crucial. The prevailing claims for extending, deepening, and accessing the reservation space cannot totally be taken as an indirect measure of its overall impact. In the absence of complementary, or alternative radical promotional/developmental measures, the distortions, parodies and paradoxes of the Reservation Policy continue to remain. In the absence of development supplements and/or alternatives, people will bank upon and politicize the Reservation Policy unrelentingly and unremittingly.

The latest National Sample Survey results relating to Scheduled Tribes reinforce the point here being driven home. Reportedly the State of Andhra Pradesh has been able to reduce poverty prevalent amongst its tribal population from 46.68 per cent in 1993-94 to 38.3 per cent in urban areas, and in rural areas from 25.66 per cent in 1993-94 to 15.92 per cent. Nowhere in this record of achievement figures the role of reservation. On the contrary, the reported factors underlying this achievement in poverty reduction are measures related to agriculture, livestock, forest products, minor irrigation and small and village industries. What is noteworthy in this N.S.S. report is the short time interval of this development. Political will, holistic approach, honest and effective backup services, people's participation, and local assets/resources generation and protection, etc., constitute the real, rapid, durable, non-controversial uplift measures rather than dependence on Reservation Policy which no doubt is a direct interventional/promotional measure that has its merits and claims in its own right benefiting, however, only small segments of the population in need of uplift. Its trickle down or seepage is almost nil. It has resulted paradoxically in pockets of prosperity in the deserts of distress. Or as some one has put it, Reservation has created a new caste, namely, the "Dalit Brahmin". That was not our aim!

Notes

1. To check evasion and ensure a vigilant implementation, the government has put in place several devices such as the National Commission for SCs and STs and the Standing Committee of the Parliament for Labour and Welfare.
2. Policy presumptions and motivations of Reservation are generally taken for granted. Impact measurement is too much and too complex for these official reports/reporters. Even the Parliament rarely discusses impact issues.
3. SC and ST Tabulations of the census and National Sample Surveys are perhaps exceptions.
4. The aggregate and cumulative effect of these processes is emergence of creamy layers and articulate vested interests. The so-called *harijan/dalit* elites align mostly in-group formations with the dominant sections of the civil society and its institutions as hijackers of plums of office, crumbs of patronage, and development benefits. The writer has personal experience of a *harijan* elite ceasely hustling for promotions every two years, becoming restless for membership in management boards, and vying for priority allotment of residential quarters, all the time using the trump card of the dalit background and

reservation. Students entering higher educational institutions on the basis of reservation prolong their stay in the hostels and the campuses shifting from one-degree programme to another and emerge as student elites and leaders for the new entrants. The second degree not of much use to them and showing therefore little interest in studies, they upset academic calendars agitating for the postponement of examinations or confront teachers with demands for undeserved favours. To buy peace by pampering students some hostel wardens give money advances to hostlers.

5. In Andhra Pradesh, Brahmins, Kapus, Balija, Telaga and Ontari castes are claiming inclusion in the OBC Reservation list. Similarly there are demands from several other castes to be grouped with SCs Determination of the inclusion/exclusion criteria has been the most baffling and contentious part of Reservation history. See, for example, the case of Karnataka in K.S. Narayana's paper. The inclusion/exclusion issue is further complicated by quota fixation for want of caste-based population census. See M.K. Premi; Satish Deshpande; and Vijayan Unni.
6. In traditional India, caste identities are defined in ritual, cultural, and status hierarchy terms. Today, the bases and reinforcers of caste identities are more secular – modern education, modern occupation, political power, wealth, demographic size, and horizontal organization. Politicization rather than Sanskritization is the option in mobility. In other words, the traditional identity bases are selectively appropriated or co-opted by the class criteria in coalition formations depending on the context and objective. The traditional caste system was dominated by the Brahaminical ideology. Even today upper castes are prone to asubliminal allegiance to this ideology (e.g. The Hindutva ideology of BJP appeals to them). However, the lower and intermediate castes which are very large in number commanding a huge heterogeneous demographic size, are more influenced by the modern, egalitarian ideologies where relations with upper castes are concerned. Mandal Reservation is a consequence of this. Kanshi Ram's BSP is a case. See Prasad Rao and Radhakrishna Murthy and Rajni Kothari.

References

Bhargava, B.S. and Avinash Samal, "Protective Discrimination and Development of Scheduled Castes: An Alternative Model for Good Governance", *The Indian Journal of Public Administration*, July-September, No.3, 1998, pp. 508-519.

Deshpande, Satish, "Caste and the Census: Symposium", *Sociological Bulletin*, 48 (1 & 2), March-September 1999, pp. 257-262.

Kothari, Rajni, "Rise of the Dalits and the Renewed Debate on Caste", *Economic and Political Weekly*, June 25, 1994, pp. 1589-1594.

Maheshwari, S.R., "Reservation Policy in India: Theory and Practice", *The Indian Journal of Public Administration*, July-September, 1997, No.3, pp. 662-97.

Narayana, K.S., "Drawbacks Impeding Success of Positive Discrimination", *The Indian Journal of Public Administration*, July-September, No.3, 1998, pp. 520-533.

Premi, Mahendra K., "Indian Census and the Social Reality Symposium", *Sociological Bulletin*, 48 (1 & 2), March-September, 1999, pp. 247-255.

Rao, C.R. Prasad and K. Radhakrishna Murty, "Dalit Consciousness and Brahminism: A Multiplex Question", *The Eastern Anthropologist*, 46(1), January-March 1993, pp. 31-46.

Unni, M. Vijayan, "The Millennium Census of India 2001: Innovators, Initiatives and Improvements", *Sociological Bulletin*, 48(1 & 2), 1999, p. 239.

10

Constitution, Law and Justice

Ambedkar's Perspective

PRAKASH LOUIS

> A people suffering oppression under a feudal system were grimly struggling to be reborn into a life of dignity and hope. The past was heavy on their shoulders, and the future uncertain. The framers of the Constitution sought to unite the vast country with its great diversity, many languages and creeds within a common-bond of the Constitutional justice on the great ideals of liberty, equality, fraternity and social justice. Framers showed an uncompromising respect for human dignity, an unquestioning commitment to equality and non-discrimination, and an abiding concern for the poor and the weak. They made the bold attempt to base the Constitutional foundations on the firm faith that all classes of people, followers of all faith, and particularly the traditionally under-privileged should all join to work for their united Constitutional salvation on the shared faith that peoples of several faiths must sink or swim together, and that in the long run prosperity and salvation are in union and not in division.[1]

These are the words of National Commission to Review the Working of the Constitution. The Commission rightly acknowledges the fact that the framing of the Constitution was a stupendous task. This is because of the fact that the framers of the Constitution had to take into account the immense diverse socio-cultural, economic and political realities of India. They also had to pay heed to the aspirations of the innumerable caste and class categories that are spread over the Indian sub-continent. The Commission also gives due credit to the framers of the Constitution that inspite of all odds against them they drafted an all-encompassing, all-enhancing and all-ensuring legal principles as the foundation for national life. Further, the Commission also in clear terms recognizes the bold step taken by the founding fathers of the Constitution that human dignity is the central focus of our Constitution.

The ostensible reason for these high praises to the framers of the Constitution is that like in many others areas in this case too, by eulogizing on some of the aspects of an issue, some of the other fundamental issues are relegated to the background. For instance, the Commission takes note of the disastrous consequences of the remnants of feudalism. But once again it has eclipsed the nefarious caste system in general and untouchability in particular. There is no mention of the barbaric and brutish caste discrimination that are carried out on those who are in the lowest rung of the Indian social order. Significantly, the Commission has also failed to explore the expedience of social principles propounded by Dr. Ambedkar. This attitude of the Commission is all the more deplorable.

Going further, one also becomes acutely aware of the reference points of the Commission. The draft of the Commission takes recourse to the World Bank Country Study which states that "India is an ancient civilization with a bright history". Two salient features of this statement needs to be stated here. Firstly, the Constitution Review Commission had to take recourse to the World Bank to tell itself and to the nation that India is an ancient civilization. Once again the World Bank has to become the saving point for the Commission to state a truth about India. This affirms the fact that not only economically but culturally too we have become bankrupt and the alien market forces have to highlight our greatness. Even if this statement is accepted, one crucial and central question remains unanswered which social categories fall under this civilized India. Do the Dalits, the Tribals, women, the most backward castes and the minorities form part of the civilization, or are they at the periphery as ever?

From the day-to-day experience of these marginalized, deprived and discriminated communities it is amply clear that they are not part of the ancient civilization of India. Though they are the toiling masses who contribute in the upholding of the Indian and society, they are the despised and discriminated segment of the Indian population.

The assiduous attempt made by the Bharatiya Janata Party (BJP), the political face of the right wing forces, the Sangh Parivar, to amend the Constitution has reduced the iota of doubt that the Sangh Parivar respects Baba Saheb Ambedkar, the architect of Indian Constitution to say the least. For the last 50 years, the proponents of the upper caste monopoly could not digest the fact that a person from the Dalit community could be the main inspiration of the Constitution. There have been violent convulsions within them about this historical reality. But they are not to sit idle. On the one hand the Brahminical forces have constituted a Constitution Review Committee to introduce changes at will. On the other had, it is alleged that they have already worked out an alternative 'Constitution of Bharat'.

In this given context, it is not only the Constitution, the law of this land but justice itself is under severe threat. In this article an attempt is made to examine the dialogical approach utilized by Dr. Ambedkar in his examination of the Indian social order as well as his perception about a just social order. In the recent past there have been various attempts made to appropriate Ambedkar. I am not entering into this debate here.[2] I have tried to read Dr. Ambedkar's writings and speeches in today's context.

Injustice Inherent in Indian Society and Polity

A careful gleaning of the Indian society and polity unravels this fact that deprived and marginalized segments of the Indian population is subjected to institutionalized injustice. This is not a new revelation. Everyone from the ruling class to the 'least person' in the Indian society is acutely aware of this historical and social reality. While the institutional frameworks and structural adjustments benefit the ruling castes and classes, the poor and the downtrodden are structurally reduced to poverty and inhuman living. Former President, K.R. Narayanan, who has emerged as the conscience keeper of this country has echoed his view in a perceptive manner: "On this anniversary of our Republic we must resolve to complete the unfinished task of land reforms that we embarked upon years ago and empower the landless poor and the small farmers who have not got any benefits from the Green Revolution. Much of the poverty and unrest in rural India – the caste conflicts and economic violence – can be traced to gross injustice in the distribution of land and to some kind of counter-revolution that is taking place, holding up the implementation of land reforms and the snatching away to whatever benefits progressive legislation had bestowed upon the poor".[3]

At this juncture it is expedient to identify few major issues which have once again rendered institutional injustice to the fate of the Dalits and the downtrodden. It is significant to note that the Approach Paper to the Tenth Five-Year Plan states that the major objective of this plan is 'Growth, Equity and Sustainability'. The paper goes on to argue that "Although growth has strong direct poverty reducing effects, the frictions and rigidities in the Indian economy can make these processes less effective, and the Tenth Plan must therefore be formulated in a manner which explicitly addresses the need to ensure equity and social justice. There are several ways in which this can be achieved".[4] It is interesting to note that the masters of planning instead of pursuing the ideals of equity in real terms divert their whole intention to the regularly trodden path of shifting the priority from industry to agriculture and from agriculture to industry. Fifty-three years of independent India has witnessed this shadow boxing in terms of planned development. And thus social justice remained only a slogan.

One can also take into account the enduring debate on caste and race that is in the air in the Indian sub-continent. UN sponsored 'World Conference Against Racism, Racial Discrimination, Xenophobia and Related intolerance' held in Durban, South Africa from 31st August to 7th September 2001. Since this global conference was aimed at debating on the various forms of discrimination, the Dalit and human rights activists have raised the issue of caste discrimination at the international forum. This has distressed the upper castes and upper class of India in an unprecedented manner. The ruling class is harping on the fact that this attempt by the Dalit and human rights activists is equal to challenging the very sovereignty of the state.[5] The spokespersons of the dominant castes are crying aloud that caste discrimination is prevalent, but that does not call for taking it up in the international forum. There are some social scientists, who like in the past, are interested in engaging in the debate if caste is race or can casteism be equated with racism. This entire process has once again exposed the upper castes and upper classes with regard to their attitude and behaviour towards the Dalits. These limited incidents highlight injustices that are heaped upon the Dalits and the downtrodden even today.

Constitution, Law and Justice

Before we proceed to examine the perspective of Dr. Ambedkar on Constitution, law and justice, let us briefly spell out the meanings of these three concepts. The *Cambridge International Dictionary of English* defines constitution as a written document which forms the set of political principles by which a state or an organization is governed especially in relation to the rights of the people it governs. From the writings and speeches of Baba

Saheb one can discern three objectives in the Constitution of India. First, the Constitution was aimed at ensuring the building up of a new social order based on liberty, fraternity and equality; second, to protect the freedom of every individual from the onslaught of autocratic, arbitrary and repressive power, third, the Constitution of India was to safeguard the lives and interest of the depressed classes in a special way.

The *Cambridge International Dictionary of English* defines law as a rule, usually made by a government, that is used to order the way in which a society behaves, or the whole system of such rules. In common parlance, law is understood as the norms and regulations of a group or collectively which are supposed to guide the behaviour pattern of the entity. Often times, law is understood as an entity in itself. But the sociology of law proceeds with this assumption that law and legal institutions both affect and are affected by the social conditions that are around them. This also takes into consideration the social foundations of legality.

With regard to the question whether law is a vehicle of social change, legal sociology for the most part has viewed law as passive rather than active agent in social change. Laws 'respond' to new circumstances and pressures. However, especially in recent years the great social effects of social change have been too obvious to ignore. The question is no longer whether law is a significant vehicle of social change but rather how it so functions and what special problems arise. Further, legislation is the most obvious way of bringing political will to bear, for the purpose of effecting social change through law. Here, once again, comes the importance of the legislatures who are supposed to be innovative and are supposed to work for common good.[6]

Some of the scholars present several attributes associated with law. "Law is a complex whole which always includes social norms that regulate human behaviour. These norms are social in character, and they form a complex whole that is 'orderly'." The order is characteristically coercive and institutionalized. Law has a degree of effectiveness sufficient to maintain itself.[7] Ambedkar's penetrative reading into the Indian social order made him become acutely aware of the fact that the Indian social order was based on the law of higher beings and lower beings, superior castes and inferior castes, pure persons and impure persons. The Hindu, Brahminical order is based on the law of unequal stratification of individuals. Hence, Ambedkar's intuition and perception led him to the beliefs and the practices of Buddhism. He saw in Buddhism a clear option for the establishment of a social order based on the values of equality, individual dignity and freedom of human beings.

The *Cambridge International Dictionary of English* defines justice as the putting of the law into action. Two other interpretations also bring out the meaning of justice. First, miscarriage of justice. This refers to the fact that the law has been carried out wrongly. By this, it is meant that there is an appropriate way of enacting the legal provisions which are supported to result in the betterment of all citizens. Second, obstructing the course of justice. This expression refers to preventing the law being put into action. But this kind of perception appears to be a dead log.

In the earlier writings justice comprised the whole of virtue and complete conformity with the approved pattern of moral conduct. The *Bible* presents the following general perception of justice: (1) that a general standard of justice or righteousness may become too vague in outline and arbitrary in use without the specification that comes from definite rules; (2) that in order to be considered just, a system of ethical or legal ordinances requires not only a conceived authoritative command but also a conceived popular consent, acceptance or mutual covenant; (3) that justice imposes a duty to perform group and individual acts of social reparation, welfare, and assistance; (4) that justice comprises the functionally related principles of impartiality and probity in rendering judgement, reciprocity in inter-personal transactions and equality of elementary rights not only between members of diverse economic classes but also between nations and races; (5) that the emotional manifestation of justice consists in passionately abhoring all forms of appression exploitation and cruelty and its behavioural manifestation consists in denouncing and combatting them.[8]

Irrespective of various theoretical frameworks, common usage continues to treat 'justice' as denoting some of the greatest of human needs and worthiest of social enterprises. In common experience human beings turn to the vocabulary of justice when they confront real or imagined instances of injustice. The ethical and biological functions of justice become evident in 'the sense of injustice'. The sense of injustice is the equipment by which a human being discerns assault, recognizes oppression of another as a species of attack upon himself, and prepares a defence. In this perspective, 'justice' means the active process of preventing or remedying what would arouse the sense of injustice. Justice then is more than a static equilibrium or a quality of the human will; it is, as common usage has always hinted, an active process or agenda or enterprise. The meaning of the term comes alive whenever one confronts injustice and 'does' justice.[9]

Ambedkar and Nation-Building

For Ambedkar, nation-building and Constitutional enforcement went hand in hand. He maintained an extreme sense of optimism that the Constitution will enhance the space for nation-building. On the other hand he was also frightened of the consequences that if political participation alone was enacted without a concurrent social change, then political democracy will become deadening: On November 25th, 1949 he made a prophetic declaration. "My mind is full of the future of our country that I feel I ought to take this occasion to give expression to some of my reflection thereon. On 26th January 1950, India will be an independent country. What would happen to her independence? Will she maintain her independence or will she lose it again? It is this thought which fills me with anxiety".[10]

This prophetic expression of Baba Saheb has been proved by the ruling caste and class of this country. More than fifty years have gone by after obtaining independence. The political independence and the sovereignty of the Indian State have been upheld intact. But for more than 70 per cent of the population, freedom and the independence means little. Their life struggle continues unmitigated. But oppression and suppression of them goes on unabated.[11]

Dr. Ambedkar had foretold the deplorable state of affairs due to caste, class and political manipulations. "This anxiety is deepened by the realization of the fact that in addition to our old enemies in the forms of castes and creeds we are going to have many political parties with diverse and opposing political creeds. Will the Indians place the country above their creed or will they place creed above the country? I do not know. But this much is certain that if the parties place creed above country our independence will be put in jeopardy second time and probably lost forever. This eventuality we must all resolutely guard against. We must be determined to defend our independence with the last drop of our blood".[12]

Dr. Ambedkar did not engage in shadow boxing about the 'impending' threat to the national sovereignty or did not figure out any 'foreign hand' in all the ills affecting the state and the society. The present political dispensation is busy projecting imminent threat to national sovereignty. It employs this trick to direct the national economy from productive sectors to consumption sector. For instance, in the last budget over Rs. 60,000 crore have been allotted for defence. But for a fundamental issue like land reform enactment it has allotted only one crore rupees.[13] Baba Saheb was well aware of the fact that in a socially skewed society, personal and political interest will over weigh against societal and national interest.

With the given data available to him Dr. Ambedkar made perspicacious and penetrating analysis of the Indian society. He cautioned his fellow citizens that "we must begin by acknowledging the fact that there is absence of two things in Indian society. One of these is equality. On the social plane, we have in India a society based on the principle of graded inequality which means elevation for some and degradation for others, on the economic plane, we have society in which there are some who have immense wealth as against many who live in abject poverty".[14]

Dr. Ambedkar goes on to maintain, "The second thing we are wanting in is recognition of the principle of fraternity... a sense of common brotherhood of all Indians... How long shall we continue to deny equality in our social and economic life? ... We must remove this contradiction at the earliest possible moment or else those who suffer from inequality will blow up the structure of political democracy which this assembly has so laboriously built up".[15] In all his writings and speeches Ambedkar did not speak of putting one social group against the other. At times he is accused of not cleansing anger that arose out of caste discrimination but is charged with stoking anger like a fire. But he warned the Indian state and society that if the ruling dispensation thought that by providing political participation they could quell the aspirations of the Dalits and the downtrodden, they are in for a historical surprise.

The Dialectics of Justice

Dr. Ambedkar engaged in an extensive discourse on the nature of social order. While propounding the basic principles of a just social order he also spelt out his unrivaled understanding of liberty, fraternity and equality. But the seminal significance of his perceptions was that they were not the product of armchair philosophy. His long drawn-out discourses emanated from the agony of the depressed masses in general and his anguish in particular. In that sense he was a real *karmayogi*, who not only propounded theories of social change but engaged in changing the very foundations of Indian social order.

Baba Saheb began his debate by raising the question "What is the character of Hindu social order? Is it a free social order?" In his analysis of the salient features of Hindu social order, Baba Saheb gave one of his perceptive analysis of the fundamental tenets of social order. He draws his arguments from the essentials of French Revolution and the Gospel traditions and goes on to spell out the foundations of a skewed Indian social order. The Marxian tradition of dialectics also enhanced his deliberations. According to Ambedkar there are two fundamental tenets of any social order. "The first is that the individual is an end in himself and that the aim and object of society is the growth of the individual and the development of the personality. Society is not above the individual and if the individual has to subordinate himself to society, it is because such subordination is for his betterment and only to the extent necessary." From years of experience within the Hindu fold where he realized that an individual gets subsumed within the caste ethos of collectivity, Ambedkar continued to demand the liberty and the freedom of the individual. He was intensely aware of the fact that the depressed and the deprived masses will be continuously demanded to sacrifice even the limited resources and space they have for their survival. Hence, he argued for individual freedom. But he goes on to maintain that any societal and national enterprise is appropriate only to the extent the individual can obtain the fullness of his/her life. "The second essential is that the terms of associated life between members of the society must be regarded by consideration founded on liberty, equality and fraternity".[16]

Dr. Ambedkar at length quotes the arguments of Beard to analyse the basic features of equality and in extension he talks of moral equality. According to Beard equality means 'exactly the same or equivalent in measure, amount, number, degree, value or quality'. But there are critics who state that in physical strength, talents, and wealth, human beings are not equal. The declaration of independence does not assert that all men are equal; it proclaims that they are 'crated' equal. Beard goes on to argue that 'moral equality' is asserted against inequalities in physical strength, talents, industry, and wealth. It denied that superior physical strength has a moral right to kill, eat, or oppress human beings merely because it is superior.

Dr. Ambedkar's views on fraternity also needs to be examined at this stage. For Dr. Ambedkar "Fraternity is the name for the disposition of an individual to treat men as the object of reverence and love and the desire to be in unity with his fellow beings". To explicitate his point of view Baba Saheb quotes from the Bible: "There is neither Jew nor Greek, there is neither slave nor free, there is neither male nor female, for you are all one in Christ Jesus".[17] Dr. Ambedkar goes on to argue that fraternity strengthens social ideals and gives to each individual a stronger personal interest in practically consulting the welfare of the others. It leads him to identify his feelings more and more with their good, or at least with an even greater degree of practical consideration for it. The good of others becomes to him a thing naturally and necessarily to be attended to like any of the physical conditions of our existence. "For a person in whom social feelings is not developed cannot but bring himself to think of the rest of his fellow-beings as rivals struggling with him for the means of happiness when he must endeavour to defeat in order that he may succeed in himself."

Here once again one can discern fundamentally contradictory perception in the view of Ambedkar and the principles of Brahminical social order. For him every person is worthy of reverence by the very fact of he or she being a human being. This sense of respect and reverence inherently provides space for filial relationship between human beings. These in turn ensure and enhance liberty and equal status of individuals, which ultimately result in the building up of a just social order.

Dr. Ambedkar in the same vein spells out the features of liberty and also examines at length its importance for a free social order. According to him liberty falls under two categories. The first one is civil liberty. For Ambedkar civil liberty refers to (i) liberty of movement which is another name for freedom from arrest without due process of law, (ii) liberty of speech (which of course includes liberty of thought, liberty of reading, writing and discussion) and (iii) liberty of action.

In Dr. Ambedkar's perspective, liberty of movement is fundamental and also most essential. Liberty of speech or freedom of opinion is necessary for intellectual, moral, political and social progress. He warns that where freedom of expression is absent, the status quo becomes stereotyped and all originality even the most necessary, is discouraged. According to Dr. Ambedkar, liberty of action means doing what one likes to do. He further argues that liberty of action means effective power to do specific things. There is no freedom where there are no means of taking advantage of it. *Real liberty of action exists only where exploitation has been annihilated, where no suppression of one class by another exists, where there is no unemployment, no poverty and where a person is free from the fear of losing his job, his home and his food as a consequence of his action* (emphasis added)[18].

The second class of liberty according to Ambedkar is political liberty. Political liberty consists in the right of the individual to share in the framing of laws and in the making and unmaking of governments. Governments are instituted for securing to men certain unalienable rights such as life, liberty and pursuit of happiness. Government must, therefore, derive its powers from those whose rights is charged with the duty to protect. This is what is meant when it is said that the existence power and authority of the government must be derived from the consent of the governed. Political liberty is really a deduction from the principle of human personality and equality. For it implies that all political authority is derived from the people, that the people are capable of directing and controlling their public as well as private lives to ends determined by themselves and by none else.

Dr. Ambedkar concludes his argument stating that these two tenets of a free social order are integrally connected. They are inseverable and insufferable. Once the first tenet is admitted, the second tenet automatically follows. Once the sacredness of human personality is admitted the necessity of liberty, equality and fraternity must also be admitted as the proper climate for the development of personality.

Dr. Ambedkar having examined the importance of the three pillars of social order in general goes on to expose the place and role of these three principles in the Indian social order. He conducts this exercise by raising penetrating questions about the tenets of Indian social order. 'Does the Hindu social order recognize the individual? Does it recognize the distinctiveness his moral responsibility? Does it recognize him as an end in himself, as a subject not merely of disabilities but also of rights even against the State? Ultimately, does the Hindu social order recognize the three tenets – liberty, equality and fraternity – of a social order.

Dr. Ambedkar further engages himself in the exploration of the social fact that the Hindu social order does not recognize the individual as a centre of social purpose. For the Hindu social order is based primarily on class or *varna* and not on individuals. The Hindu social order recognizes only five classes, that is the Brahmins, the Kshatriyas, the Vaishyas, the Shudras and the Untouchables. In the Hindu social structure, the individuals Brahmin or Shudra or the untouchables are not taken seriously. Even the family is not regarded by the Hindu social order as the unit of society except for the purposes of marriage and inheritance. The unit of Hindu society is the class or Varna. Here there is no room for individual merit and no consideration of individual justice. If the individual has a privilege, it is not because it is due to him personally as the privilege goes with the class, and if he is found to enjoy it, it is because he belongs to that class. Contrawise, if an individuals is suffering from a wrong, it is not because he by his conduct deserves it. The disability is the disability imposed upon the class and if he is found to be labouring under it, it is because he belongs to that class.

Baba Saheb goes on to explore this fact if Hindu social order regards fraternity. In search for an answer he compares the different religious traditions about origin of human species. He argues that all the religions believe that men are created by God. The Hindu religious traditions also believes that men are created by God. But they also believe that 'God created different men from different parts of his divine body'. This is the most important and more fundamental principle for the Hindus, argues Ambedkar.

According to Dr. Ambedkar, this belief reinstates two inter-related beliefs and practices. Since each class or unit or caste members are born from different parts of the body, one unit or class or caste is not the keeper of the other or well-wisher of the other. In extension it can be stated that one unit, class or caste can even be inimical to the other.

The second most crucial aspect of this belief is that since different classes, units or castes were created from different parts of the divine body, it must be divine will that they should remain separated and distinct. Dr. Ambedkar argues that it is this belief which has created in the Hindu an instinct to be different, to be separated and to be distinct from the rest of the fellow Hindus. Ambedkar quotes the *Manu Smriti* to establish his point about this distinction and separation. "In the eight year after conception, one should perform the initiation (*Upanayan*) of a Brahmin, in the eleventh year of a Kshatriya but in the twelfth that of Vaishya" (*Manu Smriti II, 36*). This religious injunction on the one hand establishes distinction between different castes and on the other, it also denied this religious rite to the *Shudras* and the untouchables.

Dr. Ambedkar goes on to present examples from various authors and finally maintains this view that the guiding principles between different castes is 'be separate', 'do not inter-marry', 'do not interdine' and 'do not touch'. Once he raises a central question, "in such a separation and distinction what fraternity can be present?" He states that far from working in a spirit of fraternity the mutual relations of castes are fratricidal. It can be stated without any exaggeration that caste has been and is the source and sustaining power of conflict in Indian society. Hence, Dr. Ambedkar rules out any possibility of fraternity existing in the Indian social order.

In the same vein Baba Saheb argues that the principle of equality is also alien to Brahminical social structure since, equality of all creation is a doctrine which is repugnant to the Hindu system. Though the Hindu traditions perceive all human beings as children of *Prajapti*, but since they were created from different parts of the body they are different. In this regard Dr. Ambedkar presents one of the powerful critiques to the Hindu social order: "the Hindu social order is indifferent to the doctrine of equality. It is equally indifferent to it as an ethical principle. It refuses to recognize that men no matter how profoundly they differ as individuals in capacity and character, are equally entitled as human beings to consideration and respect and that the well-being of a society is likely to be increased if it so plans its organization that, whether their powers are great or small, all its members may be equally enabled to make the best of such powers as they possess. It will not allow equality of circumstances, institutions and manner of life. It is against equalitarian temple".[19]

Dr. Ambedkar does not limit his discourse to these facts alone. He proceeds further to examine the principles on which the Hindu social order is constructed. Firstly, it is founded on graded inequality. Secondly, it is established on the principle of fixity of occupations for each class and continuance thereof by heredity. And finally it is brought into existence on the principle of fixation of people within their respective classes.

By demonstrating carefully the socio-historical fact that the Brahminical social order is not based on liberty, fraternity and equality, Dr. Ambedkar has once again upheld this truth that justice can never be part of the Hindu social order. On the other hand by arguing that the Hindu social order is founded on graded inequality, fixity of place and role he has established the social fact that injustice is inherent to the Hindu social order. This is the seminal contribution of Dr. Ambedkar to the understanding of Indian social order in general and the *varna* system in particular. Hence, he called for the annihilation of caste system and not reforms within the caste system.

It is in the fitness of the things to conclude this brief presentation with the immense intuition of Dr. Ambedkar:

> How to bring about the reform of the Hindu social order? How to abolish caste?... To agitate for and to organize inter-caste dinners and inter-caste marriages is like forced feeding brought about by artificial means. Make every man and woman free from the thralldom to the *Shastras*, cleanse their minds of the pernicious notions founded on the *Shastras*, and he or she will inter-dine and inter-marry, without your telling him or her to do so... you must make efforts to uproot caste.[20]

Fifty-three years of independence has proved correct the social facts propounded by Dr. Ambedkar. Even the well thought out Constitution has evaded justice to the Dalits and the downtrodden, but injustice has become the only birth right of these deprived masses. But their search for a just social order not only for themselves but for the entire Indian sub-continent will prove the beliefs and the practices of Baba Saheb that in the emancipation of the Dalits lies the liberation of the entire Indian social order.

Notes

1. Consultation Paper on Pace of Socio-Economic Change under the Constitution. National Commission to Review the Working of the Constitution. First Draft, 2001, p. 8.
2. Gopal Guru, Appropriating Ambedkar, *Economic and Political Weekly*, July 6-13, 1991, p. 1697.

3. K.R. Narayanan, former President of India. Excerpts from the Presidential speech broadcast on January 25, 1998.
4. Approach Paper to Tenth Five-Year Plan, Planning Commission, Government of India, p. 4.
5. For more details, see Prakash Louis, Casteism is Horrendous than Racism: Durban and Dalit Discourse, Indian Social Institute, New Delhi 2001.
6. *International Encyclopedia of the Social Sciences*, The Macmillan Company and the Free Press, New York, Vol. 9, p. 50-77.
7. Ibid. p. 73.
8. *International Encyclopedia of the Social Sciences*, The Macmillan Company and The Free Press, New York, Vol. 7 and 8, p. 342.
9. Ibid, p. 346.
10. *Dr. Baba Saheb Ambedkar Writings and Speeches*, Vol. XIII, Education Department, Government of Maharashtra, 1987, p. 1213.
11. For more details, see Prakash Louis, *Dalit Human Rights are for Violation: State of Human Rights in India 2000*, Indian Social Institute, New Delhi 2001, p. 33-40. Also refer to Scheduled Caste and Scheduled Tribes Commission Reports.
12. *Dr. Baba Saheb Ambedkar Writing and Speeches*, Vol. XIII, Education Department, Government of Maharashtra, 1987, p. 1213.
13. Even a cursory glance at the budgetary allocation for social sector over the years unravels the fact that the government has been steadily abdicating its responsibilities slowly and steadily and thus has driven the deprived communities to further starvation and deprivation.
14. Ibid.
15. Ibid.
16. Ibid., Vol. III, p. 95.
17. Letter of St. Paul to the Galatians 3: 28, *The Holy Bible.*
18. *Dr. Baba Saheb Ambedkar Writing and Speeches*, Vol. XIII, Education Department, Government of Maharashtra, 1987, p. 98.
19. Ibid, p. 106.
20. B. R. Ambedkar, *Annihilation of Caste*, Bheem Patrika Publications, Punjab, 1982.

11

Constitutional Justice

Ambedkar's Perspective

D.S. PRAKASA RAO

Dr. B.R. Ambedkar was an educationist, economist, advocate and administrator. He was a social reformer, political thinker, parliamentarian and constitutionalist of high order. Indeed, he was a rare combination of constitutional statesman and creative iconoclast. As described by justice Krishna Iyer he was explosive insider and expropriated Mahr, promethean humanist, a passionate rebel fighting against feudal casteism and dehumanization in life as crystalized in India by Hindu orthodoxy's pathological devotion and fidelity to the fundamentalist dogma of caste and *chathurvarna* as an inexorable and exclusive determinant of a person's family, occupational and social status and of all the attendant incidents and disabilities attached to that status which was an outrageous affront to human dignity and an unacceptable negation of the autonomy of the individual and his legitimate claim to make rational choice in exercise of his personal freedom in matters, personal or social, which involves the creative use of one's faculties for the free development and full expression of one's personality.

The epic battle that he waged for the liberation of the oppressed humanity of the Dalits and Depressed Classes, whose undisputed leader and articulate spokesman he was, from the stranglehold and appalling in humanity of the canker of casteism and the associated evil of untouchability will go down in human history as a crusader's struggle, without a parallel, for the recognition of the universal right to be human and of the principle of one-man-one value as the most basic and incontestable foundation for civilized intercourse between humans.[1]

Dr. B.R. Ambedkar's monumental contribution to our national jurisprudence is his leading role as the chairman of the Drafting Committee of the Constituent Assembly of India. As rightly pointed out by N.R. Madhava Menon, so long as Indian constitution lives and guides the destiny of nearly a fifth of human race in the subcontinent, the name and fame of Dr. B.R. Ambedkar will continue to reverberate and inspire law makers towards structuring a social order committed to equality dignity and social justice.[2]

Ambedkar's eternal search for knowledge, his incredible industry and his unflinching aim with which he raised himself from dust to doyen, from the life of a social leper to the position of a constitution maker, and his heroic struggles for raising the downtrodden to human dignity will constitute a golden chapter in the history of this nation and in the history of human freedom as well. As Dhananjay Keer strongly feels India must learn to understand his life, character and mission and know him as he is and not as he is distorted by his enemies or deified by his devotees.[3]

Any Indian with unprejudiced eyes will have little difficulty in realizing that the impartial understanding of his life and message gives us an idea that Ambedkarism, consisting of the message of Dr. B.R. Ambedkar through his political, economic and social ideology is more relevant today in India than ever before.

An attempt is made in this paper to understand Ambedkar as Constitutionalist (Upendra Baxi's 6th Ambedkar)[4] and Constitutional justice in Ambedkar's perspective containing justice in general social justice in particular, Equality,

Fraternity, Liberty, Constitutionalism, Social Democracy, Constitutional Morality as they are very much relevant today.

Let us first assimilate the social, political, legal and economic theories of Dr. B.R. Ambedkar and their impact on constitution making. After having attained the compromising path between his confrontation approach and Gandhian assimilation approach, he made a sincere attempt to accommodate and incorporate all the conflicting interests in the constitution of India.

Constitutionalism and Constitutional Morality: Ambedkar's Perspective

A constitution means a document having a special legal sanctity which sets the framework and the principle functions of the organs of the government of a state and declares the principles governing the operation of those organs. The law of the constitution of a country seeks to establish the fundamental organs of government and administration, lays down their structure, composition, powers and principal functions, defines the inter-relationship of one organ with another and regulates the relationship between the citizen and the state, more particularly the political relationship. All constitutions are the heirs of the past as well as the testators of the future and a constitution is a creature of social circumstances and conditions, though after coming into being it controls its own creator and the evolution and development of constitutional law can be safely discovered from the hidden laws of the development of the society. It is a meta-legal document, i.e., a political, social and economic document; therefore the structure of the constitution would reflect the social realities in the society and thereby considered as having a basic structure, indelible profile and essential lifestyle. The basic constitutional values are fundamentally similar in all democracies.

A country may have a constitution without having constitutionalism, for the latter concept denotes that a constitution has within itself some mechanism to control governmental powers. Constitutionalism is the antithesis of arbitrary power. One of the significant ways in which constitutionalism may be promoted is to have entrenched rights and liberties for the people.

The constitution aims at the creation of new legal norms, social philosophy and economic values which are to be effected by striking synthesis, harmony and fundamental adjustment between individual rights and social interests to achieve the desired community goals.

The dialectics of law and society in India has been determined by the historical experience during the passage from colonialism to nationalism. In this process both legal and social systems have evolved. Indian experience can be viewed as conflict resulting from a search for a balance between the use of law by elite for purposes of domination and the use of law to moderate elite domination by providing avenues of participation for the disadvantaged.

Our own time has been burgeoning 'Constitutional Justice' which has in a sense combined the forms of legal justice and the substance of natural justice. Desirous of protecting the permanent will, rather than the temporary whims, states have reasserted higher law principles through written constitution. Thus, there has been a synthesis of three separate concepts – the supremacy of certain higher principles, the need to put even the higher law in written form, and the employment of judiciary as a tool for enforcing the constitution against ordinary legislation. When the positivised higher law principles were sought to be defeated by means of constitutional amendments, the least dangerous branch has thus entered into the arena by performing its role as sentinel on the qui vive to restore the higher law principles.[5]

Constitutional Morality: Ambedkar's Perspective

Constitutional morality would mean an effective coordination between conflicting interests of different people and the administrative cooperation to resolve them amicably without any confrontation amongst the various groups working for the realization of their ends at any cost. For Ambedkar, moral fabric of the society, governed as well as the governance must be strong. In other words, public conscience, moral order and constitutional morality - ethics of politicians, that constitute the core of policy making, must be very sound and strong if democracy is to survive for long period of progress and prosperity for the common people.[6]

Dr. B.R. Ambedkar observed in the Constituent Assembly as follows:

> We must begin by acknowledging the fact that there is a complete absence of two things in Indian Society. One of these is equality. On the social plans we have in India a society based on the principle of graded inequality which means elevation for some and degradation for others. On the economic plans, we have a society in which there are some who have immense wealth as against many who live in abject poverty. On the 26th of January, we are going to enter into a life of contradictions. In politics, we will have equality and in social and economic life we will have inequality. In politics we will be recognizing the principle of one man vote one value. In our social and economic life we shall by reason of our social and economic structure, continue to deny the principle of one man one vote one value. How long shall we continue to live this life of contradictions? How long shall we continue to deny equality in our social and economic life? If we continue to deny it for long, we must remove this contradiction at the earliest possible moment or else those who suffer from inequality will blow up the structure of political democracy which this Assembly has so laboriously built up.

In recent times the emerging constitutional teleology also articulated as a quest for substantive values gave rise to an alternative system, viz., security diversity solidarity. Thus, there was a shift of emphasis from liberty, equality and fraternity to substantive principles of domestic peace and minimum of societal security, tolerance and promotion of diversity as well as social justice, supporting the legitimate political symbolism to human rights.

Viewed in this perspective the Indian Constitution drafted in the first half of this century fulfils the aspirations of the Indian people and will be an exemplary model for the world constitutionalism of 21st century with an excellent alchemical amalgam of its preambular goals of justice, liberty and equality guaranteeing fundamental rights through Part III and assuring – We, the people of India positive content of 21st century 'leit motif' security, diversity and solidarity.

Ambedkar's Social Theory and its Impact on Constitutional Philosophy

A constitution can perform many functions in a modern state. One of these tasks is to serve as a deposit for a cluster of a society's fundamental political values. A constitution can reflect these values in substantive ways by guaranteeing fundamental rights and in procedural ways by providing remedies. It also reflects society's basic values in 'allocative ways'. It mirrors basic values about who shall govern and in what direction. In addition to structuring and allocating and limiting power, a constitution performs 'aspirational goals'. Through its institutional arrangements and commandments, the constitution reflects a particular vision of a good and achievable community life.

While constitution is the process by which the government's action is effectively restrained and is understood as the process of the function of which is not only to organize but to restrain. Constitutionalism refers to limits on majority decisions, more specifically to limits that are in some sense self-imposed. Constitutionalism is both an end and means. It is both value free and value loaded. It is of both normative and empirical dimensions. It is antithesis of arbitrary power, absolute government and authoritarian form of government. It promotes accountability, responsibility and limited government.

Ambedkar gave a call to all downtrodden people: *Educate, Organize* and *Agitate* – the constitutional path for social justice and social order. He assessed the value and worth of any society in terms of its potential for stability/order, on the one hand, and on the other, dynamism and progress. Ultimately, this kind of social theory can be traced back to Western social theorists of nineteenth century – John Stuart Mill and Herbert Spencer.

Ambedkar's Social Theory was moulded by Dr. Ambedkar's personal experience of being an untouchable in his early life, and by his western education. This social thought ultimately led him to emerge as the champion of the oppressed. Because of his early sufferings due to the practice of untouchability, he determined to fight against the social evil which was at last abolished through the Constitution of India in whose drafting he played a significant role. Great persons like Budha, Phooley, Ranade, John Dewey and J.S. Mill influenced Dr. Ambedkar's social thought.

Ambedkar himself explicitly says, "if you ask me, my ideal would be a society based on Liberty, Equality and Fraternity".[7] He also defends these ideals by meeting the objections raised against them. On fraternity, he argues that an ideal society involves maximum facilities for communication between individuals and groups, and this is best achieved by fraternity. But what is fraternity? His answer is that "it is only another name for democracy". Democracy is necessary to generate what he calls "social-end osmosis" by which he means a social system that provides for "varied and free points of contact with other modes of association". And he states its attitude of respect and reverence towards fellowmen.[8]

Dr. Ambedkar's way of thinking was characterized by Dr. Jatav as social humanism. It contained following principles: (1) equality among human beings; (2) every human being as an end in himself; (3) right of every human being to social, economic, political and religious freedom; (4) to make every human being free from want and fear; (5) to maintain liberty, equality, fraternity, and to strive to secure redemption from oppression and exploitation of man by man, of class by class, and of nation by nation; (6) to stand for a democratic society under a parliamentary system of government; (7) to believe in non-violence as an instrument of social change and adopt peaceful and persuasive methods to avoid class conflicts and the possibility of civil war; (8) to avoid any 'ism' or any theory or dogma in its extreme aspect; (9) need for spiritual discipline; and (10) firm foundation of universal love, equality and human brotherhood that the Budha taught.[9]

Thus, his views are still thought provoking and continue to give inspiration to the people of India.

The Constitution of India is a very effective instrument in India to bring social change. It promotes integrity, egalitarian society, secularism, welfare society and a just social order. It discourages casteism, communalism and a feudalistic nature of society. It provides effective mechanism to translate its goals into reality. It is the duty of the people in general, the people who are called to work upon it, may be legislators, administrators judges in particular to commit themselves to constitutionalism for a better tomorrow.

Dr. Ambedkar and Equality, Social Justice and Dynamics of Indian Polity

Dr. Ambedkar asserts that it is innocent to say that Fundamental Rights are absolute and non-Fundamental Rights are not absolute. The non-Fundamental Rights are created by agreement between parties while Fundamental Rights are the gift of law. Fundamental Rights cannot be absolute. The Constitution itself permits the state directly to impose limitations instead of depending upon Supreme Court to come to the rescue of parliament by invoking police power.

Dr. Ambedkar on Equality and Social Justice

All social primary goods – liberty and opportunity, income and wealth and the basis of respect are to be distributed equally. Unless, an unequal distribution of any or all of these goods is the advantage of the least favour. To be more precise Rawls' *Concept of Justice*[10] is expressed in the following two principles (1) Each person is to have an equal right to the most extensive basic liberty for others; (2) Social and economic inequalities are to be arranged so that they are both (a) to the greatest benefit of the least advantaged, and (b) attached to the offices and positions opened to all under condition of fair equality of opportunity. This is nothing but reflexive equilibrium, which is the culmination of the human rights history. The human rights history is the history of struggles of different people in the society for justice. In the light of the above Rawls' theory of justice, one can understand the real sprit of human rights in India or elsewhere.

Robert Nisbet, an American writer, distinguishes between equality of opportunity and equality of result or condition. Equality of opportunity is of course the classical or traditional, liberal view of equality. It recognizes that individuals have unequal talents and endowments, but provides for maximum of opportunity to achieve realizing that individuals will achieve unequally. But this is consistent with Benthamite Utilitarianism. Equality of result is the more radical formulation and it is closer to contemporary liberal creed. It is an ascendant philosophy of reform, not a meekish acceptance of a sanctioned status quo. In its extreme form, however, it may not be compatible with the liberal democratic form of government. Even as Prof. Dworkin develops a conception of equality as a basis for a theory of political morality which would significantly restrict government's ability to interfere with the preferred liberties of the citizen, Rawls, who shares the distrust of Dworkin of unreconstructed utilitarianism, develops a theory of distributive justice keeping the priority of equality as the centerpiece in his notion of justice as "fairness".[11]

Dr. Ambedkar also understood the concept of justice and equality in Indian context. He says, "We must remove the contradiction (equality in politics and inequality in social and economics life) at the earliest possible moment or else those who suffer from inequality will blow up the structure of political democracy which this Assembly has so laboriously built up. What Ambedkar did not realize was that it was the advantaged who were going to abuse the constitution (without any sense of what he called fraternity) so thoroughly and completely that it would become wholly unrecognizable in its reflective existence of the pathology of its use. His fight was against the cruel forces of the society. Although a revolutionary, he had also suffered at the hands of revolution.

Ambedkar never isolated the issue of untouchability from the core question of caste system. Inspite of varied nature of his writings, we do find a central theme in his thinking around which his entire politics was also woven. He supported parliamentary democracy. His overall faith in constitutionalism, his loyalty to law and western jurisprudence, insisting on individual freedom in fact suggest a liberal imbalance. He was aware of the tension between individualism and collective good. He sought to resolve this in the framework of Buddhism.

In his '*Dharma*' he sought to reconcile democratic values with socialist values. The conflict between liberal and socialist values appears again and again in his thinking. He rejected outright the 'atomistic' individualism of liberalism but subscribed to the ideas of dignity of the individual and individual freedoms.

In one of his speeches on the All India Radio, Dr. Ambedkar categorically said that "positively, my sole philosophy may be said to be inspired in three words: liberty, equality and fraternity. Let one say that I have not – I have derived them from the teachings of my master, the Budha".

The castes are anti-national. They generate jealousy and antipathy. We must overcome all this to make our nation a reality, for fraternity can be a fact only when there is a nation.

Essential Holifeldian juristic strategy was to innovate jural relations – depressed classes have a right and state a duty to eradicate obdurate discrimination practices in civil society were under a liability to have their cultural practices redefined. The constitutional articulation of Ambedkar is remarkable in that it, in a chapter on Fundamentals Rights, creates specific offences and that the rights themselves are limitations on the power of civil society rather than that of the state (Art. 17, 23).

He understood the problems of Minorities in the following words. In this country both minorities and majorities have favoured a wrong path. It is wrong for the majorities to deny existence of minorities. It is equally wrong for the minorities to perpetuate themselves. They should merge some day into one. Minorities have loyally accepted to realize its duty not to discriminate against minorities.

Fraternity creates an inner force which pushes different sections into unity. The term 'Maitri' used by him encompasses the meaning of fraternity. Love for living beings and empathy/communion with respect to human beings are the hallmarks of fraternity.

He considered functional opposition and free and fair elections to be essential pillars of parliamentary democracy. Realizing the major weakness of parliamentary democracy, viz., slowness to respond to the demands of socio-economic change and equality, he strongly pleaded for a vigilant public opinion, effective implication of laws and responsible executive, committed legislatures and impartial judiciary. Constitution as an instrument of social engineering, while destroying old inequalities should not create new inequalities. The application of compensatory discrimination has to be gradually individualized. To leave inequality between class and class, between sex and sex, which is the soul of Hindu society, untouched and go on making legislation relating to economic problems is to make the constitution a farce and to build a place on a dung heap.

Implementation of Human Rights through Constitutional Culture: Recent Indian Experience

The constitution confers on the individual certain basic rights enforceable against the state. It can perhaps best be described as a document which, while upholding and protecting individual interest in the form of fundamental rights guaranteed against the state, envisages a positive role for it in ensuring realization of these basic rights by every individual. In other words, the fact that an individual has a right would mean the state has a duty not to interfere with it. This can be best explained in terms of Rawls' First principle of justice that each person is to have an equal right to the most extensive, total system of equal basic liberties compatible with a similar system of liberties for all.

As a result of the recognition of the need of balancing conflicting claims, the notion of rights and equality in rights has been slowly extended from the political to the economic and social spheres. This can be seen in the recognition of the right to the minimum conditions of a decent life embodied in legislation fixing minimum wage rates, in the various provisions for old age, sickness and unemployment and in the extension of opportunities for education. These measures involve a fundamental departure. They involve a repudiation of the charge so often levelled against the collectivist or socialist trend in liberal thought that it sacrifices liberty for equality. The use of the public resources or public power to assure a greater diffusion of educational opportunities to control and eliminate disease, to improve conditions of work, to abolish slums, no doubt means an interference with the liberty of some individuals, but it tends on the whole to maximize liberty.

What social liberalism has been concerned to maintain is that the principle of equal freedom must be taken more seriously than was done by the individualists, and the power of the state may be rightly used to reduce or remove arbitrary inequalities, and to ensure that the common resources should not be employed for selfish ends, but for the general well-being.[12]

Human Rights Jurisprudence: Problems and Prospects

As Justice Krishna Iyer rightly pointed out we live in an age when a new world legal order is blossoming. The universal declaration of Human Rights, the Great Covenants, the many conventions and other United Nations resolutions have woven a garment of human rights, social justice, defence of dignity and cultural development, not merely for individuals but also for homogeneous groups, communities and minorities. Alas, alongside of these advancing frontiers of humanist jurisprudence is the massive invasion, even annihilation of those very rights and claims to economic and social justice. State terrorism is a growing menace. Mini-wars and neo-imperialist, manoeuvres are proliferating.[13]

No doubt the recent teleological approach of Indian Supreme Court towards fundamental rights particularly in post-Maneka scenario[14] gave impetus to contemporary international human rights and constitutional protection of individual liberty. The protection extended from abuse of official power to official neglect is well demonstrated in the expansion of constitutional remedies, i.e., the compensation through writs, public interest litigation and the dynamics of the concept of State. The Judicial Activism in India reaches its high peak in protecting the constitutional spirit.

Here Ambedkar's views on human rights are worth quoting. A fertile human rights jurisprudence cannot avert Ambedkar's prophecy. The texts were born from, and produced some significant interventions by state and society in defence of human rights until they reach the hard rock of social reality on which so much of India's development is founded. Greed for oneself has overtaken mutual respect and concern for others. Ambedkar's hope lay in Indian society creating a sense of fraternity which may, perforce, find itself in the subaltern struggles of the oppressed was singularly absent in the highly individuated plans of the government which made atomistic individuals (and sometime their families) the beneficiaries of the programmatic concern of state planning. It is also increasingly missing from civil society. The poor are forced to fight and compete with each other. Capacity has acquitted that dimension of a social virtue in a society which had learnt to respect consequential dividends more than issues of togetherness and moral equity. Not only is there "no senses of public spirit except at a Xenophobic level", there is not even the kind of minimal honesty ascribes, some kind of special status of the rule of law or a willingness to abide by the rules. Like everything else in India the rules are up for grabs. Such as it is, the commitment to human rights lies amongst this debris – enmeshed in words, insufficiently refined in its articulations, unsupported by the social and political will of a large part of society (except in the struggle of those who fight back and their benefactors) and generally ineffectual in its capacity to honour its aims.

Curbing Challenges to Constitutional Fundamentals: The Real Tribute to Ambedkarism

The constitution of a country is the expression of the will of the people to govern themselves. It reflects the peoples aspirations. In any country the constitution is the fundamental law of the land. It is a living law. In India, at the time of making the constitution in mid-20th century after taking the advantage of the experience of various other constitutions, the constitutional makers prepared a best constitution suitable to the prevailing circumstances of the country. The Indian Constitution is tested through times. Even though the challenges were there to the very existence of the constitution in the past, it was proved successful in facing the challenges. But new challenges are developing often and some challenges posed a problem even for the survival of the country and the constitution. The 50 years constitutional working experience provides us an opportunity to understand these challenges in the past and present as impediment of achieving the constitutional goals. How far the goals were achieved even against the challenges and what are the possible solutions to make the present constitutional system more effective are to be examined.

Some have the opinion that the constitution of India is a great failure in curbing the challenges. But it is not true. If at all any failure is there, it is the failure of the people who are called to work upon the constitution. Maybe the legislators, judges, executives or the people at large in cultivating the true democratic spirit.[15]

The constitution aims at the creation of new legal norms, social philosophy and economic values which are to be effected by striking synthesis, harmony and fundamental adjustment between individual rights and social interests to achieve the desired community goals.

The dialectics of law and society in India has been determined by the historical experience during the passage from colonialism to nationalism. In this process both legal and social systems have evolved. Indian experience can be viewed as a conflict resulting from a search for a balance between the use of law by elite for purposes of domination and the use of law to moderate elite domination by providing avenues of participation for the disadvantaged.

Our experience in parliamentary government under the present constitution has been the subject of examination in the recent past mostly at the hands of politicians, power brokers, power groups and elite sections of society. Our complex plural society based with problems of mass poverty, colossal illiteracy and long periods of socio-cultural exploitation reached an intolerable state of affairs. The system may be called upon to respond or be replaced.

An activist state is one which takes interest in all forms of the activities of their subject sometimes leading to undue interference. Presently, most of the countries are very conscious of the crises of ingovernability. To adopt to the new structure of the societies, governments have chosen to de-legalize and deregulate and often transfer most of the states dominant sphere to the private. The old sovereign states shrink largely in the process of regionalization as well as globalization. These in total give a picture of diminishing state. What we should learn from this emancipated paradigm shift at the beginning of millennium, especially developing countries endeavouring to achieve better levels of economic and political living without repeating the whole dialectic process?

While the state in a liberal democracy is limited to the role of a faithful night watcher, its counterpart in a social democracy is expected to be an omnipotent caretaker, at best from credit to grave.

India is bringing about fundamental changes in the economic field aiming at globalization through liberalized economic policies. Free market has been accepted as the model in India. Foreign capital and multinationals are not only welcome but are being positively induced to participate in a big way in the economic resurgence of India. However, the free market economy which has bid good-bye to Nehruvian model of development is to be modulated to give room to the demands of social justice and social security. These contemplated changes in India's economic system will be of far reaching importance with regard to the question of reach of fundamental rights.

The liberalized policy of the recent times in India or elsewhere is the best example for this. For example, without changing the socialistic pattern envisaged in Preamble and Part III dealing with Fundamental Rights and Part IV dealing with Directive Principles of state policy of the Constitution of India, economic relations are radically changed in India.

What is the reality during the last 50 years? The country has seen the execution of various five-year plans involving huge expenditure by the government for various nation-building activities. The corrupt officers, businessmen and contractors never had it so good. No doubt the country did make some progress but a big chunk of money earmarked for developmental projects was pocketed by the white-collar criminals.

In the words of Justice Krishna Iyer, xenophilious mentality is controlling even development and simian conception of corporate greed has displaced the basic needs of the voiceless masses. Recolonism, criminalism, communalism above all corruptionism deadened democracy; paralyzed development negatived every socio economic value in the National Charter.[16]

The thesis of more market, less state and the antithesis of the constitutional call for social solidarity and welfare must merge into a synthesis immediately to achieve social justice because without social justice, no social stability will last longer, otherwise the system is going to be collapsed.

For the last 50 years no doubt development is there. But the creamy class of the society only enjoyed the benefits. Some new classes have emerged due to implementation of some positive measures like reservations, constructing irrigation projects, green revolution, information technology revolution of course without industrial revolution, etc. Due to negative factors like scams, corruption, windfalls due to uncertain, directionless economic policies, criminalization of politics, etc., also cause the emergence of class caste convergence with yawning gap between haves and have-nots.

In India at present in every caste including backward classes, scheduled castes, minorities there is a creamy class most of whom denationalize themselves and collide with global elite. This neo-rich class became the puppet in the hands of market forces which forced progressive forces to backseat in the later half of 20th century.

The middle class[17], mostly labouring class, service sector with considerable pay scales, farmers with sufficient agricultural land who are in a strong position to mould the public opinion are misguided. Market forces dominate everywhere. Social justice cannot be achieved only through reservations in public employment which is rapidly diminishing under this hostile environment. The evils in Indian democracy should be curbed. The forces of equality and freedom with untiring and uncompromising struggles like women, children, dalits, tribes, backward classes should be strengthened so that eradication of poverty, illiteracy, ignorance and rise of the level of standard of living are possible.[18]

The middle class alone can bring change provided they must be educated regarding the challenges in proper perspective. It is possible to educate, organize and agitate in true spirit of Ambedkar's Mytri, the only solution to the constitutional path for social justice and an egalitarian social order.

Notes

1. C.G. Raghavan, "Dr. B.R. Ambedkar and the Making of the Indian Constitution: Some Reflections", *Dr. B.R. Ambedkar and the Indian Constitution,* (March 2001) edited by Dr. S.G. Bhat, published by Journal Society, Dr. B.R. Ambedkar Govt. Law College, Pondicherry. p. 194-195.
2. Dr. N.R. Madhavmenono, "Education, Equality and Social Justice", *Dr. B.R. Ambedkar and the Indian Constitution*, edited by Dr. S.G. Bhat.
3. Dhananjay Keer, "Dr. Ambedkar's Life and Mission".
4. Upendra Baxi characterizes the various images of Dr. Ambedkar as follows:
   (a) The First Ambedkar: An Authentic Dalit
   (b) The Second Ambedkar: Exemplar of Scholarship
   (c) The Third Ambedkar: Activist Journalist
   (d) The Fourth Ambedkar: Pre-Gandhian Activist
   (e) The Fifth Ambedkar: Gandhisation

(f) The Sixth Ambedkar: The Constitutionalist

(g) The Seventh Ambedkar: Renunciation of Hinduism

5. A. Lakshminath - Editorial Note, *Andhra University Law Journal*, Vol. 3, 2000 (2000 AULJ 3).
6. A. Lakshminath, "Dr. Ambedkar's Perceptions and Contemporary Constitutional Perspectives", *Dr. B.R. Ambedkar and the Indian Constitution,* edited by S.G. Bhat. p. 141-142.
7. *Dr. Babasaheb Ambedkar: Writings and Speeches*, Vol. I, Education Department, Government of Maharashtra, Bombay 1979, p. 57.
8. K. Raghavendra Rao, *Babasaheb Ambedkar*, Published by Sahitya Akademi at p. 23.
9. D.R. Jatav, *Social Philosophy of Dr. B.R. Ambedkar.*
10. John Rawls, *Theory of Justice.*
11. C.G. Raghavan, supra note 1.

    For Nisbet see Grossman and Wells, *Constitutional Law and Judicial Policy Making*, second edition, 1980, New York.

    For Dworkin's right based thesis and a critique of Rawls' *Theory of Justice* and of his revision of the theory in his new work *Political Liberalism* (1993). See Lyoyd, *Introduction to Jurisprudence*, edited by Freeman, 6th edition, 1994.

    See also C.G. Raghavan's lectures on Dr. B.R. Ambedkar and Indian Constitution. C.G. Raghavan's lectures are informative, instructive and illuminating and contain rich legal research material regarding the role of Dr. Ambedkar in making of the constitution, the constitutional philosophy of Dr. B.R. Ambedkar. (Lecture I: Dr. B.R. Ambedkar and making of the Indian constitution), Concept of Justice, Equality differences between justice and equality, Racial segregation in USA - Counter part of caste system in India, Dr. Ambedkar's views on the constitutional limits to preferential treatment, reservation jurisprudence, the views of contemporary scholars like Robert Nisbet, Dworkin, Rawls on distributional equality, a critical analysis of judicial interpretation of Art. 16(1) & 16(4), (Lecture II: The outlay of untouchability in India's Republican contribution), Harmony and balance between Directive Principles and Fundamental Rights: Expanding Human Rights Dimension, Dr. Ambedkar's Dilemma regarding due process clause, (Lecture III)
12. Supra Note 10.
13. Justice V.R. Krishna Iyer, *Justice at Cross Roads*. See also Justice Krishna Iyer's, *Social Democracy and Dalit Egalite*. As C.G. Raghavan

understands, Justice Krishna Iyer's explosive critique in social democracy and Dalit egalite is the best and most balanced and well reasoned exposition of the Dalits' Rights to equal justice.

14. *Maneka Gandhi vs. Union of India*, AIR 1978, SC, 786.
15. Dr. B.R. Ambedkar's view on future of the constitution is as follows: "I shall not... enter into the merits of the Constitution. Because I feel, however good a constitution may be, it is sure to turn out bad because those who are called to work it happen to be a bad lot. However bad a constitution may be, it may turn out to be good if those who are called to work it happen to be a good lot. The working of a constitution does not depend wholly upon the nature of the constitution. The constitution can provide the organs of state such as the legislature, the executive and the judiciary. The factors on which the working of those organs of the state depend are the people and the political parties they will set up as their instruments to carry out their wishes and their policies. Who can say how the people of India and their parties will behave? Will they uphold constitutional methods of achieving their purposes or will they adopt revolutionary methods of achieving them. If they adopt the revolutionary method, however the constitution may be, it requires no prophet to say that it will fail. It is therefore futile to pass any judgement upon the constitution without reference to the part which the people and their parties are likely to play."
16. Justice Krishna Iyer, "Decadence of out Democracy (with none to protest)," 2000 *AULJ* 3, p. 1 to 2.
17. According to one understanding the family which spends its income more on liquor than education belongs to either rich class or poor class whereas the family which spends more on education than liquor is a middle class family. The Indian society now needs more middle class families irrespective of class or caste, creed or religion or region for effective distributional equality.
18. See also G. Hara Gopal, "Human Rights in the 21st Century" April 30, 2001, *The Hindu*. G. Hara Gopal observes realization of the unfulfilled pursuit of equality and freedom constitutes the greatest challenge of the 21st century to the theory and practice of the Human Rights.

12

Dr. B.R. Ambedkar

His Approach Towards Human Rights

M.A. KISHORE

Dr. Bhimrao Ramji Ambedkar belonged to the untouchables-the depressed classes in India. The indignities and deprivations his community faced moved him to take up the gauntlet to fight for their rights. Indian society was a socially stratified society i.e. different status (caste) groups were arranged in a hierarchical order, the untouchables at the lowest rung. Social stratification was not peculiar to Indian society but there had never been a case of a people, treating a section of their own people as permanent and hereditary slaves. The condition of untouchables was even worse than slaves in Europe and Central Asia. Slaves could revolt at least under certain circumstances because they were part of the larger society and were exposed to the developments around. The untouchables, however, could never revolt, because they being outcastes, were deprived from participating in common activity in society, thus being completely disabled for any sort of direct action.

The exact description of their human rights violations cannot even be attempted. The extent of violations of human rights cannot be truly imagined of a people whose mere shadow was polluting and inviting punishment. The existence of ritual impurity (untouchability) was the source of all other disabilities. The word 'Untouchable' is the most obnoxious. It was itself an epitome of their sufferings and deprivations. And all this was in the name of caste. The caste system is the evolved and a bit degenerated version of *varna* system which draws sanction from the *Shastras*, the Hindu religious textbooks. The four *varnas* are supposed to discharge their duties assigned to them by virtue of their birth in that *varna*, since birth itself is controlled by *karmas* of the previous lives. Thus, social hierarchy, social segregation, ascribed status, fixed occupation, endogamy, commensal restrictions and oppression and humiliation of lower castes and outcastes are the chief characteristics of the caste system. Caste system by its very nature is against the rights and liberties of certain sections of the society and as such is a human rights problem.

Dr. Ambedkar vehemently attacked the caste system which treats certain classes of people as less than human. He suggested practical measures to wipe out this inhuman system from the Indian society. He firmly held that either the absolute authority and sanctity of the *Shastras* had to be discarded and their rational interpretation had to be attempted to get rid of this menace or, if it does not happen, the depressed classes should come out of the fold of the caste system by switching over to another religion. The purpose of religion is to liberate the individuals, not to bind them in servitude.

Dr. Ambedkar's approach towards human rights clearly reflect in his works, writing and speeches, presentations and memoranda submitted to the various committees and above all in the Constitution of India, as he was its chief architect. He had special care of depressed classes always in mind when he formulated his views and concerns on fundamental rights, rights of the minorities, socio-economic rights in the form of Directive Principles of State Policy and special safeguards for the welfare of weaker sections of society.

The fact that Dr. Ambedkar always talked about the rights of depressed sections or minorities invites criticism from some thinkers that he had no such great regard for the rights of the individual. Rather, he was more concerned about the human rights of groups. They argue that Dr. Ambedkar analyzed Indian society in terms of collectivities, position akin to the Marxist philosophical position, although he did not endorse Marxist theory of class conflict. To quote him, "to say that individuals make up society is trivial, society is always composed of class. It may be an exaggeration to assert the theory of class conflict, but the existence of definite classes in society is a fact. Their basis may differ. They may be economic, or intellectual or social but an individual in society is always a member of a class".[1]

This criticism is not justified. To look at the individual as a member of a class does not mean that one does not have high regard in the sanctity of an individual. Dr. Ambedkar, rather, criticized Marxism and even Gandhism by observing that "both of these ideologies could not free the individual from the tyranny of the society".[2] Thus, the individual lies at the core of his philosophy. If he focussed more on human rights of dalits, as a group, it was because he realized that most of the violations of their human rights were distinctly connected to their being members of a certain class that is, they as a group were discriminated against, abused and did not enjoy the basic human rights. In comparison to the violation of human rights of an individual, here the violations were far more organized and targeted, therefore rightfully occupied Dr. Ambedkar's deep consideration. Besides, he himself was a member of that class. One who cannot fight for his own cause, cannot be expected to take up a general cause. Indeed, dalits' rights are human rights. As any class is composed of individuals, Dr. Ambedkar could not be said to have neglected the individual. As far as his general approach towards human rights is concerned, he meant them for one and all, as becomes clear from his views on Fundamental Rights. What he wanted for Depressed classes in particular, was some protections and safeguards to make them capable of asserting those rights and at the same time, to save their rights from the encroachment by the entrenched sections of society.

While assessing his theoretical position on human rights, it must be borne in mind that he did not speak much about human rights in systematic disciplinary framework. The discipline of Human Rights is post-World War II development. Although he articulated the rights of minorities in particular and all citizens in general with such zeal and clarity as unmatched by anyone of his contemporary.

He did not subscribe to the theory of Natural Rights. This theory holds some basic rights as natural and inalienable. Since State itself is the creation of man and comes into being to protect Natural Rights, these rights are not the gift of the state. Dr. Ambedkar did not agree with this view. According to him, all rights are created by the state and thus, are gifts of the state. "Fundamental Rights are the gift of the law".[3] His position resembles Legal Theory of Rights. He also held that fundamental rights are essential for the overall development of man. Thus, he beautifully combined Legal Theory of Rights with the Ethical Theory of Rights.

However, to hold that basic human rights are the gift of the State or law is a serious error of judgement. Human rights are of such supreme significance that they can well be supposed to set up a critical standard to gauge the legitimacy of particular laws. Laws can vary from place to place; human rights are constant and immutable, and hence they cannot be gift of law. Although Dr. Ambedkar's pious intentions can never be doubted, by holding Fundamental Rights to be the gift of the State, he just wanted to convey that these rights are not absolute and reasonable restrictions can be put upon their exercise. What he failed to realize properly was that these reasonable restrictions cannot be supposed to be restrictions in real sense or curtailment of rights, rather, they are just moral obligations on the part of each individual to enhance the value, intensity and universality of these rights. By conceding that human rights are the gift of the State, one is logically also conceding, whether he really means it or not, that human rights are dependent upon the sweet will of the State. The existence of human rights, in fact, does not depend upon the will of the State. A State is not capable of creating human rights by law. It can only confirm their existence and give them protection. It is the duty of the State towards its citizens. A gift does not come within the purview of duty.

Dr. Ambedkar and Fundamental Rights

Dr. Ambedkar as the champion of the downtrodden, was convinced beyond doubt as to the need for a Bill of Rights in the Indian Constitution. He had been pleading continuously for an elaborate system of fundamental rights for the minorities in particular, and for all the citizens in general. His views on fundamental rights are elaborately expressed in the memoranda submitted to the Minorities Sub-committee of the First Round Table Conference in 1930 and to the Advisory Committee of the Constituent Assembly. The latter which is itself in the form of a model Constitution was subsequently published as a book entitled *States and Minorities: What are Their Rights and How to Secure These in the Constitution of India.*

In Article II, Sections I and II of his model Constitution, he provides for the following rights for all citizens:

> ... Any privilege or disability arising out of rank, birth, person, family, religion or religious usage and custom is abolished. No deprivation of life, liberty and property without due process of law; equality before law. Equal access to all citizens to places of public resort of convenience - denial of them to any person shall be an offence.
>
> Subjecting a person to forced labour or to involuntary servitude shall be an offence. Right to vote for all, other than the young, the insane and the imprisoned. No law shall be made abridging the freedom of speech, of the Press, of Association and of Assembly except for consideration of public order and morality.

> No Bill of *ex-post facto* law shall be passed. Liberty of conscience including the rights to profess, to preach and to convert within limits compatible with public order and morality. The State shall not recognize any religion as State religion.

Dr. Ambedkar is criticized that he made the enjoyment of fundamental rights contingent upon the security of the State. As to the criticism on the provisions regarding the suspension of fundamental rights Ambedkar said that in certain cases where, for instance, the State's very life is in jeopardy, those rights must be subject to certain amount of limitation. In times of emergency the life of the State itself is in jeopardy and if the State is not able to protect itself in times of emergency, the individual himself will be found to have lost his very existence. Consequently, the superior right of the State to protect itself in times of emergency, so that it may. live to discharge its functions in order that the individual under the aegis of the State may develop, must be guaranteed as safely as the right of an individual.[4]

Justifying the inclusion of preventive detention clause in the Constitution, Dr. Ambedkar said that since some people always follow unconstitutional means to attain their objectives, tamper with public order or defence of the country, it will be necessary for the Executive to detain such persons to stop the situation from developing into an emergency. To satisfy the elaborate legal procedure is not always practicable. The exigency of the liberty of the individual cannot be placed above the interests of the State.

Thus, his concerns about the security of state are real. No doubt, liberty in any real sense is possible only if sovereignty exists and becomes more perfect as sovereignty is more completely and accurately organized. Hence, instead of being opposed to State authority, it is dependent upon it. Moreover, Dr. Ambedkar, introduced article on Preventive Detention in the Constituent Assembly not only to ensure security to the State but also to check the unlimited power of Parliament to make laws in matters of arrest. This power was given to Parliament by virtue of Article 21 (then Article 15) which states that no person shall be deprived of his life or liberty except according to 'procedure established by law'. Dr. Ambedkar said that by introducing Article 15 A (present Article 22), we are making, if I may say so, compensation for what was done earlier in passing Article 15 (present Article 21). In other words, we are providing for the substance of the law of "due process" by the introduction of Article 15A.[5]

Thus, Dr. Ambedkar conceived a system of rights with necessary limitations upon the interests of the individual and also upon the authority of State. He tried to balance individual liberty with the authority of the State. The point, however, he missed was that the Executive may not always act in a rightful manner under clause of Preventive Detention. Even in the presence of standard procedure set up by Parliament, Executive may work for narrower ends than national security. It may have its own axe to grind. There are not adequate safeguards in the Constitution to avoid this situation. Human rights are of such primary importance that whosoever violates them should have good reasons for doing so. The onus of proof should be on those who violate rights. If State is not able to prove charges, the individual should be duly compensated. People are entitled to human rights by virtue of their being human and so far as their exercise is reasonably consistent with a corresponding enjoyment of others, no one, even the State has the right to take away these rights. Human rights constitute the basis of State. How can they be opposed to State security? It may be conceded that without the existence of State, there can be no human rights. However, in order of thought and logic, the concern for human rights come first. The State comes afterwards to make that concern real – by recognizing and enforcing those rights. The need for individual security is the basis for the creation of State. Therefore, how can State security supercede the security of the individual. In fact, both are consistent with each other and are interdependent. The purpose of the State is to protect human rights. Human rights entail duty upon the individual and enable him as well to protect and strengthen the State.

Minority Rights

In advocating the rights of the minorities, Dr. Ambedkar proceeded on the assumption that national well-being and unity would depend upon the rights enjoyed by the minorities. Constitutional safeguards for the preservation of religious, cultural and linguistic identity of the minorities would bend them to unite as one nation by the bond of fraternity. It would enable the minorities to become equal partners in nation-building, thus, ultimately having the most desirable effect of merging the minority and majority, so that there would remain no need for safeguards. Speaking in the Constituent Assembly on the absoluteness of Rights of minorities, he said:

> ...that some members want that the rights of minorities should be relative, that is to say, we must wait and see what rights the minorities are given by the Pakistan Assembly before we determine the rights we want to give to the minorities in the Hindustan area. Now, Sir, with all deference, I must deprecate any such idea. Rights of minorities should be absolute rights. They should not be subject to any consideration as to what another party may like to do to minorities within its jurisdiction. If we find that certain minorities in which we are interested and which are within the jurisdiction of another State have not got the same rights which we have given to minorities in our territory, it would be open for the State to take up the matter in a diplomatic manner and see that the wrongs are rectified. But no matter what others do, I think we ought to do what is right in our own judgement and personally I think that the rights which are indicated in clause 18 are rights which every minority, irrespective of any other consideration is entitled to claim.[6]

In talking about Rights of minorities, he mainly focussed on Depressed Classes. He introduced a new parameter of 'social discrimination' as a real test to determine whether or not a social group was a minority. Thus, Depressed Classes were entitled to be treated as a real minority in India. The two memoranda he submitted to the Minorities Sub-committee of First Round Table Conference and Advisory Committee of the Constituent Assembly were in pursuance of his struggle to claim Minority status for his community. He always called Dalits as minorities.

The criticism that his aims in taking up minority issues were narrow and only served the interests of the Britishers cannot be justified. He always pressed for their legitimate rights and just demands. The demand that, before the Britishers leave, there should be a general acceptance as to the incorporation of Rights of minorities in the future Constitutional vision was not anti-national. Dr. Ambedkar had always in his mind the supreme goal of national unity and integrity. And these demands were never inconsistent with this goal. If the demands of the weaker sections were not met, then coming out of British servitude for them would have been nothing more than entering into another bond of slavery.

Dr. Ambedkar suggested a mixed type of Executive on the pattern of Switzerland as a best device to protect the minorities from the tyranny of communal majority in free India.[7] He was of the opinion that Parliamentary Executive of the British type was not suitable to India, as the majority in India would be communal majority, unlike political majority which grows and is changeable in its class composition, the admission to it is open, not fixed.

Reservations

Dr. Ambedkar had realized very early that Declaration of Rights and equality of opportunity would in practice be rendered ineffective if adequate safeguards for the protection and promotion of weaker sections were not provided in the

Constitution. Reservations would be, and has also proved to be the most effective such measure. Reservations for Depressed Classes as envisaged by Dr. Ambedkar in the Constitution are of three kinds, namely:

(i) Reservation to the Lok Sabha and State Assemblies (Articles 330 and 332).
(ii) Job reservations (Articles 16 (1), 16 (4) and 335 and
(iii) Reservation in the admissions to educational institutions (Articles 15 (4) and 46).

Initially, he wanted separate electorates for the Depressed Classes for at least first ten years, thereafter to be substituted by the joint electorates. He, however, gave up this demand at the insistence of Gandhi and with some concessions contended for joint electorates.

He was clear that reservation in jobs is not a concession or a privilege extended to Depressed Classes. It is their legitimate right. It is in recognition of their Fundamental Right to Equality [Art. 16 (1)]. He said, "We have to safeguards two things, namely, principle of equality of opportunity and at the same time satisfy the demand of communities which have not had so far representation in the State".[8] Dr. Ambedkar also held that reservation should always be for minority of seats, otherwise it would nullify the principle of equality of opportunity.

His stand has been vindicated by various Supreme Court judgements. In Thomas[9] and ABSK[10] cases, Supreme Court held that Article 16 (4) is a facet, an illustration or a method of application of Article 16 (1), because opportunity can never be equal among human beings who have unequal capacities to grasp it. Since reservation in jobs is not a permissible exception but a necessary ingredient of the right to equality of opportunity, Supreme Court has held it to be a Fundamental Right of the Scheduled Castes and Scheduled Tribes. Dr. Ambedkar's another contention that reservation should be for a minority of seats has been proved right by Supreme Court Judgement in

Indira Sawhney V. Union of India case, 1992. Supreme Court put a ceiling of 50 per cent for reservation in jobs.

Right to Vote

From the very beginning he disfavoured property or educational qualification to be eligible for the right to vote and advocated Universal Adult Suffrage. To quote him, "I understand Franchise to be the right to regulate the terms of what one might call associated life in society, i.e., to regulate the terms on which one will live in relationship with other individuals in society... Franchise is something which must be regarded as the inherent right of every individual who is capable of understanding it, then surely you can't make an inherent right of people dependent upon the convenience of your administration".[11] He also regarded Franchise as a right of self defence in the sense that individual should have the power to change the composition of Legislature whose laws directly affect the life, liberty and property of the individual. Appearing before South Borough Committee on Reforms in Indian Administration, he quoted L.T. Hobhouse:

> The success of democracy depends on the response of voters to the opportunities given to them. But conversely the opportunities must be given in order to call forth the response. The exercise of popular government is itself all education.... enfranchise itself may precisely be the stimulus needed to awaken interest. The ballot alone effectively liberates the quiet citizen from the Tyranny of the shooter and the wire-puller. An impression of existing inertness alone is not a sufficient reason for withholding responsible government or restricting the area of suffrage".[12]

His Economic Vision and Human Rights

As parliamentary democracy, in his view, was unmindful of the adverse consequences of liberty for the poor, the downtrodden and the disinherited, he was highly critical of the doctrine of *laissez faire*, which is an important aspect of western liberal democracy. According to him, liberty from the control of the State is another name for the dictatorship of the private employer.[13] To him the oppression and exploitation of the most human beings by a few was the result of lack of social ownership of the means of production. Therefore, if the new social order based on equality, liberty and fraternity was to be established, parliamentary democracy must be accompanied by State socialism. His Constitutional vision of State socialism included State ownership of land and basic industries.

A necessary corollary to his vision of State socialism was the absence of a Fundamental Right to Property, because he was of the view that this would not only generate economic inequality but further widen the gap between rich and poor, instead of reducing it. He said, "No landlord means no tenants, and no landless labourer".[14]

However, there was an extreme form of difference of opinion in the Constituent Assembly over Right to Property. The extent of difference can be judged from the fact that the Drafting Committee had to leave a blank in the Draft Constitution. This was done with an idea that this could be finalized by the Congress Party. Later on, in the Congress Party, except Nehru all gave support for making property as a Fundamental Right.[15]

Dr. Ambedkar in his model Constitution had provided a separate clause on "Protection Against Economic Exploitation". He emphasised the idea of including specific economic rights like right to work, right to adequate living wage and better standard of living in the list of fundamental rights. He doubted the value of fundamental rights for unemployed and rightly observed that a man without job was prone to relinquish his fundamental rights in order to gain his living. He could not, however, incorporate his total vision of economic structure in the Constitution. He had to be satisfied by incorporating them as Directive Principles which though are fundamental in the governance of the country but are not judicially enforceable. Circumstances permitted him this much, but even this by no means is insignificant. He brought radical reforms in the wages, working conditions and social security by introducing and pushing through the new labour legislation and modification of old one, when he became the Labour Minister. The Industrial Disputes Act, The Indian Employment Standing Orders Act, The Minimum Wages Act and The Factories Act were all inspired by his views on labour issues.

It will not be out of place to mention about his vehement criticism of the Bombay Industrial Disputes Act, 1938 which provided that strike under certain circumstances was illegal. He said, "Right to strike is nothing else than the right to freedom to one's services on any terms that one wants to obtain. And once you concede the right to freedom, you necessarily concede the right to strike...... If you accept that the right to freedom is a divine right I contend that the right to strike is a divine right".[16]

Dr. Ambedkar also prepared and introduced the Khoti Abolition Bill in Bombay Assembly in 1938. It was meant to abolish tenure of the Zamindars and secure occupancy rights to the tenants. Dhananjay Keer appropriately calls him as the first legislator in India to introduce a Bill for the abolition of the Serfdom of the agricultural tenants.

Conclusion

Thus, his struggle to secure human rights to weaker sections in particular and to all the citizens in general, was endless. He championed the cause of women also. He thought that there was some commonality in the plight of Untouchables and women, for both were the victims of *Manu Smriti.* He was instrumental in introducing Hindu Code Bill, 1951 which for the first time gave Hindu women some rights in matters of marriage, divorce, inheritance, etc.

All these show that human rights were very dear to his heart. He was a great humanist, activist, Constitutionalist and reformist. Without his unflinching support, guidance and articulation, the story of human rights, particularly that of Depressed Classes, would have been different in India.

Notes

1. B.R. Ambedkar, *Castes in India: Their Mechanism, Genesis and Development* (Paper read before the Anthropological Seminar at the Columbia University, New York, USA).
2. G.S. Lokhande, *B.R. Ambedkar: A Study in Social Democracy,* Delhi, 1977, p.4
3. Bhagwan Das (ed.), *Thus Spoke Ambedkar,* Bheem Patrika Publication, Jullundhur, 1977, Vol. 1, p. 162
4. *Constituent Assembly Debates,* Vol. VI, p. 950.
5. *Constituent Assembly Debates,* Vol. IX, p. 1497.
6. *Constituent Assembly Debates*, Vol. III, 1947, p. 504.
7. Ambedkar, *States and Minorities,* Section 3, Article II.
8. *Constituent Assembly Debates,* Vol. I, p. 59.
9. A.I.R. 1976, S.C., p. 490.
10. A.I.R. 1981, S.C., p. 298.
11. *Proceedings of Sub-committee (Franchise),* Government of India, Central Publication Branch, Calcutta, 1931, pp. 28-35.
12. *Writing and Speeches of Dr B. R. Ambedkar,* Department of Education, Government of Maharashtra, Bombay, Vol. I, 1979, p. 261.
13. Ambedkar, *States and Minorities,* Note 6, p. 100.
14. "Interview with Ambedkar", Mulk Raj Anand, *The Tribune,* Chandigarh, June 10, 1990.
15. A.M. Rajasekhariah, *B.R. Ambedkar: The Politics of Emancipation,* 1971, p.262.
16. "On the Industrial Disputes Bill", *Dr. B.R. Ambedkar's Writings and Speeches,* Department of Education, Government of Maharashtra, 1982, Vol. II, p. 208.

13

Constitution and Dr. Ambedkar's Vision for Social Change

SURESH MANE

It is commonly believed that enough has been spoken and written about the Constitution of India and its principal architect, Dr. Babasaheb Ambedkar. Some scholars have openly expressed their unhappiness over the process of Ambedkarization. It is true that much has been written and spoken by the opponents as well as by the eulogists about them. But it certainly does not mean that the theme has been dried up. There have been many areas yet to be covered, especially about Dr. Babasaheb Ambedkar, the statesman who shook not only the social and political structure but also the overall power structure in the country. Yet, the Indian social science landscape has disarticulated Babasaheb Ambedkar by studious theoretical silence – neither does the autonomous academia nor the substantially funded monopoly of governmental knowledge industries (the Indian Council of Social Science Research, the Indian Council of Historical Research, the Indian Council of Philosophical Research, the UGC, etc.) provide spaces-curricular or research for Dr. Ambedkar. He remains a totally forgotten figure.[1] Dr. Ambedkar has still remained to be understood in the proper perspective by large number of Indians. Since he articulately advocated the cause of the empowerment of broken men (marginal sections) in the society, waged an ideological war with Congress Party and Gandhi, he has been looked upon as the saviour of Scheduled Castes and Tribes in the country, and a political opponent of Gandhi and Congress politics. This kind of valuation of one of the greatest sons of this soil, Dr. Ambedkar is not only unjust but atrocious. His discourse represents, archetypically, the pervasive "fear of anonymous prosecutors" typical of the structures of paranoid knowledge.[2] There have been several efforts to demolish him. The communities of knowledge and communities of power, in their united silent conspiracy have tried their best to marginalize Babasaheb, yet his presence is felt whenever the Rule of Law or Constitution is in jeopardy. In the history of social change in modem India, Dr. Ambedkar has secured a solitary place for himself. Hence, in the process of social change, Dr. Ambedkar as well as his struggle needs to be understood in its spirit, in its various facets and dynamics.

Constitutional lawyers for a long time believed that the scope and function of Constitutional Law was to prescribe the shape and form of the political structure of society leaving the social and economic structure untouched. Dr. Babasaheb Ambedkar, the chief architect of the Constitution of India, however, had a strong conviction that, if democracy is to live up to its principle of one man, one value, the time has come to take a bold step and define both the socio-economic structure as well as the political structure of society by the law of the Constitution. As a consequence the Constitution of India is not just a pedantic legal text, but it is a living document for social change. During the process of constitution making, tall claims were made. K. Santhanam, member of the Constituent Assembly, described the situation in terms of three revolutions. "The political revolution would end with independence. The social revolution meant to get (India) out of the medievalism based on birth, religion, custom and community and reconstruct her social structure on modem foundations of law, individual merit, and secular education. The third revolution was an economic one: The transition from primitive rural economy to scientific and planned agriculture and industry".[3] Dr. Radhakrishnan believed India must have a 'socio-economic revolution' designed not only to bring about 'the real satisfaction of the fundamental needs of the common man', but to go much deeper and bring about 'a fundamental change in the structure of Indian society'.[4] President Rajendra Prasad, assured the nation that the Assembly and the government's aim was "to end poverty and squalor and its companions, hunger and disease; to abolish distinction and exploitation and to ensure decent conditions of living".[5] On 10 August, 1947, Pandit Nehru in one of his famous speeches declared that, "Long years ago we made a tryst with destiny, and now the time comes when we shall redeem our pledge, not wholly or in full measure, but very substantially".[6] Such views were held by many members of the Constituent Assembly.

Obviously, Dr. Ambedkar, being the Chairman of the Drafting Committee, made all the efforts to embody his scheme[7] and above all declared goals in the Constitution of India. In accord with the change in the philosophy of a constitutional law, and role of modern State, Dr. Ambedkar strongly pleaded to the Constituent Assembly that all countries like India which are late-comers in the field of Constitution-making should not copy the faults of other countries.[8] Having inspired and guided by the dynamics of constitutional law, in his scheme, he suggested very positive, interventionist role to the State, i.e., protection against communal executives, protection against social and official tyranny, State socialism with basic industry owned by the State and agriculture as a State industry with the backbone of the principle, of "no landlord, no tenant and no landless labourer".

The then Prime Minister Jawaharlal Nehru agreed with Dr. Ambedkar but expressed his inability to take the steps immediately. He also expressed his fear to Dr. Ambedkar in his communication that, if we tackle at this stage, very fundamental economic issues, in the process of Constitution-making, we might add to the strength of the disruptive tendencies and achieve nothing at all.[9] K.M. Munshi thanked God for failure of the nationalization proposals in the Constituent Assembly. He further said, "had the Constituent Assembly accepted the proposals of Dr. Ambedkar, an untouchable would have been the first citizen of a free India and a caste Hindu would have been relegated to a secondary status.[10]

Dr. Ambedkar strongly desired to plan economic life of the nation but failed to give a wisdom to Congress Party. In fact in 1940, the National Planning Committee had proposed that all key industries should be controlled by the State – collectivized cultivation on wastelands and lands owned by government, and co-operative farming in which private ownership would be permitted.[11] But when the time came to realize all these through the Constitution, the Congress Party opposed it, whatever may be the reasons, perhaps, best known to the front line leadership of Congress Party in the Constituent Assembly.

Indian 'Constitution is a document vibrant with a social and economic ideology geared to the goal of socio-economic justice. To lay down the foundation of this document of social restructuring in 1947, there was no one better prepared for the job of constitution-crafting than Dr. Babasaheb Ambedkar. With his vast funds of knowledge of Constitutional Law and grassroot experience of country's complex socio-economic and political issues he set out his thinking about the nation's constitutional needs. As a consequence, the doctrine of Rule of Law, Part III and IV of the Constitution, that is, Fundamental Rights and Directive Principles of State Policy, an independent judiciary as an arm of social revolution, the charter of equality, liberty and justice: social, economic and political to all, along with some constitutional safeguards to the downtrodden groups (SCs, STs, OBCs, minorities and women) form the core of social revolution. These constitutional convictions are as follows;

1. Articles 14, 15, 16 ensures equal protection of law, non-discrimination by the State on grounds of religion, caste, sex or place of birth particularly in matters relating to employment, absence of any disability or restriction among citizens in the matter of access to public places or use of places of public resort. Articles 15 and 16 commands the State to make special provisions through reservation or otherwise in favour of Scheduled Castes, Tribes, women, children as well as other backward classes of citizens
2. Article 17 abolished untouchability and made criminal prohibition of its practice in any form.
3. Articles 23 and 24 prescribes prohibition against exploitation and of traffic in human beings and forced labour.
4. Articles 25, 29 and 30 provides for equal entitlements of every person to freedom of conscience and the right to freely profess, practice and propagate ones religion, protection of interests of minorities and their right to establish and administer educational institutions.
5. Articles 38 directs the State to secure a social order for the promotion of welfare of the people by elimination of inequalities in status, facilities and opportunities including social order founded on justice: social, economic and political.
6. Article 39 lays down the State policy towards securing adequate means of livelihood for every citizen, equal pay for equal work to men and women and preventing concentration of wealth to the common detriment.
7. Article 39A assures equal justice under law and towards that end providing free legal aid to the poor.
8. Article 45 directs the State to provide free and compulsory education to all children within 10 years of the commencement of the Constitution.
9. Article 46 directs the State to promote educational and economic interests of Scheduled Castes, Scheduled Tribes

and other weaker sections and also commands the State to protect them from social injustice and all forms of exploitation. Article 335 directs the State to maintain the claims of SCs and STs to services and posts.

10. Along with the policy of reservation of job quota and in educational institutions for the SCs, STs, Articles 330, 332 and 334 provide reservation of seats for SCs and STs in the House of the People and in the Legislative Assemblies of the States.
11. Article 338 makes the provision for National Commission for the SCs and STs to advise on the socio-economic development of the SCs and STs and to evaluate their progress under the Union and States.
12. Article 340 provides for the Commission to investigate the conditions of backward classes and to make recommendations as to the steps that should be taken by the State.

Thus, along with the general constitutional guarantees, there are specific safeguards for the downtrodden groups. These provisions speak for the State's commitment and conviction to create a just, humanitarian social order, an egalitarian society premised on the constitutional spirit of liberty, equality, fraternity and justice.

In the mid of twentieth century liberal Constitutional States were held with the responsibility of the social and economic changes in the society. Accordingly, Dr. Ambedkar emphasized for such changes through the Law of Constitution. Obviously, Dr. Ambedkar regarded Part IV of the Constitution as of great value and that would serve as the guiding principle for all State actions and if the rulers dare to disobey this constitutional-national agenda will have to pay the heavy price. While justifying the constitutional placement of Directive Principles he said:

> The Draft Constitution as framed, only provides a machinery for the government of the country. It is not a contrivance to instal any particular party in power as has been done in some countries. Who should be in power is left to be determined by

> the people as it must be, if the system is to satisfy the tests of democracy. But whoever captures power will not be free to do what be likes with it. In the exercise of it, he will have to respect these instruments of instructions which are called Directive Principles. He cannot ignore them. He may not have to answer for their breach in a Court of Law. But he will certainly have to answer for them before the electorate at election time. What great value these directive principles possess will be realized better when the forces of right contrive to capture power.[12]

In fact it was Dr. Ambedkar's firm desire to make all Directive Principles of State Policy justiciable and sought for a comprehensive programme for the social and economic revolution. He along with K.T. Shah, a graduate from London School of Economics and an eminent socialist member in the Constituent Assembly strongly argued for the enforceable character of the directive principles. K.T. Shah supported Dr. Ambedkar by saying that, there must be a specified time limit within which all the Directive Principles must be made justiciable, otherwise they would be mere 'pious wishes' and so much window dressing for the social revolution.[13] Even Shri Rau, Adviser to the Constituent Assembly, after having the discussion on the issue with Justice Frankfurter and Justice Hand of US Supreme Court recommended in the draft a new paragraph providing for the States' power to make a law in pursuance of the Directive Principles in contravention to Fundamental Rights. He held the view that, occasionally it is essential for the State to invade private rights in order to raise the nation's standard of health of living, etc.[14] Unfortunately the powerful lobby in the Assembly favouring the supremacy to civil and political rights over social and economic rights emerged as victorious and accorded unenforceable status to the Directive Principles – a pool of half hearted compromises.[15] The most unfortunate part is that even the Supreme Court of India in its early several decisions echoed the voice of *status quoists.*

The record of the Constituent Assembly reveals that, Dr. Ambedkar tried a lot for socioeconomic planning and having failed finally warned that if socio-economic rights were not taken seriously future governments may fall down. But hardly any attention was paid to his warning. Although in the caste-ridden and gender-unjust social order the need for the social change through constitutional mechanism was realized, one group of persons (namely the *status quoists)* portrayed the general regulatory measures as a threat to the overall civil liberties of the people because they foresaw themselves being adversely affected by the incoming changes. The *status quoists* sought refuge in the enforceable civil and political rights provisions to defend themselves from the onslaught of change.[16] In the end, having left with no option, Dr. Ambedkar too accepted and advocated the unenforceable character of Directive Principles in the belief that half of a loaf was better than none.[17] The saddest part of the whole episode is, in the early period of constitutional interpretation the Justices of Apex Court too over-emphasised on the enforceable civil and political rights and committed a mistake of neglecting the Directive Principles. Dr. Ambedkar being unhappy over the court's approach, while speaking on the Constitutional First Amendment Bill, 1951, in the Lok Sabha, on May 18, said:

> The Directive Principles were nothing else than a series of provisions containing implicitly in them the doctrine of implied powers which the United States Supreme Court has developed, the courts should invoke them and support legislation undertaken by Parliament or State legislatures which tend to give effect to the Directive Principles embodied in the Constitution. ....I find that these Directive Principles are made a matter of fun both by judges and lawyers appearing before them. Article 37 of the Directive Principles has been made a buff of ridicule... it is not the way of disposing of the Directive Principles.

These historical developments speak in volume for the non-implementation of any of the directives, including the right to education for which the bill is pending in Parliament for years together. While commenting on this lethargic attitude of the rulers, Granville Austin, writes,

> A specific example of the indifference toward lower orders mentioned earlier has been government's avoidance of both the letter and spirit of the Directive Principles – admirable goals admittedly difficult to reach in any society. For example, Article 45 charged government to strive to provide, within ten years, free and compulsory education for children through age fourteen. But data tell that nearly one third of the 105 million children age six to ten were not in school in 1993. Drop-out rates from the first to the fifth standard approach one-third of those who enroll. Learning achievement is low. A conspiracy – except locally – to keep the poor uneducated or ill-educated is unlikely. But the higher castes seem to operate implicitly on the colonialist maxim that if you educate the natives they become restless; better that we don't equip them to challenge us.[18]

In the beginning, the Congress leadership strongly opposed the downtroddens' participation in the legislatures. In 1918, when the Backward Classes demanded the separate representation in the Legislature, Bal Gangadhar Tilak in a public meeting held in Sholapur (Maharashtra) said, he did not understand why the oil pressers, tobacco shopkeepers, washermen, etc., should want to go into Legislature. In his opinion, their business was to obey the laws and not to aspire for power to make laws.[19] Similarly, in 1942, when Lord Linlithgow invited 52 Indian representatives including the Scheduled Castes to enlist the support of all to the Central Governments in its war efforts, Vallabhhai Patel in a speech at Ahmedabad in a way of contempt said, the Viceroy sent for the leaders of the Hindu Mahasabha, he sent for the leaders of the Muslim League and he sent for Ghanchis (Oil pressers), Mochis (cobblers) and the rest.[20] In 1931, in the Second Round Table Conference, Gandhi opposed the separate electorate to the Untouchables and thereafter went on fast unto death. After 1935 election, Dr. Khare formed the Congress Ministry in the Central Provinces and included in the Ministry, Mr. Agnibhoj, an Untouchable, who was a member of the Central Provinces. On 26th July 1938, the Congress Working Committee met at Wardha and charged Khare for an act of indiscipline. Replying to the charge of indiscipline, Khare openly said that according to Gandhi the act of indiscipline consisted in the inclusion of an Untouchable in the Ministry. Khare also said that Gandhi told him that it was wrong on his part to have raised such aspirations and ambitions in the Untouchables and it was such an act of bad judgment that he would never forgive him.[21] These instances reveal the other side of the face of the Congress Party, during Gandhi's Raj.

All these developments of constitutional significance made Dr. Ambedkar worried about the downtrodden's share in the governance of the country. In the interest of democracy, he always felt the necessity of recognizing the marginal groups in the society as the equal partners in the affairs of the nation. It is therefore, since the beginning, he was very cautious about their representation and also made all possible efforts to secure it. On the issue of constitutional reforms, while giving the evidence before the Southborough Committee on Franchise, on 27th January, 1919, as a brilliant lawyer he justified the separate representation to the downtrodden classes. He argued,

> A community may claim representation only on the ground of separate interests which require protection. In India, such interests are of three kinds only: either they arise out of religious antipathies which are pretty strong in India, or out of the backward state of a community in educational matters, or out of the socio-religious disabilities to which a community may be subject. Confining ourselves to the Hindu communities there are certain communities who, besides being very backward, are suffering under a great social tyranny. The Untouchable classes must have their own men in the Council Hall to fight for the

> redress of their grievances. The non-Brahmins as a class are subjected to the social and intellectual domination of the Brahmin priesthood and may therefore rightly advocate separate representation.[22]

In a sequel to this, on the issue of a separate electorate, Dr. Ambedkar came into conflict with Gandhi in the second Round Table Conference. Despite Gandhi and Congress Party's strong opposition, Dr. Ambedkar successfully secured separate electorates for the Untouchables but had to give up due to Gandhi's coercive fast unto death, which resulted in Poona Pact, on 24 September, 1932. Thus, whatever Dr. Ambedkar achieved by the way of struggle from the Britishers he was forced to give up. To this, Dr. Ambedkar with deep sadness said, the Congress sucked the juice out of the Poona Pact and threw the rind on the face of the Untouchables.[23] In order to get rid of all these unpalatable developments permanently Dr. Ambedkar, in his memorandum to the Constituent Assembly[24] submitted the detail scheme providing for the Right to Representation in the Legislature, Right to Representation in the Executive, Method of Election, and Provision for New Settlements, but succeeded to secure only some of them.

While justifying the policy of constitutional safeguards to Scheduled Castes, Tribes he argued,

> No country has the problem of Communal majority and Communal minority is without some kind of an arrangement whereby they agree to share political power. South Africa has such an understanding. So has Canada.... Unfortunately for the minorities in India, Indian Nationalism has developed a new doctrine which may be called the Divine Right of the Majority to rule the minorities according to the wishes of the majority. Any claim for the sharing of power by the minority is called communalism while the monopolizing of the whole power by the majority is called Nationalism. Guided by such a political philosophy the majority is not prepared to allow the minorities to share the political power. Under these circumstances there is

no way left but to have the rights of the Scheduled Castes embodied in the Constitution."[25]

Dr. Ambedkar's such strong empowerment efforts has resulted into the present constitutional safeguards to Women, Scheduled Castes, Tribes and Backward Classes, in the fields of education, employment and legislatures. However, even today we continue to hear about the sporadic incidences that of the storming the Dalit habitat, stone-pelting and a Dalit woman being kidnapped and detained illegally by the dominant caste groups in an attempt to prevent her from filing in nomination papers for the Nattarmangalam Panchayat president post.[26] Even after the completion of more than 50 years of the Constitution of India, occurrence of such incidences justifies Dr. Ambedkar's quest in the process of attaining the social justice and social change.

In pursuance of the constitutional mandate, the policy of reservation quota in education and State employment has been one of the core area of State's affirmative action programme. The Indian Constitution has rejected the traditional monopolist reservation policy based on Varna culture and adopted the new constructive reservation policy premised on the principle of compensatory or distributive justice. In the Constituent Assembly and outside, the Draft Constitution was criticized for such safeguards provided to the minorities. Large number of Indians, even today, believe that Dr. Ambedkar was the solely guiding force behind this. But while moving the Draft Constitution in the Constituent Assembly, to make his position clear Dr. Ambedkar said, in this, the Drafting Committee has no responsibility and entire Constituent Assembly has done it wisely. Giving an example of Protestant minority in Ireland and their firm determination to reject the rule of majority[27] he said, no minority in India has taken the stand like them but loyally they have accepted the rule of majority and hence whether the minorities will continue or will vanish will depend upon the habits of the majority which is basically communal.[28]

From this view of Dr. Ambedkar, it can be learnt that, in the process of nation-building, he expected the governing class in India to adopt the patriotic attitude like the Japanese governing class who voluntarily surrendered their privileges and preferred to merge themselves in the common mass of the people so as to transform feudal Japan into a modern nation. It is a sad thing that, even after the constitutional commands and global environment of human rights, the governing class in India not merely refuse to surrender its power and authority but, it never loses an opportunity to demonstrate it. This attitude of those in power, government, bureaucracy, education, policy making, justice mechanism and general mass with the caste mentality has been the stumbling block in the way of achieving the social revolution agenda envisaged in the Constitution.

Dr. Babasaheb Ambedkar, being an ethnologist, was well aware about the casteist-cultural-untouchable background in which new Constitution will have to operate. Therefore, on the day of the adoption of the Constitution itself, after urging the countrymen to make political democracy a social democracy as well, he with great courage and conviction reminded the people of the country that, we must begin by acknowledging the fact that there is complete absence of two things in the Indian society. One of these is equality. On the social plane, we have in India a society based on the principle of graded inequality which means elevation for some and degradation for others. On the economic plane, we have a society in which there are some who have immense wealth as against many who live in abject poverty.

> On the 26th of January 1950, we are going to enter into a life of contradictions. In politics we will have equality and in social and economic life we will have inequality. In politics we will be recognizing the principle of one man one vote and one vote one value. In our social and economic life, we shall, by reason of our social and economic structure, continue to deny the principle of one man one value. How long shall we continue to live this life

> of contradictions? How long shall we continue to deny equality in our social and economic life? If we continue to deny it for long, we will do so only by putting our democracy in peril. We must remove this contradiction at the earliest possible moment or else those who suffer from inequality will blow up the structure of political democracy which this Assembly has so laboriously built up.[29]

Even today the Indians cannot afford to forget this message of Dr. Ambedkar in the process of creating a new just social order.

Empowerment of women is a talk of today. But to liberate the Hindu women from the bonds of lawless social laws Dr. Ambedkar, as the Law Minister of India courageously introduced the Hindu Code Bill in the Parliament.[30] This daring move of Dr. Ambedkar was guided by his quest for the constitutional culture - the culture of equality. Initially, Prime Minister Nehru assured his full support to the Bill. While supporting the Bill on 19th December 1949, Nehru stated, "We attach the greatest importance to it (Bill), not because of any particular clause or anything, but because of the basic approach to this vast problem. That is a stage in the journey, and there are other stages, economic, social and other and if society is to advance, there must be this integrated advance on all fronts".[31] But the Bill was opposed by the President of India, Dr. Prasad himself. President Rajendra Prasad expressed several objections against the Bill. His main objection was that the bill was discriminatory, as it did not apply to the personal law of the minorities and Parliament should not enact the bill on the eve of a general election and without obtaining the mandate. Dr. Prasad also made it clear to Nehru that if he pushed the Bill through, he would exercise his prerogative of addressing the House.[32] In fact, several women members in the Provincial Parliament considered the Hindu Code Bill as a testament of their faith in the Constitution. But taking into account the electoral prospects of the Congress Party in the first general election and stiff opposition within the Congress Party, Pandit Nehru dropped the Hindu Code Bill.

Despite ill health, Dr. Ambedkar worked very hard to pursue the agenda of social change through Hindu Code Bill in the country. Therefore, the treatment accorded to the Bill and finally the government's decision to drop the Hindu Code Bill was perceived by Dr. Ambedkar as a great betrayal. The governmental inaction over the Bill resulted into Dr. Ambedkar's resignation from the Law Ministry, on 27th September, 1951.[33] In his resignation statement, Dr. Ambedkar stated mainly five reasons behind his exit from the cabinet. Dropping of the Hindu Code Bill was one of the prime reasons.[34] In the resignation statement he elaborated how the government killed the Bill and the Bill died, to use, Ambedkar's phrase, "unwept and unsung".[35] Despite his several differences as stated in the resignation letter he remained in the office to get through the Bill. Because he held,

> "The Hindu Code Bill was the greatest social reform measure ever undertaken by the Legislature in this country. No law passed by the Indian Legislature in the past or likely to be passed in the future can be compared to it in point of its significance. To leave inequality between class and class, between sex and sex which is the soul of Hindu Society untouched and to go on passing legislation relating to economic problems is to make a farce of our Constitution and to build a palace on a dung heap. This is the significance I attached to the Hindu Code".[36]

Finally, time has proved that Dr. Ambedkar was right and subsequently the Hindu Code Bill was split into four Bills and were passed separately by the Parliament in 1955-56.

Dr. Ambedkar was never in favour of the cosmetic changes in the society. His life mission was to liberate broken men by the reconstruction of country's ancient, village based unjust, pyramidal caste based social order. In this endeavour he was more guided by the spirit of socio-economic democracy and not by political democracy alone. His idea of government was not for the sake of rule, but government with the constitutional obligations towards socio-economic democracy. Therefore, he visualized the government in which men in power will give their undivided allegiance to the best interest of the country and will not be afraid to amend the social and economic code of life which the dictates of justice and expediency so urgently call for.[37] Knowing fully well that Indian democracy was merely a top dressing on an undemocratic social order, Dr. Ambedkar was an ardent supporter of Parliamentary Democracy for India. In his three significant speeches[38] he again and again warned the political creed in India not to place the creed's interest above the interest of the country. Equally due to caste-culture, he was very much worried about the prospect of democracy in India. In his address on Prospect of Democracy of India, a talk for Voice of America, on 20th May, 1956, he said:

> ...caste system which have their evil effects and which militates against democracy. One such feature of the caste system lies in its being accompanied by what is called "Graded Inequality". Castes are not equal in status. They are standing above one another. They are jealous of one another. It is an ascending scale of hatred and a descending scale of contempt. This feature of the caste system has most pernicious consequences... those who want to keep up the caste system is not to improve the prospect of democracy in India but to put democracy in India in greater jeopardy.

Taking into account Dr. Ambedkar's messages and in the environment of socio-political turmoil in the country, it is essential for those who are at the helm of affairs of the nation to reconsider their strategy to bring about the social change in India.

Pre-Constitution social order in India was based upon certain inhuman as well as cruel religious practices. At the height of it, certain social lawless laws were ordained by Hindu lawgivers like Manu and others who sanctified such inhuman customs and practices. Custom of untouchability was one of them. The system was a gold mine to Hindus because they were getting millions of untouchables to serve as their retinues to enable the Hindus to maintain pomp and ceremony and to cultivate a feeling of pride and dignity befitting a master class which cannot be fostered and sustained unless there is beneath it a servile class to look down upon.[39] Dr. Ambedkar's viewpoint was that, the system of untouchability was not a merely religious system but more than that, an economic system – worse than slavery, a system of not only unmitigated economic exploitation but a system of uncontrolled economic exploitation.[40] Since untouchability was and is a problem of an attitude of Hindus, Dr. Ambedkar was of the firm view that, unless Hindus change their attitude, untouchability will not vanish. Ultimately, at least on the paper, the Constitution of India has abolished untouchability through its Article 17. This was a radical action towards the social change in the country backed by fundamental law. Government of India, through its several affirmative actions, schemes and laws has tried to put an end to the system of untouchability but due to social resistance it has not been able to achieve cent percent success. For instance:

1. It is a national tragedy that, despite such constitutional agenda of social change the weakest and vulnerable segments of our society continue to bear the stigma of untouchability and suffer from discrimination, exploitation and atrocities and brutal killings.
2. Dalit-tribal women face the triple burden of caste, class and gender. Most of them have been forced to join prostitution by socio-religious sanctions and are exploited sexually.
3. Dalits-tribals resistance to subjugation and exploitation has increased in caste conflicts and massacres. Sometime it is resulted into social boycotts and forced migration.
4. Issues related to land disputes has resulted into atrocities, rapes, and bonded labourers.
5. In some parts of the country, poor dalits and tribals have been deprived from the constitutional right to vote.

6. Law, law enforcement agencies and to a certain extent even judiciary also contribute for sufferings of marginalized people. Sometimes State police acts in a league with politicians and social police (protectors of caste culture) to exploit and oppressing Dalits-tribals.
7. Some of the State actions reflect the anti-constitution policies crushing the social revolution.
8. According to the UN Committee on Elimination of Racial Discrimination (1996) that India failed to protect its marginalized people, Untouchables and Tribals, from atrocities committed by 'high' caste Hindus, failed to punish the guilty and failed to give reparations to the victims and dismantle the institutionalized system of 'high caste' and 'low caste'.
9. Although in 545 members of the Lok Sabha, 79 members of the SCs and 41 members of STs are elected, rarely they are involved in the policy matters of the country. Most of them are slaves of their party leadership or ideology. They are like dumb driven cattles. Mostly these leaders are utilized to oppose the genuine and capable leadership and welfare programmes of SCs and STs.

The Constitution and its architects have tried a lot to bring a socio-economic revolution through peaceful democratic and constitutional means. Some constitutional safeguards although not to the level of Dr. Ambedkar's expectations have been provided in the Constitution as the affirmative action to uplift the backward classes, especially children, women, SCs and STs. But the fate of this social and economic revolution has been sealed by ruling class and the successive governments in the country. Due to neglect of social revolution aspect of the Constitution the goal of creating a 'just' society has remained merely on the paper. Taking the cognizance of this kind of pathetic situation, President of India, K.R. Narayanan in his address to the nation said:

> "we have to ponder over the condition of not only women in our society, but of the Dalits, the tribals and other weaker

sections. Untouchability has been abolished by law but shades of it remain in the ingrained attitudes nurtured by the caste system. Though the constitutional provisions of reservation in educational institutions and public services flow from our Constitution, these provisions remain unfulfilled through bureaucratic and administrative deformation or by narrow interpretations of these special provisions. It seems, in the social realm, some kind of a counter revolution is taking place in India. It is forgotten that these benefits have been provided not in the way of charity, but as human rights and as social Justice to a section of society who constitutes a big chunk of our population, and who actually contribute to our agriculture, industry and services as landless labourers, factory and municipal workers. These are signs that our privileged classes are getting tired of the affirmative action provided by Constitutional provisions."[41]

The prevailing stark realities in the country has compelled The President of India, K.R. Narayanan to observe that:

1. Fifty years into our life in the Republic we find that justice – social, economic and political – remains an unrealized dream for millions of our fellow citizens.
2. Tragically, the growth in our economy has not been uniform. It has been accompanied by great regional and social inequalities.
3. Beware of the fury of the patient and long-suffering people.
4. Our three-way fast lane of liberalization, privatization and globalization must provide safe pedestrian crossing for the unempowered India also so that it too can move towards Equality of Status and Opportunity.
5. There is our greatest national drawback: the status of women and our greatest national shame, the condition of the Dalits, the erstwhile untouchables.
6. We have to ponder over the condition of not only women in our society, but of the Dalits, the tribals and other weaker sections.

In the backdrop of age-old caste culture, when the Constitution which has been a largely Dr. Ambedkar's work, is itself under attack in the era of three by-lanes, privatization, globalization and liberalization, when Dalits-exploited segments of the society, consumers of social justice are in the state of wilderness in large number of States, how to realize the constitutional goal of social and economic change and equality is a million dollar question. This does not mean to suggest that there has been no change at all. Certainly, there has been a considerable amount of change. Several constitutional safeguards and State affirmative actions have delivered the goods. It has somewhat diminished the repressions of hierarchy and the effects of indifference among the upper castes to conditions among the lower.[42] Reservations in education, in legislatures and in government employment have brought about into universities and the political process many individuals who otherwise would have entered neither, and they attest to the paradoxical erosion of the caste system as caste allegiance facilitates upward mobility.[43] The socio-economic and political developments have weakened the traditional pillars of social structure. The social revolution has gained the ground, although it has far to go.[44] However, in these circumstances one should not think that the social change would be achieved very easily and without any kind of resistance. Action for social change calls for change of attitude, a systematic broad based, organized efforts backed by political will and governments with a constitutional zeal. Dr Babasaheb Ambedkar expected exactly that.

The Constitution of India has sought to create a new social order premised on the liberty, equality, fraternity and justice to all – Social, Economic and Political and created the State with such major constitutional responsibilities. State under the Constitution has been bestowed with duties, such as providing right to work., education, free and compulsory education, adequate means of livelihood, equal pay for equal work to both men and women, minimization of inequality in income and elimination of inequality in status and above all operation of economic system to prevent the monopoly of few. However, in the liberalized era of market economy there has been a sea change in the role of the State. With the closure and privatization of public sector, State has started withdrawing from its basic duties under the Constitution, such as stated herein above. This has created manifold problems and challenges before the socio-economic change in India. It goes without saying that the long cherished goals of growth with social justice have remained merely the slogan in the era of liberalization. Under the operation of new economic system the vulnerable groups in India are without any safety nets. The new economic policy has completely outlawed the entire chapter of Directive Principles of State Policy, especially Articles 38 and 39, from the Constitution, giving a death blow to the socio-economic revolution.

Dr. Ambedkar, his struggle and the Indian Constitution, have articulated the agenda of the social and economic revolution. The Constitution could be considered as the legacy of the struggle of Dr. Babasaheb Ambedkar. But as Granville Austin very ably said,

> ...a Constitution, however 'living', is inert. It does not 'work', it is worked – worked by human beings whose conduct may shape, whose energies it may canalize, but whose character it cannot improve, and whose tasks it cannot perform.... The politics of working the Constitution confronted Indians with two apparent incompatibilities: the first was between aspects of their culture and the pursuit of a democratic and reformed society; the second was among constitutional provisions carrying the strands of the seamless web. These difficulties had to be surmounted, circumvented, or accommodated in the conditions prevailing in the country.[45]

In this process law makers, law and interpreters of law-judges have to shoulder the major responsibility. Among all, the major burden lies on judiciary because, ultimately, it is the judges who infuse the spirit into the dead letters of law and Constitution. They are the expounders of the Constitution. To realize the goal of social change, it is they, who have to rise above the caste-communal, regional considerations and class hatred, interest as well as prejudices.

To what extent the constitutional agenda of social change has worked out is a matter of great debate. In fact, Dr. Ambedkar visualized the futility of the constitutional safeguards in the hands of majority in the country that he thought of communal character as essentially undemocratic. He held the firm view that:

> In India, the majority is not a political majority. In India, the majority is born: it is not made. That is the difference between a communal majority and a political majority. A political majority is not a fixed or a permanent majority. It is a majority which is always made, unmade and remade. A communal majority is a permanent majority fixed in its attitude. One can destroy it, but one cannot transform it.[46]

Dr. Babasaheb Ambedkar's this diagnosis of India's political as well as communal majority, and its evil effects on the constitutional institutions and functionaries, perhaps reveals the reasons for incomplete picture of social and economic change in India.

Notes

1. Upendra Baxi, Inaugural Oration on Babasaheb Ambedkar Centenary Celebration at University of Madras, on March 5, 1991. In Vibhute K.I. (ed.), *Dr. Ambedkar and Empowerment: Constitutional Vicissitudes*, University of Poona, 1993.
2. Ibid.
3. Granville Austin, *The Indian Constitution Cornerstone of Nation*, p. 26, Oxford University Press, New Delhi, Third Impression 2000.
4. Ibid. p. 27.

5. *Constituent Assembly Debates*, Vol. V, p. 2, Official Report, Reprinted by Lok Sabha Secretariat, New Delhi, Second Reprint, 1989.
6. Ibid. p.4.
7. "States and Minorities", Memorandum submitted to the Constituent Assembly, on behalf of Dr. Ambedkar's Party, the All India Scheduled Castes Federation, *Dr. Babasaheb Ambedkar Writings and Speeches*, Vol. 1, by Education Department, Government of Maharashtra, 1979.
8. Ibid. p. 412.
9. *Selected Works of Jawaharlal Nehru*, Vol. 2, p. 196, II Series, Editor S. Gopal, J. N. Memorial Fund, Teen Murthy House, New Delhi, 1984.
10. Munshi, K.M., *Pilgrimage to Freedom* Vol. I, Quoted by Ram Iqbal, Dr. Ambedkar's Political Philosophy and Indian Politics, Voice of the Weak, April, 1985.
11. Supra Note., 9.
12. On moving the Draft Constitution in the Constituent Assembly, on 4th November, 1948, Constituent Assembly Debates, Vol. VII, p. 41.
13. Supra Note, 3, P. 79.
14. Shiva Rao, *The Framing of India's Constitution: Select Documents*, Vol. III, pp. 7, 98, 226 and Supra Note 3, pp. 363-365.
15 Rajeev Dhavan, "Promises, Promises...: Human Rights In India", 39 *J.I.L.I.*, 1997, p. 150.
16. Ibid. p. 152.
17. Supra Note, 5, p. 78.
18. Granville Austin, *Working a Democratic Constitution: The Indian Experience*, p. 651, Oxford, 2000.
19. *Dr. Babasaheb Ambedkar Writings and Speeches*, Vol. 9, p. 209.
20. Ibid.
21. Ibid. p. 98.
22. *Dr. Ambedkar Writings and Speeches*, Vol. I, pp. 252-253.
23. Supra Note No. 5, p. 102.
24. "States and Minorities: What are Their Rights and How to Secure Them in the Constitution of Free India", *Dr. Ambedkar Writing and Speeches*, Vol. 1, pp. 401-403.
25. Ibid. pp. 426-428.
26. *The Hindu*, Tuesday, October 9, 2001, Chennai.
27. In the history of negotiation for preventing the partition of Ireland, Redmond said to Carson, "ask for any safeguards you like for the

Protestant Minority but let use a United Ireland." Carson's reply was 'Damn with your safeguards, we don't want to be ruled by you."

28. *Constituent Assembly Debates*, Vol. VII, p. 39.
29. *Constituent Assembly Debates*, Vol. XII, p. 979.
30. The Hindu Code Bill was introduced in the Parliament, on, 11th April, 1947.
31. *Dr. Babasaheb Ambedkar Writings and Speeches*, Vol. 14, Part 2, p. 1326, Education Department, Government of Maharashtra, 1995.
32. Munshi, K.M., *Pilgrimage to Freedom*, Vol. I, p. 286.
33. Dr. Ambedkar was the Law Minister for a period of 4 years, 1 month and 26 days.
34. (1) Prime Minister had agreed to give him additional charge of Planning department which was not given. (2) Treatment accorded to the Backward Classes and the Scheduled. Castes. (3) Ruinous foreign policy. (4) Fiction of cabinet responsibility. He said, "The Cabinet has become a merely recording and registration office of decisions already arrived at by Committees."
35. Resignation Statement of Dr. Ambedkar, *Dr. Babasaheb Ambedkar Writings and Speeches*, Vol. 14, Part 2, p. 1323, Education Department, Government of Maharashtra, 1995.
36. Ibid. pp. 1325-1326.
37. Dr. Ambedkar's Speech in the Plenary Session of the Round Table Conferences, on 20th November, 1930.
38. (1) Speech in the Constituent Assembly on 25th November 1949, (2) Address at District Law Library, Poona Bar, on 22nd December 1952, (3) Talk for Voice of America on 20th May, 1956.
39. *Dr. Babasaheb Ambedkar Writings and Speeches*, Vol. 9, pp. 196-197.
40. Ibid.
41. The President of India, Mr. K.R. Narayanan's Address to Nation on the eve of the Golden Jubilee of Republic India, On 25th January, 2000.
42. Supra Note No. 18, p. 646.
43. Shah, Ghanshyam, "Grassroots Mobilisation in Indian Politics", in Kohli (ed.) *Indian Democracy*, p. 270.
44. Supra Note No. 18, p. 667.
45. Ibid. p. 636.
46. *Dr. Babasaheb Ambedkar Writings and Speeches*, Vol. 1, p. 37, Education Department, Government of Maharashtra, 1979.

14

Backward Classes, Dalits and the Digital Divides

ABDUL MATIN

Equality has become a touchstone in modern Indian society, at least in principle, as enshrined in the Indian constitution.[1] However, practice of inequality is a social fact, which may be explained by examining the social structure of the society. Ever since Jean Jacques Rousseau in his magnum opus *The Social Contract and Discourse* pointed out the differences between natural and social inequalities (quoted in Beteille, 1977: 3-4), sociologists have evinced more interest in the latter one.[2] Social inequality stems from wealth, prestige and power in Indian society like other societies since time immemorial. Knowledge is an added dimension of source of social inequality in an era of Information and Communication Technology (ICT) and globalization. ICT is assumed to superimpose digital divide on the traditional divides. Backward classes (including dalits)[3] in India, due to unequal access to wealth, prestige and power have been unjustly treated, humiliated and exploited at various

This paper is a substantially revised version of the lecture delivered to the participants of the 20th Refresher Course in Sociology at the Academic Staff College, Jawaharlal Nehru University, New Delhi in 23 November 2000.

frontiers. Bayley (2000: 180) has pointed out that throughout the nineteenth century the broad and ill-defined category of the 'depressed' ('tribes', 'aboriginals' and 'non-Aryan castes') were outside the norms and boundaries of the Hindu 'nation'. All this began to change when Hindu nation builders began to turn their public spotlight on the faith, morals and condition of the 'depressed classes'. In order to 'uplift' such people and make them worthy co-sharers in the moral order of the nation, well-meaning reformist called for initiatives to 'promote education including cleanliness and morality' among these groups. Mohan (2001) has examined the history of dalit struggle for freedom with specific reference to the Dravidian parties in Tamil Nadu. Ambedkar had shown a great concern by championing resistance to these inequalities mainly based on social prestige. Narayan (2001) has narrated the heroes, histories and peoples' aspirations manifested through political parties by publishing books and booklets by various publishers specializing their publications on dalits dealing with the issue of social inequality and social injustice and possible remedial measures. Knowledge is an added dimension of source of social inequality in an era of ICT and globalization. This paper explores the implications of ICT on social inequality at the beginning of the 21st century in contemporary Indian society with specific reference to the backward classes. It may provide as a tentative theoretical framework for the analysis of the impact of Information and Communication Technology. It may further help in unravelling the perpetuation and intensification of contemporary social inequalities. This endeavour may help in devising a strategy for affirmative action for the backward classes (including dalits) in Indian society for digital empowerment and equity at the first quarter of the 21st century.

Information and Communication Technology (ICT)

Human being is a communicator of information. It is characteristic of human being to communicate information to other human beings. This capability of communication of very complex ideas from human being to human being has led to our present state of civilization. The history of civilization is the theory of improved means of communication of information. In the second half of the 20th century, this fact has been theorized and information has been defined in such a way that its quantities may be measured. C.E. Shannon has pointed out that information may be treated very much like a physical quantity, viz., mass or energy. In 1953, Daniel Bell predicted that information would succeed the raw materials, natural resources and energy as a commodity. The increasing complexity and competition in the global market, the vast uncontrolled information explosion, just-in-time delivery systems, and socio-economic and cultural changes are already proving that the world is now getting tuned to the information era. *It has taken many decades to realize that the new wealth is neither money nor power but information and knowledge* (emphasis added) (Shah, 1999).

Kagami (2001: 21) has pointed out that the industrial revolution started in the eighteenth century in the United Kingdom where the steam engine and other mechanical innovations dramatically increased industrial output and drastically changed social systems. The second wave of industrialization came with mass production methods represented particularly by the automotive industry at the beginning of the twentieth century. Then, the third industrial revolution came to the front during the 1980s driven by technological breakthroughs taking place in the computer industry. Toffler (1981) has described about this third wave in a greater detail. The emergence of powerful desktop computers changed existing social systems from industrial production to people's lifestyles. Especially, the appearance of the Internet has had a profound impact on society. There were around 4.5 million Internet users at the beginning of the 1990s, and the number reached 260 million in 1999. A network system such as the Internet can cross national boundaries and surpass time differences. This creates fundamental complications for current territorially based systems including regulations, laws, administration, and economic and social institutions (Kagami, 2001: 27).

Information is the next managerial asset after the following forces of production: *land, labour, machine* and *capital*[4] (emphasis added). ICT applications can be broadly categorized into three types[5]: (a) Decision support to public administrators; (b) Improving services to citizens; and (c) Empowering citizens to access information and knowledge.[6]

Income disparity brings about digital disparity, i.e., what is called 'digital divide'. It is reported that in the US among the 5.5 million White, Asian, and Pacific Islander families with an income of at least US$ 75,000, living in metropolitan areas, headed by someone with at least a college education and aged 30 to 55; about 87 per cent had computers at home, and 68 per cent had Internet connections. At the other extreme, the 1.2 million Black and Hispanic urban households with incomes below US$15,000, in which all adults lack a high school diploma or GED, and headed by someone aged 30 to 55, only 7 per cent had computers at home and only 2 per cent had Internet service. This observation can also be applied to countries on a developed, underdeveloped basis (Ibid. 28). Thus, those who can have access to the Internet can enjoy the benefits of the IT revolution but those who cannot are left behind. This gap takes place not only within one country but also between advanced and developing countries. This is applicable in the case of India in terms of 'inter' and 'intra' digital divides: wherein the latter case existing social divides in terms of caste is continuing, digital divides are superimposed and reinforced on it.

Theoretical Framework

McGaughy (2000) has pointed out five epochs of civilization. It has been summarized in Figure 14.1. The fifth epoch is of the IT which is associated with the close of the 20th century. This epoch is characterized by some as third wave. Others have considered it as de-massification.

Figure 14.1
Five Epochs of Civilization

Epochs	*Time*	*Events*	*New Dominant Cultural Technology*
First Epoch	2nd Century A.D.	Roman, Parthian, Kushan, Han Chinese	Primitive/ Ideographic Writing
Second Epoch	Mid First millennium B.C.	Buddhism, Christianity, Islam	Alphabetic Writing
Third Epoch	14th/15th Century A.D.	Renaissance	Printing in Europe
Fourth Epoch	Early 20th Century	Mass Media	Electronic Technologies
Fifth Epoch	Close of 20th Century	Information Technology (IT)	Computer Technology

Source: William McGaughy. *2000. Five Epochs of Civilizations: World History as Emerging in Five Civilizations.* Minneapolis, MN: Thrirstlerose Publications.

Manuel Castells (1996, 1997, 1998) examines the emergence of a new society, culture, and economy in light of the revolution, begun in the United States in the 1970s, in informational technology (television, computers, and so on). This revolution led, in turn, to a fundamental restructuring of the capitalist system beginning in the late 1980s and to the emergence of what Castells calls 'informational capitalism'. Also emerging were 'informational societies' (although there are important cultural and institutional differences among these societies). Both are based on 'informationalism' (a mode of development in which the main source of productivity is the qualitative capacity to optimize the combination and use of factors of production on the basis of knowledge and information (Castells, 1998: 7).[7]

Castells's analysis of information technology paradigm has five characteristics. First, these are technologies that act on information. Second, since information is part of all human activity, these technologies have a pervasive effect. Third, all systems using information technologies are defined by a 'networking logic', allowing them to affect a wide variety of processes and organizations. Fourth, the new technologies are highly flexible, allowing them to adapt and change constantly. Fifth, the specific technologies associated with information are merging into a highly integrated system (Ritzer, 2000).

Globalization refers to 'One World'. Yogendra Singh has looked upon globalization in two possible contradictory ways of knowledge and capital[8]: (a) Information age or knowledge in which skills and the service sector have become crucial than capital. (b) Globalization may also be called a neo-capitalism: importance of capital has increased than decreased. Singh has examined the impact of globalization on India in terms of culture, family, mass media, regions (north/south) and identities (Singh, 2000).

While it is global, there are differences, and Castells distinguishes among regions that lie at the heart of the new global, there are differences, and Castells distinguishes among regions that lie at the heart of the new global economy (North America NAFTA, European Union EEC, Asian Pacific ASEAN). Thus, we are talking about a regionalized, global economy. In addition, there is considerable diversity within each region and of crucial importance is the fact that while some areas of the globe are included, others are excluded and they suffer grave negative consequences. Whole areas of the world (e.g., sub-Saharan Africa) are excluded, as are parts of the privileged regions such as the inner cities in the United States.[9]

The complex relationship of IT with culture, society, polity and economy may be theorized in Figure 14.2. This tentative exercise may be looked upon as what Blaikie (2000) calls retroductive research strategy or logic of inquiry. However, the present paper is an attempt towards discerning relationship between access to information with the social structure in the Indian society.

Figure 14.2
Conceptual Framework

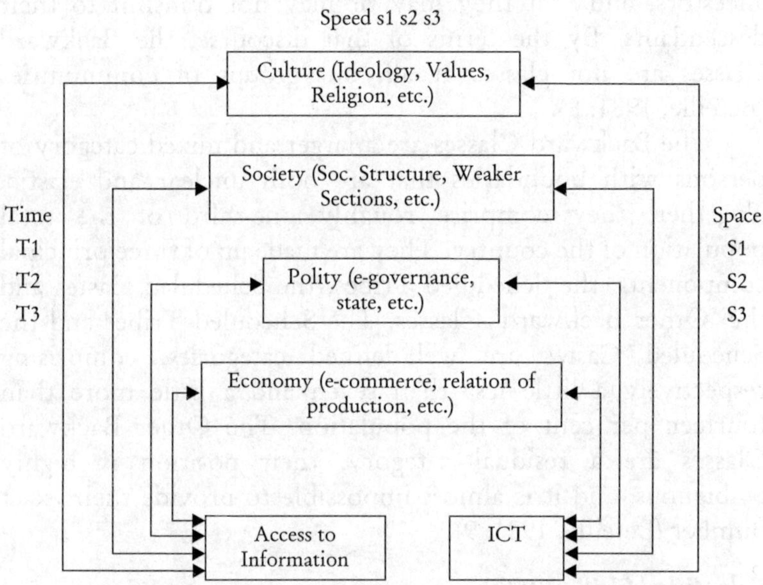

Time	Space	Speed
T1 = Pre-Modern	S1 = First World	s1 = Slow
T2 = Modern	S2 = Second World	s2 = Medium
T3 = Post-Modern	S3 = Third World	s3 = Fast

Backward Classes Including Dalits

The problem of the Backward Classes is, in its most general form, the problem of achieving equality in a world permeated by inequality. The significance of the category 'Backward Classes' lies not only in its size and extent, but also in the uniquely Indian way of defining its boundaries. This uniqueness is a reflection of specific social and historical conditions. In India, unlike other societies, 'backwardness' is viewed as an attribute not of individuals but of communities which are, by their nature, self-perpetuating. In Weberian sense, a class is a set of individuals – or, at least, families – sharing certain life chances in common that they may or may not owe to their ancestors, and that they may or may not transmit to their descendants. By the terms of that discourse, the Backward Classes are not classes at all, but groups of communities (Beteille, 1981: 8).

The Backward Classes are a larger and mixed category of persons with boundaries that are both unclear and elastic. Together, they comprise roughly one-third of the total population of the country. They are made up of three principal components, the Scheduled Tribes, the Scheduled Castes and the 'Other Backward' Classes. The Scheduled Tribes and the Scheduled Castes are well-defined categories, comprising respectively a little less than seven and a little more than fourteen per cent of the population. The Other Backward Classes are a residual category, their position is highly ambiguous; and it is almost impossible to provide their exact number (Beteille, 1981: 9).

Scheduled Tribes (STs)

According to 1991 census, the tribal population of India is 67.76 million. The tribals form 8.08 per cent of the total population of India. India has the second largest tribal population in the world. While the growth rate of population during 1981-91 is 23.79 per cent, STs growth rate has been 25.67 per cent. The highest rate of growth of STs is in Kerala followed by Gujarat and Rajasthan. The highest number of tribals according to 1991 census is in Madhya Pradesh (15.40 million), followed by Maharashtra (7.32 million), Orissa (7.03 million), Bihar (6.61 million) and Gujarat (6.16 million). In Rajasthan, West Bengal and Andhra Pradesh, the number of tribals varies between three and four million; in Assam, Meghalaya and Nagaland between one and two million; and in Arunachal Pradesh, Tripura, Manipur and Mizoram between 0.3 and 0.7 million. In Mizoram, the tribal population constitutes 95 per cent of the total population of the state. In Nagaland tribal population constitutes 89 per cent, in Meghalaya and Arunachal Pradesh 80 per cent, in Tripura 70 per cent, in Madhya Pradesh and Orissa 23 per cent, in Gujarat 14 per cent, in Rajasthan 12 per cent, and in Assam and Bihar 10 per cent. It may be noted here that because of separation of Chattisgarh and Jharkhand from Madhya Pradesh and Bihar respectively, these figures should be disaggregated.

Most of the tribals live in isolated areas. The main sources of their livelihood are agriculture and gathering of forest produce, mainly for their subsistence. They largely rely upon barter system. They spend greater part of their earnings on social and religious ceremonies. A large number of tribes are illiterate. They are victimized by unscrupulous forest contractors and money-lenders. Tribal population posses small and uneconomical land holdings because of which their crop yield is less. This is the main reason for their perpetual indebtedness. Only a small percentage of the tribal population participates in the secondary and tertiary sectors. Literacy rate among the tribal population, according to the 1991 census is 29.60 per cent as opposed to 52.21 per cent general literacy rate of the country. However, tribal literacy rate in Mizoram is 82.71 per cent and in Nagaland, Sikkim and Kerala is between 57 per cent and 61 per cent.

Scheduled Castes (SCs)

The total population of the SCs (dalits) according to 1991 census is 138.22 million (16.3 per cent of the total population). The highest number of SCs is found in Uttar Pradesh (29.2 million or 21 per cent of the total SC population in India), followed by West Bengal (11.6%), Bihar (9.1%), Tamil Nadu (7.7%), Andhra Pradesh (7.7%), Madhya Pradesh (7%), Rajasthan (5.5%), Karnataka (5.3%), Punjab (4.2%), and Maharashtra (6.3%). About 84 per cent of the SC population live in rural areas. They are working as agricultural labourers, sharecroppers, tenants, and marginal farmers. Almost all persons engaged in occupations like sweeping, scavenging and tanning are from SCs. In terms of work/occupations, according to the 1991 census, of the total scheduled caste population of 138. 2 millions, 57.49 millions (41.6%) fall in the category of workers. Out of the total workers the break-up of various occupations are as follows: 53.8 per cent are working as leather workers; 12.4 per cent as weavers; 7.9 per cent as fishermen; 6.8 per cent as toddy-tappers; 5.2 per cent as basket and rope makers; 4.6 per cent as washermen; 3.7 per cent as scavengers; 1.3 per cent as artisans; 1.3 per cent as fruit/vegetable sellers; 0.9 per cent as shoe-makers; 0.4 per cent as liquor manufacturers; 0.3 per cent as drummers; and 0.1 per cent as carpenters and iron-smiths. The remaining 1.3 per cent is engaged in other petty occupations. About two-thirds of the bonded labourers are from the scheduled castes. Literacy among the Scheduled Caste people is extremely low. It was only 13.6 per cent in 1991. Singh (1999: 12) has pointed out that the scheduled castes have reacted favourably to education for boys, less so for girls. The drop-out rate for boys is very high on account of economic reasons, in spite of government help. According to the 1961 census, the literacy rate among the scheduled castes at the national level was 10.27 per cent, which increased to 14.67 per cent in 1971 and to 21.38 per cent in 1981 (excluding Assam). Thus it is observed that over 1961-81 literacy among them has doubled. Similarly, the sex-wise literacy rate during this period also shows a positive trend. According to the 1961 census, 16.96 per cent males and 3.29 per cent females were literate. This number increased to 22.36 per cent for males and 6.44 per cent for females in 1977, which further increased to 31.12 per cent and 10.93 per cent respectively in 1981. Thus, during this period male literacy has almost doubled, whereas literacy among females has shown an increase by more than three times. Thus analysis of the literacy rate (1981 census) among the scheduled castes in rural areas (27.91% males and 8.45% females) and 36.60 per cent in urban areas (47.54% males and 24.34% females) have been returned literate. This shows that the scheduled castes living in urban areas have more opportunity to get their children educated than do their rural counterparts.

Mendelsohn and Vicziany (2000: 118-175) have pointed out towards compensatory discrimination and action against adverse discrimination as public policy towards the untouchables in modem India. They grew out of Ambedkar's approach, and consist in guarantees of seats in legislatures, positions in public employment, and educational benefits. The second policy more closely reflected Gandhi's position, and has been concerned to bring about a cessation of discriminatory behaviour on the part of caste Hindus. On the two policies it is compensatory discrimination that has captured the attention of the Indian public and Untouchables themselves (Ibid.: 118-119). They have further pointed out that untouchable literacy now lags behind that of the general population by about a decade; at the time of the 1981 Census the lag was two decades. If the recent trend persists, literacy among the Untouchables may reach the national average at the time of the 2001 Census (Ibid.: 141). However, there are great differences in the literacy of different Untouchable communities, and of course this must be reflected in divergent representation in higher education too. For example, 21 per cent of the Chamars and the Dusadhs of Bihar were literate in 1981, but only 4 per cent of the Musahars of that State (Ibid.: 144). They have concluded that compensatory discrimination is the more successful of these policies. On the other hand, the failure of the anti-discrimination action is measurable in the continuing discrimination against Untouchables throughout large parts of Indian social life (Ibid.: 145). They have argued that the condition of the Untouchables can only be adequately conceived by reference to two interlocking forms of subordination: ritual, cultural and broader social debasement on the one hand, and poverty on the other. They have observed that the post-Independence regime has failed in systematically redistributing the resources in favour downtrodden sections of the society. It has further failed in pursuing a consistent strategy of supplying 'basic needs' (health, education and simple welfare) to the poorest of the poor (Ibid.: 147). However, relatively two successful approaches to development (Kerala model and Punjab model) will necessarily work out for the huge Untouchable population to get out of poverty line. They have aptly remarked that few people now believe that Untouchables and other Indians are poor because they are brutish and stupid, but there has been no discovery of a sure-fire way of rapidly transforming the circumstances of the bottom segment of the Indian population. This is the context for the present popularity of approaches to development that rest their faith in market forces and the transforming power of globalization (Ibid.: 175).

Other Backward Classes (OBCs)

OBCs are the least homogeneous and the most loosely defined. They are mentioned in the Constitution in only the most general terms. There is no all-India list for the OBC. They are not separately enumerated in the census and, in fact, one has to work with only a rough estimate of their population. Their position was sought to be defined in more specific terms of the OBC Commission set up in 1953 under the chairmanship of Kaka Kalelkar. The Commission, which was not a standing body, could not in fact come to any tangible or agreed conclusions.

The OBCs constitute a collection of communities of rather uncertain status. Lists had earlier been prepared by the Ministry of Education and by the State Governments. The Backward Classes Commission under Kaka Kalelkar reported a good deal of ambiguity in these lists. But there was no authoritative list of 'Other Backward Classes'. The census had assumed one list; the Ministry of Education had prepared another; and it was left to the present Commission to recommend an authoritative list. The recommendations of the Commission were not, in fact, accepted as authoritative. The State Governments have in general been allowed to use their own criteria in drawing up lists of the 'Other Backward Classes'. These, in turn are not always held to be binding by the Supreme Court which, in the case of *M.R. Balaji and Others Vs the State of Mysore*, decided against the recommendation of the Nagana Gowda Commission.

The Central Government has particularly since 1961, been pressing for the adoption of economic criteria in defining the Other Backward Classes but there has been resistance to this from a number of State Governments. Some of the castes included in the earlier lists of the Other Backward Classes are fairly powerful in state politics and have therefore been in a position to exert pressure on the State Governments to have the old criteria retained. The Lingayats of Mysore and the Ezhavas of Kerala provide good instances of powerful dominant castes, which have exerted pressure on their respective State Governments for the retention of caste as the basis for defining backwardness.

It is difficult to give exact figures for the 'Other Backward Classes' because they are not enumerated separately in the census and because such lists as do exist are subject to revision from time to time. Some estimate may, however, be made of their strength by projection of the caste returns in the 1931 Census. Broadly, Other Backward Classes constitute about 1/7th of the total population of the country, being thus approximately equal in numerical strength to the Scheduled Castes and Scheduled Tribes. The core of the Other Backward Classes consists of the peasant castes of various descriptions. OBC is a residual category of the Backward Classes, which are not identifiable as SCs or STs.

Backward classes may be defined as less socially developed. Social development refers to the quality of a social system in terms of social justice it delivers, social cohesion it maintains, and quality of life it provides as an integral component of a system. Literacy and education are crucial for ensuring a better quality of life as components of social development as well as for transformation of any society.

In integrating information and communication technology, globalization on the one hand and other backward classes on the other hand, two concepts of 'cumulative inequality' and 'dispersed inequality' of Andre Beteille is very helpful. Thus, caste position of individual/group in social stratification also in terms of social status is very important.

Conclusion

In the trajectory of social transformations: from top down to bottom up approaches of development in terms of economic development to human development to social development to sustainable development approaches in Indian society the backward classes have unique experiences. These approaches have shown a great concern for social divides and concerted efforts in reducing inequality and ensuring social justice. Information Technology may be an additional source of social inequality popularly known as 'digital divides'. Will there be superimposition of digital divides on the continuing 'social divides' is a million-dollar question. Answers may be sought in terms of access to information by the socially underprivileged backward classes. In this background, the following research questions may be examined. (1) How social structure shapes information access especially the socially underprivileged? (2) How the backward classes have been responding to the new opportunity of accessing information? and (3) What are government efforts in the social sector for ensuring access to information by the socially disadvantaged so that their socio-economic conditions may improve?

Notes

1. Beteille (1981: 13) has pointed out that one can distinguish between equality in the simple sense and equality considered as a ratio. This is an old distinction in Western ethical and political philosophy, and

Aristotle makes it both in his Ethics and his Politics. In his terminology, the distinction is between 'numerical' equality and 'proportional' equality. Aristotle observes 'by the first I mean sameness or equality in number or size; by the second equality of ratios'. Aristotle deals primarily with 'proportional' equality, and his whole theory of distributive justice is based on it.

2. But, whenever sociologists study natural inequalities (e.g. age, sex), they examine its social and cultural dimensions. Beteille (1977: 4) has rightly pointed out that even if we admit that there are differences everywhere in nature, these differences are turned into social inequalities only through a process of evaluation, and evaluation is essentially a social or cultural process.
3. 'Backward classes' here refers to castes in India. Sociologists and social anthropologists have shown their great interest in studying caste in India. However, in spite of a large literature available on caste, they have been shifting their interests in studying the dimensions of the caste. For instance, initially, they were interested in the origins and theories of the caste system. Then they evinced their interests in its definitions, characteristics and empirical evidences. Lately they are inclined towards integrating origin, theories, definitions, characteristics at the one hand and empirical evidences and their analysis on the other hand Klass (1998) and Bayly (2000) are some of the examples in this direction.
4. Information Technology (IT) is the brain of hi-tech industry and telecom is the heart. IT, at a basic level, is the conversion of human intelligence and logic into software that propels the computer to crunch number. Telecom is the backbone for widespread informational growth. It provides the means to send the bytes of information soaring across the country or even to far-off countries via satellite uplinks. The reach and power of IT and telecom defy political and geographical obstacles. World Wide Web (WWW) spans across time space to put cyber-surfers in contact with each other.
5. (a) Decision support systems for public administrators focus on improving planning and monitoring development programmes. Examples of such systems include the use of GIS to plan the location of rural facilities or to identify disaster prone areas. Similarly, provision of PCs in the district rural development agencies was primarily intended to improve the monitoring of the integrated rural development programme. The case study of health workers (Bhatnagar and Schware, 2000: 35-49) illustrates how ICT could

enable fieldworkers to better plan their activities and for their supervisors to more effectively monitor their performance. Such systems are likely to be successful in the request to build them originate from public administrators interested in improving the administration of development programmes. However, if such tools are provided in a centrally sponsored scheme to administrators unwilling to change their style of administration, i.e., who are unwilling to use information and its analysis for decision-making, it is unlikely the decision support system will be used. When development programmes are not operationally dependent on such systems, their use becomes purely discretionary. (b) Improving services to citizens focus on automating the process of delivering services to citizens, and, in the process, bring in transparency. Examples of such systems need to make to government agencies. The use of ICT can shorten queues and waiting time at collection counters, improve accuracy in billing and accounts receivable and provide immediate proof of payments to citizens. The case study of collecting stamp duty for registration of property deeds (Ibid.: 76-93) exemplifies the kind of benefits that can accrue to citizens as well as the department delivering the service. Computerization of land records which has been undertaken in many districts is another example (Ibid.: 94-104). Similarly, issuance of important documents to citizens can also be done through computerized systems (Ibid.: 94-104). (c) Empowering citizens to access information and knowledge: Access to information about markets is crucial for rural producers of all varieties of goods and services because these must be exported to other regions. Often middlemen, who bring consumers and producers together, are able to seek disproportionate rent because they have access to ruling prices in different markets. Use of ICT can provide up-to-date information on markets to producers, thus increasing their bargaining power (Ibid.: 65-75).

6. Rural communities can also be helped through access to knowledge that will improve productivity in their work, health practices, and enable them to learn about their environment. A large number of innovations in farm practices, tool design and use of indigenous medication do not diffuse beyond local boundaries because of the isolation of rural communities. Much indigenous knowledge passed down from generations is also becoming extinct due to lack of preservation efforts. ICT and web technologies could make such information/knowledge visible to large cross sections of rural communities. An organized effort at diffusing such knowledge

through ICT: the Honey Bee Network is an example worth appreciation (Bhatnagar and Schware, 2000: 115-131).

7. The spread of informationalism, especially informational capitalism, leads to the emergence of oppositional social movements based on self and identity. The process by which a social actor recognizes itself and constructs meaning primarily on the basis of a given cultural attribute or set of attributes, to the exclusion of a broader reference to other social structures (Castells, 1996: 22). Such movements bring about the contemporary equivalent of what Marxists call 'class struggle'. The hope against the spread of informational capitalism and the problems it causes (exploitation, exclusion, threats to self and identity) is not the working class, but a diverse set of social movements (e.g., ecological, feminist) based primarily on identity. In the 1980s there emerged a new, increasingly profitable global informational economy. It is informational because the productivity and competitiveness of units or agents in this economy (be it firms, regions, or nations) fundamentally depend upon their capacity to generate, process, and apply efficiently knowledge-based information (Ibid.: 66). It is global because it has the capacity to work as a unit in real time by the new information and communication technologies. And it is informational, not just information-based., because the cultural-institutional attributes of the whole social system must be included in the diffusion and implementation of the new technological paradigm (Ibid.: 91).
8. T.K. Oommen has analyzed globalization in terms of the following dichotomies and trichotomy respectively: Tribe/Other; Primitive/Other; Black/Other; Oriental/Other; First World/Second World/Third World. I look upon globalization in terms of economic globalization (EG), political globalization (PG) and cultural/social globalization (C/S G). EG refers to neo-liberalism; free flow of capital from one nation-state to another nation-state; market economy. EG results into increasing economic inequalities. PG implies shift from centralization of 'power and resources' to decentralization of 'power and resources' (decentralization of 'power and resources' at the nation-state level and centralization at the global level). C/S G: culture of the market/consumer market; uniformity and homogeneity; and consumption pattern. Ethnic, Caste and Community Identities have been reviving in India because of globalization. I would like to further add two concepts of localization and glocalization. By localization, I mean identities to be more specific caste identities of backward classes in India. By glocalization, I mean

creamy layers of dalits and backward classes having an access to resources opened up by globalization in its varied scale.

9. However, as we saw above, Castells does not see the development of networks, the culture of real virtuality, informationalism, and especially their use in informational capitalism as going unchallenged. These are opposed by individuals and collectivities with identities of their own, which they seek to defend. Thus, 'God, nation, family, and community will provide unbreakable, eternal codes around which a counter-offensive will be mounted (Castells, 1997: 66). However, it is important to recognize that these counter-movements must rely on information an networks in order to succeed. Thus, they are deeply implicated in the new order to succeed. Thus, they are deeply implicated in the new order. In this context, Castells describes a wide range of social movements including the Zapatistas in Chiapas, Mexico, the American militia, the Japanese cult Aum Shinrikyo, environmentalism, feminism, and the gay movement. In Castells's view on state is that it is increasingly powerless in this new-world of the globalization of the economy and its dependence on global capital markets.

References

Ahuja, Ram. 1999. *Social Problems in India.* (Second Edition) Jaipur: Rawat Publications.

Bajpai, Nirupam and Navi Radjou. 2000. 'Raising Global Competitiveness of Tamil Nadu's IT Industry', *Economic and Political Weekly,* vol. XXXV, No. 6, February 5, pp. 449-465.

Bayly, Susan. 2000. *Caste, Society and Politics in India: From the Eighteenth Century to the Modern Age.* Cambridge: Cambridge University Press.

Beteille, Andre. 1999. *Society and Politics in India: Essays in a Comparative Perspective.* New Delhi: Oxford University Press.

—. 1988. *The Backward Classes and the New Social Order.* Delhi: Oxford University Press.

—. 1977. *Inequality Among Men.* Delhi: Oxford University Press.

Bhatnagar, Subhash and Robert Schware (eds). 2000. *Information and Communication Technology in Development: Cases from India.* New Delhi: Sage Publications.

Blaikie, Norman. 2000. *Designing Social Research: The Logic of Anticipation.* Cambridge: Polity Press.

Castells, Manuel. 1998. *End of Millennium.* Malden, Mass.: Blackwell.

—. 1997. *The Power of-Identity.* Malden, Mass.: Blackwell.

—. 1996a. 'The Net and the Self. Working Notes for a Critical Theory of the Informational Society', *Critique of Anthropology,* 16: 9-38.

—. 1996b. *The Rise of the Network Society.* Malden, Mass.: Blackwell. See 'ICTs in Rural Poverty Alleviation', *Economic and Political Weekly,* vol. xxxvi, No. 11 (March 17-23), pp. 917-920.

Galanter, Marc. 1984. *Competing Equalities: Law and the Backward Classes in India.* New Delhi: Oxford University Press.

Galanter, Marc. 1978. 'Who are the Other Backward Classes? An Introduction to a Constitutional Puzzle', *Economic and Political Weekly,* vol. xiii, nos. 43-44, pp. 1812.

Habib, Ifran. 1999. 'The Peasant and the Village Community' (Chapter IV), in Ifran Habib, *The Agrarian System of Mughal India 1556-1707.* (Second Revised Edition), New Delhi: Oxford University Press.

Habib, Irfan. 1997. 'Caste in Indian History', in Ifran Habib, *Essays in Indian History: Towards a Marxist Perception.* New Delhi: Tulika, pp. 161-179.

Heeks, Richard. 1999. ICTs, *Poverty and Development.* Working Paper No. 5, Development Informatics Working Series, Institute for Development Policy and Management, University of Manchester, (www.man.ac.uk/idpn).

Hutton, J.H. 1986. *Caste in India: Its Nature, Function, and Origins.* (Fourth Edition), Bombay: Oxford University Press.

Kagami, Mitsuhiro and Masatsugh Tsuji. 2001. *The 'IT' Revolution and Developing Countries: Late-Comer Advantage?* Chiba, Japan: IDE (JETRO).

Klass, Morton. 1998. *Caste: The Emergence of the South Asian Social System.* New Delhi: Manohar.

Matin, Abdul. 1999. 'Understanding Uneven Social Development in India (Historical and Comparative Method)', *Indian History Congress Proceedings (60th (Diamond Jubilee) Session,* Calicut University, Kozhikode.

Matin, Abdul. 1990. 'Changing Agrarian Relations in Mithila, North India'. (Unpublished Ph.D. thesis, University of Toronto).

McGaughy, William. 2000. *Five Epochs of Civilizations: World History as Emerging in Five Civilizations.* Minneapolis, MN: Thrirstlerose Publications.

Mendelsohn, Oliver and Marika Vicziany. 2000. *The Untouchables: Subordination, Poverty and the State in Modern India.* Cambridge: Cambridge University Press.

Mohan, J. 2001. *History of Dalit Struggle for Freedom: Dravidian Parties and Dalit Uprise in Tamil Nadu.* Pondicherry: Dhamma Institute of Social Sciences (Diss).

Mohanty, B.B. 2001. 'Land Distribution among Scheduled Castes and Tribes', *Economic and Political Weekly,* vol. xxxvi, no. 40, October 6, pp. 3857-3868.

Narayan, Badri. 2001. 'Heroes, Histories and Booklets', *Economic and Political Weekly,* vol. xxxvi, no. 41, October 13, pp. 3923-3934.

Nesiah, Devanesan. 2000. *Discrimination with Reason? The Policy of Reservations in the United States, India and Malaysia.* New Delhi: Oxford University Press.

Omvedt, Gail. 2001a. 'Infosys and Microsoft-I', *The Hindu,* 10 September, vol. 124, No. 215.

Omvedt, Gail. 2001b. 'Infosys and Microsoft-II', *The Hindu,* 11 September, vol. 124, No. 216.

Parry, Jonathan P. 1999. 'Two Cheers for Reservation: The Satnamis and the Steel Plant in Ramchandra Guha and Jonathan P. Parry (eds.) *Institutions and Inequalities: Essays in Honour of Andre Beteille.* New Delhi: Oxford University Press, pp. 100-127.

Ramaiah, A. 1992. 'Identifying Other Backward Classes', *Economic and Political Weekly,* vol. xxvii, no. 23, pp. 1203-1207.

Rao, Madanmohan, Sanjib Raj Bhandari, S.M. Iqbal, Anjali Sinha and Wahaj us Siraj. 1999. 'Struggling with the Digital Divide: Internet Infrastructure, Policies and Regulations', *Economic and Political Weekly,* vol. XXXVI, Nos. 46 and 47, November 20, pp. 3317-3320.

Ritzer, George. 2000. *Sociological Theory.* (Fifth Edition). New York: McGraw Hill.

Sen, Amartya. 2000. *Development as Freedom.* New Delhi: Oxford University Press.

Shah, S.L. 1999. *Information Technology.* New Delhi: Gyan Publishing House.

Singh, K.S. 1999. *The Scheduled Castes.* (Revised Edition). New Delhi: Oxford University Press.

Singh, Yogendra. 2000, *Culture Change in India: Identity and Globalization.* Jaipur: Rawat Publications.

Sinha, Dipankar. 2000. 'Info-Age and Indian Intellectuals: An Unfashionable Poser', *Economic and Political Weekly,* vol. XXXV, No. 48, November 25, pp, 4188-4194.

Srinivas, M.N. (ed.) 1997. *Caste: Its Twentieth Century Avatar.* New Delhi: Penguin Books.

Sundar, Nandini. 1999. 'The Indian Census, Identity and Inequality', in Ramchandra Guha and Jonathan P. Parry (eds.) *Institutions and Inequalities: Essays in Honour of Andre Beteille.* New Delhi: Oxford University Press, pp. 128-169.

Toffler, Alvin. 1981. *The Third Wave: The Classical Study of Tomorrow.* New York: Bantam Books.

Wankhede, G.G. 2001. 'Educational Inequalities among Scheduled Castes in Maharashtra', *Economic and Political Weekly,* vol. XXXVI, No. 18, May 5, pp. 1553-1558.

15

Dr. Ambedkar and Social Justice

Observatory Remarks

USHA KAPOOR

Social justice is a tridimensional concept – it is a prime democratic value, a prime social ethic and an instrument of social transformation. As a democrative value, it connote political equality and freedom, the acceptance of the principle of 'one man one vote'. As a social ethic, it is a matter of the rejection of caste and class barriers by clearing the social conscience of the traditional notion of inequality between man and man. As an instrument of social transformation, it provides leverage to the state to check social disparities and imbalances through legislative action.

Dr. Ambedkar was a great crusader for the rights of the downtrodden and weaker sections of Indian society. Through his speeches and writings and organized social activities and movements he tried to create self-respect among lower casts and the untouchables so that they could fight for social justice and be able to undo the indignities heaped on them for the past many centuries.[1]

Dr. Ambedkar who had been a victim of social ostracism, blatant prejudice and humiliating acts for being a Mahar, a low caste, refused to accept heinous social customs or institutions simply because they had been sanctified by religion, tradition or law-givers, for what could be more important than the dignity of man and his general well-being. Any book or school of thought, which lowered man's prestige, blurred his perspectives, generated ill will or sanctioned the exploitation of man by man, was no more than the work of the devil and deserved to be relegated into the dustbin of history. Obviously, tradition cannot be regarded as sacrosanct if it promotes slavery. Nor can religion be considered infallible if it denies human rights to a vast segment of society.[2] Since the post-Vedic period Indian society had grievously suffered from the rigid stratification of caste, which asserted their supremacy over hers as per their set gradations and held those outside the *varna* in utter contempt. This section gradually acquired the pseudonym of the untouchables and underwent ingnominious trials and tribulations for centuries[3] despite the endeavours of *Bhakti* and *Sufi* saints and more recently, socio-religious reformers. To quote Dr. Ambedkar:

> Most parts of the world have had their type of populations called the lowly. The Romans had their slaves, the Spartans had their helots, the British their villains, the Americans their negroes and the Germans their Jews. So the Hindus have their Untouchables. But none of these can be said to have been called upon to face of fate which pursues the Untouchables. Slavery, serfdom, villainage have all vanished. But untouchability still exists....The Untouchable is worse off than the Jew....Yet nobody sees to take any notice of the Untouchables – some sixty millions of souls – much less espouse their cause.[4]

Indian sacred literature got a thrashing at Dr. Ambedkar's hands as he regarded it as a creation of the Brahmins to exploit the gullible masses and classes, he regarded Brahminism as the poison which had spoiled Hinduism. He pleaded for the prescription of those texts which sanctioned inequality in society, degraded human beings and disgraced the name of religion, he felt that no intellectual class in the world had prostituted its intelligence to invent a philosophy aimed at keeping its illiterate countrymen in a perpetual state of ignorance and poverty as the Brahmins had done it India. Hinduism as contained in the *Vedas* and the *Smritis* was nothings "but a mass of sacrificial, societal, political and sanitary rules and regulations, all mixed up", he said. What is called religion by the Hindu is nothing but a multitude of commands and prohibitions."[5] Religion ought to be as matter of principle, universally applicable in their essence. But if it deprives one of freedom, promotes inhumanity and gives irrational command it needs to be discarded. "I have, therefore, no hesitation in saying that such a religion must be destroyed and I say, there is nothing irreligious in working for the destruction of such a religion.[6]

The point where Dr. Ambedkar differed from some of his contemporaries like Mahatma Gandhi, Vinayak Damodar Savarkar and Madan Mohan Malaviya was that while he wanted to do away with nefarious social institutions, the latter merely intended to mend them according to the exigencies of circumstances. While Mahatma Gandhi was totally opposed to the political segregation of the untouchables from the Hindu society, Dr. Ambedkar regarded the very idea as absurd and preposterous. The Hindu, he said were unaware of what Carson said to Raymond when the two were negotiating for a United Ireland. "Ask any safeguards you like for the Protestant Minority of Ulster, I am prepared to give them; but let us have a United Ireland under one constitution", said Raymond. To this Carson retorted: "Damn your safeguards. I do not want to be ruled by you".[7]

While Mahatma Gandhi did not regard the practice of *Varnashrama Dharma* as sinful despite its limitations, misinterpretations and distortions, Dr. Ambedkar held that the outcastes were a product of the caste system. The former saw a dichotomy between such issues as the annihilation of caste and the inter-communication between the high and the low in society and the loathsome tradition of segregating the untouchables from the mainstream of society. The latter, on other hand, argued that such issues were interrelated and interwoven into the fabric of society, rooted as they were in false religions. "The real method of breaking up the caste system was not to bring about intercaste marriages dinners and intercaste marriages but to destroy the religious notions on which caste was founded", he observed.[8]

While Mahatma Gandhi and the Congress claimed to have worked for the untouchables on humanistic grounds, Dr. Ambedkar distrusted both the Mahatma and the party. He called Gandhi a social reactionary; Gandhism as "another form of satanisam" and the Congress as "a body of middle-class Hindus supported by the Hindu capitalist whose object is not to make Indians free but to be independent of British control".[9]

Dr. Ambekar disapproved of the grand monde appellative Harijans for the dalits by arguing that this was a subtle move to segregate them. Besides, if the untouchables were the people of God, were the touchable monsters?[10] After being told by Mahatma Gandhi that he had been pondering over the problem of untouchables ever since his school days "when you were not even born" and that he had worked hard to incorporate the problems of the downtrodden sections in the programmes of the congress and made provision for providing them with monetary help, Dr. Ambedkar retorted *inter alia*:

> ....we are not prepared to have faith in great leaders and mahatmas. Let me be brutally frank about it. History tells that Mahatmas, like fleeting phantoms, raise dust but raise no level".[11]

The milieu in which Dr. Ambedkar grew up convinced him of the inadequacy of traditional methods like prayer, admonition or mild rebukes for bringing about a change of heart among the dominant caste groups and hence set him thinking on new lines during the British period. Violence as a catalyst of social change did not appear to him to be a same proposition as it is always stained with the human blood.

Mendicancy too will not help as right can never be secured by begging alone. Constitutional methods my help in achieving the target to a great extent but without ensuring a change in the perceptions of both the dominant and the dominated communities, these were likely to prove as sheer exercise in futility. Hence the need was to grasp the nature and structure of society, pinpoint the malady affecting its constituent parts, and make more and more people aware of it.[12] Dr. Ambedkar's speeches and writings were directed towards this goal.

Indian society of Dr. Ambedkar's time required both assurance and self help before it could be resuscitated from its diseased state, assurance so as to convince it of the efficacy of eliminating caste and untouchability and self help for coming out of the state of despair. Dr. Ambedkar was convinced that so long as caste barrier remained, a demarcate structure would be of no meaning to the vast majority of people. Democracy was not just a political arrangement but a system based on the twin principles of equality and fraternity. Caste could thus prove to be a major hurdle in establishing true democracy. No amount of law or constitutional provisions could change the prejudices of the higher castes against the lower caste till the former listened to the voice of their conscience and stopped perpetrating atrocities on them.[13]

Even though Dr. Ambedkar argued that the inferiority complex of the untouchables was the consequence of their "isolation, discrimination and unfriendliness of the social environment"[14] he often felt that they were themselves to blame for their miserable plight. He wanted them to change their evil habits, improve upon their bad way of living, and stay hygienic so as to be socially acceptable. He exhorted them to "educate, agitate and organize" for emancipating themselves from the hegemony of dominant caste groups. He regretted that the untouchables had never regarded self-respect or self-elevation as the keys to deliverance from poverty, privation, despair and social stigma. To quote Dr. Ambedkar:

> My heart breaks to see the pitiable sights of your faces and to hear your sad voices. You have been groaning from time immemorial and yet are not ashamed to hug your helplessness as an inevitability. Why did you not perish in the pre-natal stage instead? Why did you worsen and sadden the picture of the sorrows, poverty, slavery and burdens of the world with your deplorable, despicable, and detestable, miserable life? You had better die and relieve this world if you cannot rise to a new life and if you cannot rejuvenate yourself. As a matter of fact it is your birthright to get food, shelter and clothing in this land, in equal proportion with every individual, high or low. If you believe in living a respectable life, you believe in self-help which is the best help.[15]

By arguing that Shudras could very aptly trace their descent from the Aryan communities of the solar race and ranked as the Kshatriya *varna* before being deprived of the sacred thread as a result of continuing feuds between Brahmins and Shudra kings, Dr. Ambedkar sought to provide an ethnographic identity to the depressed sections of society.[16] He proved that there was nothing shameful in their past and that their low status was due to the machination of Brahmins who deprived them of the rights of wearing the sacred thread and imposed other social restrictions on them. Such deprivations worsened their plight and left them with little chance to protest.

Dr. Ambedkar fought a twin battle for justice – against the British Raj and against the members of high castes. He reprimanded the former for not giving top priority to the abolition of untouchability.[17] In his view the British were not interested in introducing such social reforms as would rouse the irk of the upper castes.[18] He also felt that the abrupt departure of the British from India would be deleterious to the cause of the depressed classes, as political power would then pass on to the upper castes. Hence, a viable political settlement in favour of the lower castes was necessary before the country was declared free.

Dr. Ambedkar's crusade against the higher caste Hindus stemmed from his belief that they had deliberately prevented the lower castes from rising to the cultural level attained by their counterparts. Religion sanctioned it and the tradition of ill-treating the low castes continued without opposition. To quote him:

> If the Hindu observes untouchability it is because his religion enjoins him to do so. If he is ruthless and lawless in putting down the untouchables rising against the established order, it is because his religion not only tells him that the established order is divine and therefore sacrosanct but also imposes upon him a duty to see that the established order is maintained by all means possible. If he does not listen to the call of humanity, it is because his religion does not enjoin him to regard the untouchable as human being.[19]

Dr. Ambedkar was thus convinced that caste had a religious sanction and that, any attempt to uproot it would be resisted by the orthodox. "We want equal rights in society", he wrote in the first issue of *Bahishkrit Bharat* (April 3, 1927). "We will achieve them as far as possible while remaining within the Hindu fold or if necessary by kicking away this worthless Hindu identity."[20] Dr. Ambedkar's conversion to Buddhism was a clear protest against the prevailing social system which imposed the will of the privileged few on a vast section of humanity.[21] At one stage he was so disillusioned that he went to the extent of disowning even the land of his birth, although deep within the patriot in him remained awake. During a discussion with Mahatma Gandhi on August 14, 1931, he regretfully stated:

> How can I call this land my own homeland and this religion my own wherein we cannot get water to drink? No self-respecting untouchable worth the name will be proud of his land. The

> injustice and sufferings inflicted upon us by this land are so enormous that if knowingly or unknowingly we fall a prey to disloyalty to this country, the responsibility for that act would be solely hers.... If at all I have rendered any national service...it is due to my unsullied conscience and not due to any patriotic feelings in me. If in my endeavour to secure human rights for my people who have been trampled upon in this country for ages, I do any disservice to this country, it would not be a sin....[22]

Dr. Ambedkar held that social justice alone could lead to social harmony and social stability and kindle patriotic feelings. His efforts to get the Bombay Hereditary Office Act amended for the amelioration of the Mahar community were well meant although he could not see the Act relating to the abolition of the *Watan* system on the statute book during his lifetime. It may also be noted that the *Mahar Watan* was finally abolished under the Bombay Inferior Village Watan Abolition Act in 1959.

The way Dr. Ambedkar presented the case of the depressed classes before the South Borough Committee, the Simon Commission, at the Round Table Conferences (also at the time of the Poona Pact) and before the Cripps' Mission, speaks of his erudition and his utmost concern for the welfare of millions of his countrymen. The Mahar Tank Satyagraha and the Kala Ram Mandir Satyagraha launched by him were not simply aimed at securing the right of the untouchables to drink water from a public tank or making way for their entry into a temple, but to shake off their inertia and complacency on one hand and to debunk the notions of superiority nurtured by the high caste people on other.

Dr. Ambedkar's endeavours to abolish untouchability and forced labour and to achieve the ideal of 'one man one vote' as also to ensure for the untouchables equality before the Law and reservations in various domains bore fruit when India achieved freedom. As the Chairman of the Drafting Committee of the

Constituent Assembly, he strove hard to ensure justice for Dalits. Of all human rights he considered equality of opportunities for all citizens, irrespective of their caste, as the most important one. Dr. Ambedkar succeeded in creating provisions for the political reservations of scheduled castes in legislatures as also the appointment of a Commissioner for the Scheduled Castes and Scheduled Tribes.

Dr. Ambedkar's concern for the miserable plight of women led him, on the one had, to repudiate the Laws of Manu which degraded them in clear terms and denied them the right to freedom to property, to education and to spiritual sacraments like the *upanayana*, and on the other, pleaded for their rights in a number of forums like the Viceroy's Executive Council, Legislative Council, Bombay, the Constituent Assembly and the Indian Parliament. Although he did not succeed in getting the Hindu Code Bill passed, aimed at legalizing monogamy and restoring to women the rights to property and adoption, his labour did not go waste as the Bill was later resurrected in the form of four Acts – Hindus Marriage Act, 1955, Hindu Succession Act, 1956, Hindu Minority and Guardianship Act, 1956 and Hindu Adoption and Maintenance Act, 1956.[23]

Dr. Ambedkar tried to liberate people from the clutches of religious scriptures and outworn traditions. He organized the low castes, infused in them the spirit to fight and reassert themselves, and secured for them the status of human beings. They have come out of their inferiority complex and gained new confidence. Many of them have risen to high positions by dint of hard work and with the help of reservation policy. Prejudices against them however persist.

Notes

1. The most readable biography of Dr. B.R. Ambedkar is Dhananjay Keer, *Dr. Ambedkar: Life and Mission* (Bombay: Popular Prakashan,

1971). See also W.N. Kuber, *B.R. Ambedkar* (Builders of Modern India Series), New Delhi: Government of India, 1970.

2. Dr. Ambedkar wrote in *Bahishkrit Bharat* (May 6, 1927): "We do not value Hinduism, we value human dignity. The principles of Hinduism are great, but we are not fools to be lost in dreaming about those sublime principles."
3. For this aspect see, B.R. Ambedkar, *The Untouchables* (Shravasti, Balrampur, 1969).
4. B.R. Ambedkar, *Mr. Gandhi and the Emancipation of the Untouchables*, (Jalandhar, not dated), p. 11.
5. B.R. Ambedkar, *Annihilation of Caste* (Jalandhar, 1968), p.87.
6. Ibid., p. 88.
7. "Some Questions to the Hindus and Their Friends" in B.R. Ambedkar, *Mr. Gandhi and the Emancipation of the Untouchables*, op. cit., p. 48.
8. B.R. Ambedkar, *Annihilation of Caste*, op.cit. p. 10.
9. B.R.Ambedkar, *What Congress and Gandhi Have Done to the Untouchables* (Bombay: Thacker and Co. Ltd, 1946), pp. 307-8.
10. Dhananjay Keer, op.cit., p. 301.

    "If all people were to be called Harijans, we should not object. It is no use only giving the Untouchables a sweet name. Something practical should be done to ameliorate their condition", said Ambedkar. Ibid., p. 301-2.
11. *Ibid.*, pp. 165-66.
12. Cf., N. Benjamin and B.B. Mohanty, "Ambedkar's Quest for the Right of Social Equality: An Interpretation", *Social Action*, Vol.51, no. 2, April-June 2001.
13. See Ambedkar's lectures "Labour and Parliamentary Democracy" and "Future of Parliamentary Democracy" at Delhi and Jalandhar respectively. Bhagwan Das (ed.) *Thus Spoke Ambedkar*, Vol.1 (Jalandhar: Buddhist Publishing House, 1963), pp. 43-57.
14. See Vasant Moon (ed.) *Baba Saheb Ambedkar: Writing and Speeches* (Bombay: Government of Maharashtra, 1979-1999), Vol.5, p. 418
15. Dhananjay Keer, op. cit., pp. 60-61.
16. For this aspect see, B.R.Ambedkar, *The Untouchables*, op.cit., pp. 31-83.
17. Addressing the First Round Table Conference which began on November 12, 1930, Dr. Ambedkar observed: ".... Before the British we were in the loathsome condition due to our untouchability. Has

the British Government done anything to remove it? Before the British, we could not draw water from the village well. Has the British Government secured us the right to the well? Before the British we could not enter the temples? Can we enter now? Before the British we were denied entry to the police force. Does the British Government admit us into the force? Before the British we were not allowed to serve in the military. Is that career now open to us? To none of these questions we can give an affirmative answer. Our wrongs have remained as open sores and they have not been righted, although 150 years of British rule have rolled away." Dhananjay Keer, op.cit., pp. 149-50.

18. "Although it (the British Government) had the legal powers to remove these evils, it did not amend the existing code of social and economic life because it was afraid that its intervention would give rise to resistance", said Dr Ambedkar at the First Round Table Conference. "We must have a Government in which the men in power will give their undivided allegiance to the best interests of the country..." Ibid., p. 150
19. Vasant Moon, op. cit. vol. V, p. 90.
20. For a critical appraisal of Dr Ambedkar's views on the subject see Eleanor Zelliot, "The Social and Political Thought of B.R. Ambedkar" in Thomas Pentham and Kenneth L. Deutsch, *Political Thought in Modern India,* pp. 161-175.
21. See "Reasons for Conversion", speech delivered by Dr Ambedkar in Bombay in April 1936; Editorial Note on the history of the Conversion Movement launched by Dr Ambedkar on October 13, 1935 at Yeola, District Nasik, Bombay; and Statement by Dr Ambedkar on Conversion. Bhagwan Das, *Thus Spoke Ambedkar* (On renunciation of Hinduism and conversion of untouchables), Vol. II pp. 65-276, 296-301.

    See also Valerian Rodrigues, "Dalits and Cultural Identity: Ambedkar's Prevarications on the Question of Culture", *Social Action*, Vol.50, January-March 2000; N.Benjamin and B.B. Mohanty, op.cit.
22. Dhananjay Keer, op.cit., pp. 166-167.
23. See "The Woman and the Counter Revolution" (Ambedkar's essay carrying extracts from *Manu Smriti* which have a bearing on the status of women) in Vasant Moon, op. cit., Vol.3,pp.428-437; see also, Rekha Chowdhry, "Hindu Social Order and Women: Understanding Ambedkar's Viewpoint", in Mohammad Shabbir,

B.R.Ambedkar: Study in Law and Society (New Delhi: Rawat Publications, 1997), pp.289-295; Lalitha Sreenath and M.R. Sreenath, "Dr Ambedkar, women and the weaker sections of Society" in Mohammad Shabbir, op.cit., pp. 297-317; Basant Kumar Mallik, "Ambedkar on Women's Progress" in Verinder Grover (ed.), *B.R.Ambedkar* (New Delhi: Deep and Deep Publications, 1998), pp. 467-476; D.C. Ahir, *The Legacy of Ambedkar* (Delhi: B.R. Publishing Corporation, 1990), pp. 129-134 (chapter 8).

16

Social Justice and the Indian Constitution

Ambedkar's Perspective

ZAFAR A. KHAN

Thomas Jefferson has said that justice is the fundamental law of a society. A law which the members of the society must truly feel as their own law. Where laws in a society create discrimination or social or economic inequality among its sections, they are bound to alienate its members from them, resulting in their breakdown. Even making of a fair law is not enough. It has also to be administered fairly, equally and effectively for the benefit of the community.

Social Justice Explained

Here, the question arises: what is social justice? Definition of 'social justice' cannot be put in a strait jacket. In fact, it is not only difficult, but is hard to define the term social justice. Justice Bhagwati in *Muir Mills Co Ltd v. Suti Mills Mazdoor Union*,[1] described social justice as a "very vague and indeterminate expression – without embarking upon a discussion as to the expression social justice we may only observe that the concept of social justice does not emanate from the fanciful notions of any adjudicator but must be founded on a more solid foundation.[2]

Chagla C.J. (as he then was)[3] agreed that social justice was hard to define, but submitted that court should import its own ideas of social justice in interpreting statutory provisions. Social justice was an objective of the Constitution and it was an in articulate major premise which was personal and individual to every court and every judge depending on the judge's outlook on life and society, and laws cannot be interpreted without reference to social justice to the achievement of which our country was pledged.

C.K. Allen has said:

> ...We hear much today of social justice. I am not sure that those who use the term most glibly, know very clearly what they mean by it. Some mean distribution, redistribution of wealth, some interpret it as equality of opportunity – a misleading term, as since opportunity can never be equal among human beings who have unequal capacities to grasp it; many suspect, mean simply that it is unjust that anybody should be more fortunate than themselves and the more intelligent mean that it is just – I would rather say benevolent – that every effort should be made at least to mitigate that no obstacles should be offered but rather, help afforded to practicable opportunities of self improvements.[4]

Social justice or distributive justice, or compensatory justice is a quest for justice. It is a challenge to equality, liberty and justice. It is in pursuit of "making law an instrument of social change and for reminding lawyers and judges that they are social engineers".[5] Therefore, sanction of social justice demands to have interaction with social purpose, which requires the interpretation of the eternal principles of human freedom to meet the challenging conditions of our times and the application of the fundamental principles of justice to the problems which arise in the complex industrial and commercial life of our era. Conscientiously, the Preamble of our Constitution is the culmination of securing social justice through it. Twin brethern: Fundamental Rights and Directive Principles of State Policy are directed to achieving means as well as ends of social justice. Thus, justice devoid of social justice, that is to say, socio-economic, is not meaningfully purposeful and result-oriented social justice does not aim at providing justice to 'haves' but equally cares for the 'have-nots', underdogs, disadvantaged, and under privileged populace.[6]

'Social justice' is understood as the right of the weak, aged, destitute, poor, women, children and other under-privileged persons, to the protection of the state against the ruthless competition of life. It gives the necessary adventitious aids to the under-privileged so that, they may have equal opportunity with the more advanced sections of the society in the race of life. In short, it is the balancing wheel between the 'haves' and 'have nots'.

Social justice, therefore means, justice which is not confined to a fortunate few but takes within its sweep, large masses of disadvantaged and underprivileged segments of society; justice which not only penetrates and destroys the inequalities of race, sex, power, position, or wealth but is also heavily weighed in favour of the weaker sections of humanity. Justice which brings equitable distribution of the social, material and political resources of the community; justice which the law must ensure the people that rule of law becomes meaningful and social justice a reality for them.[7]

Social justice, opines V.R. Krishna Iyer, "in our Socialist Republic is socio-economic revolution in the current miasmic milieu".[8] He further explains social justice as follows:

> The vice of social inequality assumes a particularly reprehensible form in relation to the backward classes and communities which are treated as untouchable, and so the problem of social justice is as urgent and important in India as in the problem of economic justice. I'm using the term social justice in a comprehensive sense so as to include both economic justice and social justice. The concept of social justice thus takes within its sweep the objective of removing all inequalities and affording equal

opportunities to all citizens in social affairs as well as economic activities".[9]

Part IV of the Constitution of India entitled, as "Directive Principles of State Policy" is the soul on the instrument of instructions in the nature of social policy with the direction to the state to strive to achieve the goals of social justice through the instrumentalities of law, schemes, and other mechanisms.

The concept of social justice has varied with age and time; social justice is to the millions: "to wipe every tear from every eye".[10] Be that as it may, our Constitution envisages tripartite picturesque of social justice, that is justice – social, economic and political as directed in the Preamble. Socio-economic justice is procured by the Directive Principles of State Policy: Justice – social and political, is secured by fundamental rights. The public interest law has introduced a safe inroad of public interest litigation (PIL) which has been described as 'Access to Justice'. It is a new designation of social justice; it has given a novel court process as 'Epistolary Jurisdiction' that is giving a golden key in the hands of the 'have-nots' to open the inaccessible doors of the courts to have access to justice so that the type of justice enjoined in the constitutional justice comes to be realized.

Social Justice: Dr. Ambedkar's Vision

Dr. B.R. Ambedkar's social justice vision can be equated with the sayings of Alexander Pope: "That true self-love and social justice are the same".[11] Ambedkar himself explained his social philosophy: "My social philosophy may be said to be enshrined in three words: Liberty, equality and fraternity".[12] To him, real democracy was a social democracy. According to Dr. Ambedkar, it is essential to realize that political democracy cannot succeed where there is no social and economic democracy.[13] He pleaded the realization of economic and social democracy in India, for political democracy was unreal unless preceded by economic and social democracy. Dr. Ambedkar said:

> We must begin by acknowledging the fact that there is complete absence of two things in Indian society. One of these is equality on the social plane. We have in India a society based on the principle of graded inequality which means elevation for some and degradation for others. On the economic plane, we have a society in which there are some who have immense wealth as against many who live in abject poverty – How long shall we continue to live this life of contradictions? How long shall we continue to deny equality in our social and economic life? If we continue to deny it for long, we will do so only by putting our political democracy in peril. We must remove this contradiction at the earliest possible moment or those who suffer from inequality will blow up the structure of political democracy.[14]

Dr. Ambedkar 51 years ago cautioned:

> Therefore the sooner room is made for the realization of their aspiration, the better for the few, the better for the country, the better for the maintenance of its independence and the better for the continuance of its democratic structure. This can only be done by the establishment of equality and fraternity in all spheres of life.[15]

His philosophy was occupied with social amelioration, political enlightenment and spiritual awakening. For this it attached due importance to the economic well-being of the masses. To him, political thought embodied a social dynamism because of man's attitude as a political animal and social being. He had deep faith in fundamental human rights, in the equal rights of man and women, in the dignity of the individual, in social and economic justice, in the promotion of social progress and better standards of life with peace and security in all spheres of human life. His study of social facts enriched his political philosophy.[16]

Dr. Ambedkar was dead against the Hindu cast structure as he was of the view that this structure has been primarily responsible for committing all sorts of atrocities on the various sections of the society, particularly the weaker sections and Scheduled Castes and Scheduled Tribes. He was, therefore, against *Manu Smiriti* as it gives a blank cheque to the Brahamins to commit all sorts of atrocities on Scheduled Castes and Scheduled Tribes and justify their evil designs. Barbara Roger recalls.

> A representative of untouchables (Dalits) caused quite a stir when he called for the floor microphone at the end of one long session to be placed for outside help for his people. He broke down in tears as he told the plenary that untouchables were being narrated, beaten raped and abused every day throughout India, while nobody outside knew what was happening and the people were completely friendless within India itself.[17]

According to Dr. Ambedkar the root cause of social injustice to the Shudras is the caste system in Hindu society. He observed, castes are enclosed units and it is their conspiracy with clear conscience that compels the ex-communicated to make themselves into a caste. The logic of their obdurate circumstance is merciless and it is in obedience to its force that some unfortunate groups find themselves closed out with the result that new groups by a mechanical law are constantly being converted into castes in a widening multiplicity.[18] He further maintained that the root of untouchability is the caste system and the root of the caste-system is religion attached to *varnashram*; and the root of the *varnashram* is the Brahminical religion.[19] Dr. Ambedkar's social vision is reflective in his own words:

> As an economic system permits exploitation without obligation Untouchability is not only a system of unmitigated economic exploitation, but it is also a system of uncontrolled economic

exploitation. That is because there is no independent public opinion to condemn it and there is no impartial machinery of administration to restrain it. There is no check from the police or the judiciary for the simple reasons that they are all down from the Hindus, and take side of exploiters.[20]

Indian Constitution Mandates Social Justice

Social justice is embedded in the Indian Constitution, but left social justice undefined and is a relative concept taking in its wings the time and circumstances, the people, their traditions and aspirations, this turmoil and torments, their backwardness, blood, sweat and tears.[21]

The Constitution of India brings a renaissance in the concept of social justice when it weaves a trinity of it in the Preamble, the Directive Principles of State Policies and the Fundamental Rights and this trinity is the "the core of the commitments to the social revolution;[22] this is the conscience of the constitution",[23] it is born "from the womb of the freedom struggle".[24]

The Preamble to our Constitution declares that we the people of India, having solemnly resolved to constitute India into a "Sovereign socialist secular Democratic Republic" and to secure to all its citizens justice: social, economic, political liberty of thought and expression, belief; faith; and worship; equality of status and of opportunity; and to promote among them all fraternity assuring the dignity of the individual and the unity and integrity of the nation. This indeed is social justice guaranteed by the Constitution of India because it strives to create a "balancing wheel between freedom, political and economic, and indeed, makes the survival of democracy".[25] Dr. Ambedkar concluded the debate on the preamble in these words: "I say that this preamble embodies what is the desire of every member of the house that this constitution should have its roots, its authority, its sovereignty from the people, that it has":[26]

For the establishment of social order, the people of India have been given the following fundamental rights:

(i) Right to equality.[27]

(ii) Right to freedom – freedom of speech and expression; to assemble peaceably and without arms, to form associations or unions, to move freely throughout the territory of India, to reside and settle in any part of the territory of India, to practice any profession or to carry on any occupation, trade and business;.[28] Right to life and personal liberty.[29]

(iv) Right against exploitation.[30]

(v) Right to freedom of religion.[31]

(vi) Cultural and educational rights,[32] and

(vii) Right to constitutional remedies.[33]

In addition to these, the directive principles of state policy also express in categorical terms the ideas of social justice Art.38 of the constitution requires the state *inter alia* to minimize the inequalities in income and endeavour to culminate in equalities in status, facilities and opportunities, not only amongst individual, but also amongst group of people residing in different areas or engaged in different vocations.[34] Article 39 of the Indian Constitution requires the state to make available to all the citizens adequate means of livelihood; to distribute ownership and control of material resources so as to subserve the common good; to operate the economic system in such a way that it does not result in concentration of wealth and means of production to the common detriment, that there is equal pay for equal work; to protect the health and strength of workers, men and women, and the tender age of children against abuse and that citizens are not forced by economic necessity to enter avocations unsuited to their age and strength, that children are given opportunities and facilities to develop in a healthy manner and in conditions of freedom and dignity and that childhood and youth are protected against exploitation and against moral and material abandonment.[35]

The state is also required to provide equal justice through the mechanism of free legal aid in order to ensure that opportunities for securing justice are not denied to any citizen by reason of economic or other disabilities,[36] to provide to right to work, to education and public assistance in cases of unemployment, old age, sickness and disablement and other cases of undeserved want,[37] to make provision for securing just and humane conditions of work and for maternity relief[38] to provide work, a living wage, conditions of work ensuring a decent standard of life and full enjoyment of leisure and social and cultural opportunities;[39] to secure the participation of workers in the management of undertakings establishment or other organizations engaged in industry;[40] to secure for all the citizens a uniform civil code throughout the country.[41] To provide free and compulsory education for children below the age of 14 years,[42] to promote the educational and economic interests of the Scheduled Castes and, Scheduled Tribes and other weaker sections,[43] to raise the level of nutrition and scheduled standard of living and to improve the public health, etc.[44]

To continue the reference to the constitutional provisions, part XVI of the Constitution contains special provision relating to certain classes. Article 332 provides for reservation of seats for the Scheduled Castes and Scheduled Tribes in the legislative assemblies of the states. There is however, one such reservation in favour of the socially and educationally backward classes under Article 333 which provides for the nomination of a person of the Anglo-Indian community to the legislative assembly of the state. Article 334 stipulates the period after which the reservation of seats in the central and state legislators must cease. Article 335 provides that the claims of the members of the Scheduled Castes and Scheduled Tribes shall be taken into consideration, consistently, with the maintenance of efficiency of administration in the making of appointments to services and posts in connection with the affairs of the union or of the state. Article 336 and 337 deal with the special provision respectively for appointments in certain services and educational grants for Anglo-Indian Community. Article 338 provides for a special officer for the Schedule Caste and Schedule Tribes to be appointed by the President whose duty is to investigate all matters relating to the safeguards provided for the Scheduled Caste and Scheduled Tribes and to report to the President. Article 339 provides for the appointment of a commission to report in regard to the administration of the scheduled areas and scheduled tribes. Article 340(1) provides for the appointment, by the President of a commission to investigate the conditions of socially and educationally backward classes within the territory of India and the difficulties under which they labour and to make recommendations as to steps that should be taken by the union or any state to remove such difficulties and to remove their condition, etc.[45]

These are the imperatives towards social transformation and reconstruction of the Indian society which constitute the gist of social justice. Dr. Ambedkar was of the view that social justice alone could lead to social harmony, social stability and patriotic feelings. He believed that a democracy, which enslaves the working class, a class that is devoid of education which is devoid of means of life, which is devoid of any power of organization, which is devoid of intelligence, is no democracy but a mockery of democracy.[46]

Conclusion

In India today what prevails from the perspective of social justice, as the rule of life, is not a law of life, but a regime of half-truths which is hardened to fight than if naked truth had been writ large for people to see and struggle against. The poignant contradiction between promise of justice and the harrowing human condition, as it deepens day after day, may well fuel the explosive locomotive of politico-economic change, without which the paramount national parchment over which Ambedkar and the Constituent Assembly laboured for long years, may prove a hallow jurisprudence.

Decades have passed India by; ballots have been cast periodically and governments have come and gone but social injustice, an anathema of Ambedkar's India, survives diehards with marginalized millions denied freedom and justice as a reality of life.

Dr. Ambedkar's words of 1949 vintage ring in our sensitive ears even to day. "There is great danger of things going wrong. Times are fast changing people, including our own, are being moved by new ideologies. ...if we wish, to preserve the constitution in which we have sought to enshrine the principle of government of the people, for the people and by the people, let us, resolve not to be tardy in the recognition of the evils that lie across our path – not to be weak in our initiative to remove them."[47]

In fact, social justice is the end; judicial justice is the means, the legislative and executive operations are human engineering, and together the three branches of government have to work in comity so that the constitution may fulfil what the founding fathers designed.[48]

It is obvious that social justice cannot be realized by law, or supreme lex, or social legislations alone put in the present day crisis, many more agencies have to play a significant role in achieving the objectives of social justice. Besides untouchables, there are other disadvantaged groups of the society who too are depressed and are in quicksands of injustice from knee to head and are in quest to have access to social justice. The objectives of social justice as realized by the founding fathers of Indian constitution in general and Dr. B.R. Ambedkar in particular could only be perceived pragmatically if we give an unparallel insight into it, give to disadvantaged groups of people (in both rural and urban areas) who, in their ignorance and lack of organization, are being cheated, oppressed, and denied their basic human rights and fundamental freedoms.

Notes

1. 1955, ISCR, p. 991.
2. Ibid., pp. 100 1-2.
3. In *Prakash Cotton Mills vs. Bombay, Bombay L.R.* pp. 836, 844.
4. Aspects of Justice, 1958 p. 31.
5. Justice Y.V. Chandrachud, *The Challenge of Social Justice*, Supreme Court of India Publication, Third International Congress of Appelate Judges, 1985, pp. 2-3.
6. K.L. Bhatia, "Kaleidoscopic view of Jurisprudential dimensions of Judicial Activism with reference to Swadeshi Jurisprudence: Saint or Sinner", in K.L. Bhatia (ed.), *Indian Activism and Social Change*, 1990, p. 155.
7. Justice P.N. Bhagwati, Supra Note 5 at pp. 21, 157-61, Justice V.R. Krishna Iyer, in S. Dayal (ed.), *Legal Education*, 1976, XI.
8. V.R. Krishna Iyer, *Social Justice Sunset or Dawn*, 1987, p. 23.
9. Ibid., p. 51.
10. Pandit Jawahar Lal Nehru, as quoted in Granville Austin, *The Indian Constitution: Corner Stone of a Nation*, 1972 p. 26.
11. As quoted in V. Chandra Mowli, *B.R. Ambedkar: Man and His Vision*, p. 62.
12. Speech on All India Radio on October 3, 1954, as mentioned in L.R. Balley (ed.), *Thoughts of Ambedkar*, 1989 pp. 73-74.
13. *Dr. Ambedkar's: Writings and Speeches*, Vol. 1, pp 57, 222-23.
14. Constituent Assembly Debates (CAD) Vol. XI pp. 972-981.
15. Ibid., p. 946.
16. W.N. Kuber, *Dr. Ambedkar: A Critical Study*, p. 289.
17. Massey, James, *Down-trodden*, Risk Book Services, WCC Publication, Geneva, 1997 p. 31.
18. Ambedkar B.R. "Castes in India: Their Mechanism Genesis and Development", *Indian Antiquary*, Vol. XIVI, pp. 81-85.
19. Praskah Prem, cited in, *Ambedkar: Politics and Scheduled Castes* Ashish Publishing House, New Delhi 1993 p. 52.
20. As quoted by V. Chandra Mowli, op.cit., p. 68.
21. V.R. Krishna Iyer, op. cit, pp. 5-51, 53.
22. Supra Note 8 at p. 53.
23. Ibid.
24. lbid. p. 60.

25. Ibid., p. 54.
26. CAD Vol.X-XII, p. 456.
27. Arts. 14 to 18.
28. Art. 19 (1) (a), (b), (c), (e), (g).
29. Arts. 20 to 22.
30. Arts. 23 and 24.
31. Arts. 25 to 28.
32. Art. 29 and 30.
33. Art. 32.
34. Art. 38 (2).
35. See Art. 39 (a), (b) (c) (d) (e) and (f).
36. See Art. 39-A, See Legal Aid Services Act, 1987.
37. Art. 41.
38. Art. 42.
39. Art. 43.
40. Art. 43-A.
41. Art. 44.
42. Art. 45.
43. Art. 46.
44. Art. 47.
45. Report of the Karnataka Third Backward Classes Vol. I, p. 8-9.
46. Dr. B.R. Ambedkar's: Writings and Speeches, Vol. II, p. 217.
47. CAD Vol. XI, p. 946.
48. Justice V.R. Krishna Iyer "The Judicial System: Has it a Functional Future in Our Constitutional Order", 15 (1979), *Civil and Military Law Journal*, p. 169.

17

Dr. Ambedkar's Approach Towards Human Rights

KHURRAM

Social stratification has been a fact of Indian society for around three thousand years. Different classes of people are placed on a vertical plane characterized by hereditary hierarchy of socially superior and inferior ranks. These classes are broadly, categorized as *brahmins* at the top in hierarchy followed by *kshatriyas, vaisyas* and, *sudras* at the bottom. This is known as *chaturvarna vyavastha.* This system draws its sanction from the *shastras* (the Hindu religious texts). Each of the *varna,* further consists of a number of castes or *jatis.* With the juxtaposition of *varna* with *jati,* the caste system emerges. There is a fifth category outside and below the four *varnas,* viz., untouchables or outcastes (*varna vyavastha*). Their status is the lowest in the Hindu social arrangement. However, since there is not much difference between the status of untouchables and *sudras,* untouchables can be conceived as forming part of *sudra* community for the analytical purposes. Therefore, in the context of present paper *sudras* mean a wide range of castes, with some artisan castes ranked superior and untochables at the bottom. However, whenever the term 'untouchables' is used, it excludes the reference to higher placed artisan castes. The untouchables were called as *dalits* or 'depressed classes' by Dr. Ambedkar, *harijans* by Gandhi and designated as Scheduled Castes by the Indian Constitution. These terms have been used interchangeably.

The untouchables are the most discriminated, deprived and exploited section of Indian society. They have been denied basic human rights and education. They have been forced to live in segregated localities. They have been denied free movement. The whole community has been compelled to lead a secluded life, unexposed to the developments around. For centuries, they have not been allowed to have any association or interaction with the world outside their restricted localities. In other words, they have been forced to exist at a sub-human level by the exigencies of the Hindu social order. They have been refused the fruits of civilization and culture for thousands of years. In no other part of the world has so much injustice been done and basic human rights denied to a community for so long, as has been the case with the untouchables. The exact description of their human rights violations cannot be given. The extent of violations of human rights cannot be truly imagined of a people whose mere shadow was polluting and inviting punishment. Dr. Ambedkar was born as untouchable. The indignities and deprivations his community faced, moved him to take up the gauntlet to fight for its rights. His life had been a long stretched struggle to fight for their socio-economic and political rights. He articulated and pressed hard for their legitimate claims before the Britishers and the caste Hindus. He demanded and ultimately, secured for them some special privileges as means to a greater realization of their human rights. His approach towards the rights of the depressed classes in particular, and all citizens in general, is well reflected in his various writings, speeches and representations, particularly the Memorandum submitted by him to the Advisory Committee of the Constituent Assembly.[1] Being the chief architect of the Indian Constitution, he was successful, ultimately, though not completely, in incorporating his vision of human rights in it. His role in this regard is well acknowledged. He attacked the caste-system which is the source of inequality and exploitation. He asked the *dalits* to throw up the shackles of isolation and bondage. He raised their morale and tried to make them stand on their feet. All his efforts were aimed at people who did not have the means and the capabilities to avail the rights.

Human beings need rights because of their being human. T.H. Green held that human beings, being self-conscious, aspire for, and essentially need freedom, and freedom involves rights. Another political philosopher, Laski held the rights to be essential conditions of human life. Thus, rights are required by humans to realize their freedom, their personality, their humanity. They need the rights to live with dignity. Dignity is an essential component of human self-consciousness. Therefore, it is the cornerstone of human rights. Our Supreme Court has interpreted the Fundamental Right to Life as constituting of the right to live with human dignity.[2] It is to restore the dignity of his community that Dr. Ambedkar devoted his whole life. He gave the slogan "to live with respect is the birth right of man". Human rights cannot be realized in a society where a vast section of people feel humiliated in everyday life. Without a sense of dignity, the man cannot develop faith in himself. Without having faith in himself, he cannot dare to stand for his rights. Therefore, Dr. Ambedkar continuously roused *dalits* to a sense of self-respect. He instilled confidence among them. He showed them how to fight and assert for their rights. He played the key role in securing special rights for them.[3]

While assessing his theoretical position on human rights, it must be borne in mind that he did not speak much about the rights in a systematic disciplinary framework. Human rights discourse is post-World War II development. Although, Dr. Ambedkar articulated the rights of minorities in particular, and all citizens in general, with such zeal and clarity as unmatched by any one of his contemporaries. Departing, fundamentally, from the liberal paradigm of rights, he sought the active intervention of the State. Rights were not just seen as constraints or limits on the power of the State. Apart from guaranteeing the rights, the State had to undertake certain positive obligations towards their better realization. Socialism and positive discrimination was to be followed by the State. It had to indulge in levelling process. He wanted the State to cater to the basic needs of all the citizens. Thus, his views subscribe to the Welfare theory of Rights. He does not seem to believe in the theory of Natural Rights. This theory holds some basic rights to be inherent and inalienable part of human personality. Since State is the creation of man and comes into being to protect natural rights, these rights cannot be the creation of the State. Dr. Ambedkar, on the other hand, says, "Fundamental Rights are the gift of the law".[4] Here his position resembles Legal theory of Rights. However, to hold basic human rights as the gift of law is an error of judgment. Human rights are of such supreme significance that they can well be supposed to set up a critical standard to gauge the legitimacy of particular laws. Desirability about laws can vary from place to place but the need for basic rights is same everywhere, because the needs of human personality are same everywhere. By conceding that human rights are the gift of the State, one is, also conceding, logically, whether he really meant it or not, that human rights are dependent upon the will of the State and the rights are something which the State bestows as a favour upon its citizens. While the fact is that the State is not capable of creating human rights by law. It only confirms their existence and gives them protection. It is the duty of the State towards its citizens. A gift does not come within the purview of duty. Still, the reason for Dr. Ambedkar to consider the Fundamental Rights to be the gift of the State was twofold. First, Dr. Ambedkar wanted to convey that these rights are not absolute, and reasonable restrictions can be put upon their exercise. What he failed to realize properly was that these reasonable restrictions cannot be supposed to be curtailment of rights, rather they are just meant to enhance the value, intensity and universality of these rights. Secondly, Dr. Ambedkar just wanted to convey that without the backing of laws, rights cannot be enforced. He was not wrong in holding this view. Thus, Dr. Ambedkar, can be faulted or criticized only for the selection of word 'gift', otherwise, his beliefs or intentions were never in doubt. He firmly held rights to be integral part of human personality essential for the well-being of man. He offsets the drawbacks of Legal theory of Rights by combining it with the Welfare theory of Rights.

Dr. Ambedkar's over emphasis on the rights of the *dalits* has drawn criticism from some quarters that he was more interested in the rights of a particular group, and less concerned about the individualist dimension of rights, thus his approach about human rights is narrow and parochial. This criticism is untenable. If he focused more on rights of the *dalits*, as a group, it was because he realized that most of the violations of their rights were distinctly connected to their being members of a certain group. They, as an aggregate group, were discriminated against, and denied basic human rights. In comparison to the human rights violations of particular individuals, the violations in case of *dalits*, as a group were far more organized and targeted. Therefore, the rights of *dalits*, rightfully occupied his deep consideration. Naturally, human rights have to be fought for those people who are denied rights, and not for those who violate rights. Dr. Ambedkar realized that Hindu social order did not provide the basis for the development of individuality. The group (the caste) was the unit of Hindu society, not the individual. His comprehension of group reality of Indian society can be loosely interpreted as 'oppressed groups' *vs.* 'oppressor groups.' This state was maintained by the institution of caste. Although, Dr. Ambedkar hoped that the progressive Constitution, and legislation, would enable the people to transcend their group identities and networks. With the withering away of those identities and networks, the ideology of caste domination would also crumble. Until, that took place, the *dalits* had to be given certain special rights and privileges to enable them to get out of their wretched group existence. The idea was to bring each individual on an equal plane to make society into a genuine whole where each member could realize his potential to the maximum, within his natural limits. Dr. Ambedkar's vision of democracy is that of egalitarian democracy where all individuals can claim equal status and worth, and enjoy equal access to the basic means of production. In such democracy, the State looks after the needs of all the citizens, not just the dominant or entrenched groups. The least disadvantageous, naturally, need the greatest support from the State. Thus, his aim was the growth of individual as the prerequisite of true democracy. The individual as a free but equal member of society lies at the core his philosophy. He criticized Marxism and even Gandhism by observing, "Both of these ideologies could not free the individual from the tyranny of the society."[5] Thus, Dr. Ambedkar's approach was pragmatic and all embracing. He wanted Fundamental Rights for one and all. He demanded certain *dalits* rights, not as a separate or opposite category to the Fundamental Rights, but just as a means towards the wide and comprehensive realization of the Fundamental Rights. *Dalits* rights are human rights, indeed.

Caste: A Human Rights Problem

The man in Hindu society is supposed to discharge his duties assigned to him by virtue of his birth in a given *varna* since birth itself is controlled by *karmas* of the previous lives. Hindu religious texts and traditions support this concept. Hence, a *brahmina* by virtue of his higher birth performs sacred functions, with all the privileges attached to those functions. While, a man born as *sudra*, performs the meanest jobs, the jobs which are inferior in the social consciousness. *Sudras* suffer from all the disadvantages of being confined to the menial jobs. Thus, different castes, on the basis of their occupation are assigned the ranks one above another on a vertical scale. The status of members in caste groups is ascribed and hereditary. The superiority of some *vis-à-vis* others as well as inferiority of some *vis-à-vis* others is maintained and justified as the natural order of things by the institution of the caste. According to *Manu Smriti*, a *brahmana* or a *kshatriya* could get away killing a *sudra* just by performing the fasting penance while a *sudra* had to forfeit his life for the same offence. Perhaps, in the Early Vedic Period, *varna vyavastha* was nothing more than a system of organization of society into various classes on the basis of their work. Originally, it was not conceived as a watertight compartmentalization of society into various classes on the basis of astrictive identity. However, as Dr. Ambedkar holds in his book 'The Caste in India' the class degenerated into caste and acquired ascribed status with the superimposition of endogamy over exogamy. The system was legitimized through certain religious texts written over time as a result of *brahminical* ingenuity to preserve and increase their authority and domination over society. Gradually, this system of domination and hierarchy developed an in-built mechanism of its continuity, maintenance, justification and intensification. Thus, caste system came to be characterized by social hierarchy, inequality, fixity of occupations and continuance thereof by heredity, ascribed status, endogamy, social segregation, commensal restrictions, authorization of power to upper castes on a permanent basis and continuous denial and humiliation of lower castes. There, of course, exists a sort of religious sanction behind it.

The worst victims of the hierarchised and closed social order have been the untouchables. They have suffered untouchability, the most heinous crime against human dignity ever experienced on the earth. This phenomenon, in certain respects, is unique to India. It connotes the practice of non-touching of the outcastes by the caste Hindus, implying the notion of ritual impurity. It means separation, segregation and isolation of a people within society. It has resulted in the greatest and the longest violations of human rights of a community ever experienced by humanity. The word untouchable is itself, the most obnoxious. It is an epitome of suffering and deprivations of a people. The condition of untouchables was even worse than the slaves of Europe and Central Asia. Slaves could revolt at least under certain circumstances. They were integral part of the larger society. Their masters used to take trouble to train and initiate them into higher forms of labour and culture, so as to increase their value. The untouchables, however, could never revolt because they were deprived from participating in common activity of society. Thus, they were completely disabled for any sort of direct action. They could exercise their will at the level of beasts only. All this was in the name of caste which had the religious backing. It was not merely conventional or legal, it was spiritual and moral too.

Dr. Ambedkar, vehemently, attacked such social order. He believed that if democracy had to take roots and society had to move forward, the inhuman system of caste had to be wiped out. He suggested practical measures to abolish it. He held that the rational interpretation of the *Shastras* had to be attempted and their absolute authority had to be discarded. He maintained, "the root of untouchability is the caste system, the root of caste system is religion attached to *varnashram*, and the root of *varnashram* is the *brahminical* religion, and the root of brahminical religion is authorization of power." He was not content with the abolition of untouchability and leaving the caste system intact. That kind of superficial approach would not terminate the notions of superior and inferior. According to Dr. Ambedkar the caste system could not be retained in a moderate form. There was no scope for its retention from the side of untouchables. Hinduism must get rid of it. Otherwise, the only way left out for the *dalits* would be to get rid of it altogether by giving up Hinduism itself. In the beginning, he chose the piecemeal course. He actively participated in the 'tank and temple entry' campaigns. But, soon he got disillusioned with these campaigns by seeing the caste Hindus' reaction. He also feared that the real issues of the untouchables such as reservations might get bogged down into these petty struggles. He issued a statement on 'temple entry' on 12th February 1933:

> ... if Hindu religion is to be the code of social equality, then an amendment of its code to provide temple entry is not enough. What is required is to purge it of the doctrine of *chaturvarnya*. That is the root cause of all inequality and is also the parent of the caste system and untouchability which are merely other forms of inequality. Unless it is done, the depressed classes will reject not only temple entry but also the Hindu faith. For to accept temple entry and be content with it is to compromise with evil, and to barter away the sacredness of human personality that dwells in them.[6]

This was the issue over which Dr. Ambedkar did not get along well with Gandhi. Gandhi did not want to touch any of the fundamentals of Hinduism. On the other hand, Dr. Ambedkar was convinced that without overthrowing the *chaturvarna* system which is based on graded inequality, untouchables could not be freed from the age old bondage. Far from support for the eradication of the caste system, the response to, even, the 'tank and temple entry campaigns' was not forthcoming from the caste Hindus. All this created bitterness in Dr. Ambedkar's attitude towards Hinduism. At Yeola in 1935, he asked the untouchables to abandon their efforts to obtain temple entry rights and to consider the option of switching over to another religion. The caste system was so entrenched in the Hindu social order that he could not fight it to the finish. He could not bear it for long. Ultimately, in 1956, the year in which he died, he converted to Buddhism his lacs followers.

Untouchability has been legally abolished and it is a severely punishable offence, today. But the notion of ritual impurity is still surviving in the minds of the people. Its practice is continuing, sometimes, with complete disregard to the law, and, frequently, in various concealed and subtle forms. Caste system as a system of inequality and fixity of occupations has got weakened. However, ascriptive identities have become more deep rooted due to competitive mobilizational democratic politics. *Dalits* have been able to improve their socio-economic status but they are still looked down upon with contempt. They have been given intensive protection of law, yet, violence against them has increased. They have got equal, even, some additional rights, but violations of their rights continue with impunity. Apart from direct violations of their rights as untouchables, there are other kinds of violations, too, indirectly related to their underprivileged caste status such as torture, rape and death in custody. If we look into these cases, majority of the victims are *dalits*. And these violations are attempted, often, in collusion with police is a sad commentary on the role of State in protecting human rights. Still, much is left to be done. There is need to have a fresh look at the caste system as it operates, today. The notions of higher or lower by birth have to be purged out from the social value system. There is no other way out. Caste system by its very nature is against the rights and dignity of a large number of people and as such is a human rights problem. Dr. Ambedkar recognized the problem and fought it hard, but could not succeed. It is, still a major source of human rights violations. Caste based discrimination, undoubtedly, exists as a human rights problem in India. We cannot turn our back to the issue.

The Government's stand towards the *dalits'* question at the recently held 'Conference of Racism, Racial Discrimination, Xenophobia and Related Intolerance' at Durban is a pointer. First, it tried to preclude any discussion over caste based discrimination which the *dalits* human rights groups wanted to raise at the conference. Having failed in that, the government tried hard to make it sure that caste do not find mention in the Draft Declaration or Programme of Action. The Government succeeded in this regard. Surely, caste cannot be equated with race. Nonetheless, the dark skin colour of the *dalits,* though, might not be the cause, but to an extent reinforce the notions of impurity and graded inequality. However, the question is not whether the caste can be equated with race or whether the caste issue should have been taken at a meet which was called to discuss the discrimination related to race. The real question is whether the victims, who have been suffering from similar kind of discrimination should have been prevented from presenting their case. They should have, at least, been allowed to speak. To pretend that the problem does not exist, does not solve the problem. Acceptance of the problem, whether at home or at international fora, is the precondition to an honest search for the solution. If the State has done something worthwhile or if it still is doing enough (No doubt, the Indian Constitution is one of the most progressive in the world with regard to the empowerment mechanisms for the downtrodden), then the government could have countered the arguments of the *dalit* groups at the forum. It could have committed itself to what it desires to do in future. In that case, there is no reason why the *dalit* should not have been allowed to speak. And if the State has not done enough for the *dalits* or if too much is left to be done, then it was highly improper and immoral not to let the *dalits* articulate their concerns on the subject at the Meet.

Minority Rights

Dr. Ambedkar supported adequate and effective representation to the minorities in the Legislatures, the Executives and the Public Services. He wanted statutory provisions and safeguards for preventing discrimination against the minorities. He demanded special rights and privileges to empower the minorities. He introduced a new parameter of 'social discrimination' as a real test to determine the minority. The *dalits,* according to this criteria, were to be treated as real minority. They were the most discriminated group. Hence, they had the best claim to the minority status. In fact, memoranda submitted by him, to the Minorities Sub-committee of the First Round Table

Conference as well as to the Advisory Committee of the Constituent Assembly were in pursuance of his struggle to claim minority status for his community. Dr. Ambedkar has been criticized, quite and often, for taking up minority (*dalits*) issues on the ground that his approach was narrow and served the British interests. The truth, however, is that his demands were always legitimate and consistent with the broad national interests. As regards timing, the demand that before the Britishers leave, there should be a general acceptance as to the incorporation of rights of minorities in the future Constitutional vision was not anti-national. Dr. Ambedkar had always in his mind the supreme goal of national unity and integrity. His demands were not only in consonance but an essential step towards that goal. It could not be achieved by frustrating the aspirations of a sizeable section of society. Dr. Ambedkar's assumption was that the unity and progress of the nation would depend upon how minorities were going to be treated in free India. He envisioned that the preservation of religious, cultural and linguistic identity of the minorities would help them develop the necessary confidence to integrate with the national mainstream. The special guarantees would enable the *dalits* to become equal partners in nation-building. It would forge a bond of fraternity between the majority and minority communities, thus, ultimately, having the most desirable effect of merging them. Then, there would remain no need for any special privileges and safeguards. Dr. Ambedkar stressed the responsibility of the majority to treat the minority well in the following words:

> The minorities in India have agreed to place their existence in the hands of the majority.... They have loyally accepted the rule of the majority which is basically a communal majority and not to discriminate against minorities. Whether the minorities will continue or vanish must depend upon this habit of discriminating against the minority, the minorities can have no ground to exist. They will vanish.[7]

Dr. Ambedkar made a distinction between political majority and communal majority. He was of the opinion that parliamentary executive of the British type was not suitable for India. As Indian society was communally divided, the majority secured by a party in the legislature would be a communal majority. Copying the British model would mean vesting the executive power in the hands of a communal majority. The communal majority is always closed and fixed unlike the political majority in Britain which is open and changeable in its class composition. The adoption of British model, in the opinion of Dr. Ambedkar, would make the majority community a governing class and the minority a subject class on a permanent basis. That would not be a true democracy. Therefore, to protect the minorities against the tyranny of communal executive, he proposed a strong and stable executive of highly representative character in his memorandum.[8] the representatives of different minorities in the cabinet could be elected by only the respective members of each minority in the legislature by single transferable vote. The representatives of the majority community, on the other hand, were to be elected by the whole House by single transferable vote. The executive had the fixed term under the scheme. The cabinet ministers could not be removed except by impeachment on grounds of corruption or treason. It was a very radical schema, therefore, did not find favour with the nationalists. The creation of Pakistan eliminated the chances, if any, of its adoption. The scheme, however, had the potential to tackle, perhaps, the greatest problem of democracy in modern times, viz., 'Majority *vs.* Minority syndrome'. In Dr. Ambedkar's own words, this form of executive was intended to serve the following purposes:

> (i) To prevent the majority from forming a Government without giving any opportunity to the minorities to have a say in the matter.

(ii) To prevent the majority from having exclusive control over administration and thereby make the tyranny of the minority by the majority possible.

(iii) To prevent the inclusion by the Majority Party in Executive representatives of the minorities who have no confidence of the minorities.

(iv) To provide a stable Executive necessary for good and efficient administration.[9]

Dr. Ambedkar realized very early that the Declaration of Rights and the Equality of opportunity would, in practice, be proved ineffective if adequate safeguards and special guarantees for the weaker sections were not incorporated in the constitution. Reservations in the legislatures and the public services were the most important such measure envisaged by Dr. Ambedkar. His stance, however, on the mode of representation for the depressed classes in the legislatures kept on changing. It also created much controversy over time. It was, partly, the result of his evolving ideas on the issue in the light of the development of events and, partly, due to his tussle with the Congress which was aspiring to be the sole representative of all the Hindus, including the *dalits.* Initially, in a representation to the Simon Commission in 1928, Dr. Ambedkar pleaded that the representatives of the Scheduled Castes should be elected by the joint electorates, instead of being nominated by the Government. In a memorandum submitted to the Minorities Committee at the Round Table Conference in 1931, he changed his stance by demanding separate electorates.[10] He had to revert to the joint electorates when Gandhi took to fast unto death over the Communal Award which had proposed separate electorates for the Scheduled Castes. The Poona Pact was signed between Dr. Ambedkar and Gandhi.

A clause of Primary election was stipulated in the Poona Pact. This clause proposed a preliminary round of election before the general election on a reserved seat. A panel of four candidates belonging to the Scheduled Castes was to be elected by the Scheduled Castes electorate only. Finally, only those four candidates could contest the reserved seat in a joint electorate. Clause 5 of the Poona Pact, however, limited the system of Primary election to ten years period. In the constituencies where Primary election was held in 1946, it was seen that Scheduled Castes could not get their first choice candidates elected in sufficient numbers. The Primary election was just a qualifying election. Ultimately, the choice fell on the joint electorates among which Scheduled Castes were a minority in most of the constituencies. Therefore, Dr. Ambedkar had developed strong reservations about the feasibility of the joint electorates for the untouchables. He argued that even if the provision for 'Primary election' be extended for a further period, it would not help the *dalits.* The final choice of numerical majority (caste Hindus) would prevail over the first choice of the Scheduled Castes under such kind of system. He was more keen to see the choice of the Scheduled Castes prevail rather than a Scheduled Caste candidate be elected who might not be their first choice. Therefore, in the memorandum to the Constituent Assembly, he pleaded, forcefully, in favour of separate electorates. He also asked for the abrogation of the Poona Pact which, he said, was accepted by him due to the coercive fast of Gandhi. He almost tried to give permanent colour to the separate electorates in his proposal.[11]

Ultimately Dr. Ambedkar had to contend with the joint electorates. The Constitution of India reserves seats for the Scheduled Castes and Scheduled Tribes in the central and state legislatures (Articles 330 and 332) with joint electorates. Thus, Dr. Ambedkar ended up from where he started. It appears that he used his demand for separate electorates, more as a bargaining leverage to get more and more concessions for the Scheduled Castes in lieu of it than as a real objective. This argument can be substantiated from the fact that when he really got at the helm of affairs (after becoming Chairman of the Drafting Committee), he did not press his demand to the end.

No doubt, the circumstances forced him to dilute his stance, for being in chair, he could not deflect beyond a point from the general will of the Constituent Assembly. But, at the same time, the chair put him in a strong bargaining position from where he could have brought pressure on the fellow members. He could have used that position, if he had been dead serious about the issue. But, he never threatened to walk out in case of his demand being unmet. Another purpose behind his demand for separate electorates, was to wrest the initiate from the Congress by adopting a tough posture as Congress had also demanded the joint electorates. Dr. Ambedkar succeeded, particularly, on this account.

Dr. Ambedkar asked for reservations in the Public services of India to the Scheduled Castes on the basis of their population.[12] He was clear that reservation in jobs is not a concession or a privilege extended to the depressed classes. It is their legitimate right. It is in recognition of their Fundamental Right to Equality. He said, "We have to safeguard two things, namely, principle of equality of opportunity and at the same time, satisfy the demand of communities which have not had so far representation in the State".[13] Dr. Ambedkar also held that reservation should always be for minority of seats, otherwise, it would nullify the principle of equality of opportunity.

His stand has been vindicated by various Supreme Court judgements. In Thomas[14] and ABKS[15] cases, Supreme Court held that Article 16(4) of the Constitution is a facet, and illustration or a method of application of Article 16(1) of the Constitution, because opportunity can never be equal among human beings who have unequal capacities to grasp it. Since reservation in jobs is not a permissible exception but a necessary ingredient of the Right to Equality of opportunity, Supreme Court has held it to be a Fundamental Right of the Scheduled Castes and Scheduled Tribes. Dr. Ambedkar's another contention that reservation should be for a minority of seats has been proved right by Supreme Court judgement in

Indira Sawhney v. Union of India case, 1991, Supreme Court put a ceiling of 50 per cent on reservation in jobs.

Dr. Ambedkar did not take up the demands of the religious minorities reservation in the Legislatures. Nor did he oppose their demands. If he did not take into account the like demands of the religious minorities it does not mean that his proposal was inconsistent with their demands. He did not formulate the demands of the religious minorities due to four reasons. First, he was not their representative for they had their own representatives on the ground. Second, there was inconsistency and no broad consensus over their demand. Third, the likelihood of creation of Pakistan would make their demands obsolete and uncertain. Fourth, he had far more important cause of (*dalits*) in hand and the memorandum he submitted was on behalf of *dalits*, not the general minorities. He was so much preoccupied with the problems of the *dalits*, that neither could he find any platform nor time for articulation of the concerns of religious minorities. His own community was so dispriviledged and under represented that he could not afford to divert his attention and energy to the other communities' cause. He could speak, quite logically, either for his own cause (i.e., the cause of his community) or for the general cause (Declaration of Fundamental Rights). To plead for some particular cause of any of the community other than his own was not practical and prudent under the prevailing circumstances. The *dalits* stood in the greatest need of reservation. Until the creation of Pakistan, the claims of the religious minorities were widely recognized for political representation. However, with the bifurcation of the country, the demand of political representation on a communal (religious) basis lost much of its force. The idea stood, totally, rejected. It could not find favour with Dr. Ambedkar, too. He concentrated exclusively on the demands of the Scheduled Castes. However, it does not mean that his ideas and efforts have no relevance to religious minorities. His proposal for Parliamentary-type, broad-based and fixed Executive was meant to help and protect all kinds of minorities. All the religious rights contained in the list of Fundamental Rights of the Memorandum found their place in the Constitution of India. Being its chief architect, he ensured some special rights to the minorities in the Articles 29 and 30 of the Constitution. Speaking in the Constituent Assembly on the absoluteness of the rights of the minorities, he was outright that some members want that:

> ...the rights of minorities should be relative, that is to say, we must wait and see, what rights the minorities are given by the Pakistan Assembly before we determine the rights we want to give to the minorities in the Hindustan area. Now, Sir, with all deference, I must deprecate any such idea. Rights of minorities should be absolute rights. They should not be subject to any consideration as to what another party may like to do to minorities within the jurisdiction of another State have not got the same rights which we have given to minorities in our territory, it would be open for the State to take up the matter in a diplomatic manner and see that the wrongs are rectified. But no matter what others do, I think we ought to do what is right in our judgement and personally I think that the rights which are indicated in clause 18 are rights which every minority, irrespective of any other consideration is entitled to claim.[16]

Fundamental Rights

Although Dr. Ambedkar's chief struggle centred, always, round the rights of *dalits*, he never lost sight of the fact that human rights are meant of one and all. In fact, his demand for some special privileges for the depressed classes was not an attempt to go beyond the scope of Fundamental Rights. It was, rather, an endeavour to make their rights more meaningful. His memorandum to the Constituent Assembly on behalf of depressed classes contained a comprehensive list of Fundamental Rights to be enjoyed by all the citizens. He was the chief exponent of Fundamental Rights in various debates of the Constituent Assembly bear testimony to this fact. A brief summary of the Fundamental Rights contained in his memorandum to the Constituent Assembly is as follows:

> Any privilege or disability arising out of rank, birth, person, family, religion or religious usage and custom will be abolished. The State shall not deprive any person of life, liberty and property without due process of law; nor deny to any person equal protection of law. All citizens will possess equal civil rights and will have equal access to all places, institutions, conveyances and amenities which are dedicated to, or maintained for the use of the public. No citizen shall be disqualified to hold any public office or exercise any trade or calling by reason of his or her religion, caste, creed, sex or social status. Every citizen will have the right to reside in any part of India subject to public order and morality. But the Right of Settlement from one state to another may be curtailed in case of certain undesirable persons. The Union Government shall guarantee protection against persecution of a community as well as against internal disorder or violence arising in any part of India. Subjecting a person to forced labour and involuntary servitude will be an offence. Unreasonable or unlawful searches and arrest will be prohibited. Right to vote for all, other than the immature, imprisoned and insane. No law or order shall be made abridging the freedom of Speech, of Press, of Association and of Assembly except for consideration of public order and morality. No post facto law shall be passed. Liberty of conscience including the right to profess, to preach and to convert within limits compatible with public order and morality. No person shall be compelled to become a member of any religious association, submit to any religious instruction, perform any act of religion or pay any tax, the proceeds of which are specifically appropriated for the use of any religious community of which he is not a member. Every religious association shall be free to regulate and administer its affairs, within the limits of the laws applicable to all. The State shall not recognize any religion as State religion. All offences under this

section shall be deemed to be cognizable offences. The Union Legislature shall make laws in this regard.

It becomes clear that most of the Fundamental Rights conceptualized by Dr. Ambedkar, finally, found their place in the Constitution of India. The Right to Life, The Right to Equality, the right to various kinds of freedoms including the right against arbitrary arrest are all there in the Indian Constitution. It is interesting that inspite of all his inclination towards socialism, the Right to Property was still sacrosanct (though not absolute) for him. The property could not be taken away without due process of law. Some provisions of the memorandum could not find explicit mention in the Constitution of India. For instance, the right of communities against genocide or the provision that State shall not recognize any religion as State religion. Nevertheless, the Right to Life along with the Right to Equality covers the protection against Genocide while the latter anomaly was made up by inserting the word 'Secular' in the Preamble of the Constitution by the Forty Second Constitutional Amendment in 1976. After the creation of Pakistan, the subtle distinction between Residence and Settlement, and the conditions attached to 'Resettlement', in the memorandum, lost their significance. Hence, no need was felt to include those provisions in the Constitution. Ambedkar held the Right to Vote in very high regard and included it in his list of Fundamental Rights. He regarded franchise as a right of self-defence in the sense that individual should have the power to change the composition of Legislature whose laws directly affect him. Appearing before South Borough Committee on Reforms in Indian Administration, he quoted L.T. Hobhouse, "The success of democracy depends on the response of voters to the opportunities given to them. But, conversely, the opportunities must be given in order to call forth the response. The exercise of popular government is itself an education.... enfranchise itself may, precisely, be the stimulus needed to awaken interest. The ballot alone, effectively, liberates the quiet citizen from the tyranny of the shooter and the wirepuller. An impression of existing inertness alone is not a sufficient reason for withholding responsible government or restricting the area of suffrage".[17] How prophetic these words have proved to be in Indian context can be gauged from the fact of increasing political participation of the depressed classes after independence. Dr. Ambedkar believed in the principle of 'one vote one value'. Therefore, he disfavoured property or educational qualifications for voting. He was not in favour of weighted voting, which was, at that time, still continuing in Britain. He argued, beautifully:

> .... poorer the individual the greater the necessity of enfranchising him. In every society based on private property, the terms of associated life as between owners and workers are from the start set against the workers. If the welfare of the workers is to be guaranteed from being menaced by the owners, the terms of this associated life must be constantly resettled. But this can hardly be done unless the franchise is disassociated from property and extended to all propertyless adults.[18]

As remedy against invasion of Fundamental Rights, the Memorandum prohibited the State from making any law or issuing any order violative of Fundamental Rights. The Supreme Court was vested with the authority to issue writs of *Habeas Corpus, Quo Warranto, Prohibition, Certiorari* and *Mandamus* to redress the violation of Fundamental Rights. However, Fundamental Rights could be abridged or suspended in case of 'invasion' or 'rebellion'. All these provisions were carried into the Constitution of India. A staunch defender of Fundamental Rights, notwithstanding, Dr. Ambedkar was instrumental in introducing the provisions relating to suspension of these rights during emergency. As to the criticism that the enjoyment of Fundamental Rights was made contingent upon the security of the State, Dr. Ambedkar argued in the Constituent Assembly:

> … in certain cases where, for instance, the State's very life is in jeopardy, those rights must be subject to certain amount of limitation…. In times of emergency the life of the State itself is in jeopardy and if the State is not able to protect itself in times of emergency, the individual himself will be found to have lost his very existence. Consequently, the superior right of the State to protect itself in times of emergency, so that it may …. live to discharge its functions in order that the individual under the aegis of the State may develop, must be guaranteed as safely as the right of an individual.[19]

In so far as the survival of the State is concerned, the curtailment of Rights is justifiable. But Dr. Ambedkar had gone as far as justifying the provision of Preventive Detention, even, in normal times. That provision was embodied as Article 22 in the chapter of the Fundamental Rights in the Constitution. Dr. Ambedkar justified its inclusion, in the Constituent Assembly, on the ground that it was necessary for the Executive to detain such persons in advance who are suspected of tampering with the public order or defence of the country. To satisfy the elaborate legal procedure is not always practicable. In this way, a situation could be stopped from developing into an emergency. According to him, the exigency of the liberty of the individual cannot be placed above the interests of the State. Instead of being opposed to State authority, it is dependent on it. The more important reason for Dr. Ambedkar to introduce a clause on Preventive Detention in the Constituent Assembly, however, was to check the unlimited power of the Parliament to make laws in matters of arrest. This power had been given to the Parliament by virtue of Article 21 (then, Article 15 of the draft) of the Constitution. It states that no person shall be deprived of his life or liberty except according to 'procedure established by law'. Now, by virtue of this Article, the Parliament had got unlimited power to establish whatever procedure it deemed fit in matters of arrest. Dr. Ambedkar argued in the Constituent Assembly, "by introducing Article

15A (present Article 22 of the Constitution), we are making, if I may say so, compensation for what was done earlier in passing Article 15 (present Article 21). In other words, we are providing for the substance of the law of 'due process' by the introduction of Article 15A (present Article 22)".[20]

Thus, Dr. Ambedkar advocated Preventive Detention not only to ensure the security of the State but also to limit the power of the State. He conceived a system of rights with necessary limitations upon the interests of the individual as well as authority of the State. The point he missed, however, was that even in the presence of standard procedure set up by the Parliament under clause of Preventive Detention, the Executive might not act, always, in the rightful manner. It might have its own axe to grind, thus, work for narrower ends than national security. Adequate safeguards to avoid such situation were not inserted in the Constitution. The suspension of human rights in times of emergency can be justified, because it is the duty of the State to divert and concentrate all its energy and resources towards its own protection. However, under normal circumstances (when the State's survival is not in question), the preventive detention cannot be justified. Although, Dr. Ambedkar supported it to checkmate the power of the Parliament, he could not foresee its abuse by the Executive. And that is precisely, what has occurred in last three decades.

It is commonplace how various Acts of Preventive Detention have been misused. The most widely abused laws have been Maintenance of Internal Security Act (MISA; enacted in 1971 and repealed in 1978) and Terrorist And Disruptive Activities (Prevention) Act (TADA; enacted in 1985 and repealed in 1995). These laws were grossly misused as instruments of arbitrary arrest and suppression by the government. The number of detenus (mostly, political opponents or dissidents of the Congress Party) during 1975-76 had soared upto 1,75,000 under MISA. TADA was applied with impunity even in those states where terrorism was non-existent. Most people were arrested in Gujarat – a terrorism free state. The conviction rate in TADA throughout the country has been less than even one per cent. Thousands of under trials under TADA, despite its revocation in 1995 are, still, lying in jails. Just recently, forty-five under trails who had spent an average of seven years in Mysore jail in connection with the so-called 'Veerappan associates cases' were acquitted by a TADA court. Despite all the shortcomings and misuse of earlier Preventive Detention Acts, the NDA government has brought an Ordinance on the pattern of TADA, just a few weeks before the winter session of the Parliament. It is entitled 'Prevention of Terrorism Ordinance' 2003 (POTO). Now it has got the status of an Act. Such legislations, without adequate safeguards, instead of curbing disruptive and divisive tendencies, weaken the integrity and security of the nation in the long run. The menace is more so in the hands of a government which pursues sectarian and anti-minorities agenda.

Fundamental Rights are of such primary importance that whosoever violates them should have good reasons for doing so. The onus of proof should be on those who encroach the rights, unlike TADA or POTA under which the arrested person has to prove his innocence. If the State is not able to prove the charges after keeping the individual in preventive detention, the individual should be duly compensated. There should be scope for severe punishment to the authorities who act malafides. People are entitled to human rights, because rights are so essential to realize their humanity. In so far as the exercise of rights is reasonably consistent with a corresponding enjoyment by others, even the State has no right to curb or take away the rights. Some Rights have been specified as Fundamental, precisely, because modern societies have come to affirm their sanctity and inviolability. That is to say, these rights do not admit any kind of trade offs. These rights provide the conditions of peace, security, happiness and prosperity. Thus, the concern for Rights constitute the basis of the state. The security of the State cannot be allowed to supersede this concern. No doubt, the security of the State is also desired for the same ends which the rights are supposed to promote, viz., peace, happiness and prosperity. The individual cannot be secure without the State being secure and the State cannot be secure, unless, the individual is secure. Thus, the interests of both are not contradictory but complementary. Nevertheless, the interests of the rulers and the interests of the subjects are, sometimes, contradictory. It is the ruling elite which manipulates and misuses the Preventive Detention laws in the name of law and order or security of the State. The law and order cannot be a substitute for good governance. Detentions without trials for as long as one year with no grounds shown for the arrest are no alternate for efficient investigations, speedy trials and equitable justice. The arrest should not precede the charges. Freedom can be curtailed only for the sake of freedom. It cannot been tailed to make up for the lapse in good governance. Necessarily, ways and means other than encroaching the rights have to be found to maintain law and order.

State Socialism as Protection Against Exploitation

Human rights can be realized at two fronts – at 'consciousness' level and at 'development' level. The realization can be enhanced at the 'consciousness' level by deepening the awareness about the rights, and by developing the confidence, among the people. At 'developmental' level, the rights can be realized by improving the material conditions, particularly of the disadvantageous groups. Dr. Ambedkar worked at both the fronts. He realized that Fundamental Rights will have no meaning for the poor, the unemployed and the dispossessed. He asked, "....if a person who is unemployed is offered a choice between a job of some sort, with some sort of wages, with no fixed hours of labour and with an interdict on joining a union and the exercise of his right to freedom of speech, association, religion etc., can there be any doubt as to what his choice will be. How can it be otherwise? The fear of starvation, the fear of losing a house, the fear of losing savings, if any, the fear of being compelled to take children away from school.... are factors too strong to permit a man to stand out for his Fundamental Rights".[21] Dr. Ambedkar suggested 'State Socialism' as a way out. It was to be an adjunct of Fundamental Rights. In fact, he proposed it as a remedy against invasion of Fundamental Rights.[22] He was of the opinion that the oppression and exploitation of the masses by a few individuals was due to the lack of collective ownership of the means of production. If the new social order based on equality, liberty and fraternity had to be established, parliamentary democracy must be accompanied by State socialism. His vision of socialism included State ownership of land and key industries. Insurance would be the monopoly of the state.

Dr. Ambedkar, was not a Marxist, not withstanding. He believed that the State could play positive role. He did not subscribe to the irreconcilability of conflict between the classes. He was not in favour of snatching, forcefully, the property from the rich without any regard to their claims to the property. There was no scope for violence in his scheme. He believed in the sanctity of the Right to Property. Therefore in his scheme, the individual had to be duly compensated in the form of debenture equal to the value of the land or industry to be overtaken by the State. The debenture-holder was to be entitled, even, to the interest on the debenture. He was to be gradually repaid in instalments out of the State revenue. Thus, Dr. Ambedkar, beautifully, interwove the Right to Property in his scheme of State Socialism. The scheme had the potential to solve the problem of extreme inequality in Indian society without any side effects. Yet, it was quite a radical proposal, therefore, did not find favour in the Constituent Assembly. It was not adopted. As a result, the gap between the haves and have-nots, instead of being bridged, has further widened after the independence. Half-baked land reform measures were undertaken in half-hearted manner. The policy of progressive taxation was adopted with large scope for corruption and inefficiency. Ceilings on expansion of land and industry were implemented with a number of loopholes. All these measures were bound to fail, and they failed, miserably. The inequality persists with greater elan.

Dr. Ambedkar proposed State Socialism as a means towards fuller realization of Fundamental Rights. On the contrary, the scheme is criticized on the grounds that it severely restricts the scope of Fundamental Rights. The criticism, however, is based on narrow conception of Fundamental Rights. Fundamental Rights are not absolute. If by restricting some of the rights, the intensity, universality and scope of the rights, as a whole, can be increased, then it is worth it. For what is the purpose of rights? Is it to secure the freedom to some and deny it to others? Or is it to provide the conditions of good living to a few individuals and deprive the rest of the people from enjoying those conditions? If the purpose is the maximum possible liberty to all the individuals, then curtailing the unlimited right to property to increase the freedom and the capabilities of the masses fits well in the truer and holistic conception of Fundamental Rights. Here, the connection between individual liberty and the shape and form of the economic structure of society becomes apparent. Dr. Ambedkar perceived liberty within the social context. He criticized the notion that liberty increases in proportion to the decrease in intervention by the State. He said "it is true that where the State refrains from intervention what remains is liberty. But this does not dispose of the matter. One more question remains to be answered. To whom and for whom is this liberty? What is called liberty from the control of the State is another name for the dictatorship of the private employer".[23] Thus, only by removing the control of the rich over the economic life, the poor can be freed from the exploitation. By limiting the Right to Property, the liberty can be brought at the doorstep of each individual. Genuine liberty cannot usher unless political equality is complemented by economic equality. Only then, can democracy live up to its principle of 'one man one value' and Fundamental Rights become achievable for all. The State intervention in economic affairs, therefore, does not diminish but enlarges and widens the scope of liberty.

Although, Dr. Ambedkar held the Right to Property in high esteem, at the same time, he was highly critical of the doctrine of *laissez faire* (a policy of non-interference by the State in economic matters). This doctrine could not ensure liberty to all. The consolidation of holdings could not have any meaning for the landless. In Dr. Ambedkar's scheme, the property is an individual as well as a social right. It is an individual right in the sense that property cannot be taken away without due compensation. It is a social right in the sense that property has to be enjoyed by all in relation with each other. It is not a privilege to be enjoyed by individuals in an isolated context. Apart from gratifying the individual, it has a social purpose to fulfil. The individualist and the socialist dimensions of the Right to Property are coalesced in Dr. Ambedkar's vision of socialism. This consummation was to be protected and effected by the Constitution.

Dr. Ambedkar realized the implications of leaving the economic structure of society untouched by the Constitution. His scheme marked a departure from the Western Constitutions which prescribed the form of political structure, but not the economic structure of the society. To translate the principle of 'one man one vote' (existing in Western democracies) into 'one man one value' (the ultimate goal of democracy), it was essential, in the opinion of Dr. Ambedkar, to prescribe the form of economic structure in the Constitution itself. This task could not be left to the will of the Legislature. He said, "the successful invocation by the less powerful of the authority of the Legislature is a doubtful proposition. Having regard to the fact that, even, under adult suffrage all Legislatures and Government are controlled by the more powerful, an appeal to the Legislature to intervene is a very precarious safeguard against the invasion of the liberty of the less powerful".[24] Dr. Ambedkar could not, however, get his economic ideas incorporated in the Constitution. Given the socio-economic composition of the Constituent Assembly, there were few takers for his radical ideas. He had to contend with getting only some of his ideas enshrined as Directive Principles in the Constitution.

It would not be out of place to mention, in brief, Dr. Ambedkar's efforts towards improving the economic conditions of the workers and the tenants. He took great interest in 'urban labour' and 'agricultural tenancy' problems. He prepared and introduced Khoti Abolition Bill in Bombay Assembly in 1938. It was meant to abolish tenure of the *zamindars* and secure occupancy rights to the tenants. Dhananjay Keer, appropriately, calls him the first legislator in India to introduce a Bill for the abolition of the serfdom of the agricultural tenants. Dr. Ambedkar, vehemently, criticized the Bombay Industrial Disputes Act, 1938. It declared the strike as illegal under certain circumstances. Dr. Ambedkar held the "Right to strike is nothing else than the right to freedom to one's services on any terms that one wants to obtain. And once you concede the right to freedom, you, necessarily, concede the right to strike".[25] He brought radical reforms in the wages, the working conditions and the social security of the workers when he became the Labour Minister. The Industrial Disputes Act, the Indian Employment Standing Orders Act, the Minimum Wages Act, the Factories Act were all inspired by his views on labour issues.

Women's Rights

Like *dalits,* women have also faced suppression for thousands of years. They were also denied education and free movement. Their growth (mental, spiritual, physical and cultural) has been dwarfed due to social restrictions on their sphere of activity outside the four walls of their homes. Even, being part of the larger society, they have faced torture and humiliation in their daily lives. They could not protest, because, like *dalits,* their low position in the society was also justified through the Hindu *Shastras.* Thus, like *dalits,* the women, too, had low status in

Indian society. The problems of both were intertwined in the sense that the Hindu social order did not recognize the equal worth of human dignity. Therefore, some sections were bound to be at the receiving end. Dr. Ambedkar held the pitiable condition of women to be a direct manifestation of the caste system. The inequality cherished by the caste system, in his opinion, had a direct bearing on the unequal status of women. They were also victims of the *Manu Smriti* and the flawed interpretation of the Hindu *shastras*. Thus, the struggle for the rights of the *dalits* as well as women had some common elements. The problems of both had common roots. The roots lay in the ideology which had bred and justified inequality. Therefore, the change in their status could be brought by annihilating that ideology. The transformation could also be brought with the help of a positive law.

Dr. Ambedkar took the initiative to draft and introduce the Hindu Code Bill in the Constituent Assembly. The Bill sought to abolish polygamy among the Hindus. It proposed the right to property and the right to divorce for women. The absence of these rights was incompatible with the Fundamental Rights of Liberty and Equality enshrined in the Constitution of India. The Bill tried to codify the Hindu laws which were in a scattered form. He proposed to reform these laws on seven different matters, viz., (i) the right to property of a deceased Hindu dying intestate, to both male and female, (ii) the order of succession among different heirs to the property of a deceased dying intestate, (iii) the law of maintenance, (iv) marriage, (v) divorce, (vi) adoption, and (vii) minority guardianship. Despite the very moderate nature of the Bill, Dr. Ambedkar could not get it passed due to its opposition by many conservative caste Hindus. In protest against the failure of the Bill, Dr. Ambedkar resigned his seat in the cabinet. Although, his efforts did not, entirely, go waste. Later, the original Bill was split into four different Bills with slight changes. Those were passed as the Hindu Marriage Act, 1955; the Hindu Succession, Act 1956; the

Hindu Minority and Guardianship Act, 1956; and the Hindu Adoption and Maintenance Act 1956.

Concluding Remarks

It is to the credit of Dr. Ambedkar that he grasped fully, the difference between the struggle for the independence of the country (Right to Self-determination of the people of India) and the struggle for the emancipation of the *dalits* (their Right to live with dignity as equal members of society). The former was being fought against a discrete alien power. It had reached its crescendo and the country was on the verge of Independence. The latter was being fought within the society and was aimed not at overthrow but transformation. The enemy, here, was an age old ideological system which was quite complex and well entrenched. This struggle was in its infancy and could not be accomplished in a single stroke. It was likely to continue after the Independence. The former struggle could be won without even eradicating the ideology of Imperialism or Colonialism. However, the latter struggle could not be won without annihilating the ideology of *chaturvarnya.* Being conscious of the difference, Dr. Ambedkar tried his best not to allow the latter to get absorbed in the former. It was important to maintain the distinct identity of the *dalits'* struggle at that juncture, if it could help their cause. They had always been the victims. It was quite logical for them to make a noise when they got some strength and opportunity. The British rule did no more harm to them than the previous ages. So, the assumption that their struggle served the British interests, from their point of view, is baseless. *Dalits* had their legitimate concerns which had to be addressed before the Constitution of free India took shape. If their demands had not been met, then, coming out of the British servitude would have been nothing more than entering into another bond of slavery for them.

The allegation that Dr. Ambedkar divided the Indian society on a permanent basis by separating the *dalits'* concerns from the general society, smacks of either ignorance or contempt. The caste divisions were, already, acute but not so manifest in the absence of competitive political mobilization process. The problem was bound to surface and intensify once the democratic process had started off. If unaddressed, these divisions could lead to the disruption of the social fabric of India. For its proper solution, a problem has to be understood, recognized and addressed in the right perspective. That is, precisely, what Dr. Ambedkar did. His exclusivist agenda for the *dalits* was just a means towards a noble goal of their fuller integration with the Indian society based on relationship of equality and fraternity. Thus, Dr. Ambedkar did a yeoman service to the cause of nation-building. His contribution towards the integration and consolidation of Indian society is immense.

Dr. Ambedkar's ideas were deeply rooted in the reality of Indian society. He had clear understanding that human rights could not become a reality for a large number of people in India, unless the socio-economic structure is transformed. He proposed radical but practical measures in this regard. His scheme of State Socialism was designed to change the whole set of hierarchised and unequal relationship. It was aimed at not just the *dalits* but all the poor and the dispossessed people who were most vulnerable to the violations of human rights. The scheme could not be materialized due to the vested interests in the Constituent Assembly. Dr. Ambedkar visualized a broad representative Executive to protect the minorities, but in vain. He envisaged reservations for the depressed classes in the Legislatures and the Public Services. The reservations have borne some fruit but far below the desired level. His approach was not just restricted to the Constitution or the law. The real task before him was to change the social consciousness, the very mindset, which had justified social inequality for ages. Nothing short of transforming the ideological foundations of Indian society would achieve the purpose. The objective was twofold in this regard. First, the caste Hindus had to be impressed to change their indifferent and discriminatory attitude towards the *dalits* and treat them as equals. This could be pursued, as Dr. Ambedkar did, by making efforts towards the eradication of *varna* system, beseeching re-interpretation of the *shastras* and, invoking the ideals of equality and justice. Second, the more important objective was to make the discriminated community stand on its own feet. Neither the change of heart among the caste Hindus, nor the various empowerment mechanisms would bring them out of their predicament, unless, the *dalits* developed faith in themselves. Merely the availability, even, the accessibility, to the Rights was not enough. They had to be empowered, psychologically, to assert and realize their rights. Here the contribution of Dr. Ambedkar was tremendous. All his efforts were devoted towards inculcating a sense of dignity and self-worth among the *dalits.*

He was more of human rights activist than a theoretician. Although none has articulated the rights of the vulnerable sections in India, more ably than Dr. Ambedkar. His efforts are unparalleled in the history of the human rights movement. Without his guidance, articulation and support, the story of human rights of *dalits* would have been different. No doubt, Dr. Ambedkar was the greatest champion of human rights, India has ever produced.

Notes

1. *States and Minorities: What are their Rights and How to Secure them in the Constitution of Free India,* Memorandum on the safeguards for the Scheduled Castes prepared and submitted by Ambedkar to the Constituent Assembly on behalf of All India Scheduled Castes Federation, 1947.
2. See *Francis Coralie Mullin v. Administrator, Union Territory of Delhi,* A.I.R. 1981, SC, 746.
3. G.S. Lokhande, *B.R. Ambedkar: A Study in Social Democracy*, 1977, p.4.
4. Bhagwan Das (edited), *Thus Spoke Ambedkar*, Bheem Patrika Publication, Jallandhar, 1977, Vol. I, p. 162.

5. Prem Prakash, cited in *Ambedkar: Politics and the Scheduled Castes*, Ashish Publishing House, New Delhi, 1993, p. 52.
6. Dhananjay Keer, *Dr. Ambedkar: Life and Mission*, Edition III, 1971 p. 230.
7. *Constituent Assembly Debates*, Vol. VII, (4th November 1946). Note that the full text of this speech is reproduced in Appendix B.
8. Clause I, Section III, Article II entitled 'Provisions for the Protection of Minorities' in Memorandum, *States and Minorities: What are Their Rights and How to Secure Them in the Constitution of Free India*, 1947.
9. Appendix I (Explanatory Notes), Clause I, Section III, Article II of Memorandum, *States and Minorities: What are their Rights and How to Secure them in the Constitution of Free India*, 1947.
10. Supplementary Memorandum on the claims of the Depressed Classes for special representation, submitted to the Round Table Conference in 1931 by Dr. Bhimrao Ambedkar and Rao B.R. Srinivasan; reproduced in D. Keer, *Dr. Ambedkar: Life and Mission*, Edition III, 1971, pp. 315-317.
11. Separate electorates could be done away with only if the resolution to that effect could be passed by the Scheduled Castes members of a freshly constituted House. See Clause 2, Part III, Section IV, Article II of *States and Minorities....*, 1947.
12. Clause 3, Part I (Safeguards for the Scheduled Castes), Section IV, Article II of *States and Minorities....*, 1947.
13. *Constituent Assembly Debates*, Vol. I, p. 59.
14. *State of Kerala v. Thomas*, A.I.R. 1976, Supreme Court, 490.
15. *A.B.K. Singh v. Union of India*, A.I.R. 1981, Supreme Court, 298.
16. *Constituent Assembly Debates*, Vol. VI, p. 950.
17. *Writings and Speeches of Dr. B.R. Ambedkar*, Department of Education, Govt. of Maharashtra, Bombay, Vol. I, 1979, p. 261.
18. Memorandum to Simon Commission cited in *Writings and Speeches of Dr. B.R. Ambedkar*, Vol. II, Department of Education, Govt. of Maharashtra, 1979, pp. 337-338.
19. *Constituent Assembly Debates*, Vol. VI, p. 950.
20. *Constituent Assembly Debates*, Vol. IX, p. 1497.
21. Appendix I (Explanatory Notes), Clause 4, Section II, Article II, *States and Minorities...*, 1947.

22. Clause 4, subtitled 'Protection against Economic Exploitation', in section II titled 'Remedies against Invasion of Fundamental Rights', Article II, *States and Minorities...*, 1947.
23. Appendix I (Explanatory Notes), Clause 4, Section II, Article II, *States and Minorities...*, 1947.
24. Ibid.
25. 'On the Industrial Disputes Bill', *Writings and Speeches of Dr. B.R. Ambedkar*, Department of Education, Govt. of Maharashtra, Vol. II, 1982, p. 208.

18

Ambedkarite Vision of Mineral Resources Development Policy and Law

Reflections on Humanistic and Labour-Oriented Jurisprudence in Retrospects and Prospects

MD. ZAFAR MAHFOOZ NOMANI

Besides Ambedkar's much publicized constitutional stewardship of social justice, egalitarian social order and democratic republicanism his vision of national development of natural and mineral resources abound in profundity. Beseeched with the national structuring he meticulously indoctrinated developmental polices[1] with greater circumspection to augur social engineering and consensual model of society. An inquiry into his economic thoughts and developmental vision broadly encapsulates four major policies such as water policy, mineral policy,[2] labour policy and agricultural or land policy. Since India has been endowed with rich mineral resources he pains-takingly thrashed out mining policy for greater common good than to serve the goals of truncated capitalism and colonialism. Envisioning social justice to go along with economic justice he fashioned the national economic policies to the ultimate benefaction of marginalized and oppressed segment of society.[3] Keeping this goal paramount he not only turned the mineral policy but also rejuvenated geological institution to promote development with human face. Viewed in this perspective Ambedkarite mineral resources development policy and legislative activism is an interesting discourse on development, equity and justice. Apart from the inflow of capital and growth of economy the legal policy was heavily influenced by tender concerns of exploitative imperialist order, subjugation of proletariat, casualisation of Indian working class and sustainable use of mineral resources.

India has a dubious distinction of extensive mining for developmental pursuits and undermining the environmental social imperatives.[4] The legal framework centering around *Indian Mines Act, 1952; Mines and Mineral (Development and Regulations) Act, 1957; Mineral Concession Rule, 1988* are generally castigated on being oblivious to ecological sustainability, social accountability, health and safety of workers and innocent population. The pro-active developmental base of mining legislation has been severely contested in the wake of environmental catastrophe, health and safety and social security. Equally significant is the fact that most of mining operations are taking place in tribal hinterlands witnessing gradual encroachment on the entitlement of land, cultural identity and social development of scheduled castes and tribes. In the wake of wide spread criticism of nationalization and de-nationalization saga, frequency of legal amendments and pronouncement of Mineral policy of 1993, a contemporary restatement of Ambedkarite vision of mining law and policy merits greater attention and focus. The paper underlines the imperative and relevance of Ambedkarite vision of mineral resource development for refurbishing sustainable and inter-sectoral equity.

Evolutionary Phase

The evolution and development of mining policy and law can be traced back to Ambedkar's appointment as labour member of the Viceroy's Council on the 20th July 1942 and election to membership of advisory committee for the utilization branch of Geological Survey of India (GSI).[5] After the assumption of these assignment Ambedkarite vision started radiating.[6] At the first instance he piloted numerous amendments into mining legislation and secondly rationalized the term of reference of geological committee.[7] During the Constitutional Assembly Debates (CAD) he informed the House that the GSI has three main duties; first, to carry out the necessary field work for proving mineral deposits, second, to initiate, where necessary, preliminary mining operations, and third, to conduct experimental work as may be necessary to solve problems in redressing, smelting and other problems of production that may be capable of solution by the utilization of India's minerals.[8] The functional ambit of the utilization branch was prioritized under six dimensional heads such as opening of the lead and zinc mines of Zawar in Udaipur state in Mewar; development of Rajputana mica mines; working of sulphur deposits in Baluchistan; operation on wolfram in Bengal and the Central Provinces; examination of certain deposits in Bihar; and search for certain minerals, stones and salts and other related substances.[9] While answering another querry he established the fundamental linkages between the Utilization Branch of GSI and the Board of Scientific and Industrial Research (BSIR). The BSIR deals with three things, namely, inventions, heavy chemicals and naturally occurring salts. The Utilization Branch deals with the discovery of minerals. Obviously, their functions are different. Dr. Fox, in charge of the GSI, was the chairman of the Committee on Heavy Chemicals, which was working under the BSIR. On the other hand, the Director of Scientific and Industrial Research is a member of the advisory committee to the Utilization Branch of the GSI, and, secondly, by this arrangement, the House will see that exchange between the two departments has been arranged.[10]

In spite of these institutional arrangements there has been criticism of Government's action on many counts. He stated that there was a neglect of India's mineral resources, and, secondly, he suggested that the Utilisation Branch was started more for the purpose of providing occupation for evacuees from Burma. He regretted heavily that India's mineral resources were not taken in hand earlier than it was done. There were three principal difficulties in the way of India's undertaking a project. It is to be admitted that up to the present time the GSI had no qualified official mining personnel. Unfortunately, the GSI has acted merely as an inspectorate of mines rather than as a technical body of experts who were engaged in developing the mineral resources of India.[11] Secondly, there is a certain amount of shyness in the mineral exploitation due to the risks involved in opening up mineral deposits. There was a general belief prevalent in India, probably due to long disuse of mining operations in the country, that India was not well endowed with minerals other than those which were suitable for export, such as manganese and mica. He submitted to the House that while we may regret that we have not tackled the business much earlier than we have done, one ought to say that better late than never.[12]

With regard to the employment of Burmese evacuees, he pointed out before the House that we really had no choice. We have been suffering from lack of official mining personnel. Burma was the only place where mining, such as, lead and zinc, was carried on an extensive scale. Burma is the only place where mining engineers were trained and there is no doubt that the project will herald a better future for India. He also expressed satisfaction over the amendments and the initiative of Utilisation Branch.[13] He drew the attention of the honourable members who have moved these amendments to bear in mind that this Committee is not an Executive Committee but purely an Advisory Committee. The object of the Committee is to bring together experts and the representatives of trade and industry together. The composition has been devised in order that principal object may be achieved. There are sixteen members on this Committee, five experts on the Committee, five representatives of trade and industry. First of all, there is the Director of Geological Survey, the Director of the BSIR, one representative of Mining and Metallurgical Industrial Institute, one representatives of the Indian Mining Association and representative of the Indian Mining Federation: these constitute a body of experts as representative of trade and industry with two seats to steel industry and Secretary Department on this Committee. The object of the Committee is really to bring experts who will tell the industrialist and the representative of the trade what minerals they are in a position to prove and representative of the trade and industry will tell the experts how they could be commercially exploited. Bearing in mind the principal object of Committee, there is really not much scope left for the inclusion of what I might call general opinion in the country.[14] On the question of representatives of the general public he rejected the amendments because it will be too unwieldy for doing the business which it will be called upon to undertake. As a via media he suggested that the constitution of the Committee already provides for the nomination of four Members by the Labour Member and without committing myself to any particular line of using this power of nomination I think it is perfectly possible that one member of the house may find a place on it through nomination.[15] Ambedkarite vision of mineral policy and law is partly influenced by the labour policy specially the need for a coherence in labour legislations. The diversity of labour legislation had been a source of industrial disharmony and at times the provincial considerations dominate over considerations of general and national importance.[16] The tripartite objectives of Labour Conference such as the promotion of uniformity in labour legislations, laying down of a procedure for the settlement of industrial disputes, and matters of employees has deeply influenced the mineral policy and law.[17]

Mineral Policy

While formulating the mineral resource policy for India Ambedkar stated before the Legislative Assembly in 1945 that there is great degree of ignorance and misunderstanding. He therefore formulated the policy statement on mines and minerals which hitherto the Government has not outlined and explained fully.[18] The virtual absence of mineral policy owes greatly to the passivity the of the GSI. To dispel many apprehensions and chaos he admitted that the mineral policy was heavily overshadowed by industrial policy. Minerals necessarily play a great role in the industrial development of the country and if the country has no industrial policy, obviously there cannot be a mineral policy at all. The reconstruction of the economic and industrial life to this country in the post-war period played very small part in the industrialization of the country. If there has been no mineral policy, the fault is not of the GSI but the Government of the day and similar organizations which were interested in the economic and industrial life of the country. The GSI did not play the part that geological surveys in other parts of the world do play, and is largely due to the fact that departments have always been understaffed with trained personnel.[19]

The Government of India has taken a decision to have a drive in favour of bringing about the industrialization of the country. The mineral policy of the Government of India has been set out in Section 14 of the Second Report on Reconstruction and Planning. The major thrust of mineral policy falls into two parts: in the first place, we propose to reconstitute the GSI in order to make it a more potent instrument for the furtherance of our policy. Accordingly, a detailed scheme of expansion of the survey has been drawn up and administratively approved for engineering geology, industrial utilization of minerals, central mineral development, geological works, oil development, establishment of a natural history museum and a publicity. The second part of our mineral policy consists of legislations, which the Government propose to initiate for the purpose of establishing control over minerals by taking into consideration the following circumstances.[20] One, the importance of the mineral from the defence point of view on all India mineral development; two, the technical nature of the mineral;

three, the purposes for which the mineral is used; four, the value of the mineral or of the provisions will fall into two classes, or rather divide the minerals into two classes: those which will be subjected to general control, and under general control we propose to confine ourselves to the granting of prospecting and mining leases, the terms and conditions of such licenses and termination thereof. Then there will be other minerals, which will be selected for more detailed control. The detailed control will include besides the power to grant licenses, the power to control the method of mining, of processing, of grading, of standardizing, to direct improvement of mining and procuring methods, and also the power to initiate research for increased utilization and for other necessary purposes.[21]

In the contemplated legislation there will undoubtedly be provisions for dealing with the export of minerals outside India. The question whether we can completely stop the export of our minerals necessarily depend upon shall we be able to import those minerals. India is in fact deficient in such important minerals as oil, copper, lead, zinc, tin and sulphur. Therefore, export has to be considered in the light of the effect it may produce on our ability to import things of which we have a deficiency. The safest is to regulate the export of those minerals of which we are in short supply and which are necessary for the industrial development of the country,[22] and secondly to see that our minerals are not exported in a raw condition but that we establish in our own country such industries as will enable us to process the raw material before it is exported. The policy favoured a moratorium on oil concession including granting of mining and prospecting licenses. The moratorium was introduced mainly because the Government of India did not desire that various oil companies should dissipate or engage for their own prospecting purpose, technical personnel which is so deficient in its supply in this country, moratorium will last till the end some time thereafter. So far as the question of granting licenses is concerned the matter, is in the hands of the Provincial Governments. Moreover it is closely connected with another important matter, namely, the provisions contained in Sections 111 to 118 of the *Government of India Act* and which is being debated in the House on a separate resolution. Regarding coal policy such as mining, grading, marketing and utilization of inferior coal he maintained that it will require a good deal of co-operation of the owners of mines and all those who are in the trade in order that our legislation may be fruitful to take as part of our post-war policy.[23] In conclusion he summed up that an all pervasive and dynamic mineral policy would depend upon three circumstances such as industrial resurgence in the country. The ultimate mineral policy will be depend upon two other considerations, namely the constitutional and legal framework position, and federal friendly distribution of authority between the provinces and the Centre.[24]

Mining Legislations

Ambedkarite legal policy of mineral resources manifested in numerous legislations such as *Indian Mines Act, 1923; Coal Mines Safety (Stowing) Act, 1939; Mines Maternity Benefit Act, 1943* and *Indian and Coal Mines Act.* Indian Mines (Amendment) Bill was introduced to provide labour welfare, social security and just utilization of mineral resources. It obligated upon the mine owners to provide pithead baths equipped with shower baths and locker rooms for the use of men employed in mines and of similar and separate places and rooms for the use of women in mines where women are employed and for prescribing either generally or with particular reference to the numbers of men and women ordinarily employed in a mine, the number and standards of such places and rooms. While introducing the Bill, Ambedkar observed that it is bound to improve the self-respect of the miner. It was long over due because Coal Mines Advisory Committee has unanimously proposed that pit-head baths should be an obligation of the colliery owners. To actualize this objective the Bill provides rule-making power to the government for prescribing pit-head bath.[25] The Bill does nothing more than exempt Government from following the usual procedure in the matter of making rules under the Coal Mines Act which are prescribed by Section 31.[26] It says that any Rules made under the Act shall be first published and then passed. We wish to exempt the rules that we propose to make under the provisions of this Bill from the provision of previous publication.[27] The reason for providing such exemption is that we are very anxious that liability not only should be imposed but should be carried out immediately, we wish to avoid delay. The Government is anxious to have this system of pit-head baths introduced in all coal mines and prepared to offer ten per cent of the capital cost of the baths to colliery owners if they undertake to provide such baths within twelve months.[28] In Ambedkar's views shower bath would be far more effective in the matter of cleaning the person of a worker in coal mines than immersion in water or holding oneself under a running tap. With regard to the question of soap, I can give the assurance to the House that we do intend to provide soap to every miner under certain regulations, and I think the House need have no anxiety on that account. The Indian Mines Act, 1923 was amended to incorporate these concerns.[29]

Coal Sector

Dr. B.R. Ambedkar along with H.C. Prior, Secretary, Labour Department, and R.S. Nimbkar, Labour Welfare Adviser to the Government of India, visited Dhanbad to study working conditions in the coalfield of Jharia. During their stay at Dhanbad, they discussed with employers an employees, proposals to increase the production of coal and to deal with the situation arising out of the labour shortage in the fields. Also the question of giving concessions to the collierry labour and improve welfare conditions immediate steps to secure food and other concessions for the workers.[30] The team went deep and down to 400 feet underground for the inspection of stowing operations.[31] He also brought certain amendments to the Coal

Mines Safety (Stowing) Act of 1939 to administer the fund which is raised by the levy on coal and to spend it on the stowing of coal mines in order to prevent fires in the mines.[32] In the course of the administration of this Act, it has been found that there were certain defects which need to be remedied. The Bill proposes to deal only with three of such questions because it has been found that they are the most urgent and need immediate attention. The first question is the one which relates to the amendment dealing with the functions of the Board and prescribes the object on which the money arising out of this fund could be spent. Secondly, it allows the Board to grant stowing materials and other assistance to owners or agents and managers of mines for stowing operation. The Act also permits the Board to execute other operations in furtherance of the objects of the Act, and fourthly, it permits the Board to spend money on research work connected with stowing.[33] It has been found that Section 8 did not make any provision for permitting the Board to spend money on stowing operations undertaken by itself.[34] This was found to be a great lacuna. It is necessary in the opinion of the experts that such a power should be given to the Board and consequently the first amendment which clause 2 of the Bill proposes to make is to alter the wording of sub-clause (iii) of clause (1) of Section 8, by permitting the Board to undertake stowing directly by itself and to spend on that purpose out of the fund which it controls.

The Second Amendment to the Bill relates to Section 10. Section 9, sub-clause (3) of the Bill Coal Mines Safety (Stowing) Act permits the Chief Inspector of Mines to issue an order on the owner or the agent of a coal mine, and to require him to take such protective measures as may be necessary in the interest of the safety of coal.[35] The Act also makes such an order an appealable order, but it has been found that while the order issued by the coal mining expert or the inspector is an appealable order, there is no provision made in the Act to permit the owner to go to the appellate body and obtain stay or execution of the order issued against him by the Inspector of

Coal Mines. It has been suggested that this is an unfortunate provision and there should be a right of appeal, but there should not be a provision for the stay of execution of the original order. This lacuna is sought to be removed by the addition of a proviso to Section 10 of the present Act and this is done by clause 3 of the present Bill.[36] The Third Amendment which is sought to be made in the Act relates to the question whether the Board should or should not have authority to undertake stowing by itself. Stowing is an important function. Its purpose is to save coal. It has been found that there are some mines which are abandoned, over which there is nobody to exercise any control, and most persons, it has been found, very easily abandon mines whenever they find that the coal underneath has caught fire. There are cases where the ownership of a mine is in dispute or where the owner is not in a position to undertake stowing operations himself. Consequently in such cases there is nobody on whom the liability for stowing could be imposed nor is there anybody on whom an order could be served. To avoid such a situation, it is felt that power must be given to the Board in order that the Board might itself undertake the work of stowing. Incidentally, if the Board is to perform such a task it must also be given the power to enter upon the land which is the property of the mine owner.[37] This is sought to be done by a new clause which empowered the Board to undertake the stowing and also to have the power to enter upon the premises.[38] He maintained that the Bill is a very simple measure and hardly needs any more explanation; moreover there have never been known that there has been any point of difference or dispute between the Coal Mining Stowing Board and the coal owners.[39]

Mica Industry

India is the world's leading producer of sheet mica, which is mined mainly in the Hazaribagh and Gaya districts in Bihar, and Nellore in Madras, and to a minor extent in other districts in Madras and in Tonk and Ajmer-Merwara in Rajputana;

about 80 per cent coming from Bihar and most of the remainder from Nellore. This pre-eminence in the world's markets, is due largely to the excellent quality of the so-called "Bengal ruby" mica of Bihar, but also to the great manual dexterity of the aboriginals, mainly women, who trim and split the mica with crude soft-iron sickles (or shears in Nellore).[40] Most of the mica exported from India goes to the United Kingdom and the United States. With the employment of higher temperatures of voltages in generators, as radio and television are developed, as the number of motor-cars and aeroplane increases and even as the electron is brought under control, mica becomes increasing important. It is considered indispensable for commutator segments, for motors and generators; commutator V-rings, motors generators; armatures (high temperature and high voltage); aeroplane motor spark plugs; radio tubes' transformers; and radio condensers.[41]

"The Government of India is prepared to do its best to put mica industry on a sound and stable footing" observed Dr. B.R. Ambedkar addressing a mica conference between representative of the Government of India, the Bihar government, trade associations and spokesmen of mica labour, held at Kodarma (Bihar).[42] He also emphasized and referred to the fact that electro-technical industries depended on mica for their existence and that mica was a strategic material without which defence of the country would be impossible. World production of sheet mica in metric tons in 1913 was 17,018 of which India's production was 14,598 – practically 81.7 per cent. And yet the mica industry had played next to no part in the industrial affairs of India. He said: "We hear a great deal about the cotton, textile and jute industries but it is seldom that one comes across any reference to India's mica industry". Ambedkar pointed out that there were two sets of causes – first, that mica produced was not consumed in India. Mica was entirely exported and the Indian people, therefore, were unconcerned. Profits were derived from the outside world and the consuming public were not interested in the mica industry. The second set of causes included the ineffective and unorganized state of the industry. He quoted figures to show that the production of sheet mica in India in metric tons had increased from 1,714 in 1905 to 14,598 in 1937. Another indication of the industry's colossal growth was the fact that in the dry season the industry employed 60,000 workers in mines and factories and about 1,00,000 as home splitters. In spite of its enormous growth, he said, there was no big organization in the mica industry comparable with the Millowners' Association or the Northern India Employers' Federation.[43]

The Government of India, said Dr. Ambedkar, realized that after the war, India might not retain its monopoly in mica to the same degree as today, which would deal with both the immediate and ultimate problems of the mica industry.[44] The terms of reference were: working of the mica control order on long-term policy, and the review of any orders that may have been passed by the government in connection with that order; the present system of marketing both inland and abroad; standardization of quality; the extent to which alternative sources of supply may have jeopardized or are likely to jeopardize the position of this country as a principal supplier of muscovite mica and the extent to which other materials that may be used as substitutes for mica may have displaced or are likely to displace mica in this country for the manufacture of finished goods; research and development; the desirability of setting up suitable machinery, whether by appointment of a central mica committee or otherwise, to watch the interest of the mica trade and industry.[45] Dr. Ambedkar said the inquiry Committee would consist of cross section experts such a whole-time Chairman, two part-time members, one experienced in inland trade and the other in the export trade and a whole time Secretary. There would be seven assessors with the Committee, two representatives of the Government of Bihar, two representing Bihar dealers, one each representing the

Madras and Rajputana to mica trade, and one representing mica labour. In addition, the Committee would be assisted by two technical advisers, one of whom would be the Director of the Geological Survey of India and the other a representative of the Board of Scientific and Industrial Research Inquiry Committee.[46] It was suggested that the Committee might also go into the question of postwar reconstruction as regards the mica industry.

Earlier, the Conference discussed measures intended to meet the immediate needs of the industry. These included proposals regarding prohibition of the purchase, sale or transfer of certain types of mica, the vesting of District Magistrates and Provincial Governments with a certain amount of discretionary authority in granting certificates, of godowns for the storage of mica and improvements in the administrative machinery.[47] He also implored that the mica industry should not exploit labour[48] because India's monopoly was based on cheap labour. Ambedkar also desired that Government would require that labour must be assured a living wage, fair conditions of employment and general welfare, in the interest of maintaining labour welfare.[49] It was indicated to amend the Mica control order 1940, to provide for these. The labour member proposed for medical attention, housing facilities, water supply and impose a welfare and development cess.[50] In order to have a first hand comprehension of mica industry and labour problems, Dr. Ambedkar visited a mica mine and went down about 400 feet by means of ladder installed in the mines.[51] The welfare of mica workers has also attracted the attention of Ambedkar while thrashing out legal policy for mineral resources of India. In 1945, he moved mica mines labour welfare fund bill to constitute a fund for the financing of activities to promote the welfare of labour employed in the mica mining industry, out of the levy on the export of mica in order to constitute a fund for the welfare.[52] This fund will be utilized for cure of diseases, diseases directly attributable to mining operations, working conditions and configuration of the natural vegetation of the mining area.[53] Since welfare activities are conspicuous by their total absence, the obligation imposed upon the employer is to bear the cost of medical aid and house and outside house welfare schemes.[54]

Labour Welfare

In the arena of mining legislation he has taken up the issue of maternity benefits on first priority. Under the Mines Maternity Benefit Act, a woman working in the mine is entitled to maternity benefit for a period of 8 weeks, at the rate of 8 annas per day, this period preceding of 8 weeks is divided into two parts of four weeks each, one part preceding delivery and another part succeeding delivery. The four weeks before delivery is a period of optional rest during which a woman may work and get full wages or absent herself and get the maternity benefit, with regard to four weeks succeeding delivery, it is a period of compulsory rest during which the woman must not work. While introducing the Mines Maternity Benefit Amendment Bill in 1943 he held that it is unlawful and criminal for her to work, and be content only with the maternity benefit. Section 5 of the Maternity Benefit Act provides for the payment of maternity benefit if absent from work. Now, it has been suggested that these words, particularly 'absent from work' or rather work are words which are ambiguous".[55] To butteress his contention he compared Section 5 with the five different Maternity Benefit Acts which have been passed in the different provinces and came to the conclusion for deletion of the words which have caused this ambiguity from Section 5 and make the section read to the effect that 'for every day during the four weeks preceding delivery the woman would be entitled to maternity benefit'.[56]

In view of special needs of feminine working force in the mineral sector Ambedkar moved the Mines Maternity Benefit (Amendment) Bill in 1945. The Mines Maternity Benefit Act, 1941 was passed to cover cases of maternity benefit for woman working on surface.[57] Then underground not withstanding the fact that the lifting of the ban is of a temporary character, it is necessary to amend the Act in order to provide for cases of pregnant women to give some benefit to the women working underground. It is to give some benefit to the women working underground that this amendment is intended. The provision of this Bill are mainly two. There is already in the Act a provision which prohibits woman working after delivery for four weeks. We now propose to add a provision, prohibiting woman working underground before confinement. That period will be a period of ten weeks underground for ten weeks before her confinement. Similarly, there is a provision for the benefit to be given to her. That benefit will be at the rate of twelve annas per day for fourteen weeks in all – ten weeks before confinement and four weeks after confinement. The qualifying condition for enabling her to earn the benefit is 90 days work underground within a period of six months. These are mainly the provisions of this Bill.[58] However, the Bill was referred to Select Committee with instructions to report by 2nd April, 1945.

The Bill, has been considerably modified by the Select Committee on two counts. The first change was with regard to the period of prohibition of pregnant woman on woman working under-ground. The original Bill provided that the prohibition should operate for the ten weeks before confinement and for four weeks after confinement. The Select Committee has made no change in the period originally proposed, for prohibition before confinement. But with regard to the period of prohibition after confinement, the changes they have made are somewhat extensive. In the first place, the period of prohibition is extended from four weeks to thirty-six weeks. This period of thirty-six weeks is broken up into two parts: there is a period of complete prohibition which is followed by a period of partial prohibition. The period of complete prohibition, is extended by the Select Committee from four weeks to twenty-six weeks. The period of partial prohibition is again made subject to two different prescriptions dependent upon the existence or non-existence of a creche. During the period of partial prohibition, a woman is not to work underground for more than four hours if there is no creche, and, secondly, she is not to work underground for more than four hours at any time even if there is a creche.[59] These are the changes made by the Select Committee with regard to the period of prohibition on work underground.

Coming to the question of maternity benefits to be paid to a woman working underground, the Select Committee has made the following changes. Originally the Bill had laid down two conditions which a woman working underground was required to satisfy before she become entitled to maternity benefit. Those conditions were, firstly, a minimum period of work extending to six months in a mine before confinement, and the second condition was minimum of 90 days work underground during such period of six months. The Select Committee has removed the first condition, namely the requisite period of six months of service in a mine, so that under the amended Bill all that a woman need do is to satisfy the condition of having worked for ninety days underground within the period of six months prior to delivery and she becomes entitled to maternity benefit.[60]

The Select Committee has also made certain amendments with regard to the period of benefit. In the original Bill, the period of benefit was ten weeks before confinement and four weeks after confinement. Similarly changes have been made in the amount of benefit. Originally the amount of benefit was eight annas per day. The Select Committee has changed it to six rupees a week, which is a little less than fourteen annas a day. Then the whole of the period of benefit is now declared to be a period of authorized leave, so that during this period an employer is not entitled to dismiss a woman. Another important provision made was that the woman is entitled to the benefit of a woman doctor if the woman demands it, a provision which did not exist in the original Bill. Under the Amendment Bill, a woman is not only entitled to get the maternity benefit of a woman on the surface from eight to twelve annas but also an increase of fifty per cent over the previous benefit, admissible to her under the original Act. These important changes introduced by the Select Committee were accepted and passed accordingly.[61]

Gender Employment

Regarding lifting of ban on employment of women underground work in coal mines, Ambedkar expressed dissatisfaction because the Government of India was never serious with regard to this convention of preventing women working underground to which they had given their consent in the year 1939.[62] The Government had accepted the principle of prohibiting woman working underground long before the convention came into existence and the matter, was first in the year 1923 when it brought in a Bill for the amendment of the Indian Coal Mines Act. Not only did the Government of India accept the principle but they framed regulations with the definite and deliberate object of eliminating woman labour from working underground.[63] At the same time he also implored that we are dealing with an emergency and lifting of the prohibition from allowing woman to work underground is not an idle act or a wanton act on the part of the Government. But it is an Act which is amply justified by the facts and the circumstances of the case. The conduct of the Government must be judged in the emergency and these two circumstances has the Government failed to do something which it ought to have done? Has the Government done something which it was needless for it to do?[64] He submitted that judging it in the light of these two considerations which I have mentioned, I have no hesitation in saying that the Government's action is perfectly justified. Though he agreed that international convention does not contain a clause for its own suspension, every nation has got a right to break an international convention or an international treaty under certain circumstances of shortage of coal labour. This is also justified on the terrain, of grow-more-food campaign started by the Government of India. Anyone who dispassionately considers employment in coal mines as against the results of the grow-more-food campaign and the increased opportunities for employment in military works can well understand why there should have been shortage of labour in coal mines. It is quite clear to everyone that work under coal mines is the most uncongenial work, even dangerous. Nobody likes it; any workman who gets an opportunity to work on the surface is bound to take the earliest opportunity to leave the coal mines.[65] The grow-more-food campaign and the military works are those works which provide an opportunity to the coal miner to obtain what I call less dangerous and more congenial piece of work. The second thing was shortage of labour. To meet the shortage of labour he justified the employment of woman strictly in consonance with social justice. Woman shall be paid the same wages as men for the first time in any industry. The principle has been established of equal pay for equal work irrespective of the sex was adopted under Ambedkar's advocacy of human right.[66] To ensure full dignity, woman shall not be required to work in a gallery which is less than 52½ feet. Ambedkar assured that these notifications will last during the period of the war. While concluding the emergent circumstances to allow woman to work in coal mines he kept the matter absolutely fluid to be revoked at any time. It is a purely emergency and temporary measure and Government have no intention of continuing a minute longer than the necessities of the time.[67]

Since August 1943, when the ban on woman working in underground mines was first withdrawn, there has been a consistent and insistent protest throughout the country against this undesirable action. The Government of India are fully aware that they have not only violated an international pledge but that they have considerably shocked and offended world opinion. The All-India Woman's Conference, moved adjournment motion asking the ban be re-imposed immediately.[68] Ambedkar justified the temporary lifting of ban on the ground of war exigencies, boosting of coal production and defence of national interests. He articulated his arguments on three counts such as fall in production, rise of collieries and shortage of labour force. In the year 1941, the total raising were 29,381,000 tons. In 1942 they fell to 29,270,000 and in 1943, the critical year in which we were forced to lift this ban, the total production of coal had fallen to 23,453,000. Thus within a year there was a fall of something like 6,628,000 tons. It is unnecessary for me to dilate on the fact that coal is one of the most important raw materials both for industry as well as for the war effort.[69] It was impossible for any Government to sit with folded hands and to watch with indifference what might be called a tremendous fall in the production of so important a material as coal. In 1941, the total number of collieries in operation was 440. In 1941, they had risen to 670 and in 1943 the number had gone up to 706. In the ordinary course of circumstances, this enormous increase in the number of collieries in 1943 should have given us a larger quantity of coal than we actually had, but we were faced with this most curious phenomenon, namely, that on the one hand we had an increase of 366 collieries while on the other we had a fall of 6,628,000 tons of the coal.[70] In the year 1941 the total number of worker's number employed in coal mines was 2,11,601. In 1942 the total number employed was 2,08,742. In 1943 it was 2,05,822. Comparing them with the number of mines opened, it will be seen that here again we had a very strange phenomenon, namely, that although the mines had increased, the labour force had decreased considerably. In fact the total decrease was 4,879. But this does not complete the story. In fact the number of coal cutters that are employed was 55,691. In 1942 they fell to 51,438, and in 1943 they fell to 45,306, a drop of 10,385. It is no use having a very large labour force round about the coal mines if you have not got a sufficient number of coal cutters. The coal cutters had dropped because of new industrial establishments, military works, alternative employments, higher wages, advantage on surface, than underground.[71] There is shortage of coal in England and in other countries but there, women are not allowed to work underground, why should then we allow woman to work underground in India. The answer to that is twofold. In the first place, in other countries like England, where women are not allowed to work underground, they have the alternative remedy of conscription. They can compel people and they do compel people to go and work in coal mines. I have very recently read a report that in Belgium, the 1941 class recruits required to serve in the army instead of being sent to the front were sent by the Belgium Government to go into coal mines.[72] That power, as the House will realize is not available to us and therefore we could not follow that remedy. The Government of India had taken certain steps practically from 1992 with a view to close the employment of women underground and a dwindling proportion ceased to work in coal mines in 1937.[73] Ambedkar finally realized that if these women are removed from underground work in the present condition, the distress will be so great in the miners' homes that it will outweigh the evils of allowing them underground.[74] There is shortage of coal in England and in other countries but there women are not allowed to work underground, why should then we allow women to work underground in India? Now, Sir, the answer to that is twofold. In the first place in other countries like England, where women are not allowed to work underground, they have the alternative remedy of conscription. They can compel people and they do compel people to go and work in coal mines.

Contemporary Scenario

Ambedkarite legacy perpetuated in the legal policy prescription of post-independent India. The governing agenda by and large centres around his vision of mineral resource development. Therefore, it is not surprising that the mineral policy of the Government premised on the following assumptions. This mineral policy was broadly successful in keeping a strict control over extraction and export. This policy was reversed by new liberal economic policy and new Mineral Policy 1993.[75] The major objectives and the strategies of the new mineral policy are:

(i) exploration and identification of mineral wealth on land off-shore;
(ii) development of mineral resources taking into account the national and strategic considerations;
(iii) minimization of adverse effects of mineral development on the forests, environment and ecology through appropriate measure;
(iv) promotion foreign trade in minerals; and
(v) promotion of research and development in minerals.[76]

The National Mineral Policy of allowing domestic and foreign enterprises to invest in mineral extraction and export. However it is generally opined that there are numerous shortcomings in the present policy prescription most notably the entry of private sector, long term national interests and adverse impact on the environment.[77] The Government is therefore, keeping close watch on the functioning of private and public sector mineral units on the count of the protection of the environment and national development.[78]

The Mines and Minerals (Development and Regulation) Act, 1957, (MMDR) and the Mines Act, 1952, together with the rules and regulations framed under them constitute the basic laws governing the mining sector in India.[79] The relevant rules in force under the MMDR Act, are the Mineral Concession Rules, 1960, and the Mineral Conservation and Development Rules, 1988. The health and safety of the workers is governed by the Mines Rules, 1955 created under the jurisdiction of the Mines Act, 1952.[80] The Mineral Concession Rules, 1960 outlines the procedures and conditions for a prospecting license or mining lease. The Mineral Conservation and Development Rules, 1988 lays down guidelines for ensuring mining on scientific basics, while at the same time, conserving the environment. The provisions of Mineral Concession Rules and

Mineral Conservation and Development Rules are, however, not applicable to coal, atomic minerals and minor minerals.[81] The minor minerals are separately notified and come under the purview of the State Governments. The State Government for this purpose formulated the Minor Mineral Concession Rules. The international and national legal framework of mineral resources in India includes mainly the following Conventions, Statutes and Rules:

- Mines and Minerals (Development and Regulation) Act, 1957
- The Mineral Conservation and Development Rules, 1988
- Granite Conservation and Development Rules, 1999
- Cess and Other Taxes on Minerals (Validation) Act, 1992
- Goa, Daman and Diu Mining Concessions Act, 1992
- Forest (Conservation) Act and Rules, 1980 (sec. 2)
- Oil Mines Regulations, 1984 (Reg. 91, 94, 96)
- The Environment Impact Assessment Notification, 1994
- Labour Safety and Health Convention, 1995
- Mineral Conservation and Development Rules (MCDR) Forms
- Mineral Concession Rules (MCR) Forms
- Granite Conservation and Development Rules (GCDR) Forms 12

Conclusion

Beside these regulations there are environmental, ergonomic and social conventions having direct and incidental bearing on the mineral development most notably Indigenous and Tribal Population Convention, 1957, Safety and Health in Mines Convention, 1995. Ambedkarite vision of mineral resources development policy and law in the contemporary India still holds solid ground and symbiotic relevance. The spate of legislative reforms suggested in the arena of mining legislations, more specifically the coal and mica sectors are widely practiced and solemnized. The unique dovetailing of human aspirations, gender sensitization and labour mobilization in the conspectus of mining and mining related labours statutes stood the test of time. This is also a pointer to the industrial harmony and social integrity of the working class of the country. India while experiencing the second generation reform of liberalization, privatization and globalization structural adjust programmes, and labour reform can draw more saner advises from the Ambedkarite advocacy for human rights. Such an introspection and prospection seems more befitting when second National Labour Commission has been constituted for radicalizing the labour and industrial laws and policies to suit the needs of Indian working class.

Notes

1. *See,* Md. Zafar Mahfooz Nomani, 'Ambedkar on Indian Federalism: An Appraisal of Water Law and Policy in Contemporary Perspective', XXII (1&2), *The Academy Law Review,* 179-191 (1998).
2. *See,* Peter Robb, 'Meaning of Labour in Indian Social Context' in Peter Robb (Ed.) *Dalit Movements and the Meaning of Labour in India: SOAS Studies on South Asia, 1-67 (1996).*
3. V.D. Nagar and K.P. Nagar, *Economic Thoughts and Policy of Dr. B.R. Ambedkar,* 135-143 (1992).
4. Md. Zafar Mahfooz Nomani, 'Impact of Mining on Environment and Human Population: An Appraisal of Law and Policy', Paper presented in National Seminar on the Impact of Environmental Degradation Human Population in the New Millennium, January 2001, Dhanbad.
5. C.B. Khairmode, *Dr. Bhimrao Ramji Ambedkar* (Marathi Biography) Vol. 9-113 (1987).
6. Vasant Moon (Ed.), *Dr. Babasaheb Ambedkar: Writing and Speeches,* X (1991).
7. *Id* at 30.
8. *Id* at 31.
9. *Id* at 31-32.

10. *Id* at 32.
11. *Ibid.*
12. *Id* at 33.
13. *Ibid.*
14. *Id* at 34.
15. *Id* at 35.
16. *Id* at 13.
17. *Id* at 14.
18. *Id* at 237.
19. *Id* at 238.
20. *Id* at 239.
21. *Id* at *240.*
22. *Ibid.*
23. *Id* at *241.*
24. *Id* at *242.*
25. Section *30, Indian Mines Amendment Bill.*
26. *Id* at *323.*
27. Section *31, The Indian Mines Amendment Bill.*
28. *Id* at 324.
29. *Id* at 325.
30. *Id* at 129.
31. *Id* at 130.
32. Section *8, The Coal Mines Safety (Stowing) Act*, 1939.
33. *Id* Section 31.
34. *Id* at 145.
35. Section 10, *The Coal Mines Safety (Stowing) Act*, 1939.
36. *Id* at 146.
37. *Ibid.*
38. Section 10-A, *The Coal Mines Safety (Stowing) Act*, 1939.
39. *Id* at 147.
40. *Id* at 176.
41. *Id* at 177.
42. *Id* at 172.
43. *Id* at 174.
44. *Id* at 172.
45. *Id* at 173.

46. *Ibid.*
47. *Id* at 175.
48. *Id* at 173.
49. *Id* at 175.
50. *Id* at 176.
51. *Id* at 174-75.
52. *Id* at 373.
53. *Id* at 375.
54. *Id* at 376
55. *Id* at 87.
56. *Id* at 88.
57. *Id* at 264.
58. *Id* at 265.
59. *Id* at 274.
60. *Id* at 275.
61. *Id* at 276
62. *Id* at 139.
63. *Id* at 140
64. *Id* at 141.
65. *Id* at 142.
66. *Id* at 143
67. *Id* at 144
68. *Id* at 253
69. *Id* at 254
70. *Id* at 255.
71. *Ibid.*
72. *Id* at 256.
73. *Id* at 257.
74. *Id* at 258.
75. Ruddar Datt and K.P.M. Sundharam, *Indian Economy*, 90 (1999).
76. *Id* at 90-91.
77. *Id* at 71.
78. *See*, Ramnathan and Mehta, *Reports on Guidelines for Integrating Environmental Concerns with Exploitation of Mineral Resources*, (1988).

79. C.M. Jariwala, 'Mining and Environment: Indian Law Scenario', 37(4) *Journal of India Law Institute*, 434 (1995).
80. *Id* at 435.
81. *Id* at 436.
82. Centre for Education and Communication, *Mining for Whom: A Dossier on Mines and Minerals*, 124 (2000).

19

Constitutional Paradigm Reflecting Baba Saheb's Ideology of Social Justice

S.D. SHARMA AND PRITI

Social justice is the concept of distribution of benefits throughout society. It concerns such matters as the regulation of wages and profits, the protection of person's rights through the legal system and the allocation of housing, medicine and other welfare benefits. Distribution of benefits is known as distributive justice or social justice. Aristotle described distributive justice as "distribution of honours or money or the other things that fall to be divided among those who have a share in the constitution".[1] In every country constitution is the main source of social and distributive justice. Constitution formulates the social justice in definite ways. The good whose distribution is referred to may consist either of valued individual status (happiness, wants, satisfaction, etc.) or resource, external to the individual (wealth, education, job etc.). The principle of social justice itself may either state simply how the good is to be divided (equal division is the most straight forward example), or it may specify some property of the individual which will determine what his share of the good shall be (for instance allocation of basic needs).

In India, Constitution provides social justice to the Indian people. Baba Saheb Dr. Ambedkar was the great architect of the Indian Constitution. He was the chairman of the constitutional drafting committee. The constitutional provisions - The Preamble, Art 15(3), 16(4), 4A, 4B, 17, 18, 23, 24, 29, 30 and DPSP reflect the ideology and philosophy or Baba Saheb's attachment to social justice.

The Preamble of the Indian Constitution is the mirror of social justice. It provides social, economic and political justice to the citizen of sovereign, socialist, secular, democratic republic of India. The Constituent Assembly held its first meeting on 9, December 1946. The first task of the Assembly was the formulation of the objectives and the guiding principles which were to form the basis of the Constitution. The resolution of the Preamble and object of the Constitution was discussed in the Constituent Assembly for eight days, i.e., December 13 to 19 and again between January 20 and 22, 1947.

Before the actual work of the Constituent Assembly had commenced in full swing, Dr. Ambedkar proposed a memorandum entitled 'States and Minorities': what are their rights and how to secure them in the constitution of free India, on 15 March 1947. This proposal of Baba Saheb shows the social justice aspect for the minorities in free India. Although no cognizance was taken of this memorandum. But the feeling of Dr. Ambedkar was a special protection to the minorities and weaker section of the society. Many amendments were suggested to the preamble by L.N. Sahu, Pattabi Sitaramayya, G. Durgabhai, Pandit Thakurdass Bhargava, B.V. Keshkar, T.T. Krishnamachari, M. Anantasayam Ayyangar, K. Santhanam, Atul Chandra Guha, Upendranath Burman and K.T. Shah. Besides the amendments, the Drafting Committee itself at a meeting presided over by Dr. B.R. Ambedkar, proposed amendments to the draft preamble. After the long debate, the Preamble of Indian Constitution was passed by the Constituent Assembly. Thus, the Preamble as modified by the 42nd Amendment now reads:

> We, the people of India, having Solemnly resolved to constitute India into a Sovereign Socialist Secular Democratic Republic and to secure to all its citizens; social, economic and political justice, liberty of thought, expression, belief, faith and worship, equality of status and opportunity and to promote among them all, fraternity assuring the dignity of the individual and the unity and integrity of the Nation.
>
> In our Constituent Assembly this twenty-sixth day of November 1949, do hereby ADOPT, ENACT AND GIVE TO OURSELVES THIS CONSTITUTION.

The Preamble shows the Sovereignty of India. The question arose that where is the Sovereignty? Baba Saheb answered this question in the Constituent Assembly that the declaratory part of the Preamble consisted of the statement: "We, the people of India, in our Constituent Assembly, this day, do hereby adopt, enact and give to ourselves this Constitution"; he asked whether it did not mean clearly that the sovereignty is vested with people? It was quite a different question which they had nothing to do with the point which they were debating whether the Constitution should have validity if it was passed by the Constituent Assembly or whether it would have validity only when it was passed by a referendum, he added quoting the Preamble of the Constitution of the United States which reads as, we the people of the United States, do ordain and establish this Constitution of the United States of America, he asked that if the representatives of 13 states assembled in a small conference in Philadelphia passed a Constitution, and said that what they did was in the name of the people, basing on it their sovereignty as to why a body of 292 people, representing the country in their representative's capacity could not say that they were enacting in the name of the people of India. Regarding the apprehension that the sovereignty might not be located elsewhere or bartered away, he assured the House that nobody desired that there should be anything in the Constitution which had the remotest semblance of having been derived from the Sovereignty of the British Parliament, stating that they wished to delete every vestige of the Sovereignty of the British Parliament, he added that the association of India with British Common Wealth did not in any way derogate from the Sovereignty of the people as it was a treaty entered into between two sovereign countries. Beyond doubt, the Preamble embodied the desire of the members of the House that the Constitution should have its roots in the people, and derive authority and Sovereignty from the people.[2]

The above constitutional debate of Dr. B.R. Ambedkar established that there is a Sovereignty of people in India. It means people of India are politically supreme within the country, because as per Austin, sovereign should be political supreme, indivisible, unlimited and illimitable.[3] The purpose of social justice is to provide all essential things to the people, if the people of India are supreme, it means they demand the government, which is elected by themselves, the essential things which are required for themselves. If the government does not fulfil the demand of the people, in such situation or circumstances government has no right to remain in power. The Sovereignty of people's theory of Dr. Ambedkar shows the real social justice to the Indian people. In September 1976 by the 42nd amendment of Constitution the 'Socialist' word was incorporated in the Preamble. At the time of 42nd constitutional debate from 25 October 1976 to 4 November 1976 members from the both the Houses welcomed the addition of the 'Socialist' word in the Preamble. Socialist word clearly indicates the constitutional social justice to the people of India. Although this is the after independence development of constitutional social justice but to amend the constitution on the line of social justice as 'Socialist' in the Preamble, it was the impact of Dr. Ambedkar's philosophy which compelled the parliament to amend the Constitution on such lines.

Besides the Preamble there are provisions of constitutional social justice in the part III of the Constitution. Art 14 prescribes equality before law. Art 15 prohibits discrimination on the ground of religion, race, caste, sex or place of birth. Art 15(2) lays down that, "No citizen shall on the grounds only of religion, race, caste, sex, place of birth or any of them, be subject to any disability, liability, restriction or condition with regard to (a) access to shops, public restaurants, hotels and places of public entertainment or (b) the use of wells, tanks, bathing ghats, roads and places of public resort maintained wholly or partly out of state funds or dedicated to the use of the general public".

Art 15(2)(a) and (b) is the clear and direct provision of constitutional social justice against the social discrimination. This provision relates to equality in the society. At the time of Constituent Assembly debate, Dr. B.R. Ambedkar expressed his views in favour of real social justice with regard to Art 15(2). He said "All of us desire that this unfortunate class should be entitled to the same privileges as members of the other communities without any let or hindrance from any body".[4] Again he said if any community or person will violate this provision it will impose duty on the state to stop such type of violation through the law, because the Constitution contains ample provision and nothing more is really necessary. Baba Saheb opposed K.T. Shah's amendment that in Art 15(3) there should be added[5] 'Scheduled castes' and 'Scheduled Tribes' along with women and children. Dr. Ambedkar said I am afraid it may have just the opposite effect:

> The object which all of us have in mind is that the scheduled caste and scheduled tribes should not be segregated from the general public. For instance, none of us, I think would like that a separate school should be established for the scheduled caste when there is a general school in the village open to the children of the entire community. If these words are added, it will probably give a handle for a state to say Well, we are making special provision for the scheduled castes. To my mind they can safely say so by taking shelter under the article, if it is amended

in the manner the Professor wants it. I, therefore, think that it is not a desirable amendment.

The above opinion of Dr. Ambedkar indicates that in real sense he wants social justice for scheduled castes and scheduled tribes within the Indian society. Although in Article 15(4) there is a provision of "Nothing in this Article or in clause (2) of the Article 29 shall prevent the state from making any special provision for the advancement of any socially and educationally backward classes of citizens or for the Scheduled Castes and the Scheduled Tribes". In this Article it used the words "scheduled castes and the scheduled tribes". But it is quite different to Article 15(3) because here it used the words "for the advancement of any socially and educationally", it shows that for the advancement of scheduled castes and scheduled tribes, state can make special provisions. In Article 15(3) there is no such type of provisions as Article 15(4). Therefore, Dr. Ambedkar opposed the K.T. Shah's amendment.

Dr. Ambedkar recognized Untouchability as a crime under fundamental rights.[6] This Article does not propose to give any special privileges and safeguards to some minority community, but is proposes to save one sixth of the Indian population from perpetual subjugation and despair, from perpetual humiliation and disgrace. The custom of untouchability has not only thrown millions of Indian population in to the dark abyss of gloom and despair, shame and disgrace, but it has also eaten into the very vitality of our nation.[7] At the time of Constituent Assembly debate untouchability provision of draft constitution was as "No one shall on account of his religion or caste be treated or regarded as an 'Untouchable' and its observance in any form may be made punishable by law".[8] After a long debate of Constituent Assembly it was passed as "Untouchability is abolished and its practice in any form is forbidden." The enforcement of any disability arising out of Untouchability shall be an offence punishable in accordance with law.[9] Article 17 which makes the practice of untouchability an offence must be read with Art 35(a)(ii) which confers upon Parliament the exclusive power to make laws prescribing punishment for those acts which are declared to be offences under Part-III. Art 35(b) continues existing laws which provide punishment for any act which is made an offence under Part III, subject to adaptation or modification under Article 372. In the exercise of the powers conferred by Art 35, Parliament has enacted the untouchability (offences) Act 1955, untouchability (offences) amendment and miscellaneous provisions Act 1976 and Scheduled Caste and Scheduled Tribes (Prevention of Atrocity) Act, 1989. Art 17 protects an individual from discriminatory conduct not only on the part of the state but even on the part of private person. Therefore, the state is under the constitutional obligation to protect the socially weaker section of the society from discrimination.

Article 17 and Art 15(3) of the Constitution are related to each other. At the time of framing of these Articles, Dr. Ambedkar expressed his views that:

> There is no doubt that there is no difference of opinion between the members of the House desire that the untouchable class should be entitled to the privileges as member of the other communities without any let or hindrance from anybody. This purpose is carried out entirely by the provisions contained in Article 11 (i.e., Art 17), which specifically deals with untouchability instead of leaving it to Parliament or to the state to make it crime; the article itself declares that any such interference with their rights shall be treated as an offence punishable by law. If the member's view is that there should be a provision in the constitution dealing generally with acts which interfere with provision in the constitution in Art 9 (i.e., Art 15), I would like to draw his attention to Article 27 (of draft const) in the constitution which places an obligation on Parliament to make laws declaring such interference to be offences punishable by law. The reason why such power is given to parliament is

> because it is felt that any offence which deals with the fundamental rights should be uniform throughout the territory of India, which would not be the case if this power was left to the different states and provinces to regulate as they like. My submission therefore is that so as this point is concerned, the constitution contains ample provision and nothing more is really necessary.[10]

Article 15(3), 16(4) and 17 provide social justice, and Article 17, to the extreme, confers on state the power to legislate by making penal provisions against untouchability. According to Article 15(3), "Nothing in this article shall prevent the state from making any provision for reservation of appointment or posts in favour of any backward class of citizens which, in the opinion of the state, is not adequately represented in services under the state". It means that state can legislate the matters relating to reservation in favour of backward class. At the time of Constituent Assembly debates Dr. Ambedkar clarified the purpose of reservation in favour of backward class in the following words:

> There are three points of view, which it is necessary for us to reconcile if we are to produce a workable proposition which will be accepted by all of the three points of view, the first is that there shall be equality of opportunity for all citizens. It is the desire of many members of this House that every individual who is qualified for a particular post should be free to apply for that post, to sit for examination and to have his qualifications tested so as to determine whether he is fit for the post or not and that there ought to be no hindrance in the operation of this principle of equality of opportunity. Another view mostly shared by a section of the House is that, if this principle is to be operative and it ought to be operative in their judgment to its fullest extent – there ought to be no reservation of any sort for any class or community at all, that all citizens, if they are qualified, should be placed on the same footing of equality so far as the public services are concerned. That is the second point of

> view we have. That we have quite a massive opinion which insist that, although theoretically it is good to have the principle that there shall be equality of opportunity, there must at the same time be a provision made for the entry of certain communities which have so far been outside the administration. As I said, the Drafting committee had to produce a formula which would reconcile these three points of view, firstly, that there shall be equality of opportunity, secondly that there shall be reservations in favour of certain communities which have not so far had a proper look in so to say into the administration.[11]

The above idea of Dr. Ambedkar proved the reservation for backward classes who were socially backward at the time of independence. Baba Saheb wanted to uplift these persons to give them adequate representation in administration. This type of his ideology proved the fruitful social justice for these who were in real sense socially backward in Indian society. This ideology of Dr. Ambedkar was strengthened after the constitutional 77th amendment Act, 1995. According to this amendment, reservation was given to the Scheduled Castes and Scheduled Tribes in the matter of promotion, which in the opinion of the state, are not adequately represented in the services under the state.[12] Again Art. 16 was amended in 2000, thereby inserting clause '4B' to Art. 16 by the Constitution (Eighty First Amendment) Act, 2000. As per this amendment "Nothing in this Article shall prevent the state from considering any unfilled vacancies of a year in accordance with any provision for reservation made under clause (4) or clause (4A) as a separate class of vacancies to be filled up in any succeeding year or years and such class of vacancies of the year in which they are being filled up for determining the ceiling of fifty per cent reservation on total number of vacancies of that year." Again Indian Parliament enacted the Constitution (Eighty second Amendment) Act 2000 to give adequate representation to the scheduled caste and the scheduled tribes in administration. As per this amendment a new "privies", inserted in Art

335 which reads, "Provided that nothing in this article shall prevent in making of any provision in favour of the members of the scheduled castes and the scheduled tribes for relaxation in qualifying marks in any examination or lowering the standards of evaluation for reservation in matters of promotion to any class or classes of services or posts in connection with the affairs of the union or of a state". [13]

These new provisions of the Constitution reflects the feeling of Dr. Ambedkar to give equal status and representation in the administration. Dr. Ambedkar gave separate right to minorities to establish and administer educational institutions. He said "we are permitting a community which has established its institution for the advancement of its religious or its cultural life, to give such institution in the school".[14] This observation of Baba Saheb shows that he wanted to give the minorities, educational right by establishing minority institutions in India. According to this right it was easy to achieve the social justice for minorities. In this way Dr. Ambedkar expressed his views in favour of minorities and other weaker sections of the Indian society.

The very important part of social justice is there in the Constitution in part IV of the Directive Principles of the state policy. Although this part is not enforceable by any court, but the principles therein laid down are nevertheless fundamental in the governance of the country and it shall be the duty of the state to apply these principles in making laws. Dr. Ambedkar said "It is not the intention to introduce in this part these principles as mere pious declarations. It is the intention of the Assembly that in future both the legislature and the executive should not merely pay lip service to these principles enacted in this part, but that they should be made the basis of all executive an legislative action that may be taken hereafter in the matter of the governance of the country.

This debate of Dr. Ambedkar imposed pious duty on the future governance to implement the provisions of Directive Principles as social justice. In Directive Principles of State

Policy Article 38, 39A, 40, 41, 42, 43, 43A, 45, 46, and 47 are directly connected with social justice and the philosophy of Dr. Ambedkar. These provisions are:

> State to secure a social order for the promotion of welfare of the people, the certain principles of policy to be followed by the state, e.g., men and women have equal right of adequate means of livelihood, the ownership and control of the material resources of the community are so distributed as best to subserve the common good, the operation of the economic system does not result in the concentration of wealth and means of production to the common detriment, equal pay for equal work, health and strength of workers, men and women and tender age of children are not abused and that citizens are not forced by economic necessity to enter avocations unsuited to their age or strength, childhood and youth are protected against exploitation and against moral and material abandonment.[15] Equal justice and free legal aid,[16] organisation of village Panchayats, right to work, to education and to public assistance in certain cases, provisions for just and human conditions of work and maternity relief, living wage for workers, provisions for free and compulsory education for children, promotion of educational and economic interests of scheduled casts, scheduled Tribes and other weaker sections, duty of the state to raise the level of nutrition and the standard of living and to improve public health, etc.

In conclusion, it can be said that the Indian Constitution is a 'Social Document'[17]; the chief of the drafting committee of the constitution, Dr. B.R. Ambedkar had personal experience of caste-based discrimination. The Constitution of India incorporated his ideologies which resolved to establish a new social order based on justice – social, economic and political, liberty of thought, expression, belief, faith and worship, equality of status and opportunity and fraternity assuring dignity of the individual and integrity of nation.[18] The Indian Constitution is unique in legitimizing affirmative state action for bringing about equality. The fundamental rights do not merely contain civil and political rights traditionally known as civil liberties, such as freedom of speech and expression, religion, right to personal liberty, but also contains provision such as abolition of untouchably, prohibition of traffic in human beings and forced labour and prohibition of employment of children in hazardous employment. These provisions enjoin upon the state to pass suitable legislation for making these fundamental rights enforceable. These fundamental rights are social rights.[19] The real strength is also given through Directive Principles of State Policies. These provisions of Indian Constitution are the paradigm of Baba Saheb's ideology of social justice. Credit goes to Baba Saheb's philosophy of social justice who is rightly named as the 'Architect' of our Constitution. Being chairman of Constitutional Drafting Committee his thoughts were full of justice from Preamble to other provisions in the Constitution.

Notes

1. Nicomachean ethics, Vol. II.
2. K.C. Markandan, *The Preamble* (1984) pp. 61-62.
3. G.W. Keeton, *The Elementary Principles of Jurisprudence* (1949) pp. 40-48.
4. CAD, Vol. VII, p. 661.
5. Article 9 of the Draft Constitution.
6. Article 17 of the Indian Constitution.
7. Dr. Manmohan Dass, CAD Vol. VII, 666.
8. Draft Constitution, Article 11.
9. The Constitution of India, Article 17.
10. CAD Vol. VII, p. 661.
11. CAD, Vol. VII, p. 701.
12. Sec. 2 of the 77th Amendment of Indian Constitution, Act 1995.
13. Received the Assent of the President of on 8-9-2000. Act published in Gaz. of India, 8-9-2000 Part II-S1, Ext. P. 1 (No. 49).
14. CAD, Vol. VII, p. 884.

15. Inserted by the Constitution (Forty-Fourth Amendment) Act, 1978 sec. 9.
16. Inserted by the Constitution (Forty-Second Amendment) Act, 1976 sec. 7.
17. Granville Austin, *The Indian Constitution: Cornerstone of a Nation*, (1999) p. 50.
18. See Preamble of the Constitution.
19. S.P. Sathe, *The Unfinished Agenda: The Constitution at the Crossroads*, 42 JILE (2000) p. 173.

20

Ambedkar's Contribution to Social Justice

An Overview

S.S. DHAKTODE

Dr. B.R. Ambedkar was a multi-dimensional personality. He was an apostle of millions of downtrodden, voice of dumb millions, a revolutionary social reformer, a financial expert, brilliant economist, a great liberal humanist, discerning lawyer, outstanding constitutional expert, a political thinker, an able parliamentarian, an activist journalist, a man of letters, religious revivalist, a bibliophile par excellence and an imminent educationalist, all rolled into one.

Dr. B.R. Ambedkar's authority as a constitutional expert can best be summarised in his own quote:

> The Hindu wanted Vedas, and they sent for Veda Vyas who was not a caste Hindu. Hindus wanted an epic, and they sent for Valmiki who was an untouchable. The Hindus wanted a Constitution and they sent for me.

However, his contribution in the field of social justice was the most outstanding. Even Lord Mountbatten had the same perception. Dr. B.R. Ambedkar was a social revolutionary par excellence. His entire life and mission was dedicated to the upliftment of the downtrodden and fighting social apartheid in India.

India's revolution for social justice, initiated by Mahatma Phule, reached its pinnacle through the Herculean efforts of Dr. B.R. Ambedkar to emancipate the oppressed and suppressed people in India.

Pre-independence Period

Dr. B.R. Ambedkar's struggle for social justice dates back to Pre-Independence era. Mahad Tank Satyagraha and Kalaram Temple entry movements are major landmarks of his movement for social justice. Basically, this was fight for the human rights of the downtrodden.

The Mahad Satyagraha in 1927 finally culminated in the burning of the copy of *Manu Smriti*. His temple entry movement was in a sense unsuccessful, but these attempts for equality aroused an awakening in the minds of the depressing classes.

Simon Commission and Starte Committee

Dr. B.R. Ambedkar submitted a statement to the Simon commission and demanded protection for the depressed classes through adequate representation based on their population and social status. He demanded that the education of depressed classes shall be recognised as the first charge on the revenue of the Province, the right of the Depressed Classes to unrestricted recruitment in the army, navy and police, priority in the recruitment of Depressed Classes to all posts for a period of thirty years. Further, he demanded that the Depressed Classes, i.e., the Untouchables must be recognised as distinct minority separate from the Hindu community.

State Committee had been constituted by Government of Bombay in 1928 to enquire into the educational, economic and social conditions of Depressed Classes and to recommend necessary measures for their uplift.[1] Dr. B.R. Ambedkar was a prominent member of this Committee which recommended scholarship and students' hostels, recruitment of depressed classes in police and army. On the social front, the Committee recommended legislation to prevent the system of devdasis; and that social boycott be checked by legislation.[2]

Round Table Conferences

At the Round Table Conferences held in London during 1930-32, Dr. Ambedkar played pivotal role in putting forward the miserable conditions of Depressed Classes in India before the British parliamentarians. He demanded the abolition of the untouchability in future Constitution of India. Secondly, he demanded safeguards to ensure the right to adequate representation in the legislature.

Under tremendous pressure he had to sign the Poona Pact on 24 September, 1932 by agreeing to amend the communal Award for saving life of M. Gandhi. Dr. Ambedkar was terribly disappointed and lost faith in the British and hopes of securing social justice for the Depressed Classes under the British rule.

Legislative Efforts under British India

In 1937, Dr. B. R. Ambedkar was elected to the Bombay Legislative Assembly. During his tenure as the legislator, he worked for the welfare of the labourers. As a nominated member of the Viceroy's Executive Council, he asserted for the establishment of Minimum Wages Act and maintenance of proper industrial labour relations. As a member of the Advisory Committee on Minorities, he argued for separate electorates to the depressed people. In all these activities, his objective was the upliftment of depressed people, educationally, economically and socially.

Social Justice through Land Reforms

Dr. B.R. Ambedkar's concern for social justice for the poor and toiling masses is very much evident in his advocacy for the allotment of economic landholding to the landless. One of his greatest contributions was his efforts to abolish all sorts of serfdom in agricultural tenancy.

Not only he laid down the principles of macro economic management, but kept the interest of poor and Dalit marginal farmers uppermost in his mind. He was aware of the possibility of the failure of land reforms. Hence, he advocated nationalisation of land, a system of democratic socialism giving rise to the public sector economy.

Social Justice: Constitutional Provisions

Dr. B.R. Ambedkar's quest for social justice is clearly evident in his approach when he drafted the Indian Constitution which has twin objectives: First, to usher in an egalitarian social order guaranteeing social justice to every citizen and second, to protect the liberties of the people from onslaughts of autocratic and arbitrary use of executive authority. Indian Constitution is a unique statute book for upliftment of the downtrodden and disinherited.

Social justice in India is sought to be evolved through the process of rule of law which itself is an integral part of social justice. The freedoms guaranteed under the Constitution are not an end in itself, but the means to achieve social justice.

While understanding "Social Justice" in context of ancient India, we come across a serious contradiction. *Vedas* stand testimony to the insistence on equality as is evident from the following two quotes[3]:

अज्येष्ठासो अकनिष्ठास एते।
सं भ्रातरो वावृधुः सौभागाय॥

— ऋग्वेद-मण्डल 5, सूक्त 60 मंत्र - 5

समानी प्रपा सह वोन्नभागः।
समाने योको सह वो यूनज्मि।
आराः नाभिमिवाभितः॥

— अर्थर्ववेद - समज्ञानावसूक्तः

Then, how come that *Chaturvarna*, based on graded equality, come into existence?

To him, democracy was nothing but union of three principles of liberty, equality and fraternity; and absence of any one from the trinity would defeat the very purpose of democracy. Dr. B.R. Ambedkar's ideal was a society based on these three principles. He said, "Democracy is not merely a form of government. It is primarily a mode of associated living. It is essentially an attitude of respect and reverence towards the fellowmen leading to social endosmosis.[4]

Replying to the debate on final reading of the Draft Constitution he said, "On the 26th Jan 1950, we are going to enter into a life of contradiction. In politics, we will have equality and in social and economic life, we will have inequality.[5]

He was convinced that political democracy unaccompanied by social and economic democracy was illusory for the common man. In fact, he was in favour of incorporating the right to work as a fundamental right in the Constitution.[6]

As a Law Minister, Dr. B.R. Ambedkar introduced a very revolutionary bill called "Hindu Code Bill" ensuring equality between men and women. The male dominated Indian Society rose in revolt against the bill, and the bill did not get the support of Congress Party.

Knowing that the plight of women not being much different from that of the downtrodden people, he had introduced gender justice in the Constitution – something which even the American Constitution also does not have till now. Thus, emancipation of women was an essential ingredient of the concept of social justice perceived by Dr. Ambedkar. It was painful irony of circumstances that the portrait of Dr. B.R. Ambedkar, the chief architect of Indian Constitution could not find a place in the Central Hall of Parliament until 12th April 1990.

Fundamental Rights and Direct Principles of State Policy

The fundamental rights create political equality and liberty. Fundamental rights in Indian Constitution are more elaborate and comprehensive than in the Bill of Rights in any other Constitutions. Fundamental Rights guaranteeing equality before the law and equal protection of law (Article 14), prohibition of discrimination on the basis of religion, race and caste, sex and birth place (Article 15), equal opportunity in matters of public employment (Article 16), abolition of untouchability (Article 17) and prohibition of traffic in human beings and forced labour (Article 23) are important constitutional provisions for preventing discrimination and promoting social justice.

But, the social and economic rights were laid down under the Directive Principles of State Policy. They are not mandatory provisions, and as such non-justiciable rights. Even in the Directive Principles, which strive to create a welfare state and a just social order devoid of economic exploitation of poor people, specific provisions for social justice for all citizens of India were incorporated. Article 38, which contain the essence of Directive Principles, states, "The State shall strive to promote the welfare of the people by securing and protecting, as effectively as it may, a social order in which justice – social, economic and political – shall inform all the institutions of national life." Realising the importance of economic structure of Society to retain Parliamentary Democracy and to prescribe State Socialism, Dr. B. R. Ambedkar was in favour of inscribing in the constitution itself, the principles and structure of the economic life of the people. But he could not achieve this as he knew that Indian Society, by and large, was in favour of small concessions to the underprivileged people but not ready for radical reforms.

Special Provisions

Special Provisions relating to Scheduled Castes (SC) and Scheduled Tribes (ST), the Anglo-Indian and the socially and educationally Backward Classes constitute Part XVI of the Indian Constitution. Articles 330 and 332 provide for reservation of seats SC and ST in Parliament and Legislative

Assemblies of the State respectively. Articles 331 and 333 provide for representation of the Anglo-Indian Community by nomination. Article 338 provides for appointment of Special Officer for SC and ST whose duty is to investigate all matters relating to the safeguards provided for SC and ST and to report to the President.

Even Dr. Punjabrao Deshmukh, while expressing his satisfaction over Ambedkar's excellent commentary on the Constitution said that Dr. Ambedkar would, perhaps, have shaped the Constitution differently, if he had scope to do it.[7] Therefore, it was with some justification that Dr. Ambedkar said "Hinduism is bankrupt, there is in it nothing upon which to base a democracy. There is in it no sense of justices.[8] Indian Constitution is not only a code of constitutional provisions, but also a blueprint for desired social change.

Dr. B.R. Ambedkar had a deep insight into societal problems in India and drafted an ideal Constitution to provide a code to the State to usher in a peaceful social revolution in India.

Our Constitution is secular and socialistic. Dr. B.R Ambedkar made elaborate provisions in Indian Constitution to eradicate untouchability to facilitate equality and social justice for the downtrodden people of India.

Dr. B.R. Ambedkar wanted economic and social equalities before political equality. He preferred social justice to the freedom of this country, while Mahatma Gandhi wanted the freedom of the country first. This difference of view between the two great leaders set off a bitter struggle between them.

Although Dr. B.R. Ambedkar said, "I came into the Constituent Assembly with no greater aspiration than to safeguard the interests of Scheduled Caste", he addressed himself to the task of securing social justice for all the backward classes in the country. Besides, he couched the Constitution in wider and clear perspective of nationalism, social democracy, justice and humanity.

The name of Dr. B.R. Ambedkar will be written in golden letters in the history of India as a Social revolutionary par excellence.

The three words of *Rousseau,* viz, Equality, Liberty and Fraternity had revolutionised France in 1789. This trinity influenced Dr. B.R. Ambedkar and galvanised his sensitive mind for the struggle for the upliftment of downtrodden people of India.

Article 31 of the Constitution says that "the State shall strive to promote the welfare of the people by securing and protecting a social order based on social, economic and political justice".

Dr. B.R. Ambedkar was so convinced about the extreme importance of Directive Principles of state policy for the upliftment of the downtrodden, that in the original draft constitution, Directive Principles also were included as the fundamental rights.

Reservations

Hindu social order is regulated by the principle of graded inequality. This principle governed the law of slavery, laws of marriage, law of punishment, law of *sanskars* and *sanyas.*[9] In order to remove social inequalities and to achieve goal of social justice, a unique plan of reservation system was incorporated into the Constitution so as to effect 'protective discrimination' in favour of underprivileged classes which were subjected to historical injustice since time immemorial.

However, the doctrine of 'protective discrimination' embodied in Articles 15(4) and 16(4) ate of Article 29(2) cannot be stretched beyond a particular limit.[10] Palkiwala has opposed implementation of Mandal report recommending 27 per cent seats for OBC as it would violate the basic structure of the Constitution, But this contention does not hold much water, as the full bench of Supreme Court has approved the Mandal Commission Report.

Safeguards for Minorities

Because of his concern for unity and integrity of India, social justice for the underprivileged people, he justified the incorporation of the safeguard for minorities in the Constitution.

Journalism: A Tool for Social Justice

Dr. B.R. Ambedkar's life was a search for social justice. His every activity and movement was directed to achieve social justice for the weaker section of the society. He started fortnightly *Mook Nayak* in 1920 and the fortnightly continued under different names, viz., *Bahishkrit Bharat* in 1927 and *Equality* in 1932. He extensively wrote in these publications and *Janata, Samata* and *Prabuddha Bharat* as a crusader against caste oppression and discrimination.

Indian Constitution contains many legislations for abolishing the liabilities of dalits and to impart them special opportunities for advancement in education and remployment, thereby securing their overall upliftment.

Untouchability is abolished by Constitution, bonded labour is forbidden by law. The Civil Rights Act goes a long way to remove injustices heaped on the depressed classes in India.

It is pertinent to recall in this context that American Constituent Assembly failed to abolish slavery, instead it constitutionalised slavery,[12] Which lead to the bloodiest civil war in America.

Politics for Social Justice

His greatest contribution to the political thought was his advocacy and practice of ethical politics - politics based on ethics, morality and social justice.

Dr. B.R. Ambedkar was an exceptional statesman who used politics for achieving administrative and economic reforms and social justice. He never indulged in politics for sake of politics.

His ideals and ideologies including those concerning political struggle and social movements would keep guiding the

Dalits in their struggle for basic human rights and liberation from mental slavery.

Social Justice: Dr. B.R. Ambedkar vis-à-vis Mahatma Gandhi

Dr. B.R. Ambedkar had to fight on many fronts for the emancipation for his followers. His bitterest fight was, however with Mahatma Gandhi. Both Mahatma Gandhi and Dr. B.R. Ambedkar struggled for social justice for the Dalit people.

According to Tartakov,[13] while Mahatma Gandhi was the untouchables' representative for the world, it was Dr. B.R. Ambedkar who truly represented them within India.

This assertion has grave repercussions as Dr. B.R. Ambedkar opposed almost every move that Gandhi made with regards to the untouchables. Mahatma Gandhi championed for the eradication of untouchability while supporting *Chaturvarna.* Because of this inherent contradiction, Dr. B.R. Ambedkar considered Mahatma Gandhi's claim to be an honorary Harijan as a pretentious and condenscending insult.[14]

Dhamma and Social Justice

He wrote magnum opus "The Buddha and his Dhamma". According to him, religion is personal and Dhamma (teachings of Buddha) has social connotation. Righteousness and morality incorporated in social justice are essential ingredients of Dhamma. Dr. B.R. Ambedkar appreciated the fact that morality and not God is of prime importance in Buddhism; and characterised the uprise of Buddhism as not only a religious revolution but-as a social revolution as well.

Present Scenario

Inspite of constitutional provisions meant for the educational and social advancement of Dalits the social evils continue. The economic wrongs perpetuate year after year and atrocities continue. This contention can be substantiated from the Reports of the Commissioner for Scheduled Castes and Scheduled Tribes submitted year after year.

Social inequalities have widened and caste remains a crucial factor with social order and politics.

Inspite of constitutional provision, heavy backlog in SC/ST appointments exist.

In brief, Dr. B.R. Ambedkar's vision of social justice through Constitutional means remains unfulfilled to a great extent.

It was misfortune of India that the *Mahaparinirvana* of Dr. B.R. Ambedkar took place in 1956. Had he lived few more years, very impressive social transformation would have taken place in India.

Concluding Remarks

Pandit Jawaharlal Nehru had the following comment about Dr. Ambedkar's achievement in social justice.

"Dr. B.R. Ambedkar is a person who revolted against everything that is oppressive in Hindu Society."

Welsh actor and film maker Kenneth Griffith has summed up, during his BBC interview, Dr. B.R. Ambedkar's greatness in social justice in the following words.

"If there is one thing, I wish to do before I die, it is to produce a film on Dr. Ambedkar."

His contributions in social justice for the underpriveleged people of India were acknowledged, though belatedly, when Government. of India, under the Prime Ministership of Shri V.P. Singh, conferred the nation's highest civilian honour the Bharat Ratna on Dr. Ambedkar posthumously at new Delhi on 14 April, 1990 for his innumerable services he rendered to the oppressed and toiling masses. It is precisely for Dr. Ambedkar's contribution in realm of social justice, Government of India observed the year 1990-91 as the year of social justice in his memory. This contribution of Dr. B.R. Ambedkar should remind us Plato's monumental work "The Republic" which depicts his dream of society embodying the principles of justice.

Dr. B.R. Ambedkar's real place in history is perhaps due to the fact that his life and mission of social justice have a message whose relevance is universal and permanent. Perhaps, he was of the view that social justice alone could lead to social harmony and rekindle patriotic feelings among all citizens, thus strengthening unity of India.

Notes

1. D. Jeevan Kumar in "Ambedkar and Social Justice" Vol. I Babasaheb Dr. Ambedkar Birth Centenary Celebration Committee G.O.I., 1992 p. 268.
2. K.N. Kadam (ed) Dr. B.R. Ambedkar and the Significance of His Movements: A Chronology (Bombay: Popular Prakashan, 1991) p. 27.
3. R.G. Vidhu, in Dr. Ambedkar: Social Justice and Indian Constitution, ed. K. L. Bhatia, Deep and Deep Publication, New Delhi, 1994 p. 65.
4. Vasant Moon, Dr. Babasahib Ambedkar's Writings and Speeches, Vol. 1.
5. B.R. Ambedkar: The Quest for Social Justice – A.M. Rajasekhariah, Uppal Publishing House, New Delhi, 1989, p. 220.
6. The framing of India's Constitution "Select Documents". Vol. II, ed. B. Shiva Rao, p.100.
7. B.R. Ambedkar: The Quest for Social Justice – A. M. Rajsekhariah, Uppal Publishing House, New Delhi, 1989 p. 29-30.
8. Quoted in C. S. Braden: *War, Communism and World Religions,* 1953 p. 158.
9. B.R. Ambedkar, The Hindu Social Order: Its Essential Principles.
10. A.I.R. 1985 SC p. 1531.
11. The Framing of India's Constitution "Select Documents". Vol. 4 ed. B. Shiva Rao, p. 430.
12. Section 2 and 9 of Article 2 of American Constitution.
13. Tarkatov, Gary M., "Art and Identity: The Rise of a New Buddhist Imagery," *Art Journal*, 49 (Wine 90) p. 409.
14. Dalton, Dennis: *Mahatma Gandhi: Non-violent Power in Action*, New York, Columbia University Press, 1993 p. 30-90.

